Private Pilot
ORAL EXAM GUIDE

JASON BLAIR
Based on original text by Michael D. Hayes

FOURTEENTH EDITION

COMPREHENSIVE PREPARATION
FOR THE FAA CHECKRIDE

AVIATION SUPPLIES & ACADEMICS, INC.
NEWCASTLE, WASHINGTON

Private Pilot Oral Exam Guide
Fourteenth Edition
by Jason Blair
based on original text by Michael D. Hayes

Aviation Supplies & Academics, Inc.
7005 132nd Place SE
Newcastle, Washington 98059
asa@asa2fly.com | 425-235-1500 | asa2fly.com

Copyright © 2025 Aviation Supplies & Academics, Inc.
First edition published 1992. Fourteenth edition published 2025.

See the Reader Resources at **asa2fly.com/oegp** for additional information and updates relating to this book.

All rights reserved. No part of this publication may be reproduced, stored in a retrieval system, or transmitted in any form or by any means without the prior written permission of the copyright holder. No part of this publication may be used in any manner for the purpose of training artificial intelligence systems or technologies. While every precaution has been taken in the preparation of this book, the publisher, Jason Blair, and Michael D. Hayes assume no responsibility for damages resulting from the use of the information contained herein.

None of the material in this book supersedes any operational documents or procedures issued by the Federal Aviation Administration, aircraft and avionics manufacturers, flight schools, or the operators of aircraft.

ASA-OEG-P14
ISBN 978-1-64425-518-6

Additional formats available:
eBook EPUB   ISBN 978-1-64425-519-3
eBook PDF   ISBN 978-1-64425-520-9

Printed in the United States of America
2028   2027   2026   2025   9 8 7 6 5 4 3 2 1

Library of Congress Control Number: 2025931709

Contents

About the Author...vii
Introduction...ix

1 Pilot Qualifications and Limitations 1
    A. Certification, Currency, and Proficiency 2
    B. Privileges and Limitations...7
    C. Medical Certificates 13
    D. Federal Aviation Regulations (Part 91) and Pilot Operating
       Limitations 18

2 Aircraft Airworthiness Requirements.................................... 23
    A. Aircraft Certificates and Documents...24
    B. Aircraft Maintenance Requirements 34

3 Preflight Procedures 47
    A. Preflight Assessment 48
    B. Flight Deck Management..53
    C. Engine Starting...57
    D. Taxiing...59
    E. Before Takeoff Check 72

4 Postflight Procedures 77
    A. After Landing, Parking, and Securing.......................................78
    B. Aviation Security..81

5 Human Factors 85
    A. Flight Physiology 86
    B. Single-Pilot Resource Management...104
    C. Aeronautical Decision Making 105
    D. Risk Management...107

Contents

E. Task Management 112
F. Situational Awareness 115
G. CFIT Awareness 117
H. Automation Management...118

6 Aircraft Systems 121
A. Aircraft Flight Controls...122
B. Engine System Components 126
C. Fuel System..135
D. Electrical System..138
E. Pitot/Static Flight Instruments..144
F. Gyroscopic Flight Instruments 151
G. Magnetic Compass 154
H. Avionics Systems 156
I. Anti-Icing and Deicing Systems 161
J. Other Systems 163

7 Performance and Limitations 167
A. Aerodynamics 168
B. Weight and Balance..183
C. Aircraft Performance..187

8 Airport Operations 201
A. Communications, Light Signals, and Runway Lighting
Systems 202
B. Traffic Patterns 216

9 National Airspace System 231
A. General 232
B. Controlled Airspace..233
C. Uncontrolled Airspace..251
D. Special Use Airspace..252
E. Other Airspace Areas..257
F. Airspace Classification Summary 264

iv Aviation Supplies & Academics

Contents

10 Weather Information...**269**
    A. Weather Sources...270
    B. Weather Products..275
        Observations 275
        Aviation Weather Forecasts..................................279
        Aviation Weather Charts 287
    C. Meteorology..291

11 Cross-Country Flight Planning **309**
    A. Flight Planning..310
    B. Pilotage and Dead Reckoning..............................314
    C. Basic Calculations..324
    D. VFR Flight Plan 326
    E. Navigation Systems and Radar Services...............330
    F. Diversion and Lost Procedures 340

12 Night Operations **347**
    A. Night Vision 348
    B. Airport Lighting 352
    C. Airplane Equipment 356
    D. Pilot Equipment..359
    E. Night Flight Operational Environment 361
    F. Night Regulations and Currency..........................366

13 Emergency Equipment and Survival Gear.....................**369**

14 Scenario-Based Training **379**
    Introduction 380
    Scenario-Based Questions..381

Appendix 1   Maneuvers Table 405
Appendix 2   Applicant's Practical Test Checklist............................407
Appendix 3   Operations of Aircraft Without/With an MEL 411

About the Author

Jason Blair is an active single- and multi-engine instructor and an FAA Designated Pilot Examiner (DPE) with over 6,000 hours total time, over 3,500 hours of instruction given, and more than 3,500 hours in aircraft as a DPE. In his role as an Examiner, he has issued more than 2,500 pilot certificates. Blair has worked for and continues to work with multiple aviation associations with his work focusing on pilot training and testing. His experience as a pilot goes back over 30 years, as an instructor spans over 20 years, and includes more than 100 makes and models of aircraft flown. Blair has written and continues to write for multiple aviation publications with a focus on training and safety.

In addition to ASA's Oral Exam Guide series, Blair is also the author of four books in ASA's Aviator's Field Guide series: *Buying an Airplane, Owning an Airplane, Tailwheel Flying,* and *Middle-Altitude Flying.*

Introduction

The *Private Pilot Oral Exam Guide* is a comprehensive guide designed for student pilots who are involved in training for the Private Pilot Certificate.

This guide is equally applicable to those training at FAA Part 141 training providers or those who are training under Part 61 and not affiliated with a specific FAA-approved school. The guide is beneficial to private pilots who wish to refresh their knowledge or who are preparing for a flight review, and it could even be paired with ASA's *Guide to the Flight Review*.

The *Private Pilot for Airplane Category Airman Certification Standards* (FAA-S-ACS-6) specifies the areas in which knowledge must be demonstrated by the applicant before a pilot certificate or rating can be issued. This *Private Pilot Oral Exam Guide* has been designed to enhance and highlight a pilot's knowledge of those areas. It contains questions and answers organized into thirteen chapters representing those areas of knowledge required for the practical test.

At any time during the practical test, an FAA examiner may ask questions pertaining to any of the subject areas within these divisions. The focus of the Airman Certification Standards (ACS) is for an examiner to evaluate the pilot's knowledge, actual demonstrated skills, and risk management ability related to topic areas. This is done through scenario-based testing. Some of the ways examiners will propose scenarios are highlighted in Chapter 14 to help prepare an applicant to apply knowledge beyond a rote level to understanding, application, and correlation levels of learning.

For additional reference, several appendixes have been included at the end of this guide. Appendix 1 provides a maneuvers table summarizing the objectives and minimum acceptable standards of performance for the maneuver tasks in the ACS. Appendix 2 contains the "Applicant's Practical Test Checklist" to be used when making final preparations for the checkride. Appendix 3, "Operations of Aircraft Without/With an MEL," depicts the typical sequence of events a pilot,

Introduction

operating with or without a minimum equipment list, should follow when inoperative equipment is discovered to be on board.

You may supplement this guide with other comprehensive study materials as noted in brackets at the end of each answer; for example: [PA.I.A.K3; 14 CFR 61.53, FAA-H-8083-25]. The first item provided is the ACS code for the relevant Area of Operation and Task from the *Private Pilot for Airplane Category Airman Certification Standards* (FAA-S-ACS-6). Additional references pertaining to the questions can be found in the ACS, listed under the Tasks corresponding to the provided ACS code. The next references in the brackets are other study materials for which abbreviations and corresponding titles are listed below.

Be sure that you use the latest revision of these references when reviewing for the test. Also, check the ASA website at **asa2fly.com /oegp** for the most recent updates to this book due to changes in FAA procedures and regulations as well as for Reader Resources containing additional relevant information. Future updates may also contain additional study material and new FAA information regarding the Private Pilot checkride.

14 CFR Part 1	*Definitions and Abbreviations*
14 CFR Part 21	*Certification Procedures for Products and Articles*
14 CFR Part 23	*Airworthiness Standards: Normal Category Airplanes*
14 CFR Part 43	*Maintenance, Preventive Maintenance, Rebuilding, and Alteration*
14 CFR Part 45	*Identification and Registration Marking*
14 CFR Part 47	*Aircraft Registration*
14 CFR Part 61	*Certification: Pilots, Flight Instructors, and Ground Instructors*
14 CFR Part 67	*Medical Standards and Certification*
14 CFR Part 91	*General Operating and Flight Rules*
14 CFR Part 99	*Security Control of Air Traffic*
47 CFR Part 87	*Telecommunication: Part 87 Aviation Services*
49 CFR Part 830	*NTSB: Notification and Reporting of Aircraft Accidents or Incidents and Overdue Aircraft, and Preservation of Aircraft Wreckage, Mail, Cargo, and Records*

49 CFR Part 1542	*Airport Security*
AC 00-46	*Aviation Safety Reporting Program*
AC 20-105	*Reciprocating Engine Power-Loss Accident Prevention and Trend Monitoring*
AC 20-125	*Water in Aviation Fuels*
AC 21-40	*Guide for Obtaining a Supplemental Type Certificate*
AC 39-7	*Airworthiness Directives*
AC 43-12	*Preventive Maintenance*
AC 61-67	*Stall and Spin Awareness Training*
AC 61-91	*WINGS—Pilot Proficiency Program*
AC 61-134	*General Aviation Controlled Flight into Terrain Awareness*
AC 68-1	*BasicMed*
AC 89-3	*FAA-Recognized Identification Areas*
AC 90-48	*Pilots' Role in Collision Avoidance*
AC 90-66	*Non-Towered Airport Flight Operations*
AC 90-100	*U.S. Terminal and En Route Area Navigation (RNAV) Operations*
AC 90-114	*Automatic Dependent Surveillance–Broadcast Operations*
AC 91-63	*Temporary Flight Restrictions (TFR) and Flight Limitations*
AC 91-73	*Parts 91 and 135 Single Pilot, Flight School Procedures During Taxi Operations*
AC 91-78	*Use of Electronic Flight Bags*
AC 91-92	*Pilot's Guide to a Preflight Briefing*
AC 107-2	*Small Unmanned Aircraft Systems (Small UAS)*
AC 117-3	*Fitness for Duty*
AC 120-27	*Aircraft Weight and Balance Control*
AC 120-71	*Standard Operating Procedures and Pilot Monitoring Duties for Flight Deck Crewmembers*
AERONAV FAQ	*FAA Aeronautical Information Systems: Frequently Asked Questions*

Private Pilot Oral Exam Guide xi

Introduction

AFM	*FAA-Approved Airplane Flight Manual*
AIM	*Aeronautical Information Manual*
AWC	*Aviation Weather Center (aviationweather.gov)*
CAMI OK-06-033	*Basic Survival Skills for Aviation*
Chart Supplement	*FAA Chart Supplements*
DAT	*ASA Dictionary of Aeronautical Terms*
FAA CUG	*FAA Aeronautical Information Services Aeronautical Chart User's Guide*
FAA FRAT	*FAA Fly Safe Fact Sheet: Flight Risk Assessment Tools*
FAA-H-8083-1	*Aircraft Weight and Balance Handbook*
FAA-H-8083-2	*Risk Management Handbook*
FAA-H-8083-3	*Airplane Flying Handbook*
FAA-H-8083-9	*Aviation Instructor's Handbook*
FAA-H-8083-15	*Instrument Flying Handbook*
FAA-H-8083-16	*Instrument Procedures Handbook*
FAA-H-8083-19	*Plane Sense: General Aviation Information*
FAA-H-8083-25	*Pilot's Handbook of Aeronautical Knowledge*
FAA-H-8083-28	*Aviation Weather Handbook*
FAA-H-8083-30	*Aviation Maintenance Technician Handbook— General*
FAA-H-8083-31	*Aviation Maintenance Technician Handbook— Airframe*
FAA OTC Med Guide	*Over-the-Counter (OTC) Medications Reference Guide*
FAA-P-8740-2	*Density Altitude*
FAA-P-8740-24	*Winter Flying Tips*
FAA-P-8740-35	*All About Fuel*
FAA-P-8740-36	*Proficiency and the Private Pilot*
FAA-P-8740-41	*Medical Facts for Pilots*
FAA-P-8740-47	*Radio Communications Phraseology and Techniques*

FAA-S-ACS-6	*Private Pilot for Airplane Category Airman Certification Standards*
FAA GA Preflight	*General Aviation Pilot's Guide to Preflight Weather Planning, Weather Self-Briefings, and Weather Decision Making*
FAA GA Survival	*FAA Safety Briefing: General Aviation Survival*
FAA Safety ALC-25	*Flight Review Prep Guide*
FAA Safety: Bias	*FAA Safety Briefing: Just a Bit Biased—How to See and Avoid Dangerous Assumptions*
FAA Safety Briefing	*Passenger SAFETY Briefing*
FAA Sustainability	*Working to Build a Net-Zero Sustainable Aviation System by 2050 (www.faa.gov/sustainability)*
FSSAT	*Flight School Security Awareness Training*
P/CG	*FAA Pilot/Controller Glossary*
POH	*Pilot's Operating Handbook*
SAFO	*FAA Safety Alert for Operators*
SAFO 11004	*Runway Incursion Prevention Actions*
SAIB CE-11-17	*FAA Special Airworthiness Information Bulletin—Instruments (Maneuvering Speed)*
Sectional Chart Legend	*FAA Section Chart legend*
TCDS	*Type Certificate Data Sheet*
TSA	*Transportation Security Administration*

Most of these documents are available on the FAA's website (www.faa.gov). ASA also reprints many of these federal publications and makes them available in printed and ebook formats and in training and study applications.

Pilot Qualifications and Limitations

1

Chapter 1 **Pilot Qualifications and Limitations**

A. Certification, Currency, and Proficiency

1. What are the eligibility requirements for a Private Pilot (Airplane) Certificate?

a. Be at least 17 years of age.

b. Be able to read, speak, write, and understand the English language.

c. Hold at least a current Third-Class Medical Certificate.

d. Received the required ground and flight training endorsements.

e. Meet the applicable aeronautical experience requirements.

f. Pass the required knowledge and practical tests.

Exam Tip: The evaluator may ask you to demonstrate that you're current and eligible to take the practical test. When preparing for your practical test, verify that you have the required hours and that you're current, and don't forget to double-check all of your endorsements (especially the 90-day solo flight endorsement). Make sure that you have totaled all the logbook columns and that the entries make sense.

[PA.I.A.K1; 14 CFR 61.103]

2. What are the requirements to remain current as a private pilot?

a. Within the preceding 24 months, a pilot must have accomplished a flight review given in an aircraft for which that pilot is rated by an authorized instructor and received a logbook endorsement certifying that the person has satisfactorily completed the review.

b. To carry passengers, a pilot must have made, within the preceding 90 days:

- Three takeoffs and three landings as the sole manipulator of the flight controls of an aircraft of the same category, class, and type (if a type rating is required).

- If the aircraft is a tailwheel airplane, the landings must have been made to a full stop in an airplane with a tailwheel. If the takeoffs and landings were in a tailwheel aircraft, the currency will apply for tricycle-gear aircraft, but not vice versa.

2   Aviation Supplies & Academics

Chapter 1 **Pilot Qualifications and Limitations**

- If operations are to be conducted during the period beginning 1 hour after sunset and 1 hour before sunrise, with passengers on board, the pilot-in-command (PIC) must have, within the preceding 90 days, made at least three takeoffs and three landings to a full stop during that period in an aircraft of the same category, class, and type (if a type rating is required) of aircraft to be used.

Exam Tip: Many pilots confuse what *category*, *class*, and *type* mean when being asked during the practical test. Be sure to understand what category, class, and type refer to with regard to currency. This is not referring to "make and model" of aircraft as it is during solo authorizations as a student pilot.

[PA.I.A.K1; 14 CFR 61.56, 61.57]

3. With respect to certification, privileges, and limitations of pilots, define the terms *category*, *class*, and *type*.

Category—A broad classification of aircraft, e.g., airplane, rotorcraft, glider.

Class—A classification of aircraft within a category having similar operating characteristics, e.g., single-engine land, multi-engine land.

Type (type rating)—A specific make and basic model of aircraft including modifications that do not change its handling or flight characteristics, e.g., Boing 737, King Air 350, Cessna 525 (Citation), or Gulfstream IV.

[PA.I.A.K2; 14 CFR Part 1]

4. Are you required to log all of your flights?

No. You are only required to document and record the training and aeronautical experience used to meet the requirements for a certificate, rating, or flight review and the aeronautical experience required for meeting the recent flight experience requirements. However, a best practice is to log all of your flights to show continued proficiency, potentially to meet insurance requirements, and in the event that you need those flights to help you remain current.

[PA.I.A.K1; 14 CFR 61.51]

Chapter 1 **Pilot Qualifications and Limitations**

5. What must a pilot do to regain currency to fly if their flight review is more than 24 months in the past?

If a pilot's flight review is more than 24 months overdue, they must complete a new flight review before acting as pilot-in-command (PIC) of an aircraft, as required by 14 CFR §61.56. A flight review consists of at least one hour of ground instruction and one hour of flight training conducted by an authorized flight instructor. During the flight review, the instructor will assess the pilot's knowledge of current regulations, procedures, and airspace, as well as evaluate their piloting skills.

Until the flight review is completed or an alternative is met, the pilot is not current and cannot legally serve as PIC.

[PA.I.A.K1; AC 61-98, 14 CFR 61.19, 61.56]

6. Are there any other activities a pilot can accomplish that can be substituted for a flight review?

A pilot can meet the flight review requirement through other FAA-approved activities. These include:

- *Earning a new certificate or rating*—Successfully completing a practical test for a new pilot certificate or rating, such as an Instrument Rating or a Commercial Pilot Certificate, also fulfills the requirement.
  Note: Receiving a tailwheel, complex, high-performance, or high-altitude endorsement does not meet the requirements of a flight review unless the CFI additionally is willing to sign an endorsement for a flight review.

- *Participating in FAA Wings Program*—Completing a phase of the FAA's Pilot Proficiency Program (WINGS) also satisfies the flight review requirement. This involves completing specific knowledge and flight activities tailored to enhance safety.

[PA.I.A.K1; 14 CFR 61.56]

7. Explain the difference between being current and being proficient.

Being *current* means that a pilot has accomplished the minimum FAA regulatory requirements within a specific time period and can exercise the privileges of their certificate. It means that the pilot is legal to make a flight, but it does not necessarily mean that they are proficient or competent to make that flight.

Chapter 1 **Pilot Qualifications and Limitations**

Being *proficient* means that a pilot is capable of conducting a flight with a high degree of competence; it requires that the pilot have a wide range of knowledge and skills. Being proficient is not just about being legal in terms of the regulations but about being smart and safe in terms of pilot experience and proficiency.

[PA.I.A.R1; FAA-H-8083-2, FAA-P-8740-36]

8. How will establishing a personal minimums checklist help a pilot reduce risk?

Professional pilots live by the numbers, and so should you. Pre-established numbers can make it a lot easier to come to a smart go/no-go or diversion decision, than would the vague sense that you probably can deal with the conditions you face at any given time. A written set of personal minimums also makes it easier to explain tough cancelation or diversion decisions to passengers who are, after all, trusting their lives to your aeronautical skill and judgment.

[PA.I.A.R1; FAA-H-8083-25]

9. The airplane you normally rent has been grounded due to an intermittent electrical problem. You ask to be scheduled in another airplane. During preflight of the new airplane, you discover that it has avionics you're unfamiliar with. Should you go ahead and depart on your VFR flight?

Pilot familiarity with all equipment is critical in optimizing both safety and efficiency. If a pilot is unfamiliar with any aircraft system, this will add to workload and can contribute to a loss of situational awareness. This level of proficiency is critical and should be looked upon as a requirement, not unlike carrying an adequate supply of fuel. As a result, pilots should not look upon unfamiliarity with the aircraft and its systems as a risk control measure but instead as a hazard with high-risk potential. Discipline is the key to success.

[PA.I.A.R2; FAA-H-8083-2]

Private Pilot Oral Exam Guide 5

Chapter 1 **Pilot Qualifications and Limitations**

10. If a pilot's permanent mailing address changes, and the pilot fails to notify the FAA Airmen Certification Branch of the new address, how long may the pilot continue to exercise the privileges of a pilot certificate?

30 days after the date of the move.

[PA.I.A.K4; 14 CFR 61.60]

11. What flight time can a pilot log as second-in-command time?

A person may log second-in-command (SIC) time only for flight time during which that person:

a. Is qualified in accordance with the SIC requirements of 14 CFR §61.55 and occupies a crewmember station in an aircraft that requires more than one pilot by the aircraft's type certificate; or

b. Holds the appropriate category, class, and instrument rating (if a class or instrument rating is required) for the aircraft being flown, and the type certification of the aircraft or the regulations under which the flight is being conducted requires more than one pilot.

[PA.I.A.K1; 14 CFR 61.51]

12. How can a pilot utilize the PAVE model to minimize risk in their flight operations?

The PAVE model—which stands for **P**ilot, **A**ircraft, en**V**ironment, and **E**xternal pressures—is a framework designed to help pilots systematically evaluate risks before and during flight. When used in conjunction with setting personal minimums, the PAVE model can serve as an effective tool for mitigating risk and enhancing flight safety.

Pilot—The pilot component emphasizes assessing your physical, mental, and emotional readiness to fly. Personal minimums can include limits on fatigue, illness, stress, and medication (following the IMSAFE checklist). For instance, a pilot may set a personal minimum of eight hours of sleep before a flight or decide not to fly if feeling unwell or under excessive stress. By defining these limits, pilots can avoid situations where their decision-making, reaction times, or situational awareness are compromised.

Aircraft—The aircraft factor evaluates whether the aircraft is suitable and properly equipped for the flight. Personal minimums

6 Aviation Supplies & Academics

Chapter 1 **Pilot Qualifications and Limitations**

in this area could involve specifying the minimum fuel reserve, acceptable maintenance status, or equipment requirements, such as ensuring the plane is equipped with IFR-certified instruments for flights in marginal weather. For example, a pilot might decide never to take off with less than one hour of fuel reserve, even if regulations allow less. These minimums ensure the aircraft is in optimal condition and reduces the likelihood of mechanical failure during critical moments.

enVironment—This element focuses on weather, terrain, and other external conditions. Personal minimums could include weather conditions like ceiling and visibility limits, crosswind components, or turbulence tolerance. For example, a pilot might decide not to depart if crosswinds exceed 10 knots or if visibility drops below 3 statute miles, even if legally permissible. Such boundaries protect pilots from operating in conditions beyond their skill level or comfort zone.

External Pressures—External pressures relate to time constraints, passenger demands, or personal commitments that might influence decision-making. Personal minimums can involve setting strict policies to avoid "get-there-itis," such as canceling a flight if conditions are marginal or delaying departure until safety is ensured. This protects against making unsafe choices due to perceived obligations.

By proactively defining personal minimums within the PAVE framework, pilots can limit exposure to risks, ensure better decision-making, and prioritize safety over convenience. Adhering to these self-imposed limits fosters discipline, reduces complacency, and ensures consistent risk management practices.

[PA.I.A.R1; FAA-H-8083-25]

B. Privileges and Limitations

1. What privileges and limitations apply to a private pilot?

No person who holds a Private Pilot Certificate may act as PIC of an aircraft that is carrying passengers or property for compensation or hire; nor may that person, for compensation or hire, act as PIC of an aircraft. A private pilot:

a. May act as PIC of an aircraft in connection with any business or employment if it is only incidental to that business or

Private Pilot Oral Exam Guide 7

Chapter 1 **Pilot Qualifications and Limitations**

employment and does not carry passengers or property for compensation or hire.

b. May not pay less than the pro rata share of the operating expenses of a flight with passengers, provided the expenses involve only fuel, oil, airport expenditures, or rental fees.

c. May act as PIC of a charitable, nonprofit, or community event flight described in 14 CFR §91.146, if the sponsor and pilot comply with the requirements of that regulation.

d. May be reimbursed for aircraft operating expenses that are directly related to search and location operations, provided the expenses involve only fuel, oil, airport expenditures, or rental fees, and the operation is sanctioned and under the direction and control of local, state, or federal agencies or organizations that conduct search and location operations.

e. May demonstrate an aircraft in flight to a prospective buyer if the private pilot is an aircraft salesperson and has at least 200 hours of logged flight time.

f. May act as PIC of an aircraft towing a glider or unpowered ultralight vehicle, provided they meet the requirements of 14 CFR §61.69.

g. May act as PIC for the purpose of conducting a production flight test in a light-sport aircraft intended for certification in the light-sport category under 14 CFR §21.190, provided they meet the requirements of §61.113.

[PA.I.A.K2; 14 CFR 61.113]

2. Explain the statement: "A private pilot may not pay less than the pro rata share of the operating expenses of a flight."

Pro rata means proportional. The pilot may not pay less than a proportional share of the operating expenses of a flight with passengers, provided the expenses involve only fuel, oil, airport expenditures, or rental fees.

[PA.I.A.K2; 14 CFR 61.113]

Chapter 1 **Pilot Qualifications and Limitations**

3. **The annual inspection for your aircraft is now due, and you ask several friends that fly with you regularly to contribute money to help you pay for the inspection. Do the regulations allow for these contributions?**

No. A private pilot may not pay less than the pro rata (proportional) share of the operating expenses of a flight with passengers, provided the expenses involve only fuel, oil, airport expenditures, or rental fees.

Note: The regulation applies to the operating expenses of a flight and does not allow for the sharing of fixed or long-term operating costs of the airplane with passengers.

[PA.I.A.K2; 14 CFR 61.113]

4. **To act as a required pilot flight crewmember of a civil aircraft, what must a pilot have in their physical possession or readily accessible in the aircraft?**

a. A pilot certificate (or special purpose pilot authorization)

b. A photo identification

c. A medical certificate (with certain exceptions as provided in 14 CFR §61.3)

[PA.I.A.K4; 14 CFR 61.3]

5. **While you are performing a preflight inspection on your aircraft, an inspector from the Federal Aviation Administration (FAA) introduces herself and says she wants to conduct a ramp inspection. What documents are you required to show the inspector?**

Each person who holds a pilot certificate, medical certificate, authorization, or license required by 14 CFR Part 61 must present it and their photo identification for inspection upon a request from the Administrator; an authorized NTSB representative; any federal, state, or local law enforcement officer; or an authorized representative of the TSA.

[PA.I.A.K4; 14 CFR 61.3]

Chapter 1 **Pilot Qualifications and Limitations**

6. What is the definition of a *high-performance airplane*, and what must you do to act as pilot-in-command of such an airplane?

A high-performance airplane is one with an engine of more than 200 horsepower. To act as PIC of a high-performance airplane you must have:

a. Received and logged ground and flight training from an authorized instructor in a high-performance airplane, or in a flight simulator or flight training device that is representative of a high-performance airplane, and been found proficient in the operation and systems of that airplane.

b. Received and logged a one-time endorsement in your logbook from an authorized instructor who certifies you are proficient to operate a high-performance airplane.

Note: The training and endorsement required by this regulation is not required if the person has logged flight time as PIC of a high-performance airplane or in a flight simulator or flight training device that is representative of a high-performance airplane prior to August 4, 1997.

[PA.I.A.K2; 14 CFR 61.31]

7. You are flying in a single-engine, high-performance, complex airplane. You hold a Private Pilot Certificate with an Airplane Single-Engine Land Rating, but you don't have a high-performance or complex airplane endorsement. Your friend, who has those endorsements, is acting as PIC for the flight. Can you log PIC time for the time you act as sole manipulator of the controls? Explain.

Yes, 14 CFR §61.51 governs the logging of PIC time and states that a sport, recreational, private, commercial, or airline transport pilot may log PIC time for the time during which that pilot is "sole manipulator of the controls of an aircraft for which the pilot is rated, or has . . . privileges."

Note: This means you can log PIC time, but you cannot act as PIC. For pilots to act as PIC, they must be properly rated in the aircraft and authorized to conduct the flight, which would include having

10 Aviation Supplies & Academics

Chapter 1 **Pilot Qualifications and Limitations**

the required endorsements for complex and high-performance airplanes as required by 14 CFR §61.31.

[PA.I.A.K2; 14 CFR 61.31, 61.51]

8. What is the definition of a *complex airplane*, and what must you do to act as pilot-of-command of such an airplane?

A *complex airplane* is defined as an airplane that has retractable landing gear, flaps, and a controllable-pitch propeller, including airplanes equipped with a full-authority digital engine control (FADEC). To act as PIC of such an airplane, you must have:

a. Received and logged ground and flight training from an authorized instructor in a complex airplane or in a flight simulator or flight training device that is representative of a complex airplane and have been found proficient in the operation and systems of the airplane.

b. Received a one-time endorsement in your logbook from an authorized instructor who certifies you are proficient to operate a complex airplane.

Note: The training and endorsement required by this regulation is not required if the person has logged flight time as PIC of a complex airplane or in a flight simulator or flight training device that is representative of a complex airplane prior to August 4, 1997.

[PA.I.A.K2; 14 CFR 61.1, 61.31]

9. To operate a tailwheel aircraft, what training must a pilot have completed?

No person may act as pilot-in-command of a tailwheel airplane unless that person has received and logged flight training from an authorized instructor in a tailwheel airplane and received a logbook endorsement from an authorized instructor who found the person proficient in the operation of a tailwheel airplane. This training and endorsement are not required if the person logged pilot-in-command time in a tailwheel airplane before April 15, 1991.

[PA.I.A.K2; 14 CFR 61.31]

Private Pilot Oral Exam Guide 11

Chapter 1 **Pilot Qualifications and Limitations**

10. When would a pilot of an aircraft require specific training and logbook endorsements with regard to flying at higher altitudes?

No person may act as pilot-in-command of a pressurized airplane that has a [manufacturer designated] service ceiling or maximum operating altitude (whichever is lower) above 25,000 feet MSL unless that person has completed the ground and flight training specified and has received a logbook or training record endorsement from an authorized instructor certifying satisfactory completion of the training.

[PA.I.A.K2; 14 CFR 61.31]

11. What regulatory requirements must be met prior to a pilot acting as PIC of an aircraft towing a glider?

To act as pilot-in-command (PIC) of an aircraft towing a glider, a pilot must meet the requirements outlined in 14 CFR §61.69. These include holding at least a Private Pilot Certificate and having logged at least 100 hours of PIC time in the aircraft category, class, and type (if required). The pilot must additionally receive ground and flight training in glider towing operations from an authorized instructor and obtain a logbook endorsement certifying proficiency and must have performed at least three actual or simulated glider tows in the preceding 12 months while accompanied by a qualified pilot or as PIC.

[PA.I.A.K2; 14 CFR 61.69]

12. As a private pilot, can you accept payment from a friend to fly a package somewhere for them? Do the regulations allow you to accept this offer? Can you fly the friend instead of a package?

As a private pilot, you cannot accept payment to fly a package or passengers under most circumstances, as it would violate FAA regulations. 14 CFR §61.113 states that a private pilot may not act as pilot-in-command of an aircraft for compensation or hire.

If a friend asks you to fly a package somewhere, you cannot accept payment or reimbursement for this service. Doing so would qualify as compensation, and transporting goods for hire falls under commercial operations, which require at least a Commercial Pilot Certificate. The only permissible scenario is if the flight is

Chapter 1 **Pilot Qualifications and Limitations**

incidental to your own personal purpose and you do not receive any form of compensation.

When flying a friend, you can share the pro-rata expenses of the flight, which means the costs of fuel, oil, airport fees, or rental fees must be equally shared among all occupants, including yourself. For instance, if you and your friend agree to split the fuel cost for a personal trip, this is allowed, provided there is no intent to profit from the flight.

As a private pilot, you are limited to sharing expenses or conducting flights for personal, non-commercial purposes.

The FAA offers additional resources to help determine if a flight might be commercial in nature at www.faa.gov/charter.

[PA.I.A.K2; 14 CFR 61.113]

C. Medical Certificates

1. To exercise the privileges of a Private Pilot Certificate, what medical certificate is required, and how long is it valid?

You must hold at least a Third-Class Medical Certificate. The medical certificate expires at the end of the last day of:

a. The 60th month after the month of the examination shown on the certificate, if on the date of your most recent medical examination you were under the age of 40.

b. The 24th month after the month of the examination shown on the certificate, if on the date of your most recent medical examination you were over the age of 40.

Note: A pilot may alternately meet the regulatory requirements under BasicMed.

[PA.I.A.K3; 14 CFR 61.23]

2. What can a pilot do if they develop a condition that prevents them from obtaining a medical certificate?

At the discretion of the Federal Air Surgeon, a Statement of Demonstrated Ability (SODA) may be granted, instead of an authorization, to a person whose disqualifying condition is static or nonprogressive and who has been found capable of performing pilot duties without endangering public safety. A SODA does not

Chapter 1 **Pilot Qualifications and Limitations**

expire and authorizes a designated Aviation Medical Examiner to issue a medical certificate of a specified class if the examiner finds that the condition described on its face has not adversely changed.

[PA.I.A.K3; 14 CFR 67.401]

3. Spring has finally arrived, and the weather looks great, so you decide to rent an airplane and go fly. However, your allergies are causing you a problem, and you have just taken your medication. Can you still go fly? Explain.

The safest rule is not to fly while taking any medication, unless approved to do so by the FAA. Some of the most commonly used over-the-counter (OTC) drugs, antihistamines and decongestants, have the potential to cause noticeable adverse side effects, including drowsiness and cognitive deficits. 14 CFR prohibits pilots from performing crewmember duties while using any medication that affects the body in any way contrary to safety. If there is any doubt regarding the effects of any medication, consult an Aviation Medical Examiner (AME) before flying.

Note: Information on the FAA's "Do Not Issue/Do Not Fly" medications can be found at www.faa.gov/ame_guide/pharm /dni_dnf.

[PA.I.A.K3; FAA-H-8083-25, 14 CFR 61.53, 91.17]

4. If you take a medication that is not on the do-not-fly list, how long should you wait to be able to fly again?

The FAA offers information on its Pharmaceuticals (Therapeutics): Medication Guidelines for Pilots webpage that can help you decide how long you should wait to fly. For many over-the-counter medications, it is recommended for pilots to wait at least five dosage intervals after the last dose before flying. For example, for a medication taken every 8 hours, the pilot would multiply 8 times 5 to get 40 hours; therefore, the pilot must wait at least 40 hours after taking their last dose of the medication before they could fly.

More information and specific medication information can be found at www.faa.gov/pilots/medical_certification/medications.

[PA.I.A.K3; FAA-H-8083-25]

14 Aviation Supplies & Academics

Chapter 1 **Pilot Qualifications and Limitations**

5. Where can you find a list of the medical conditions that may disqualify you from obtaining a medical certificate?

The standards for medical certification are contained in 14 CFR Part 67 and the requirements for obtaining medical certificates can be found in Part 61.

[PA.I.A.K3; FAA-H-8083-25, 14 CFR Part 61, Part 67]

6. What requirements must be met to fly under BasicMed?

a. Hold a current and valid U.S. driver's license.

b. Hold or have held a current and valid medical certificate issued by the FAA on or after July 14, 2006.

c. Answer the health questions on the Comprehensive Medical Examination Checklist (CMEC).

d. Get your physical examination by any state-licensed physician, and have that physician complete the CMEC every 4 years (48 calendar months). (Be sure to keep your copy of the CMEC.)

e. Take a BasicMed online medical education course every 24 calendar months. Keep the course completion document issued to you by the course provider.

[PA.I.A.K5; AC 68-1]

7. What privileges and limitations apply when flying under BasicMed?

You can conduct any operation that you would otherwise be able to conduct using your pilot certificate and a Third-Class Medical Certificate, except you are limited to:

a. Fly with no more than six passengers.

b. Fly an aircraft that has a maximum takeoff weight of not more than 12,500 pounds, excluding transport category helicopters.

c. Fly an aircraft that is authorized to carry no more than seven occupants (i.e., six passengers plus the pilot).

d. Flights within the United States at an indicated airspeed of 250 knots or less and at an altitude at or below 18,000 feet MSL.

e. You may not fly for compensation or hire.

[PA.I.A.K5; 14 CFR 61.113, AC 68-1]

Private Pilot Oral Exam Guide 15

Chapter 1 **Pilot Qualifications and Limitations**

8. What is required to maintain BasicMed privileges?

a. Be sure you have a CMEC that shows that your most recent physical examination was within the past 48 months. Keep the completed, signed CMEC in a safe place.

b. Be sure you are being treated by a physician for medical conditions that may affect the safety of flight.

c. Be sure you have a course completion certificate that was issued by a BasicMed medical training course provider within the past 24 calendar months.

[PA.I.A.K5; AC 68-1]

9. If a private pilot does not have a current medical certificate (but has not been denied one), and they have not completed the requirements for BasicMed, may the pilot operate as a pilot-in-command of any aircraft?

If a private pilot does not have a current medical certificate but has not been denied, and has not completed the requirements for BasicMed, they may still operate as a sport pilot. A pilot acting as a sport pilot is not required to have a medical certificate; instead, they are only required to hold a valid driver's license as their compliance with medical requirements.

Any aircraft that may be flown by a sport pilot may be flown by a private pilot exercising the privileges of sport pilot when they do not have a medical certificate. During such a time that they do not have a medical certificate (as long as it has not been denied or revoked) and they have not complied with BasicMed, they can still operate aircraft authorized for sport pilot operations.

[PA.I.A.K2; 14 CFR 61.315]

10. What are some examples of general medical conditions that are temporarily disqualifying?

The FAA identifies some medical conditions as "temporarily" disqualifying for medical compliance. These may include conditions such as acute infections, anemia, and peptic ulcers, along with others. Pilots who do not meet medical standards may still be qualified under special issuance provisions or the exemption process. This may require that either additional medical information be provided or practical flight tests be conducted.

Chapter 1 **Pilot Qualifications and Limitations**

Several general medical conditions can temporarily disqualify a pilot from flying until resolved or medically cleared by an Aviation Medical Examiner (AME). These conditions are often considered temporary if they affect the pilot's ability to safely operate an aircraft but can improve with treatment or recovery over time. Examples include:

a. *Respiratory infections*—Conditions like colds, sinus infections, or bronchitis can impair breathing, disrupt equilibrium, or cause significant discomfort during altitude changes due to pressure differences.

b. *Ear and sinus issues*—Blocked sinuses or ear infections can lead to severe pain or even temporary hearing loss, particularly during ascent or descent, due to changes in cabin pressure.

c. *Gastrointestinal disorders*—Conditions such as severe diarrhea, food poisoning, or other gastrointestinal upsets can cause dehydration, weakness, or distraction, posing a safety risk in flight.

d. *Acute injuries*—Sprains, fractures, or any injury that limits mobility, reaction time, or ability to operate aircraft controls are disqualifying until healed sufficiently.

e. *Psychological conditions*—Temporary stress, anxiety, or depression related to life events can impair decision-making, focus, or situational awareness.

f. *Medication side effects*—Using certain medications, such as strong painkillers, sedatives, or antihistamines, can result in drowsiness or impaired cognition, making a pilot unfit to fly.

Pilots are responsible for self-assessing their fitness to fly, guided by the IMSAFE checklist (**I**llness, **M**edication, **S**tress, **A**lcohol, **F**atigue, **E**motion). If experiencing a temporary condition, a pilot should ground themselves and consult an AME as needed before resuming flight duties.

[PA.I.A.K3; AIM 8-1-1, 14 CFR 61.53]

11. When must a pilot report suspension of driving privileges for driving under the influence of alcohol (DWI/DUI) or drug use?

A pilot is required to report any motor vehicle action related to alcohol or drug use, such as a conviction, suspension, or revocation

Private Pilot Oral Exam Guide 17

Chapter 1 **Pilot Qualifications and Limitations**

of driving privileges. This notification must be made within 60 days of the action.

The report must be submitted in writing to the FAA's Security and Investigations Division. It's important to note that the requirement applies regardless of whether the DUI results in a criminal conviction or administrative penalty, such as a license suspension.

Additionally, pilots are required to disclose any alcohol- or drug-related convictions on their next medical certificate application (FAA Form 8500-8), even if they have already reported the incident separately.

[PA.I.A.K3; 14 CFR 61.15]

D. Federal Aviation Regulations (Part 91) and Pilot Operating Limitations

1. If an inflight emergency requires immediate action by the pilot, what authority and responsibilities does the pilot have?

a. The PIC is directly responsible for, and is the final authority as to, the operation of that aircraft.

b. In an inflight emergency requiring immediate action, the PIC may deviate from any rule in Part 91 to the extent required to meet that emergency.

c. Each PIC who deviates from a Part 91 rule shall, upon request from the Administrator, send a written report of that deviation to the Administrator.

[PA.I.A.K2; 14 CFR 91.3]

2. What does the FAA consider careless or reckless operation of an aircraft?

14 CFR §91.13, Careless or Reckless Operation, states the following:

a. *Aircraft operations for the purpose of air navigation*—No person may operate an aircraft in a careless or reckless manner so as to endanger the life or property of another.

b. *Aircraft operations other than for the purpose of air navigation*—No person may operate an aircraft, other than for the purpose of air navigation, on any part of the surface of an airport used by aircraft for air commerce (including areas used

18 Aviation Supplies & Academics

Chapter 1 **Pilot Qualifications and Limitations**

by those aircraft for receiving or discharging persons or cargo), in a careless or reckless manner so as to endanger the life or property of another.

[PA.I.A.K2; 14 CFR 91.13]

3. Under what conditions can an object be dropped from an aircraft?

No pilot-in-command of a civil aircraft may allow any object to be dropped from that aircraft in flight that creates a hazard to persons or property. However, this section does not prohibit the dropping of any object if reasonable precautions are taken to avoid injury or damage to persons or property.

[PA.I.A.K2; 14 CFR 91.15]

4. What must a pilot know about the requirements for the use of seat belts for crew and passengers during flight?

No pilot may take off a US-registered civil aircraft (except a free balloon that incorporates a basket or gondola, or an airship type certificated before November 2, 1987) unless the pilot-in-command of that aircraft ensures that each person on board is briefed on how to fasten and unfasten that person's safety belt and, if installed, shoulder harness.

No pilot may cause to be moved on the surface, take off, or land a US-registered civil aircraft (except a free balloon that incorporates a basket or gondola, or an airship type certificated before November 2, 1987) unless the pilot-in-command of that aircraft ensures that each person on board has been notified to fasten his or her safety belt and, if installed, his or her shoulder harness.

[PA.II.B.K1; 14 CFR 91.107]

5. If operating an aircraft in close proximity to another, such as in formation flight, what regulations apply?

No person may operate an aircraft:

a. So close to another aircraft as to create a collision hazard.

b. In formation flight except by arrangement with the pilot-in-command of each aircraft in the formation.

c. Carrying passengers for hire in formation flight.

[PA.I.A.K2; 14 CFR 91.111]

Private Pilot Oral Exam Guide 19

Chapter 1 **Pilot Qualifications and Limitations**

6. According to regulations, where is aerobatic flight of an aircraft not permitted?

No person may operate an aircraft in aerobatic flight:

a. Over any congested area of a city, town, or settlement;

b. Over an open-air assembly of persons;

c. Within the lateral boundaries of the surface areas of Class B, Class C, Class D, or Class E airspace designated for an airport;

d. Within 4 NM of the center line of a Federal airway;

e. Below an altitude of 1,500 feet above the surface; or

f. When flight visibility is less than 3 SM.

[PA.I.A.K2; 14 CFR 91.303]

7. Define *aerobatic flight*.

For the purposes of 14 CFR §91.303, aerobatic flight means an intentional maneuver involving an abrupt change in an aircraft's attitude, an abnormal attitude, or abnormal acceleration, not necessary for normal flight.

[PA.I.A.K2; 14 CFR 91.303]

8. When are parachutes required on board an aircraft?

a. Unless each occupant of the aircraft is wearing an approved parachute, no pilot of a civil aircraft carrying any person (other than a crewmember) may execute any intentional maneuver that exceeds:

- A bank angle of 60° relative to the horizon; or
- A nose-up or nose-down attitude of 30° relative to the horizon.

b. The above regulation does not apply to:

- Flight tests for pilot certification or rating; or
- Spins and other flight maneuvers required by the regulations for any certificate or rating when given by a CFI or ATP instructing in accordance with 14 CFR §61.67.

[PA.I.A.K2; 14 CFR 91.307]

Chapter 1 **Pilot Qualifications and Limitations**

9. **If a pilot lives in a state that has legalized marihuana, may the pilot carry marihuana on board an aircraft during flight?**

While some states have legalized marihuana, the federal government regulates airspace, and regulations still prohibit a pilot from carrying marihuana on board an aircraft operated in the National Airspace System.

The FAA regulations in §91.19 state that:

a. Except as provided in paragraph (b) of this section, no person may operate a civil aircraft within the United States with knowledge that narcotic drugs, marihuana, and depressant or stimulant drugs or substances as defined in Federal or State statutes are carried in the aircraft.

b. Paragraph (a) of this section does not apply to any carriage of narcotic drugs, marihuana, and depressant or stimulant drugs or substances authorized by or under any Federal or State statute or by any Federal or State agency.

[PA.I.H.K2; 14 CFR 91.19]

10. **What does the FAA consider passenger-carrying flying that is done for the benefit of a charitable, nonprofit, or community event?**

Charitable event means an event that raises funds for the benefit of a charitable organization recognized by the Department of the Treasury whose donors may deduct contributions under section 170 of the Internal Revenue Code (26 U.S.C. Section 170).

Community event means an event that raises funds for the benefit of any local or community cause that is not a charitable event or non-profit event.

Non-profit event means a passenger-carrying event that raises funds for the benefit of a non-profit organization recognized under State or Federal law, as long as one of the organization's purposes is the promotion of aviation safety.

[PA.I.A.K2; 14 CFR 91.146]

Private Pilot Oral Exam Guide 21

Chapter 1 **Pilot Qualifications and Limitations**

11. Can a pilot volunteer their time to fly for a charity, nonprofit, or community event?

Yes, however the FAA has very specific requirements related to a pilot flying for a charitable, nonprofit, or community event. Limitations include minimum flight times for a private pilot (500 hours of flight time) unless exemptions are offered (such as the EAA Young Eagles program), and flights must be conducted from an FAA-approved location, in an FAA-approved aircraft, and within a radius of 25 NM. There are size limitations on the aircraft that can be used, and flights must be in day VFR conditions.

Reimbursement of the operator of the aircraft is limited to that portion of the passenger payment for the flight that does not exceed the pro rata cost of owning, operating, and maintaining the aircraft for that flight, which may include fuel, oil, airport expenditures, and rental fees. The beneficiary of the funds raised cannot be in the business of transportation by air.

Passenger-carrying flights or series of flights are limited to a total of four charitable events or non-profit events per year, and one community event per year, with no event lasting more than three consecutive days. Pilots and sponsors of events described in this section are limited to no more than four events per calendar year.

At least seven days before the event, each sponsor of an event described in 14 CFR §91.146 must furnish to the responsible Flight Standards office for the area where the event is scheduled additional information for approval.

[PA.I.A.K2; 14 CFR 91.146]

Aircraft Airworthiness Requirements

2

Chapter 2 **Aircraft Airworthiness Requirements**

A. Aircraft Certificates and Documents

1. What documents are required on board an aircraft prior to flight?

Remember: SPARROW+CE

Supplements (14 CFR §91.9)

Placards (14 CFR §91.9)

Airworthiness certificate (14 CFR §91.203)

Registration certificate (14 CFR §91.203)

Radio station license—if operating outside of US (FCC 47 CFR §87.18)

Operating limitations—Airplane flight manual (AFM)/pilot's operating handbook (POH) and supplements, placards, markings (14 CFR §91.9)

Weight and balance data—current (14 CFR §23.2620)

Compass deviation card (14 CFR §23.1547)

External data plate/serial number (14 CFR §45.11)

Exam Tip: During the practical test, your evaluator is required to examine the various required aircraft documents (SPARROW) in the preflight inspection, as well as the currency of any aeronautical charts, EFB data, etc., and then ensure they are on board the aircraft for the flight. Prior to the test, verify that all the necessary aircraft documentation, onboard databases, and charts are current and available.

[PA.I.B.K1; 14 CFR 91.9, 91.203]

2. What is an airworthiness certificate?

An airworthiness certificate is issued by the FAA to an aircraft that has been proven to meet the minimum design and manufacturing requirements and is in condition for safe operation. Under all circumstances, the aircraft must meet the requirements of the original type certificate or it is no longer airworthy. Airworthiness certificates come in two different classifications: standard airworthiness and special airworthiness.

[PA.I.B.K4; FAA-H-8083-25]

24 Aviation Supplies & Academics

Chapter 2 **Aircraft Airworthiness Requirements**

3. What is the difference between standard and special airworthiness certificates?

Standard airworthiness certificates (white paper) are issued for normal, utility, acrobatic, commuter, or transport category aircraft. Special airworthiness certificates (pink paper) are issued for primary, restricted, or limited category aircraft and light-sport aircraft.

[PA.I.B.K4; FAA-H-8083-25]

4. What is an experimental airworthiness certificate?

A special airworthiness certificate in the experimental category is issued to operate an aircraft that does not have a type certificate or does not conform to its type certificate yet is in a condition for safe operation. Additionally, this certificate is issued to operate a primary category kit-built aircraft that was assembled without the supervision and quality control of the production certificate holder.

[PA.I.B.K4; FAA-H-8083-25]

5. Does an airworthiness certificate have an expiration date?

No. A standard airworthiness certificate remains valid for as long as the aircraft meets its approved type design, the aircraft is in a condition for safe operation, and the maintenance, preventative maintenance, and alterations are performed in accordance with 14 CFR Parts 21, 43, and 91.

[PA.I.B.K1; FAA-H-8083-25]

6. Where must the airworthiness certificate be located?

The airworthiness certificate must be displayed at the cabin or flight deck entrance so that it is legible and visible to passengers or crew.

[PA.I.B.K1; 14 CFR 91.203, FAA-H-8083-19]

7. If the airplane flight manual (AFM) for an aircraft you are about to fly is missing, what substitution may be made, if any?

If the AFM for the aircraft is missing, a pilot may not legally fly the aircraft unless an acceptable substitution is available. The AFM is considered a required document under 14 CFR §91.9, which

Private Pilot Oral Exam Guide 25

Chapter 2 **Aircraft Airworthiness Requirements**

states that the aircraft must be operated in accordance with the operating limitations specified in its approved flight manual or, if applicable, its pilot's operating handbook (POH).

For most modern aircraft, the AFM is specific to the aircraft model and sometimes even the individual aircraft based on its equipment and modifications. If the original AFM is missing, the pilot can substitute an identical, approved replacement manual for the same make and model. This replacement must be approved by the FAA or provided by the manufacturer and include all current supplements, procedures, and limitations relevant to the aircraft.

If no approved replacement is available, the aircraft is not legal to fly until the AFM is replaced. In such cases, the operator must contact the manufacturer or obtain a certified copy of the AFM from the FAA or authorized sources.

Flying without the required operating manual is a violation of federal regulations and compromises the pilot's ability to ensure safe and legal operation.

[PA.I.B.K1; 14 CFR 91.9, FAA-H-8083-25]

8. Are airplane flight manual (AFM) supplements required on board an airplane for flight?

Airplane flight manual (AFM) supplements are required to be on board an airplane for flight if they apply to the specific aircraft configuration or modifications. Under 14 CFR §91.9(a), pilots must comply with the operating limitations specified in the AFM, including any required supplements.

AFM supplements are typically issued when additional equipment, systems, or modifications are installed on the aircraft. For instance, the installation of a GPS unit, autopilot, or specific avionics may necessitate a supplement that provides updated operating procedures, limitations, and performance data. These supplements become part of the official operating documentation for the aircraft. Supplements must be physically or electronically available with the primary AFM for reference during flight.

[PA.I.B.K1; 14 CFR 91.9, FAA-H-8083-25]

Chapter 2 **Aircraft Airworthiness Requirements**

9. For an aircraft to be considered airworthy, what two conditions must be met?

a. The aircraft must conform to its type design (type certificate). This is attained when the required and proper components are installed consistent with the drawings, specifications, and other data that are part of the type certificate. Conformity includes applicable supplemental type certificate(s) (STC) and field-approval alterations.

b. The aircraft must be in a condition for safe operation, referring to the condition of the aircraft in relation to wear and deterioration. For an aircraft to be operated with inoperative equipment, it must be permitted in accordance with an approved minimum equipment list, kinds of operation equipment list, or have been deemed airworthy and returned to service by an FAA-approved maintenance provider.

[PA.I.B.K1; FAA-H-8083-19]

10. Explain how a pilot determines if an aircraft conforms to its approved type design and is in a condition for safe operation.

a. To determine that the aircraft conforms to its type design, a pilot must determine that the maintenance, preventive maintenance, and alterations have been performed in accordance with Parts 21, 43, and 91 and that the aircraft is registered in the United States. The pilot does this by ensuring that all required inspections, maintenance, preventive maintenance, repairs, and alterations have been appropriately documented in the aircraft's maintenance records. If any inoperative equipment is present, it must have been appropriately returned to service. The return to service must include any documentation to do so in the aircraft's logbooks by an appropriately authorized maintenance provider. If the item will be allowed to be inoperative, it must be placarded inoperative and disabled and the aircraft must have been deemed to still be airworthy with the inoperative equipment.

b. To determine that the aircraft is in condition for safe operation, the pilot conducts a thorough preflight inspection of the aircraft for wear and deterioration, structural damage, fluid leaks, tire wear, inoperative instruments and equipment, etc. If an unsafe

Private Pilot Oral Exam Guide 27

Chapter 2 **Aircraft Airworthiness Requirements**

condition exists or inoperative instruments or equipment are found, the pilot uses the guidance in 14 CFR §91.213 for handling the inoperative equipment.

[PA.I.B.K1; 14 CFR Part 21]

11. What records or documents should be checked to determine that the owner or operator of an aircraft has complied with all required inspections and airworthiness directives?

The maintenance records (aircraft and engine logbooks). Each owner or operator of an aircraft shall ensure that maintenance personnel make appropriate entries in the aircraft maintenance records indicating the aircraft has been approved for return to service.

[PA.I.B.K1c; 14 CFR 91.405]

12. Who is responsible for ensuring that an aircraft is maintained in an airworthy condition?

The owner or operator of an aircraft is primarily responsible for maintaining an aircraft in an airworthy condition. The pilot-in-command is responsible for verifying that this has been completed prior to a flight.

[PA.I.B.K1e; 14 CFR 91.403]

13. Describe some of the responsibilities an aircraft owner has pertaining to aircraft documents, maintenance, and inspections of their aircraft.

Aircraft owners must:

a. Have a current airworthiness certificate and aircraft registration in the aircraft.

b. Maintain the aircraft in an airworthy condition including compliance with all applicable airworthiness directives.

c. Ensure maintenance is properly recorded.

d. Keep abreast of current regulations concerning the operation of that aircraft.

e. Notify the FAA Civil Aviation Registry immediately of any change of permanent mailing address, the sale or export of the aircraft, or the loss of citizenship.

28 Aviation Supplies & Academics

Chapter 2 **Aircraft Airworthiness Requirements**

f. Have a current FCC radio station license if equipped with radios, including an emergency locator transmitter (ELT) if operated outside of the United States.

[PA.I.B.K1e; FAA-H-8083-25]

14. What are airworthiness directives (AD)?

An airworthiness directive (AD) is the medium by which the FAA notifies aircraft owners and other potentially interested persons of unsafe conditions that may exist because of design defects, maintenance, or other causes, and specifies the conditions under which the product may continue to be operated. ADs are regulatory in nature, and compliance is mandatory. It is the aircraft owner's or operator's responsibility to ensure compliance with all pertinent ADs. Airworthiness directives may be found on the FAA's website at www.faa.gov/regulations_policies/airworthiness_directives and drs.faa.gov.

[PA.I.B.K1c; FAA-H-8083-25]

15. What are the two types of ADs?

ADs are divided into two categories: Those of an emergency nature requiring immediate compliance prior to further flight, and those of a less urgent nature requiring compliance within a specified period of time.

[PA.I.B.K1c; FAA-H-8083-19]

16. When are emergency ADs issued?

An emergency AD is issued when an unsafe condition exists that requires immediate action by an owner/operator. The intent of an emergency AD is to rapidly correct an urgent safety-of-flight situation. All known owners and operators of affected US-registered aircraft or those aircraft that have an affected product installed will be sent a copy of an emergency AD.

Exam Tip: Be capable of finding and explaining the status of all ADs and recurring ADs that exist for your aircraft. Locate and tab prior to the practical test.

[PA.I.B.K1c; FAA-H-8083-19]

Chapter 2 **Aircraft Airworthiness Requirements**

17. How can a pilot determine if all applicable airworthiness directives have been complied with for an airplane?

While it is the responsibility of the owner/operator of an aircraft to ensure that airworthiness directives (ADs) are complied with when maintenance is conducted, it is the responsibility of the pilot to ensure that this has been done prior to beginning a flight.

To determine applicable ADs for an aircraft, a pilot or operator must follow a systematic process to ensure compliance with FAA regulations. ADs are legally enforceable rules issued by the FAA to address safety issues in aircraft, engines, propellers, or other components.

It requires that the pilot or maintenance provider identify the make, model, and serial number of the aircraft and its major components, such as the engine, propeller, and avionics. Many ADs are specific to certain serial numbers or configurations. They should inspect the aircraft's logbooks and maintenance records, which should contain documentation of all previously complied-with ADs, including their completion dates and methods of compliance.

The FAA's Dynamic Regulatory System (DRS) (see drs.faa.gov) or an alternative commercial service may be used to find applicable ADs. It is best to work with a certified Airframe and Powerplant (A&P) Mechanic to address outstanding ADs.

[PA.I.B.K1c; FAA-H-8083-25, 14 CFR 91.417]

18. Do all ADs only need to be checked at annual inspections?

No; airworthiness directives are not limited to being checked only during annual inspections. AD compliance is required at all times to maintain an aircraft's airworthiness, and the specific timing and frequency of AD checks depend on the nature of each directive.

ADs may have different compliance requirements:

a. *One-time compliance*—Some ADs mandate a single inspection, modification, or replacement within a specified time or flight hours. Once completed, no further action is necessary unless otherwise noted.

b. *Recurring compliance*—Other ADs require repeated inspections or maintenance actions at regular intervals, such as every 100 flight hours or annually. These must be tracked separately from routine inspections.

30 Aviation Supplies & Academics

Chapter 2 **Aircraft Airworthiness Requirements**

c. *Immediate action*—Certain ADs, especially emergency ADs, require immediate compliance before the next flight due to critical safety concerns.

d. *Special situations*—Some ADs are conditional, becoming applicable only if specific equipment is installed or under certain operating conditions.

While annual inspections are a convenient time to verify AD compliance, the aircraft owner or operator is responsible for ensuring all applicable ADs are met before the aircraft is flown. Maintenance records must reflect AD compliance, and pilots must confirm adherence as part of preflight preparations and operational planning.

Some ADs will come up between inspections, and a pilot should ensure they will not be starting a flight with an AD that is past due.

[PA.I.B.K1c; 14 CFR 91.213]

19. While reviewing the aircraft logbooks, you discover that your aircraft is not in compliance with an AD's specified time or date. Are you allowed to continue to operate that aircraft until the next required maintenance inspection? Do the regulations allow any kind of buffer?

The assumption that AD compliance is only required at the time of a required inspection (e.g., at a 100-hour or annual inspection) is not correct. The required compliance time/date is specified in each AD, and no person may operate the affected product after expiration of that stated compliance time without an Alternative Method of Compliance (AMOC) approval for a change in compliance time.

[PA.I.B.K1c; AC 39-7]

20. May a pilot overfly a due airworthiness directive (AD) in order to get back to their home base or travel to maintenance?

Most ADs do not allow for flight beyond the due time. Unless a specific allowance is stipulated in the AD to get the aircraft somewhere for maintenance, the aircraft must not be flown until the AD has been complied with. In most cases, special flight permits are also not issued unless all ADs have been complied with.

(continued)

Private Pilot Oral Exam Guide 31

Chapter 2 **Aircraft Airworthiness Requirements**

A pilot cannot legally overfly a due airworthiness directive, even to return to a home base or travel to a maintenance facility, without specific FAA authorization. ADs are mandatory safety regulations, and compliance with their deadlines is essential to ensure the aircraft remains airworthy.

If an AD is due and the required action has not been completed, the aircraft is considered unairworthy. Operating an unairworthy aircraft violates FAA regulations, specifically 14 CFR §91.7, which prohibits flights in unairworthy aircraft.

[PA.I.B.K1c; 14 CFR 91.213]

21. You determine that you need to fly your aircraft with an expired AD to another airport where a repair facility can do the work required by the AD. How can you accomplish this?

Unless the AD states otherwise, you may apply to the FAA for a special flight permit following the procedures in 14 CFR §21.199.

[PA.I.B.K1c; AC 39-7, 14 CFR 21.199]

22. What is a type certificate data sheet?

The FAA issues a type certificate when a new aircraft, engine, propeller, etc., is found to meet safety standards set forth by the FAA. The type certificate data sheet (TCDS) lists the specifications, conditions, and limitations under which airworthiness requirements were met for the specified product, such as engine make and model, fuel type, engine limits, airspeed limits, maximum weight, minimum crew. Information on the TCDS by make and model can be found on the FAA website at drs.faa.gov/search.

[PA.I.B.K1; FAA-H-8083-30]

23. What is a supplemental type certificate?

A supplemental type certificate (STC) is the FAA's approval of a major change in the type design of a previously approved type-certificated product. The certificate authorizes an alteration to an airframe, engine, or component that has been granted an approved type certificate. Sometimes alterations are made that are not specified or authorized in the TCDS. When that condition exists, an

Chapter 2 **Aircraft Airworthiness Requirements**

STC will be issued. STCs are considered a part of the permanent records of an aircraft and should be maintained as part of that aircraft's logs.

[PA.I.B.K1; FAA-H-8083-3, FAA-H-8083-30, AC 21-40]

24. What is an aircraft registration certificate?

Before an aircraft can be flown legally, it must be registered with the FAA Aircraft Registry. The Certificate of Aircraft Registration, which is issued to the owner as evidence of the registration, must be carried in the aircraft at all times.

[PA.I.B.K1a; FAA-H-8083-25]

25. Does an aircraft's registration certificate have an expiration date?

Yes. A Certificate of Aircraft Registration issued in accordance with 14 CFR §47.31 expires seven years after the last day of the month in which it is issued. The Aircraft Registration Application (pink copy) is valid until the applicant receives the aircraft registration certificate, the application is denied by the FAA, or 12 months have elapsed during which the registration is pending on the aircraft.

[PA.I.B.K1a; 14 CFR 47.31, 47.40]

26. Where can you find information on the placards and marking information required to be in the airplane?

The principal source of information for identifying the required airplane flight manuals (AFM), approved manual materials, markings, and placards is the FAA type certificate data sheet or aircraft specification issued for each airplane eligible for an airworthiness certificate. The required placards are also reproduced in the "Limitations" section of the AFM or as directed by an AD.

[PA.I.B.K3; FAA-H-8083-25, 14 CFR 91.9, 23.2610]

27. What are several examples of placards and markings required in the airplane?

Placards—Day-Night-VFR-IFR placard, "Flight Maneuvers Permitted" placard, "Caution Control Lock Remove before Starting," "Maneuvering Speed," "Compass Calibration Card," etc.

(continued)

Private Pilot Oral Exam Guide   33

Chapter 2 **Aircraft Airworthiness Requirements**

Markings—Airspeed indicator markings; flight deck control markings; fuel, oil, and coolant filler openings; etc.

[PA.I.B.K3; 14 CFR 23.2610]

28. What are Special Airworthiness Information Bulletins (SAIB)? Are they regulatory?

Special Airworthiness Information Bulletins (SAIBs) are informational notices issued by the FAA to communicate important safety information to aircraft owners, operators, and maintenance personnel. Unlike airworthiness directives (ADs), SAIBs are not regulatory and do not mandate any specific actions. Instead, they serve as recommendations to address potential safety issues that may not require immediate corrective action or do not warrant the issuance of an AD.

SAIBs can cover a wide range of topics, including maintenance practices, operational concerns, and potential defects in aircraft, engines, propellers, or systems. They are often issued to highlight concerns discovered during FAA oversight activities or based on reports from manufacturers, operators, or other aviation stakeholders.

While SAIBs are non-regulatory, compliance with their recommendations can significantly enhance safety by addressing issues proactively. For instance, a SAIB may suggest inspecting a particular component or adopting new maintenance procedures. These actions, while optional, can help operators avoid more severe problems in the future.

[PA.I.B.K1c; FAA-H-8083-25]

B. Aircraft Maintenance Requirements

1. What are the required tests and inspections to be performed on an aircraft? Include inspections for instrument flight rules (IFR).

Remember: AAV1ATE

Annual inspection within the preceding 12 calendar months (14 CFR §91.409)

Airworthiness directives and life-limited parts compliance, as required (14 CFR §91.403, §91.417)

34 Aviation Supplies & Academics

Chapter 2 **Aircraft Airworthiness Requirements**

VOR equipment check every 30 days (for IFR ops) (14 CFR §91.171)

100-hour inspection, if used for hire or flight instruction in aircraft a CFI provides (14 CFR §91.409)

Altimeter, altitude reporting equipment, and static pressure systems tested and inspected (for IFR ops) every 24 calendar months (14 CFR §91.411)

Transponder tests and inspections, every 24 calendar months (14 CFR §91.413)

Emergency locator transmitter, operation, and battery condition inspected every 12 calendar months (14 CFR §91.207)

Exam Tip: Be prepared to locate all the required inspections, ADs, life-limited parts, etc., in the aircraft and engine logbooks, and be able to determine when the next inspections are due. Create an aircraft status sheet that indicates the status of all required inspections, ADs, life-limited parts, etc., and/or use post-it notes to tab the specific pages in the aircraft and engine logbooks. Write the due date of the next inspection on the post-it note. A critical ability is to be able to demonstrate compliance at the time of flight with any recurring AD inspections.

[PA.I.B.K1b; 14 CFR 91.171, 91.207, 91.409, 91.411, 91.413]

2. What is an annual inspection, and which aircraft are required to have annual inspections?

An annual inspection is a complete inspection of an aircraft and engine as required by the regulations that is required to be accomplished every 12 calendar months on all certificated aircraft.

[PA.I.B.K1b; FAA-H-8083-25]

3. Who can complete an annual inspection for an aircraft?

Only an A&P (airframe and powerplant rated) mechanic holding an Inspection Authorization (IA) can conduct an annual inspection.

[PA.I.B.K1b; FAA-H-8083-25]

Private Pilot Oral Exam Guide 35

Chapter 2 **Aircraft Airworthiness Requirements**

4. When is an aircraft required to have 100-hour inspections?

a. All aircraft under 12,500 pounds (except turbojet/turbopropeller-powered multiengine airplanes and turbine-powered rotorcraft) used to carry passengers for hire.

b. Aircraft used for flight instruction for hire, when provided by the person giving the flight instruction.

Note: Technically, an aircraft that was rented or leased but not used to carry passengers for hire or flight instruction would not require a 100-hour inspection.

[PA.I.B.K1b; FAA-H-8083-25, 14 CFR 91.409]

5. Who can complete a 100-hour inspection for an aircraft?

Either an FAA-authorized A&P mechanic or an A&P mechanic with an additional IA certification may complete a 100-hour inspection on an aircraft.

[PA.I.B.K1b; 14 CFR 91.409]

6. What is the difference between an annual inspection and a 100-hour inspection?

The main difference is who is allowed to perform these inspections. Only an A&P mechanic with an IA can perform an annual inspection. 100-hour inspections may be performed by any A&P mechanic (no IA required). Part 43, Appendix D (Scope and Detail of Items to Be Included in Annual and 100-Hour Inspections) contains a list of items to be checked during inspections.

[PA.I.B.K1b; 14 CFR Part 43]

7. If an aircraft has been on a schedule of inspection every 10 hours, under what condition may it continue to operate beyond the 10 hours without a new inspection?

The 100-hour limitation may be exceeded by not more than 10 hours while en route to a place where the inspection can be done. The excess time used to reach a place where the inspection can be done must be included in computing the next 100 hours of time in service. During this time, the aircraft may not be operated for compensation or hire or for flight instruction purposes.

[PA.I.B.K1b; 14 CFR 91.409]

Chapter 2 **Aircraft Airworthiness Requirements**

8. **A 100-hour inspection was due at 3,302.5 hours. The 100-hour inspection was actually done at 3,309.5 hours. When is the next 100-hour inspection due?**

A 100-hour inspection can be over flown to a maintenance location, but it will not reset the hours at which the next inspection will be due. While in this case the inspection was done at 3,309.5 hours, it was due at 3,302.5 hours and thus the next will be due at 3,402.5 hours. The only way to reset the hours for the 100-hour inspection would be to complete an annual inspection. For example, if an IA mechanic completed an annual inspection at 3,309.5 hours instead of a 100-hour inspection, the next 100-hour inspection would then be due at 3,409.5 hours.

[PA.I.B.K1b; FAA-H-8083-25, 14 CFR 91.409]

9. **If the annual inspection date has passed, can an aircraft be operated in flight to a location where the inspection can be performed?**

An aircraft overdue for an annual inspection may only be operated under a special flight permit issued by the FAA for the purpose of flying the aircraft to a location where the annual inspection can be performed. However, all applicable ADs that are due must be complied with before the flight.

[PA.I.B.K1d; FAA-H-8083-25]

10. **After aircraft inspections have been made and defects have been repaired, who is responsible for determining that the aircraft is in an airworthy condition?**

The pilot-in-command of a civil aircraft is responsible for determining whether that aircraft is in a condition for safe flight. The pilot-in-command shall discontinue the flight when unairworthy, mechanical, electrical, or structural conditions occur.

[PA.I.B.K1e; 14 CFR 91.7]

11. **What instruments and equipment are required for an aircraft by regulation for VFR (visual flight rules) day flight?**

For VFR flight during the day, the following are required:

Anticollision light system—aviation red or white for small airplanes certificated after March 11, 1996.

(continued)

Private Pilot Oral Exam Guide 37

Chapter 2 **Aircraft Airworthiness Requirements**

Tachometer for each engine.

Oil pressure gauge for each engine.

Manifold pressure gauge for each altitude engine.

Altimeter.

Temperature gauge for each liquid-cooled engine.

Oil temperature gauge for each air-cooled engine.

Fuel gauge indicating the quantity in each tank.

Flotation gear—if operated for hire over water beyond power-off gliding distance from shore.

Landing gear position indicator, if the airplane has retractable gear.

Airspeed indicator.

Magnetic direction indicator.

Emergency locator transmitter (if required by 14 CFR §91.207).

Safety belts (shoulder harnesses for each front seat also required in aircraft manufactured after 1978).

Remember: A TOMATO FLAMES.

Note: Additional aircraft equipment is required for night flight. Refer to Chapter 12 for more information on this requirement.

[PA.I.B.K3; 14 CFR 91.205]

12. While en route on a VFR cross-country, you notice that your left fuel tank indicator is inoperative during a descent to your first fuel stop. Can you legally continue your cross-country flight? If yes, what actions are required?

Since FAA regulations stipulate that the aircraft must have a "fuel gauge indicating the quantity in each tank," the flight would not be able to proceed. The pilot would need to proceed with procedures to fix or obtain special approval to fly with the inoperative equipment.

[PA.I.B.K3a; FAA-H-8083-25, 14 CFR 91.205]

13. What is a minimum equipment list?

The minimum equipment list (MEL) is a precise listing of instruments, equipment, and procedures that allows an aircraft to be operated under specific conditions with inoperative equipment. The MEL is the specific inoperative equipment document for a particular make and model aircraft by serial and registration numbers (e.g., BE-200, N12345). The FAA-approved MEL includes only those

Chapter 2 **Aircraft Airworthiness Requirements**

items of equipment that the FAA deems may be inoperative and still maintain an acceptable level of safety with appropriate conditions and limitations. A MEL should be considered a "permission to operate with inoperative" list, not a list of minimum equipment that must be operating for a flight.

Note: Do not confuse an MEL with the aircraft's equipment list. They are not the same.

[PA.I.B.K3b; FAA-H-8083-25]

14. For an aircraft with an approved MEL, explain the decision sequence a pilot would use after discovering the position lights are inoperative.

With an approved MEL, if the position lights were discovered inoperative prior to a daytime flight, the pilot would make an entry in the maintenance record or discrepancy record provided for that purpose. The item is then either repaired or deferred in accordance with the MEL. Upon confirming that daytime flight with inoperative position lights is acceptable in accordance with the provisions of the MEL, the pilot would leave the position lights switch OFF, open the circuit breaker (or do whatever action is called for in the procedures document), and placard the position light switch as INOPERATIVE.

[PA.I.B.K3b; FAA-H-8083-25]

15. Explain the limitations that apply to aircraft operations being conducted using an MEL.

The use of an MEL for a small, non-turbine-powered airplane operated under 14 CFR Part 91 allows for the deferral of inoperative items or equipment. The FAA considers an approved MEL to be a supplemental type certificate (STC) issued to an aircraft by serial number and registration number. Once an operator requests an MEL, and a letter of authorization (LOA) is issued by the FAA, the MEL then becomes mandatory for that aircraft. All maintenance deferrals must be done in accordance with the terms and conditions of the MEL and the operator-generated procedures document. Most light general aviation aircraft do not have established MEL lists.

[PA.I.B.K3b; FAA-H-8083-25]

Chapter 2 **Aircraft Airworthiness Requirements**

16. What is a *kinds of operation equipment list* (KOEL)

A kinds of operation equipment list (KOEL) is a document associated with an aircraft's pilot's operating handbook (POH) or airplane flight manual (AFM). It specifies the equipment required for the aircraft to be considered airworthy for specific types of operations, such as day or night flights, visual flight rules (VFR), or instrument flight rules (IFR). It is specific to make and model, not specific to an individual aircraft (e.g., N1234).

A KOEL may be used similarly to a MEL in that it defines what equipment may be allowed to be inoperative under specific conditions, but also what must be functional based on the aircraft's certification and intended use. It includes items like navigation lights, instruments, autopilots, deicing equipment, alternators, or other equipment depending on the type of operation. For instance, for IFR operations, functioning gyroscopic flight instruments would typically be required, but under VFR conditions it might be allowed for a backup battery or alternator to be inoperative.

Developed based on the aircraft's type certificate, the KOEL ensures compliance with 14 CFR §91.213, which governs operations with inoperative equipment. Pilots reference the KOEL to determine if an inoperative item affects the airworthiness of their aircraft for their intended flight.

Unlike an MEL, which requires FAA approval for specific aircraft, the KOEL is a manufacturer-provided document that is universally applicable to the aircraft model it pertains to. Pilots may use it to make informed go/no-go decisions, ensuring the aircraft's configuration meets regulatory and operational safety requirements.

[PA.I.B.K3c; FAA-H-8083-25]

17. What regulations apply concerning the operation of an aircraft that has had alterations or repairs that may have substantially affected its operation in flight?

No person may operate or carry passengers in any aircraft that has undergone maintenance, preventative maintenance, rebuilding, or alteration that may have appreciably changed its flight characteristics or substantially affected its operation in flight until an appropriately rated pilot with at least a Private Pilot Certificate:

Chapter 2 **Aircraft Airworthiness Requirements**

a. Flies the aircraft;

b. Makes an operational check of the maintenance performed or alteration made; and

c. Logs the flight in the aircraft records.

[PA.I.B.K1b; 14 CFR 91.407]

18. Can a pilot legally conduct flight operations with known inoperative equipment onboard?

Yes, under specific conditions. Part 91 describes acceptable methods for the operation of an aircraft with certain inoperative instruments and equipment that are not essential for safe flight. They are:

a. Operation of an aircraft with a minimum equipment list (MEL) or kinds of operation equipment list (KOEL), as authorized by 14 CFR §91.213(a); or

b. Operation of an aircraft without a MEL or a KOEL under 14 CFR §91.213(d).

Exam Tip: Know this regulation well. Unfamiliarity with 14 CFR §91.213 is a common weakness of applicants at all levels. You must demonstrate that you know this regulation and how to apply it.

[PA.I.B.K3a; 14 CFR 91.213]

19. How can a pilot deactivate an item or system on an aircraft if it has become inoperative, and make a flight legal to proceed?

To legally proceed with a flight after an item or system becomes inoperative, a pilot must follow the guidance in 14 CFR §91.213 (for aircraft without a minimum equipment list [MEL] or kinds of operation equipment list [KOEL]).

The following steps should be followed:

a. *Determine airworthiness impact*—The pilot must assess whether the inoperative item affects the aircraft's airworthiness or safety for the planned operation. Reference the type certificate data sheet (TCDS), kinds of operation equipment list (KOEL), pilot's operating handbook (POH), installed equipment list, STCs, or FAA regulations. If the item is required for the flight (e.g., lights for night VFR), the flight cannot proceed without repair.

(continued)

Private Pilot Oral Exam Guide 41

Chapter 2 **Aircraft Airworthiness Requirements**

b. *Check for airworthiness directives (ADs)*—Verify that no applicable ADs require the item to be operational. If an AD applies, compliance is mandatory.

c. *Placard the item*—If the item is determined to be nonessential for the planned operation, it must be deactivated or turned off. Place a placard (e.g., "INOPERATIVE") near the control or item to indicate its status.

d. *Record the inoperative item*—Document the issue in the aircraft's maintenance log. This may be done if the item is eligible for preventative maintenance by the pilot. If not, it will require an FAA approved maintenance certificate holder to disable, placard, and record the work related to the inoperative item.

[PA.I.B.K2; 14 CFR 91.213]

20. What limitations apply to aircraft operations conducted using the deferral provision of 14 CFR §91.213(d)?

When inoperative equipment is found during preflight or prior to departure, the decision should be to cancel the flight, obtain maintenance prior to flight, or defer the item or equipment. Maintenance deferrals are not used for inflight discrepancies. The manufacturer's POH/AFM procedures are to be used in those situations.

[PA.I.B.K3a; FAA-H-8083-25]

21. During the preflight inspection in an aircraft, you find a piece of equipment that is inoperative. Describe how you will determine if the aircraft is still airworthy for flight.

The pilot must determine if the aircraft can be operated without the piece of equipment for the type of flight operation intended to be completed. The pilot should follow this sequence:

a. Does the aircraft have an approved minimum equipment list (MEL) or kinds of operations equipment list (KOEL) that includes the affected equipment and allows operation with it inoperative?

b. Is the inoperative equipment included in the type certificate data sheet for the aircraft?

Chapter 2 **Aircraft Airworthiness Requirements**

c. Is the inoperative equipment required by 14 CFR §91.205, §91.207, or any other rule of 14 CFR Part 91 for the specific kind of flight operation being conducted (for example, VFR, IFR, day, night)?

d. Is the inoperative equipment required to be operational by an AD?

If the equipment is specifically allowed to be inoperative by an approved MEL/KOEL, the pilot may operate the flight with the equipment inoperative. If this is not the case, the pilot will need to have the equipment disabled and placarded inoperative or have it removed, and the aircraft must be returned to service by a maintenance professional who would also need to complete documentation in the aircraft maintenance logs of the activity.

Note: See Appendix 3 for further explanation of this regulation.

Exam Tip: If an instrument or equipment item is inoperative in your aircraft, be able to explain how you will determine if the aircraft is airworthy and legal for flight and be able to show where proper documentation of the inoperative equipment was completed in the aircraft maintenance logs.

[PA.II.A.K3; 14 CFR 91.213(d), AC 91-67, FAA-H-8083-25]

22. What are special flight permits, and when are they necessary?

A special flight permit may be issued for an aircraft that may not currently meet applicable airworthiness requirements but is capable of safe flight. These permits are typically issued for the following purposes:

a. Flying an aircraft to a base where repairs, alterations, or maintenance are to be performed or to a point of storage.

b. Delivering or exporting an aircraft.

c. Production flight testing new-production aircraft.

d. Evacuating aircraft from areas of impending danger.

e. Conducting customer demonstration flights in new-production aircraft that have satisfactorily completed production flight tests.

[PA.I.B.K1d; 14 CFR 21.197, 91.213]

Private Pilot Oral Exam Guide   43

Chapter 2 **Aircraft Airworthiness Requirements**

23. How are special flight permits obtained?

If a special flight permit is needed, assistance and the necessary forms may be obtained from the local FSDO (Flight Standards District Office) or Designated Airworthiness Representative (DAR). Typically, this will be obtained from the FSDO office in which the flight is originating. The preferred process to complete this is using the FAA's Airworthiness Certification (AWC) —Applicant Portal at awc.faa.gov/AWCExternalApplicant.

[PA.I.B.K1d; FAA-H-8083-25, 14 CFR 21.197]

24. Who can perform maintenance on an aircraft?

An FAA-certificated A&P mechanic, an A&P mechanic with Inspection Authorization (IA), an appropriately rated FAA-certificated repair station, or the aircraft manufacturer.

[PA.I.B.K1; FAA-H-8083-25]

25. Define *preventive maintenance*.

Preventive maintenance means simple or minor preservation operations and the replacement of small standard parts not involving complex assembly operations. Certificated pilots, excluding student pilots, sport pilots, and recreational pilots, may perform preventive maintenance on any aircraft that is owned or operated by them provided that aircraft is not used in air carrier service. 14 CFR Part 43, Appendix A, identifies typical preventive maintenance operations, which include such basic items as oil changes, wheel bearing lubrication, and hydraulic fluid (brakes, landing gear system) refills.

Exam Tip: Know where to look in the regulations for items approved for preventive maintenance: Part 43, Appendix A, Paragraph C—Preventive Maintenance.

[PA.I.B.K2; FAA-H-8083-25, 14 CFR Part 43 Appendix A, AC 43-12]

26. What logbook entry information is required of the person performing preventive maintenance?

All pilots who maintain or perform preventive maintenance must make an entry in the maintenance record of the aircraft. The entry must include a description of the work, the date of completion of

44 Aviation Supplies & Academics

Chapter 2 **Aircraft Airworthiness Requirements**

the work performed, and an entry of the pilot's name, signature, certificate number, and type of certificate held.

[PA.I.B.K2; FAA-H-8083-25, 14 CFR 43.3]

27. You have just completed the first leg of a long cross-country flight and notice that the oil level is approaching the one-quart-low mark. As a private pilot, can you add the quart of oil yourself or is a mechanic required?

A pilot is authorized to add oil to an engine under the FAA's allowed list of "preventive maintenance" provisions.

[PA.I.B.K2; 14 CFR Part 43 Appendix A(c)]

28. During your preflight inspection, you discover that the left main tire on your aircraft has a large flat spot with nylon cord showing. You wisely decide that this is unacceptable, and the tire should be replaced before flight. Do the regulations allow the pilot to perform this maintenance, or must a licensed mechanic (A&P) perform it?

A pilot is authorized to change a tire under the FAA's allowed list of "preventative maintenance" provisions.

[PA.I.B.K2; 14 CFR Part 43 Appendix A(c)]

29. While inspecting the engine logbook of the rental aircraft you are planning to fly, you notice that the engine has exceeded its time between overhaul (TBO). Is it legal to fly this aircraft?

Yes. TBO is computed by the engine manufacturer and is a reliable estimate of the number of hours the engine could perform reliably within the established engine parameters and still not exceed the service wear limits for overhaul for major component parts such as the crankshaft, cam shaft, cylinders, connecting rods, and pistons. TBO times are make and model specific, and the recommended overhaul times are usually identified in the engine manufacturer's service bulletin or letter. For 14 CFR Part 91 operations, compliance with the TBO is not a mandatory maintenance requirement.

[PA.I.B.R1; AC 20-105]

Private Pilot Oral Exam Guide 45

Chapter 2 **Aircraft Airworthiness Requirements**

30. What are several good reasons for aircraft owners to comply with TBO times recommended by the manufacturer?

a. An overhaul at TBO will ensure safety and reliability.

b. An engine overhaul at TBO is usually less expensive than one for an engine that has been run an additional 200 or 300 hours.

c. Running the engine past TBO usually accelerates the overall wear of the engine due to bearing movement outside tolerances, loss of protective materials such as plating or nitrating on the cylinder walls, and vibration caused by engine reciprocating parts that have worn unevenly and are now out of balance.

Study Tip: Chapter 2 of the FAA-H-8083-30 provides an excellent overview and an in-depth explanation of the maintenance regulations, publications, forms, and records required to design, build, and maintain aircraft. Consider it as an additional reference when studying the ACS Airworthiness task prior to your checkride.

[PA.I.B.K1; AC 20-105]

Preflight Procedures

3

Chapter 3 Preflight Procedures

A. Preflight Assessment

1. Explain how a pilot can perform an effective self-assessment before flight.

Prior to each and every flight, all pilots must do a proper physical self-assessment to ensure safety. One of the best ways to accomplish this is to use the IMSAFE checklist to determine physical and mental readiness for flying:

Illness—Am I sick? Illness is an obvious pilot risk.

Medication—Am I taking any medicines that might affect my judgment or make me drowsy?

Stress—Am I under excessive stress or psychological pressure?

Alcohol—Have I been drinking within 8 hours? Within 24 hours?

Fatigue—Am I tired and not adequately rested?

Emotion—Am I emotionally upset?

[PA.I.H, PA.II.A.R; FAA-H-8083-25]

2. What is the purpose of performing a preflight inspection on the airplane?

The purpose of the preflight inspection is to ensure that the airplane meets regulatory airworthiness standards and is in a safe mechanical condition prior to flight.

[PA.II.A.K; FAA-H-8083-3]

3. Who is responsible for ensuring that an aircraft is maintained in an airworthy condition?

The owner or operator of an aircraft is primarily responsible for maintaining an aircraft in an airworthy condition.

[PA.II.A.K2; 14 CFR 91.403]

4. Who is responsible for determining that an aircraft is airworthy and in a condition for safe flight?

The pilot-in-command of a civil aircraft is responsible for determining whether that aircraft is in condition for safe flight. The pilot-in-command shall discontinue the flight when unairworthy mechanical, electrical, or structural conditions occur.

[PA.II.A.K2; 14 CFR 91.7]

48 Aviation Supplies & Academics

Chapter 3 **Preflight Procedures**

5. **For an aircraft to be considered airworthy, what two conditions must be met?**

   a. The aircraft must conform to its type design (type certificate). This is attained when the required and proper components are installed consistent with the drawings, specifications, and other data that are part of the type certificate. Conformity includes applicable supplemental type certificate(s) (STC) and field-approval alterations.

   b. The aircraft must be in a condition for safe operation, referring to the condition of the aircraft in relation to wear and deterioration.

   [PA.II.A.K2; FAA-H-8083-19]

6. **Explain how a pilot determines if an aircraft conforms to its approved type design and is in a condition for safe operation.**

   a. To determine that the aircraft conforms to its type design, a pilot must determine that the maintenance, preventive maintenance, and alterations have been performed in accordance with Parts 21, 43, and 91 and that the aircraft is registered in the United States. The pilot does this by ensuring that all required inspections, maintenance, preventive maintenance, repairs, and alterations have been appropriately documented in the aircraft's maintenance records.

   b. To determine that the aircraft is in condition for safe operation, the pilot conducts a thorough preflight inspection of the aircraft for wear and deterioration, structural damage, fluid leaks, tire wear, inoperative instruments, and equipment, etc. If an unsafe condition exists or inoperative instruments or equipment are found, the pilot uses the guidance in 14 CFR §91.213 for handling the inoperative equipment.

   [PA.II.A.K2; 14 CFR Parts 21, 43, and 91]

7. **When approaching the airplane on the ramp to begin the preflight inspection, what should a pilot be looking for?**

   The pilot should make note of the general appearance of the airplane, looking for discrepancies such as misalignment of the landing gear and airplane structure. The pilot should also take note of any distortions of the wings, fuselage, and tail, as well as skin damage and any staining, dripping, or puddles of fuel or oils.

   [PA.II.A.K; FAA-H-8083-3]

Private Pilot Oral Exam Guide   49

Chapter 3 **Preflight Procedures**

8. According to most POH/AFM documents, what is the recommended sequence when beginning the inspection of the outer wing surfaces and tail section of the airplane?

Generally, the POH/AFM specifies a sequence for the pilot to inspect the aircraft that begins from the cabin entry access opening and then continues, in a counterclockwise direction, until the aircraft has been completely inspected.

[PA.II.A.K3; FAA-H-8083-3]

9. How would a pilot determine if a fuel sample obtained during the preflight inspection contained the incorrect grade of fuel or had signs of water contamination?

During a preflight inspection, a pilot uses a fuel sampler to verify the fuel's quality and check for contamination. To determine if the fuel contains the incorrect grade or water contamination, the pilot performs a visual inspection of sumped fuel.

Correctly graded aviation fuel has a distinct color. For instance, 100LL (low-lead) avgas is blue, while Jet A fuel is clear or straw-colored. If the sample's color does not match the expected grade, it may indicate contamination or refueling with the wrong fuel type. Water contamination appears as clear bubbles or distinct layers, as water is denser than fuel and settles at the bottom of the sample container. Fuel additionally has a specific odor. A smell inconsistent with avgas or jet fuel could suggest improper fuel or contamination.

If contamination or incorrect fuel is suspected, the pilot should drain additional samples until clean fuel is observed. If contamination persists, it must be addressed by maintenance personnel before flight. Do not fly until the issue is resolved.

[PA.II.A.S2; AC 20-125, FAA-H-8083-25]

10. Why is it important to inspect the airplane with reference to an appropriate checklist?

Checklists are guides for use in ensuring that all necessary items are not only checked but checked in a logical sequence. The pilot should never assume that the checklist is merely a crutch for poor memory but instead should consider the checklist a necessary tool used to accomplish a complex task thoroughly and efficiently.

[PA.II.A.S1; FAA-H-8083-3]

50 Aviation Supplies & Academics

Chapter 3 **Preflight Procedures**

11. What requirement must pilots understand about placards in an aircraft?

Pilots must understand that placards in an aircraft are legally required markings that convey essential information about operating limitations, safety instructions, or equipment functionality. They are installed to comply with Federal Aviation Regulations (FARs) and the aircraft's type certificate.

Placards often address critical operational restrictions, such as weight limits, approved fuel grades, or prohibited maneuvers. Pilots must ensure all placards are present, legible, and adhered to during flight, as missing or illegible placards may render the aircraft unairworthy.

[PA.II.A.K2; POH/AFM, TCDS]

12. In addition to items specified in the POH/AFM for inspection, what are other areas of concern to a pilot when inspecting the exterior structure of the aircraft?

a. A pilot should be aware of critical areas such as spar lines and wing, horizontal, and vertical attach points including wing struts and landing gear attachment areas. The airplane skin should be inspected in these areas, as load-related stresses are concentrated along spar lines and attachment points.

b. Spar lines are lateral rivet lines that extend across the wing, horizontal stabilizer, or vertical stabilizer. Pilots should pay close attention to spar lines looking for distortion, ripples, bubbles, dents, creases, or waves, as any structural deformity may be an indication of internal damage or failure.

c. A pilot should inspect around rivet heads, looking for cracked paint or a black-oxide film that forms when a rivet works free in its hole.

[PA.II.A.K3; FAA-H-8083-3]

13. Describe the additional inspections that may be required when conducting the preflight inspection of an airplane equipped with integrated flight deck (IFD) glass-panel avionics.

Ground-based inspections may include verifying that the flight deck reference guide is in the aircraft and accessible; checking of system-driven removal of Xs over engine indicators; checking

Private Pilot Oral Exam Guide 51

Chapter 3 **Preflight Procedures**

pitot/static and attitude displays; testing of low-level alarms and annunciator panels; setting of fuel levels; and verification that the avionics cooling fans, if equipped, are functional. The POH/AFM specifies how these preflight inspections are to take place.

[PA.II.B.S3; FAA-H-8083-3]

14. Explain the different types of airplane logbooks that should be available for inspection prior to flight.

Each airplane has a set of logbooks that include airframe and engine—and in some cases, propeller and appliance—logbooks, which are used to record maintenance, alterations, and inspections performed on a specific airframe, engine, propeller, or appliance.

[PA.II.A.K2; FAA-H-8083-3]

15. Where are the airplane logbooks located and when should they be inspected?

It is important that the logbooks be kept accurate, secure, and available for inspection. Airplane logbooks are not normally kept in the airplane. It should be a matter of procedure by the pilot to inspect the airplane logbooks or a summary of the airworthy status prior to flight to ensure that the airplane records of maintenance, alteration, and inspections are current and correct.

[PA.II.A.K2; FAA-H-8083-3]

16. How can the use of the PAVE checklist during preflight help a pilot to assess and mitigate risk?

Use of the PAVE checklist provides pilots with a simple way to remember each category to examine for risk during flight planning. The pilot divides the risks of flight into four categories:

Pilot—Illness, medication, stress, alcohol, fatigue, emotion (I'M SAFE), proficiency, currency.

Aircraft—Airworthiness, aircraft equipped for flight, proficiency in aircraft, performance capability.

enVironment—Weather hazards, type of terrain, airports/runways to be used, conditions.

External pressures—Meetings, people waiting at destination, desire to impress, desire to get there, etc.

[PA.II.A.R; FAA-H-8083-9]

52 Aviation Supplies & Academics

Chapter 3 **Preflight Procedures**

B. Flight Deck Management

1. Do the regulations require pilots to provide a pre-takeoff safety briefing to their passengers?

Yes. No pilot may take off an aircraft unless the PIC of that aircraft ensures that each person on board is *briefed* on how to fasten and unfasten that person's safety belt and, if installed, shoulder harness. Also, no pilot may cause to be moved on the surface, take off, or land an aircraft unless the pilot-in-command of that aircraft ensures that each person on board has been *notified* to fasten that person's safety belt and, if installed, a shoulder harness.

[PA.II.B.K1; 14 CFR 91.107]

2. Which persons on board an aircraft are required to use seat belts, and when is such use required?

Each person on board a US-registered civil aircraft must occupy an approved seat or berth with a safety belt, and if installed, shoulder harness, properly secured during movement on the surface, takeoff, and landing. However, passengers who have not reached their second birthday and do not occupy or use any restraining device may be held by an adult who is occupying a seat or berth, and a person on board for the purpose of engaging in sport parachuting may use the floor of the aircraft as a seat.

[PA.II.B.K1; 14 CFR 91.107]

3. Explain the items that should be included in a passenger preflight briefing.

Remember: SAFETY

Seat belts fastened for taxi, takeoff, landing. Shoulder harnesses fastened for takeoff, landing. Seat position adjusted and locked in place.

Air vents (location and operation). All environmental controls (discussed). Action in case of any passenger discomfort.

Fire extinguisher (location and operation).

Exit doors (how to secure; how to open). Emergency evacuation plan. Emergency/survival kit (location and contents).

Traffic (scanning, spotting, notifying pilot). Talking (sterile cockpit expectations).

Your questions? (Speak up!).

[PA.II.B.K1; FAA Safety Briefing]

Private Pilot Oral Exam Guide   53

Chapter 3 **Preflight Procedures**

4. When are flight crewmembers required to keep their seat belts and shoulder harnesses fastened?

During takeoff and landing and while en route, required flight crewmembers shall keep their seat belt fastened while at their station. During takeoff and landing, this includes shoulder harnesses, if installed, unless it interferes with other required duties.

[PA.II.B.K1; 14 CFR 91.105]

5. Why is the use of sterile cockpit procedures important when conducting taxi operations?

Pilots must be able to focus on their duties without being distracted by non-flight-related matters unrelated to the safe and proper operation of the aircraft. Refraining from nonessential activities during ground operations is essential. Passengers should be briefed on the importance of minimizing conversations and questions during taxi as well as on arrival, from the time landing preparations begin until the aircraft is safely parked.

[PA.II.B.S4; AC 91-73]

6. What are examples of hazards a pilot should consider when assessing flight deck management risk?

a. Equipment, checklists, charts, etc., not readily available or not secured.

b. Not briefing crew and passengers.

c. Poor ADM, SRM, CRM.

d. Improper use of systems or equipment, to include automation and portable electronic devices.

e. Flying with unresolved discrepancies.

[PA.II.B.R; FAA-S-ACS-6]

7. How can a pilot mitigate hazards and reduce the risk present when managing the flight deck?

a. Secure all items in the aircraft.

b. Conduct an appropriate passenger briefing, including identifying the pilot-in-command (PIC); use of safety belts, shoulder harnesses, and doors; passenger conduct; sterile aircraft; propeller blade avoidance; and emergency procedures.

Chapter 3 **Preflight Procedures**

   c. Properly program and manage the aircraft's automation, as applicable.

   d. Appropriately manage risks by utilizing ADM, including SRM/CRM.

[PA.II.B.R; FAA-S-ACS-6]

8. May portable electronic devices be operated on board an aircraft?

Aircraft operated by a holder of an air carrier operating certificate or an aircraft operating under IFR may not allow the operation of electronic devices on board their aircraft. Exceptions are portable voice recorders, hearing aids, heart pacemakers, electric shavers, or any other device that the operator of the aircraft has determined will not cause interference with the navigation or communication system of the aircraft on which it is to be used.

[PA.II.B.R1; 14 CFR 91.21]

9. Are navigational databases required to be updated prior to a VFR flight? What about for an IFR flight?

Databases must be updated for IFR operations and should be updated for all other operations. However, there is no requirement for databases to be updated for VFR navigation. It is not recommended to use a moving map with an outdated database in and around critical airspace. Databases are updated every 28 days and are available from various commercial vendors. For IFR operations, all approach procedures to be flown must be retrievable from the current airborne navigation database.

[PA.II.B.R1; FAA-H-8083-15, AIM 1-1-17, AC 90-100]

10. Explain what the FAA policy is for carrying current charts.

The specific FAA regulation, 14 CFR §91.103, Preflight Action, states that each pilot-in-command shall, before beginning a flight, become familiar with all available information concerning that flight. Although the regulation does not specifically require it, you should always carry current charts with you in flight. Expired charts may not show frequency changes or newly constructed obstructions, both of which, when unknown, could be a hazard.

[PA.II.B.K3; AERONAV FAQ]

Private Pilot Oral Exam Guide 55

Chapter 3 **Preflight Procedures**

11. Is a pilot required to have paper charts when flying, or may they use charting on a digital device such as a tablet?

An electronic flight bag (EFB) can be used during all phases of flight operations in lieu of paper reference material when the information displayed meets established criteria.

The inflight use of EFB systems to depict images in lieu of paper reference material is the decision of the aircraft operator and the pilot-in-command.

[PA.I.D.K1a, PA.I.D.R7; AC 91-78]

12. What criteria must an electronic flight bag (EFB) meet to be used for charting in lieu of the use of paper charts?

a. The EFB system does not replace any system or equipment (e.g., navigation, communication, or surveillance system) that is required by 14 CFR Part 91.

b. The EFB system on board the aircraft displays only information that is functionally equivalent to the paper reference material which the information is replacing or is substituted for.

c. The interactive or precomposed information being used for navigation or performance planning is current, up to date, and valid, as verified by the pilot.

d. The operator complies with the requirements of 14 CFR §91.21 to ensure that the use of the EFB does not interfere with equipment or systems required for flight.

[PA.I.D.K1a, PA.I.D.R7; AC 91-78]

13. When using an EFB for charting information, how can a pilot ensure they have current and up-to-date information?

Data on an EFB device will require updating to ensure that the pilot has the most current charting and airport information. Pilots are encouraged to ensure that data is current prior to using it. Pilots should check database versions and data content in the application/ software prior to using it for navigation, flight planning, or informational purposes. A pilot should be able to demonstrate on a practical test how they can show that the data on their device is current.

[PA.I.D.K1a, PA.I.D.R7; AC 91-78]

Chapter 3 **Preflight Procedures**

14. What are some best practices with regard to reliability and backup options for flight when using portable EFB devices?

EFB devices can fail or run out of power. Pilots are encouraged to have backup options such as traditional paper charts, backup secondary devices, or alternate power sources to provide power if the battery dies. This could include power from the aircraft charging or a backup battery pack that is carried along with a charging cable. Pilots should also be aware that some devices can overheat, and they should be prepared to handle such a scenario.

[PA.I.D.K1a, PA.I.D.R7; AC 91-78]

15. With regard to cargo carried in an aircraft, what is the responsibility of the pilot?

A pilot must make sure cargo carried in an aircraft:

a. Is properly secured by a safety belt or other tiedown having enough strength to eliminate the possibility of shifting under all normally anticipated flight and ground conditions;

b. Is packaged or covered to avoid possible injury to passengers;

c. Does not impose any load on seats or on the floor structure that exceeds the load limitation for those components;

d. Is not located in a position that restricts the access to or use of any required emergency or regular exit, or the use of the aisle between the crew and the passenger compartment; and

e. Is not carried directly above seated passengers.

[PA.II.B.K4; 14 CFR 91.525]

C. Engine Starting

1. Explain why it is important to call "Clear" prior to starting an aircraft engine.

The pilot needs to ensure that the ramp area surrounding the airplane is clear of persons, equipment, and other hazards that could come into contact with the airplane or the propeller. Just prior to starter engagement, the pilot should always call "CLEAR" out of the side window and wait for a response from anyone who may be nearby *before* engaging the starter.

[PA.II.C.R1; FAA-H-8083-3]

Private Pilot Oral Exam Guide 57

Chapter 3 **Preflight Procedures**

2. Describe several other precautions that can be taken to reduce risk prior to engine start.

The pilot should always check the area behind the airplane prior to engine start as a standard practice. At all times before engine start, the anti-collision lights should be turned on. For night operations, the position (navigation) lights should also be on.

[PA.II.C.R1; FAA-H-8083-3]

3. Explain why an engine start procedure in the winter would be different from one in the summer.

a. Batteries can lose a high percentage of their effectiveness in cold weather.

b. Oil can become partially congealed, and turning the engines is difficult for the starter or by hand.

c. There is a tendency to overprime, which results in washed-down cylinder walls and possible scouring of the walls. This results in poor compression and, consequently, harder starting.

d. Sometimes aircraft fires have been started by over prime when the engine fires while the exhaust system contains raw fuel. Other fires are caused by backfires through the carburetor.

[PA.II.C.K1; FAA-P-8740-24]

4. When starting the engine, are there any limitations on the amount of time the starter can be operated?

Starter motors are not designed for continuous duty. Their service life may be drastically shortened during a prolonged or difficult start, as an excess buildup of heat can damage internal starter components. Avoid continuous starter operation for periods longer than 30 seconds without a cool-down period of at least 30 seconds to 1 minute (some POH/AFMs specify longer cool-down routines). Reference your POH/AFM.

[PA.II.C.K3; FAA-H-8083-3, POH/AFM]

5. Explain how an airplane engine is started through the use of external power.

Some aircraft have receptacles to which an external ground power unit (GPU) may be connected to provide electrical energy for starting. These are very useful, especially during cold weather starting. Procedures for use of external power are not the same for

58 Aviation Supplies & Academics

Chapter 3 **Preflight Procedures**

all aircraft. Follow the manufacturer's recommendations in the POH/AFM.

[PA.II.C.K2; FAA-H-8083-3, POH/AFM]

6. In warm weather, how long should it take for the oil pressure to rise and provide an indication on the oil pressure gauge?

In most conditions, oil pressure should rise to at least the lower limit within 30 seconds. To prevent damage, the engine should be shut down immediately if the oil pressure does not rise to the POH/AFM values within the required time.

[PA.II.C.K3; FAA-H-8083-3, POH/AFM]

7. Identify hazards that a pilot should consider prior to conducting an engine start procedure.

a. Propeller safety.

b. Use of external power unit.

c. Engine limitations during starting.

d. Engine fire due to excessive priming.

e. Foreign object debris (FOD) around the airplane.

[PA.II.C; FAA-S-ACS-6]

D. Taxiing

1. Describe several sources of information that a pilot can reference for current airport data and conditions.

a. Aeronautical charts.

b. *Chart Supplement*

c. Notices to Airmen (NOTAMs).

d. Automated Terminal Information Service (ATIS) broadcasts.

e. GPS navigation databases and charting apps.

[PA.II.D.K1; FAA-H-8083-25]

Private Pilot Oral Exam Guide 59

Chapter 3 **Preflight Procedures**

2. Preflight planning for taxi operations should be an integral part of the pilot's flight planning process. What information should this include?

a. Review and understand airport signage, markings, and lighting.

b. Review the airport diagram and planned taxi route and identify any hot spots.

c. Review the latest airfield NOTAMs and ATIS (if available) for taxiway/runway closures, construction activity, etc.

d. Conduct a pre-taxi/pre-landing briefing that includes the expected/assigned taxi route and any hold short lines and restrictions based on ATIS information or previous experience at the airport.

e. Plan for critical times and locations on the taxi route (complex intersections, crossing runways, etc.).

f. Plan to complete as many aircraft checklist items as possible prior to taxi.

g. Brief passengers on the importance of minimizing discussions, questions, and conversation during taxi (maintain a sterile cockpit).

[PA.II.D; AC 91-73]

3. What is the purpose of an airport diagram and where can they be found?

Full page airport diagrams are designed to assist in the movement of ground traffic at locations with complex runway/taxiway configurations and provide information for updating geodetic position navigational systems aboard aircraft. Airport diagrams are available for download at www.faa.gov/airports/runway_safety /diagrams/. They can also be found in the *Chart Supplement*, the US Terminal Procedures Publication (TPP), GPS navigation databases, and many charting apps.

[PA.II.D.K1; AIM 9-1-4]

4. Explain why it is important to review NOTAMs prior to conducting taxi operations.

Notices to Airmen (NOTAMS) will include information on temporarily closed runways and taxiways. Depending on the reason for the closure, duration of closure, airfield configuration,

60 Aviation Supplies & Academics

Chapter 3 **Preflight Procedures**

and the existence and the hours of operation of an ATC tower, a visual indication may not always be present. Pilots should always check NOTAMs and ATIS prior to taxi for information on taxiway and runway closures, construction, and other airport changes that would affect their departure or arrival.

[PA.II.D.K1; FAA-H-8083-25]

5. What is a runway incursion?

A runway incursion is "any occurrence in the airport runway environment involving an aircraft, vehicle, person, or object on the ground that creates a collision hazard or results in a loss of required separation with an aircraft taking off, intending to take off, landing, or intending to land."

[PA.II.D.R4; FAA-H-8083-25]

6. Where are runway incursions most likely to occur?

Runway incursions most likely to cause accidents generally occur at complex, high-volume airports characterized by parallel/intersecting runways, multiple taxiway/runway intersections, complex taxi patterns, and the need for traffic to cross active runways. Historical data also shows that a large number of runway incursions involve general aviation pilots and often result from misunderstood controller instructions, confusion, disorientation, and/or inattention. Nearly all runway incursions are caused by human error.

[PA.II.D.R4; FAA-H-8083-25]

7. What is an airport hot spot?

A hot spot is a runway safety-related problem area on an airport that presents increased risk during surface operations. Typically, hot spots are complex or confusing taxiway–taxiway or taxiway–runway intersections. The area of increased risk has either a history of or potential for runway incursions or surface incidents due to a variety of causes, such as but not limited to airport layout; traffic flow; airport marking, signage and lighting; situational awareness; and training. Hot spots are depicted on airport diagrams as open circles or polygons designated as HS 1, HS 2, etc.

[PA.II.D.R4; Chart Supplement]

Private Pilot Oral Exam Guide   61

Chapter 3 **Preflight Procedures**

8. What are three major areas that contribute to runway incursions?

a. *Communications*—Misunderstanding the given clearance; failure to communicate effectively.

b. *Airport knowledge*—Failure to navigate the airport correctly; unable to interpret airport signage.

c. *Cockpit procedures for maintaining orientation*—Failure to maintain situational awareness.

[PA.II.D.R4; FAA-H-8083-3]

9. Identify hazards that should be considered when conducting taxi operations at a controlled airport.

a. Activities and distractions in the flight deck; pilot/passenger communications.

b. Confirmation or expectation bias as related to taxi instructions.

c. A taxi route or departure runway change.

d. ATC/pilot communications; not using standard phraseology, misunderstanding.

e. Loss of situational awareness.

f. Runway incursion.

[PA.II.D; FAA-S-ACS-6, AC 91-73]

10. Explain the terms *confirmation bias* and *expectation bias*.

Confirmation bias—The human tendency to look for information to confirm a decision already made. This occurs when we only look for, listen to, or acknowledge information that confirms our own preconceptions. We tend not to seek out or pay attention to evidence that could disconfirm the belief.

Expectation bias—When we have a strong belief or mindset toward something we expect to see or hear, and act according to those beliefs. This often occurs on the ground while taxiing where a pilot expects a particular taxi route and perceives the clearance as expected rather than as given by ATC.

Note: The result of either, if uncorrected, may lead to an error. Either case results in the pilot continuing with a plan despite clues indicating the situation is not as perceived. Fatigue tends to

62 Aviation Supplies & Academics

Chapter 3 **Preflight Procedures**

stop pilots from taking extra steps to verify perceived reality and contributes to expectation and confirmation bias susceptibility.

[PA.II.D.R2; FAA Safety: Bias, FAA-H-8083-2]

11. What can a pilot do to mitigate confirmation and expectation biases?

Understand that expectation bias often affects the verbal transmission of information. When issued instructions by ATC, focus on listening, and repeat to yourself in your head exactly what was said, and then apply that information actively. Does the clearance make sense? If something doesn't make sense (incorrect call sign, runway assignment, altitude, etc.), then query the controller about it.

[PA.II.D.R2; FAA Safety: Bias]

12. Explain the recommended practices that can help prevent runway incursions and assist a pilot in maintaining situational awareness during taxi operations.

a. A current airport diagram should be available for immediate reference during taxi.

b. Monitor ATC instructions/clearances issued to other aircraft for the big picture.

c. Focus attention outside the cockpit while taxiing.

d. Use all available resources (airport diagrams, airport signs, markings, lighting, and ATC) to keep the aircraft on its assigned taxi route.

e. Cross-reference heading indicator to ensure turns are being made in the correct direction and that you are on the assigned taxi route.

f. Prior to crossing any hold short line, visually check for conflicting traffic; verbalize "clear left, clear right."

g. Be alert for other aircraft with similar call signs on the frequency.

h. Understand and follow all ATC instructions, and if in doubt—ask!

[PA.II.D.R4; AC 91-73]

Private Pilot Oral Exam Guide 63

Chapter 3 **Preflight Procedures**

13. What information should a pilot always read back when receiving taxi instructions from a controller?

a. The runway assignment.

b. Any clearance to enter a specific runway.

c. Any instruction to hold short of a specific runway or to line up and wait.

Note: Good operating practice dictates that pilots read back *all* ATC taxi instructions to ensure that the pilot has received and clearly understands the instruction.

[PA.II.D.K2; AIM 4-3-18]

14. When issued taxi instructions to an assigned takeoff runway, are you automatically authorized to cross any runway that intersects your taxi route?

No. Aircraft must receive a runway crossing clearance for each runway that their taxi route crosses. When assigned a takeoff runway, ATC will first specify the runway, issue taxi instructions, and state any hold short instructions or runway crossing clearances if the taxi route will cross a runway. When issuing taxi instructions to any point other than an assigned takeoff runway, ATC will specify the point to which to taxi, issue taxi instructions, and state any hold short instructions or runway crossing clearances if the taxi route will cross a runway. ATC is required to obtain a read back from the pilot of all runway hold short instructions. Additionally, ATC is not authorized to clear a pilot to cross more than a runway at a time. If a pilot has been issued a clearance across a runway that would require them to cross another one first, they should query ATC for clarification before proceeding.

[PA.II.D.K2; AIM 4-3-18]

15. When should a pilot request progressive taxi instructions?

If the pilot is unfamiliar with the airport, or if for any reason confusion exists as to the correct taxi routing, a request may be made for progressive taxi instructions, which include step-by-step routing directions.

[PA.II.D.K2; AIM 4-3-18]

64 Aviation Supplies & Academics

Chapter 3 **Preflight Procedures**

16. What are several good reasons to write down taxi instructions, especially at larger or unfamiliar airports?

Writing down taxi instructions, especially complex instructions, can reduce a pilot's vulnerability to forgetting part of the instructions and provides a reference for read-back of instructions to ATC. It can also be used as a means of reconfirming the taxi route and any restrictions at any time during taxi operations.

[PA.II.D.K2, AC 91-73]

17. Describe the various types of taxiway markings.

Markings for taxiways are yellow and consist of the following types:

a. *Taxiway centerline*—Single continuous yellow line; aircraft should be kept centered over this line during taxi; however, being centered on the centerline does not guarantee wingtip clearance with other aircraft or objects.

b. *Taxiway edge*—Used to define the edge of taxiway; two types, continuous and dashed.

c. *Taxiway shoulder*—Usually defined by taxiway edge markings; denotes pavement unusable for aircraft.

d. *Surface painted taxiway direction*—Yellow background with black inscription; supplements direction signs or when not possible to provide taxiway sign.

e. *Surface painted location signs*—Black background with yellow inscription; supplements location signs.

f. *Geographic position markings*—Located at points along low-visibility taxi routes; used to identify the location of aircraft during low-visibility operations.

[PA.II.D.K3, AIM 2-3-4]

18. What are the three types of runway holding position markings?

a. *Runway holding position markings on taxiways*—These markings identify the locations on taxiways where aircraft **must stop** when a clearance has not been issued to proceed on to the runway.

(continued)

Private Pilot Oral Exam Guide   65

Chapter 3 **Preflight Procedures**

b. *Runway holding position markings on runways*—These markings identify the locations on runways where aircraft **must stop**. These markings are located on runways used by ATC for LAHSO and taxiing operations.

c. *Holding position markings on taxiways located in runway approach areas*—These markings are used at some airports where it is necessary to hold an aircraft on a taxiway located in the approach or departure area of a runway so that the aircraft does not interfere with the operations on that runway.

[PA.II.D.K3, AIM 2-3-5]

19. You're taxiing up to your departure runway and have been instructed to hold short of that runway. On which side of the runway holding position markings (four yellow lines, two solid and two dashed) does ATC expect you to hold?

Hold prior to the two solid yellow lines. When instructed by ATC, "Hold short of Runway XX," the pilot **must stop** so that no part of the aircraft extends beyond the runway holding position marking. An aircraft exiting a runway is not clear of the runway until all parts of the aircraft have crossed the applicable holding position marking.

[PA.II.D.K3, AIM 2-3-5]

20. Describe the various types of runway markings (precision instrument runway).

Markings for runways are white and consist of the following types:

a. *Runway designators*—Runway number is the whole number nearest one-tenth the magnetic azimuth of the centerline of the runway, measured clockwise from the magnetic north.

b. *Runway centerline marking*—Identifies the center of the runway and provides alignment guidance during takeoff and landings; consists of a line of uniformly spaced stripes and gaps.

c. *Runway aiming point marking*—Serves as a visual aiming point for a landing aircraft; two rectangular markings consist of a broad white stripe located on each side of the runway centerline and approximately 1,000 feet from the landing threshold.

66 Aviation Supplies & Academics

Chapter 3 **Preflight Procedures**

d. *Runway touchdown zone markers*—Identifies the touchdown zone for landing operations and are coded to provide distance information in 500-foot increments; groups of one, two, and three rectangular bars symmetrically arranged in pairs about the runway centerline.

e. *Runway side stripe markings*—Delineate the edges of the runway and provide a visual contrast between runway and the abutting terrain or shoulders; continuous white stripes located on each side of the runway.

f. *Runway shoulder markings*—May be used to supplement runway side stripes to identify pavement areas contiguous to the runway sides that are not intended for use by aircraft; painted yellow.

g. *Runway threshold markings*—Used to help identify the beginning of the runway that is available for landing. Two configurations: either eight longitudinal stripes of uniform dimensions disposed symmetrically about the runway centerline, or the number of stripes is related to the runway width.

[PA.II.D.K3, AIM 2-3-3]

21. Describe the six types of signs installed at airports.

a. *Mandatory instruction sign*—Red background/white inscription; denotes an entrance to a runway, critical area, or prohibited area.

b. *Location sign*—Black background/yellow inscription/yellow border; do not have arrows; used to identify a taxiway or runway location, the boundary of the runway, or identify an ILS critical area.

c. *Direction sign*—Yellow background/black inscription; identifies the designation of the intersecting taxiway(s) leading out of an intersection that a pilot would expect to turn onto or hold short of.

d. *Destination sign*—Yellow background/black inscription, and contain arrows; provides information on locating runways, terminals, cargo areas, civil aviation areas, etc.

e. *Information sign*—Yellow background/black inscription; used to provide the pilot with information on areas that can't be seen

Private Pilot Oral Exam Guide 67

Chapter 3 **Preflight Procedures**

from the control tower, applicable radio frequencies, noise abatement procedures, etc.

f. *Runway distance remaining sign*—Black background/white numeral inscription; indicates the distance of the remaining runway in thousands of feet.

[PA.II.D.K3, AIM 2-3-7 to 2-3-13]

22. Describe the following types of airport taxiway and runway lighting: runway edge lights, lights marking the ends of the runway, runway end identifier lights, taxiway edge lights, and taxiway centerline lights.

a. *Runway edge lights*—White. On instrument runways, yellow replaces white on the last 2,000 feet or half the runway length (whichever is less) to form a caution zone for landings.

b. *Lights marking the ends of the runway*—Emit red light toward the runway to indicate the end of the runway to a departing aircraft, and green light outward from the runway end to indicate the threshold to landing aircraft.

c. *Runway end identifier lights (REIL)*—Provide rapid and positive identification of the approach end of a particular runway. The system consists of a pair of synchronized flashing lights located laterally on each side of the runway threshold. REIL may be either omnidirectional or unidirectional facing the approach area.

d. *Taxiway edge lights*—Emit blue light; used to outline the edges of taxiways during periods of darkness or restricted visibility conditions.

e. *Taxiway centerline lights*—Steady-burning, green lights; used to facilitate ground traffic under low-visibility conditions.

[PA.II.D.K3, AIM 2-1-4, 2-1-10]

23. Describe the different visual wind direction indicators at airports without operating control towers.

a. *Segmented circle*—Located in a position affording maximum visibility to pilots in the air and on the ground and providing a centralized location for other elements of the system.

b. *Wind direction indicator*—A wind cone, windsock, or wind tee installed near the operational runway to indicate wind direction.

Chapter 3 **Preflight Procedures**

c. *Landing direction indicator*—A tetrahedron indicates the direction of landings and takeoffs. It may be located at the center of a segmented circle and may be lit for night operations. The small end of the tetrahedron points in the direction of landing.

d. *Landing strip indicators*—Installed in pairs within the airport segmented circle to show the alignment of landing strips.

e. *Traffic pattern indicators*—Arranged in pairs in conjunction with landing strip indicators and used to indicate the direction of turns when there is a variation from the normal left traffic pattern.

[PA.II.D.K4, AIM 4-3-4]

24. During calm or nearly calm wind conditions, at an airport without an operating control tower, a pilot should be aware of what potentially hazardous situations?

Aircraft may be landing and/or taking off on more than one runway at the airport. Also, aircraft may be using an instrument approach procedure to runways other than the runway in use for VFR operations. The instrument approach runway may intersect the VFR runway. It is also possible that an instrument arrival may be made to the opposite end of the runway from which takeoff is being made.

[PA.II.D.R4, AC 91-73]

25. When taxiing, describe several precautionary measures a pilot should take prior to entering or crossing a runway.

Towered airport—Prior to entering or crossing any runway, the pilot must be positive that ATC has cleared them to enter or cross that runway. Pilots should scan the full length of the runway and also scan for aircraft on final approach. If there is any confusion about the scan results, the pilot should stop and ask ATC to clarify the situation.

Non-towered airport—Listen on the appropriate frequency (CTAF) for inbound aircraft information and always scan the full length of the runway, including the final approach and departure paths, before entering or crossing the runway. Self-announce your position and intentions and remember that not all aircraft are radio-equipped.

[PA.II.D.R4, AC 91-73]

Private Pilot Oral Exam Guide   69

Chapter 3 **Preflight Procedures**

26. How can a pilot use aircraft exterior lighting to enhance situational awareness and safety during airport surface operations?

To the extent possible and consistent with aircraft equipment, operating limitations, and pilot procedures, pilots should illuminate exterior lights as follows:

a. *Engines running*—Turn on the rotating beacon whenever an engine is running.

b. *Taxiing*—Prior to commencing taxi, turn on navigation/position lights and anti-collision lights.*

c. *Crossing a runway*—All exterior lights should be illuminated when crossing a runway.

d. *Entering the departure runway for takeoff*—All exterior lights (except landing lights) should be on to make your aircraft more conspicuous to aircraft on final and to ATC.

e. *Cleared for takeoff*—All exterior lights, including takeoff/landing lights, should be on.

*Strobe lights should not be illuminated during taxi if they will adversely affect the vision of other pilots or ground personnel.

[PA.II.D.K5, AC 91-73; SAFO]

27. Explain how a pilot can mitigate the risk of a runway incursion if it becomes necessary to taxi in low-visibility conditions.

During low-visibility conditions, all available resources should be used during taxi. Resources include the airport diagram, the heading indicators, and airport signs, markings, and lighting. These resources help keep the aircraft on its assigned taxi route, and not crossing any runway hold lines without clearance.

[PA.II.D.K6e; AC 91-73]

28. What practices should a pilot follow regarding taxiing and runway incursion avoidance at non-towered airports?

Unless otherwise stated in the airport *Chart Supplement* for the airport reference to departure procedures, departing aircraft should monitor/communicate on the appropriate CTAF from startup, during taxi, and after departure, so to be aware of any inbound aircraft that could present a traffic conflict. While runway incursions are commonly thought to be relevant only at towered

70 Aviation Supplies & Academics

Chapter 3 **Preflight Procedures**

airports, they can easily occur at non-towered airports where a controller is not additionally helping provide sequencing of taxiing traffic and that which is taking off or landing.

[PA.II.D.K6b; AC 90-66]

29. When taxiing an airplane, what is considered a safe taxi speed?

A safe taxi speed is typically no faster than a brisk walking pace (5–10 knots) in congested or tight areas, such as near terminals, ramps, or during turns. This speed ensures the pilot has sufficient time to react to obstacles, other aircraft, or ground personnel.

On long, unobstructed taxiways, the speed may be increased slightly, provided it allows for safe control of the aircraft, typically not exceeding 15–20 knots. However, the speed must always be adjusted for conditions such as wet, icy, or uneven taxiways, which may reduce traction and braking effectiveness.

Pilots should prioritize maintaining positive control of the aircraft at all times, avoiding sudden turns or braking that could cause a loss of control. Adhering to a safe taxi speed helps minimize the risk of collisions or accidents on the ground, ensuring smooth and controlled ground operation.

[PA.II.D.S6; FAA-H-8083-3]

30. What basic precaution should be taken when taxiing over grass or loose gravel?

When taxiing over grass or loose gravel, pilots should exercise caution to prevent damage to the aircraft and maintain control. Taxi at a slow speed to reduce the risk of propeller or engine damage from debris kicked up by the wheels or propeller.

Use smooth, controlled inputs on the throttle, brakes, and rudder to avoid sudden movements that could cause skidding or loss of control, especially on uneven surfaces. Keep the nose wheel or tail wheel aligned to prevent digging into the ground, which could lead to tipping or damage.

Additionally, be vigilant for obstacles, such as rocks, ruts, or tall grass, that might obstruct the taxi path. If possible, follow established paths or tracks to avoid soft spots or loose terrain. These precautions help ensure safe taxi operations while minimizing the risk of damage to the aircraft.

[PA.II.D.S6; FAA-H-8083-3]

Private Pilot Oral Exam Guide 71

Chapter 3 **Preflight Procedures**

E. Before Takeoff Check

1. Explain the purpose of performing a before-takeoff checklist.

The before-takeoff check is the systematic POH/AFM procedure for checking the engine, controls, systems, instruments, and avionics prior to flight. Its purpose is to verify the airplane is ready and safe for flight.

[PA.II.F.K1; FAA-H-8083-3]

2. Why do aircraft checklists call for the engine run-up/magneto checks to be performed just before takeoff instead of prior to taxi?

Several reasons:

a. Taxiing to the run-up position usually allows sufficient time for the engine to warm up to at least minimum operating temperature. Most engines require that oil temperature reach a minimum value before takeoff power is applied.

b. Taxiing to a run-up position near the takeoff end of a runway provides a suitable location that is free of debris. Otherwise, the propeller may pick up pebbles, dirt, mud, sand, or other loose objects that could damage the propeller and also damage the tail of the airplane.

[PA.II.F.S5; FAA-H-8083-3]

3. When performing the magneto check before takeoff, explain why there is a small decrease in RPM when the ignition switch is first moved from BOTH to RIGHT, and then from BOTH to LEFT.

During the magneto check, the engine's ignition system is tested to ensure proper operation. When the ignition switch is moved from "BOTH" to one magneto, the small RPM drop occurs because only one set of spark plugs (powered by that magneto) is firing in each cylinder, rather than both sets firing simultaneously.

With only one spark plug operating per cylinder, combustion efficiency slightly decreases, causing the engine to lose a small amount of power. This RPM drop is normal and indicates that each magneto is functioning independently. However, if the drop exceeds the manufacturer's specified limit or the engine runs

72 Aviation Supplies & Academics

Chapter 3 **Preflight Procedures**

rough, it could signal a problem, such as fouled spark plugs or a malfunctioning magneto.

[PA.II.F.K1c; FAA-H-8083-25]

4. **When checking the carburetor heat (if equipped), during the before-takeoff check, explain why a drop in RPM occurs.**

The use of carburetor heat causes a decrease in engine power, sometimes up to 15 percent, because the heated air is less dense than the outside air that had been entering the engine. This enriches the mixture. A mixture that is too rich or too lean will result in the engine losing power, which is indicated by a loss of RPM (on fixed-pitch propellers).

[PA.II.F.K1; FAA-H-8083-25]

5. **Explain how a pilot should properly position the airplane in the run-up area prior to performing the before-takeoff check.**

a. To minimize overheating, the airplane should be headed as nearly as possible into the wind.

b. The airplane should be positioned clear of other aircraft and the taxiway.

c. There should not be anything behind the airplane that might be damaged by the propeller airflow blasting rearward.

d. The airplane should be allowed to roll forward slightly to ensure that the nose wheel or tail wheel is in alignment with the longitudinal axis of the airplane.

[PA.II.F.S3; FAA-H-8083-3]

6. **If the engine stops running when switched to one magneto or if the RPM drop exceeds the allowable limit, what does this indicate about the ignition system?**

The cause could be fouled plugs, broken or shorted wires between the magneto and the plugs, or improperly timed firing of the plugs. It should also be noted that no drop in RPM is not normal, and in that instance, the aircraft should not be flown.

[PA.II.F.K1b; FAA-H-8083-25]

Private Pilot Oral Exam Guide   73

Chapter 3 **Preflight Procedures**

7. **Identify the hazards that can exist while performing a before-takeoff checklist.**

   a. Division of attention while conducting the before-takeoff checks.

   b. Unexpected runway changes by ATC.

   c. Takeoff emergency procedures; failure to brief.

   d. Wake turbulence.

   e. Failure to brief of the potential for powerplant failure and other malfunctions during takeoff.

   [PA.II.F.R4; FAA-S-ACS-6]

8. **Explain what a pilot can do to minimize the possibility of overheating the engine during the engine run-up prior to takeoff.**

   To minimize overheating during engine run-up, it is recommended that the airplane be headed as nearly as possible into the wind and, if equipped, engine instruments that indicate cylinder head temperatures should be monitored. Cowl flaps, if available, should be set according to the POH/AFM.

   [PA.II.F.S5; FAA-H-8083-3]

9. **How should a pilot scan the approach area for possible landing traffic prior to taxiing onto a runway or landing area in preparation for takeoff?**

   Before taxiing onto a runway or landing area for takeoff, a pilot should conduct a thorough and systematic scan of the approach area to ensure it is clear of landing traffic. Use a deliberate left-to-right or right-to-left scan to check the full approach path, including both final approach and base legs, for incoming aircraft. This scan should include the full extent of the airspace visible from the aircraft's position. Monitor the appropriate traffic frequency for any calls from landing aircraft. Listen for position reports or announcements indicating nearby traffic. Use aircraft equipment like ADS-B (if available) to identify any nearby traffic not immediately visible. If needed, adjust the aircraft's position on the taxiway to improve the view of blind spots caused by obstructions or the aircraft's structure. Double-check the approach path, as traffic may enter the area during the scan. Taking these precautions

74 Aviation Supplies & Academics

Chapter 3 **Preflight Procedures**

ensures the runway is clear, preventing conflicts with landing traffic and enhancing safety for all aircraft.

[PA.III.B.S6; FAA-H-8083-25]

10. What are some elements of a good pre-takeoff emergency briefing a pilot should conduct?

A good pre-takeoff emergency briefing ensures the pilot and passengers are prepared for potential emergencies during takeoff. It should confirm that seat belts are fastened, ensure that passengers are familiar with emergency exits and door operations if necessary, and explain the importance of following any pilot instructions during an emergency.

The briefing should include actions if an emergency is encountered prior to liftoff, what the response will be if an emergency is encountered after liftoff (either if there is runway remaining or if no runway is remaining), what the response will be if a turn back to the airport is not possible, and/or at what point a return to the airport could be made. This requires the pilot to determine prior to takeoff key points and critical altitudes so the decisions do not need to be made while an emergency is happening.

The briefing should take into account traffic, runway options, terrain and obstacles in the area, and other airport-specific factors that may influence emergency decisions.

By addressing these elements, the pilot ensures everyone on board is aware of the procedures and can act quickly and confidently in an emergency.

An example pre-takeoff emergency briefing might sound like this:

"During the takeoff if we encounter any engine troubles, we will retard the throttle and come to a stop if we have not already lifted off. If we have lifted off, but have runway remaining, we will retard the throttle, land, and come to a stop in the remaining runway or off the end of the runway. If we have climbed to an altitude where no runway is remaining, but not high enough that a turn back to the airport can be made, we will proceed straight forward with turns no more than 30° left or right and pick the best landing site unless power is sufficient to maintain altitude. If we have reached sufficient altitude to turn back to the airport, we will turn back toward the airport and land on the closest runway."

(continued)

Private Pilot Oral Exam Guide 75

Chapter 3 **Preflight Procedures**

Exam Tip: Have a pre-determined MSL altitude at which you would be able to make a turn back to the airport. This should be an altitude that is clearly high enough to execute a 180° turn back. A best practice is to determine what the loss of altitude is during a 180° gliding turn, double that, and then add that to the takeoff runway elevation. For example, if the takeoff elevation is 1,000 feet MSL, and a pilot determined that a 180° gliding turn would generate a loss of 500 feet of altitude, they might double this and add that number (1,000) to the takeoff elevation, 1,000 feet MSL, to get 2,000 feet MSL. This is the hard number the pilot would keep in mind, and they would not attempt to turn back to the airport below this altitude unless the aircraft was making sufficient power to maintain altitude.

Note: Some aircraft are equipped with emergency parachute systems. If the aircraft you will be using for the test is so equipped, be familiar with the best practices and manufacturer's recommendations and requirements related to their use.

[PA.II.F.R4; FAA-H-8083-3]

Postflight Procedures

4

Chapter 4 **Postflight Procedures**

A. After Landing, Parking, and Securing

1. After landing, when is it considered safe to begin performing the after-landing checklist items?

The after-landing checks should be performed only after the airplane is brought to a complete stop beyond the runway holding position markings. There have many cases of a pilot mistakenly grasping the wrong handle and retracting the landing gear instead of the flaps due to improper division of attention while the airplane was moving.

[PA.XII.A.K1; FAA-H-8083-3]

2. After landing at an airport with an operating control tower, when is an airplane considered clear of the runway?

A pilot or controller may consider an aircraft that is exiting or crossing a runway to be clear of the runway when all parts of the aircraft are beyond the runway edge and there are no restrictions to its continued movement beyond the applicable runway holding position marking. Runway holding position markings generally designate the entry or exit positions to the runway environment. A pilot is advised to taxi clear of these to be considered clear of the runway.

[PA.XII.A.S3; AIM 4-3-21]

3. While taxiing to parking, what are several examples of collision avoidance procedures a pilot might employ to mitigate risk and avoid an accident?

a. Be familiar with the parking, ramp, and taxi environment. Have an airport diagram, if available, out and in view at all times.

b. The pilot's eyes should be looking outside the airplane and scanning from side to side while looking both near and far to assess routing and potential conflicts.

c. Be vigilant of the entire area around the airplane to ensure that the airplane clears all obstructions. If there is any doubt about a safe clearance from an object, the pilot should stop the airplane and check the clearance.

d. A safe taxiing speed should be maintained. The speed should be slow enough so that when the throttle is closed, the airplane can be stopped promptly.

78 Aviation Supplies & Academics

Chapter 4 **Postflight Procedures**

e. When yellow taxiway centerline stripes are present, the pilot should visually place the centerline stripe so it is under the center of the airplane fuselage.

[PA.XII.A.S2; FAA-H-8083-3]

4. When approaching the ramp for parking and maneuvering with power into or near the parking spot, what precautions should be taken?

Maneuver the airplane so that the tail is not pointed at an open hangar door, toward a parked automobile, or toward a group of bystanders in the area. Blowing dirt, small rocks, and debris is not only discourteous and thoughtless, but it could result in personal injury and serious damage to the property of others.

[PA.XII.A.S2; FAA-H-8083-3]

5. On an unfamiliar ramp, why would a pilot want to inspect their tie-down spot prior to parking and shutdown?

Foreign object debris (FOD) and other unknown objects can be a significant hazard that could cause damage to the aircraft and subject other aircraft and/or people nearby to the flying FOD.

[PA.XII.A.S5; FAA-H-8083-3]

6. After parking and shutdown, what are several considerations a pilot should have when securing the aircraft?

a. Unless parking in a designated, supervised area, the pilot should select a location and heading that will prevent the propeller or jet blast of another aircraft from striking the aircraft broadside.

b. Consider the existing (or forecast) wind when parking the airplane. Whenever possible, the aircraft should be parked headed into the existing wind.

c. Consider allowing the airplane to roll straight ahead enough to straighten the nose wheel or tail wheel.

d. Consider whether the tiedown method actually secures the aircraft. Check rope, chain, and hook integrity.

e. If using ropes as tiedowns, consider whether the knot used will be effective.

[PA.XII.A.S5; FAA-H-8083-3]

Private Pilot Oral Exam Guide 79

Chapter 4 **Postflight Procedures**

7. After the aircraft is safely hangered or tied down, what other actions can a pilot take to further enhance the safety and security of the airplane?

Flight controls should be secured, and any security locks should be in place. Also consider utilizing pitot tube covers, cowling inlet covers, rudder gust locks, window sunscreens, and propeller security locks to enhance safety.

[PA.XII.A.S5; FAA-H-8083-3]

8. Describe inspections and procedures a pilot should perform when conducting a post-flight inspection of an aircraft.

A pilot should always use the recommended procedures in the airplane's POH/AFM. A post-flight inspection is similar to a preflight inspection and should include the following:

a. Inspect near and around the cowling for signs of oil or fuel streaks and around the oil breather for excessive oil discharge.

b. Inspect under wings and other fuel tank locations for fuel stains.

c. Inspect landing gear and tires for damage and the brakes for any leaking hydraulic fluid.

d. Inspect cowling inlets for obstructions.

e. Check oil levels and bring quantities to POH/AFM levels.

f. Add fuel based on the immediate use of the airplane.

g. If the airplane will be inactive, it is a good operating practice to fill the fuel tanks to prevent water condensation from forming inside the tank.

[PA.XII.A.S4; FAA-H-8083-3]

9. If a possible mechanical problem is detected during a post-flight inspection, what procedure should be followed?

Document the problem and notify maintenance personnel. A maintenance problem that is detected during a post-flight inspection and appropriately documented will allow maintenance personnel more time to make appropriate repairs and prepare the aircraft for subsequent flights. If the airplane is a rental or belongs to a flying club or flight school, there is usually a "squawk" sheet or book for the airplane where the pilot can document the discrepancy.

[PA.XII.A.K2; FAA-H-8083-3]

Chapter 4 **Postflight Procedures**

10. When boarding or deplaning passengers, what is the safest, most effective procedure to follow to reduce the possibility of an accident?

The engine of a fixed-wing aircraft or of a helicopter should always be shut down prior to boarding or deplaning passengers. The pilot can be most effective in ensuring that their passengers arrive and depart the vicinity of the airplane safely by stopping the engine completely at the time of loading and unloading, or in instances when the engine must be running, by providing a definite means of keeping them clear of the propeller if it is left in motion.

[PA.XII.A.R4; FAA-H-8083-3]

B. Aviation Security

1. What are several actions you can take to enhance aircraft security?

a. Always lock your aircraft.

b. Keep track of door/ignition keys and don't leave keys in unattended aircraft.

c. Use secondary locks (prop, tie down, throttle, and wheel locks) or aircraft disabler if available.

d. Lock hangar when unattended.

[PA.XII.A.R3; TSA, 49 CFR 1542]

2. What is a Security Identification Display Area (SIDA)?

A SIDA is a limited access area that requires a badge issued in accordance with procedures in 49 CFR Part 1542. A SIDA can include the air operations area (AOA) (e.g., aircraft movement area or parking area) or a secured area, such as where commercial passengers enplane. The AOA is not required to be a SIDA, but a secured area is always a SIDA. Movement through or into a SIDA is prohibited without authorization and proper identification being displayed. If you are unsure of the location of a SIDA, contact the airport authority for additional information. Airports that have a SIDA will have a description and map detailing boundaries and pertinent features available.

[PA.XII.A.R3; AIM 2-3-15, 49 CFR 1542]

Chapter 4 **Postflight Procedures**

3. **What type of airport security procedures should you review regularly to prevent unauthorized access to aircraft at your airport?**

    a. Limitations on ramp access to people other than instructors and students.

    b. Standards for securing aircraft on the ramp.

    c. Securing access to aircraft keys at all times.

    d. New auxiliary security items for aircraft (prop locks, throttle locks, locking tie downs).

    e. After-hours or weekend access procedures.

    [PA.XII.A.R3; FSSAT, 49 CFR 1542]

4. **Give some examples of what you would consider suspicious activity at an airport.**

    a. Aircraft with unusual modifications (such as modified N-numbers) or activity.

    b. Unfamiliar persons loitering for extended periods in the vicinity of parked aircraft.

    c. Anyone making threats.

    d. Events or circumstances that do not fit the pattern of lawful, normal activity at an airport.

    e. Pilots appearing to be under the control of others.

    [PA.XII.A.R3; TSA, 49 CFR 1542]

5. **When witnessing suspicious or criminal activity, what are three basic ways for reporting the suspected activity?**

    If you determine that it's safe, question the individual. If their response is unsatisfactory and they continue to act suspiciously:

    a. Alert airport or FBO management.

    b. Contact local law enforcement if the activity poses an immediate threat to persons or property.

    c. Contact the 866-GA-SECURE hotline to document the reported event.

    [PA.XII.A.R3; TSA, 49 CFR 1542]

Chapter 4 **Postflight Procedures**

6. What is the purpose of the 866-GA-SECURE phone number?

866-GA-SECURE is a toll-free hotline operated by the Transportation Security Administration (TSA) Security Operations Center. It is staffed 24/7 to take reports of suspicious or criminal activity occurring at general aviation airports. TSA personnel will document the reported activity, collect your personal contact numbers, and pass the information on to the appropriate regulatory office within the TSA.

Note: Calling 866-GA-SECURE will not dispatch local law enforcement. In the event of an immediate emergency, 911 or local law enforcement should be contacted first.

[PA.XII.A.R3; TSA, 49 CFR 1542]

7. What are several sources of information available to pilots interested in additional guidance on aviation security?

TSA's *Security Guidelines for General Aviation Airport Operators and Users* is a set of federally endorsed guidelines that offers an extensive list of options, ideas, and suggestions for the airport operator, sponsor, tenant and/or user to choose from when considering security enhancements for GA facilities.

Flight School Security Awareness Training for Aircraft and Simulators is an online training course designed to raise the general security awareness levels of employees working in the flight training industry.

[PA.XII.A.R3; TSA, FSSAT, 49 CFR 1542]

Human Factors 5

Chapter 5 **Human Factors**

A. Flight Physiology

1. What is hypoxia?

Hypoxia is a state of oxygen deficiency in the body sufficient to impair functions of the brain and other organs.

[PA.I.H.K1a; AIM 8-1-2]

2. Give a brief explanation of the four forms of hypoxia.

Hypoxic—Any condition that interrupts the flow of oxygen into the lungs. This is the type of hypoxia encountered at altitude due to the reduction of the partial pressure of oxygen.

Hypemic—Any condition that interferes with the ability of the blood to carry oxygen, such as anemia, bleeding, carbon monoxide poisoning, smoking, and certain prescription drugs.

Stagnant—Any situation that interferes with the normal circulation of the blood arriving to the cells. Heart failure, shock, and positive G-forces will bring about this condition.

Histotoxic—Any condition that interferes with the normal utilization of oxygen in the cell. Alcohol, narcotics, and cyanide all can interfere with the cell's ability to use oxygen in support of metabolism.

[PA.I.H.K1a; FAA-H-8083-25]

3. Where does hypoxia usually occur, and what symptoms should one expect?

Although a deterioration in night vision occurs at a cabin pressure altitude as low as 5,000 feet, other significant effects of altitude hypoxia usually do not occur in the normal healthy pilot below 12,000 feet. From 12,000 feet to 15,000 feet of altitude, judgment, memory, alertness, coordination, and ability to make calculations are impaired, and headache, drowsiness, dizziness and either a sense of well-being or belligerence occur. The effects are worse above 15,000 feet.

[PA.I.H.K1a; AIM 8-1-2]

86 Aviation Supplies & Academics

Chapter 5 **Human Factors**

4. What factors can make a pilot more susceptible to hypoxia?

The altitude at which significant effects of hypoxia occur can be lowered by a number of factors. Carbon monoxide inhaled in smoking or from exhaust fumes, lowered hemoglobin (anemia), and certain medications can reduce the oxygen-carrying capacity of the blood. Small amounts of alcohol and low doses of certain drugs such as antihistamines, tranquilizers, sedatives, and analgesics can, through their depressant action, render the brain much more susceptible to hypoxia. Extreme heat and cold, fever, and anxiety increase the body's demand for oxygen, and hence its susceptibility to hypoxia.

[PA.I.H.K1a; AIM 8-1-2]

5. How can hypoxia be avoided?

Hypoxia is prevented by heeding factors that reduce tolerance to altitude, by enriching the inspired air with oxygen from an appropriate oxygen system, and by maintaining a comfortable, safe cabin pressure altitude. For optimum protection, pilots are encouraged to use supplemental oxygen above 10,000 feet during the day, and above 5,000 feet at night. If supplemental oxygen is not available, a fingertip pulse oximeter can be very useful in monitoring blood oxygen levels.

[PA.I.H.K1a; AIM 8-1-2]

6. What are the regulations concerning the use of supplemental oxygen on board an aircraft?

a. *At cabin pressure altitudes above 12,500 feet MSL up to and including 14,000 feet MSL*—For that part of the flight at those altitudes that is more than 30 minutes, the required minimum flight crew must be provided with and use supplemental oxygen.

b. *At cabin pressure altitudes above 14,000 feet MSL*—For the entire flight time at those altitudes, the required flight crew must be provided with and use supplemental oxygen.

c. *At cabin pressure altitudes above 15,000 feet MSL*—Each occupant must be provided with supplemental oxygen.

[PA.I.H.K1a; 14 CFR 91.211]

Private Pilot Oral Exam Guide 87

Chapter 5 **Human Factors**

7. Why does the FAA recommend that a pilot utilize oxygen at lower flight altitudes during night flight than daytime flight?

Night vision is directly affected by lack of oxygen because color acuity is degraded and peripheral vision is limited when the body is hypoxic. While hypoxia is technically not experienced at a lower altitude at night than during daylight conditions, some of the symptoms of hypoxia are more readily noticed and present greater risk at night than they do during daytime flight.

[PA.I.H.K1a; AIM 8-1-2, FAA-H-8083-3]

8. What is hyperventilation?

Hyperventilation is an abnormal increase in the volume of air breathed in and out of the lungs, and it can occur subconsciously when a stressful situation is encountered in flight. This results in a significant decrease in the carbon dioxide content of the blood. Carbon dioxide is needed to automatically regulate the breathing process. Hyperventilation can be caused by overly stressful situations or reactions, and pilots may have passengers who are fearful of flying experience it in some cases.

[PA.I.H.K1b; AIM 8-1-3]

9. What symptoms can a pilot expect from hyperventilation?

As hyperventilation blows off excessive carbon dioxide from the body, a pilot can experience symptoms of lightheadedness, suffocation, drowsiness, tingling in the extremities, and coolness, and react to them with even greater hyperventilation. Incapacitation can eventually result from uncoordination, disorientation, and painful muscle spasms. Finally, unconsciousness can occur.

[PA.I.H.K1b; AIM 8-1-3]

10. How can a hyperventilating condition be reversed?

The symptoms of hyperventilation subside within a few minutes after the rate and depth of breathing are consciously brought back to normal. The buildup of carbon dioxide in the body can be hastened by controlled breathing in and out of a paper bag held over the nose and mouth.

[PA.I.H.K1b; AIM 8-1-3]

Chapter 5 **Human Factors**

11. If a pilot has a passenger experiencing hyperventilation, what should they do?

The first priority for the pilot should be operation of the aircraft and maintenance of safe flight. If workload allows, or with the help of another passenger, the passenger may be assisted. A common practice that might help to stabilize the passenger's breathing is to have them breathe into a bag. If the condition persists, the pilot may elect to divert their flight if flying cross-country or return to the airport if flying locally.

[PA.I.H.K1b; AIM 8-1-3]

12. What is sinus block and what are the symptoms? How can it be prevented?

During ascent and descent, air pressure in the sinuses equalizes with the aircraft cabin pressure through small openings that connect the sinuses to the nasal passages. Either an upper respiratory infection, such as a cold or sinusitis, or a nasal allergic condition can produce enough congestion around an opening to slow equalization, and as the difference in pressure between the sinus and cabin mounts, eventually plug the opening. This *sinus block* occurs most frequently during descent.

A sinus block can occur in the frontal sinuses, located above each eyebrow, or in the maxillary sinuses, located in each upper cheek. It will usually produce excruciating pain over the sinus area. A maxillary sinus block can also make the upper teeth ache. Bloody mucus may discharge from the nasal passages.

A sinus block is prevented by not flying with an upper respiratory infection or nasal allergic condition. Adequate protection is usually not provided by decongestant sprays or drops to reduce congestion around the sinus openings. Oral decongestants have side effects that can impair pilot performance.

If a sinus block does not clear shortly after landing, a physician should be consulted.

[PA.I.H.K1c; AIM 8-1-2]

13. What is ear block?

As the aircraft cabin pressure decreases during ascent, the expanding air in the middle ear pushes the Eustachian tube open. The air then escapes down to the nasal passages and equalizes in pressure with

Private Pilot Oral Exam Guide 89

Chapter 5 **Human Factors**

the cabin pressure. But during descent, the pilot must periodically open the Eustachian tube to equalize pressure. Either an upper respiratory infection, such as a cold or sore throat, or a nasal allergic condition can produce enough congestion around the Eustachian tube to make equalization difficult. Consequently, the difference in pressure between the middle ear and aircraft cabin can build to a level that will hold the Eustachian tube closed, making equalization difficult if not impossible. An ear block produces severe pain and loss of hearing that can last from several hours to several days.

[PA.I.H.K1c; AIM 8-1-2]

14. How is ear block normally prevented from occurring?

Ear block can normally be prevented by swallowing, yawning, tensing muscles in the throat or, if these do not work, by the combination of closing the mouth, pinching the nose closed, and attempting to blow through the nostrils (Valsalva maneuver). It is also prevented by not flying with an upper respiratory infection or nasal allergic condition.

[PA.I.H.K1c; AIM 8-1-2]

15. What is spatial disorientation?

Orientation is the awareness of the position of the aircraft and of oneself in relation to a specific reference point. Spatial disorientation specifically refers to the lack of orientation with regard to position in space and to other objects.

[PA.I.H.K1d; FAA-H-8083-15]

16. What causes spatial disorientation?

Orientation is maintained through the body's sensory organs in three areas:

a. *Visual*—The eyes maintain visual orientation.

b. *Vestibular*—The motion sensing system in the inner ear maintains vestibular orientation.

c. *Postural*—The nerves in the skin, joints, and muscles of the body maintain postural orientation.

When human beings are in their natural environment, these three systems work well. However, when the human body is subjected to the forces of flight, these senses can provide misleading information resulting in disorientation.

[PA.I.H.K1d; FAA-H-8083-15]

Chapter 5 **Human Factors**

17. What are several examples of illusions that can lead to spatial disorientation?

According to the FAA *Aeronautical Information Manual* (*AIM*) paragraph 8-1-5 (Illusions in Flight), spatial disorientation can occur when a pilot's perception of position, motion, or attitude is inconsistent with reality, often caused by illusions. Several common illusions that can lead to spatial disorientation include:

a. *The leans*—Occurs when a gradual, unnoticed bank is corrected to level flight, giving the sensation of banking in the opposite direction.

b. *Coriolis illusion*—Results from rapid head movement in a prolonged constant-rate turn, causing the sensation of tilting or tumbling.

c. *Graveyard spiral*—Happens when a pilot in a prolonged turn loses the sensation of turning, leading to increased bank and descent while attempting to "correct."

d. *Somatogravic illusion*—During rapid acceleration, such as during takeoff, the body senses a nose-up attitude, potentially causing the pilot to push the nose down.

e. *Inversion illusion*—A sudden transition from climb to level flight may cause the sensation of tumbling backward.

f. *False horizon*—Occurs when visual cues, such as clouds or terrain, are mistaken for the horizon, resulting in an inaccurate perception of aircraft attitude.

g. *Autokinesis*—A stationary light appears to move when stared at in darkness.

[PA.I.H.K1d; AIM 8-1-5]

18. What is the cause of motion sickness, and what are its symptoms?

Motion sickness is caused by continued stimulation of the inner ear, which controls a person's sense of balance. The symptoms are progressive and include loss of appetite, saliva collecting in the mouth, perspiration, nausea, disorientation, headaches, and possible vomiting. The pilot may become incapacitated if it becomes severe enough.

[PA.I.H.K1e; FAA-H-8083-25]

Private Pilot Oral Exam Guide 91

Chapter 5 **Human Factors**

19. What action should be taken if a pilot or his passenger suffers from motion sickness?

If suffering from airsickness while piloting an aircraft, best practices to help include opening up air vents or windows (if allowed), loosening clothing, using supplemental oxygen, and focusing vision on a point outside the airplane. Avoid unnecessary head movements. Terminate the flight and land as soon as possible if symptoms do not subside.

[PA.I.H.K1e; FAA-H-8083-25]

20. What is carbon monoxide poisoning?

Carbon monoxide is a colorless, odorless, and tasteless gas contained in exhaust fumes. When inhaled, even in minute quantities over a period of time, it can significantly reduce the ability of the blood to carry oxygen. Consequently, effects of hypoxia occur.

[PA.I.H.K1f; AIM 8-1-4]

21. How does carbon monoxide poisoning occur in an aircraft, and what symptoms should a pilot be alert for?

Most heaters in light aircraft work by air flowing over the manifold. The use of these heaters while exhaust fumes are escaping through manifold cracks and seals is responsible for several nonfatal and fatal aircraft accidents from carbon monoxide poisoning every year. A pilot who detects the odor of exhaust or experiences symptoms of headache, drowsiness, nausea, dizziness, or fatigue while using the heater should suspect carbon monoxide poisoning. Pilots should be vigilant for these symptoms, particularly when flying in older aircraft or after maintenance involving the exhaust system.

[PA.I.H.K1f; AIM 8-1-4]

22. What action should be taken if a pilot suspects carbon monoxide poisoning?

A pilot who suspects this condition to exist should immediately shut off the heater and open all air vents and land as soon as safely possible to address the issue. Immediate diversion to a nearby suitable airport is recommended, as the effects of carbon monoxide are additive and the aeromedical effects do not immediately go

Chapter 5 **Human Factors**

away with venting of the cabin. Immediate diversion to a nearby suitable airport is recommended, as the effects of carbon monoxide are additive and the aeromedical effects do not immediately go away with venting of the cabin If symptoms are severe, or they continue after landing, the pilot should seek medical treatment.

[PA.I.H.K1f; AIM 8-1-4]

23. When should a pilot be particularly alert for the possibility of carbon monoxide poisoning?

A pilot should be particularly alert for the possibility of carbon monoxide (CO) poisoning during flights in piston-engine aircraft, especially when the cabin heating system is in use. CO can enter the cabin through leaks in the exhaust system, as the cabin heat is often generated by air flowing over the exhaust manifold. Cold weather operations are a primary concern since cabin heat is more frequently used, increasing the risk if there are exhaust leaks. Pilots should also be cautious during extended engine operation at high power settings, as increased exhaust flow can exacerbate leaks.

[PA.I.H.K1f; AIM 8-1-4]

24. What is one of the main differences in symptoms between carbon monoxide poisoning and altitude-based hypoxia?

Altitude-based hypoxia commonly leaves pilots and/or passengers feeling good, and potentially euphoric. Carbon monoxide poisoning commonly causes nausea or ill-feeling symptoms. These distinctions can be key in helping to differentiate between the two potential risks.

[PA.I.H.K1f; AIM 8-1-4]

25. Define the term *stress* and explain what the two main categories of stress are.

Stress is the body's response to physical and psychological demands placed upon it. The two main categories are:

Acute stress (short term)—Involves an immediate threat that is perceived as danger. This is the type of stress that triggers a fight-or-flight response in an individual, whether the threat is real or imagined.

(continued)

Private Pilot Oral Exam Guide   93

Chapter 5 **Human Factors**

Chronic stress (long term)—Defined as a level of stress that presents an intolerable burden, exceeds the ability of an individual to cope, and causes individual performance to fall sharply.

[PA.I.H.K1g; FAA-H-8083-25]

26. The term *stressor* is used to describe an element that causes an individual to experience stress. What are the three types of stressors?

Physical stressors—Include conditions associated with the environment, such as temperature and humidity extremes, noise, vibration, and lack of oxygen.

Physiological stressors—Include fatigue, lack of physical fitness, sleep loss, missed meals (leading to low blood sugar levels), and illness.

Psychological stressors—Related to social or emotional factors such as a death in the family, a divorce, a sick child, a demotion, etc. They may also be related to mental workload such as analyzing a problem, navigating an aircraft, or making decisions.

[PA.I.H.K1g; FAA-H-8083-25]

27. What is the definition of *fatigue*?

Fatigue is a physiological state of reduced mental or physical performance capability resulting from lack of sleep or increased physical activity. It can reduce a crewmember's alertness and ability to safely operate an aircraft or perform safety-related duties.

[PA.I.H.K1h; AC 117-3]

28. What are the two types of fatigue and when are they likely to occur?

Acute (short-term) fatigue—Occurs after a period of strenuous effort, excitement, or lack of sleep. Rest after exertion and eight hours of sound sleep ordinarily cures this condition. A proper diet is also helpful.

Chronic (long-term) fatigue—Has psychological roots and occurs over an extended period of time. Continuous high stress levels as well as underlying disease can produce chronic fatigue. It is not relieved by proper diet and adequate rest and sleep, and it usually requires treatment by a physician.

[PA.I.H.K1h; FAA-H-8083-25]

94 Aviation Supplies & Academics

Chapter 5 **Human Factors**

29. **How will a pilot's performance be affected by fatigue or prolonged stress?**

Degradation of attention and concentration, impaired coordination, and decreased ability to communicate seriously influence the pilot's ability to make effective decisions.

[PA.I.H.K1h; FAA-H-8083-25]

30. **Describe the common symptoms of fatigue.**

a. Measurable reduction in speed and accuracy of performance.

b. Lapses of attention and vigilance.

c. Delayed reactions.

d. Impaired logical reasoning and decision-making, including a reduced ability to assess risk or appreciate the consequences of actions.

e. Reduced situational awareness.

f. Low motivation to perform optional activities.

[PA.I.H.K1h; AC 117-3]

31. **Define the term *dehydration*. Describe the effect it has on a pilot and the corrective actions that should be taken.**

Dehydration is the term given to a critical loss of water from the body. The first noticeable effect of dehydration is fatigue, which in turn makes top physical and mental performance difficult, if not impossible. If the lost fluid is not replaced, additional symptoms may include dizziness, headache, weakness, nausea, tingling of hands and feet, abdominal cramps, and extreme thirst. If left untreated, it can progress to more severe symptoms such as confusion, rapid heartbeat, and low blood pressure.

Corrective actions for dehydration involve replenishing fluids and electrolytes. Move to a cooler environment, rest, and slowly drink water or oral rehydration solutions. Avoid excessive intake of sugary or caffeinated beverages, as they can worsen dehydration. If symptoms persist or worsen, seek medical attention.

[PA.I.H.K1i; FAA-H-8083-25]

Chapter 5 **Human Factors**

32. What are several causal factors that increase a pilot's susceptibility to dehydration?

Causes of dehydration are hot flight decks and flight lines, wind, humidity, and diuretic drinks (coffee, tea, caffeinated soft drinks). Flying for long periods in hot summer temperatures or at high altitudes increases susceptibility to dehydration since dry air at high altitudes tends to increase the rate of water loss from the body.

[PA.I.H.K1i; FAA-H-8083-25]

33. What is the definition of *hypothermia*?

The average body temperature for the human body is 98.6°F. Any deviation from this normal temperature, even as little as one to two degrees, will reduce efficiency. Hypothermia, or exposure, is defined as body core temperature below 95°F. As the body core temperature drops, so does mental and physical efficiency.

[PA.I.H.K1j; CAMI OK-06-033]

34. Explain how heat can be lost from the body.

a. *Conduction*—The primary cause of heat loss. A transfer of heat occurs when the body comes in contact with something colder than itself.

b. *Radiation*—The body will continually radiate heat from exposed areas. Fifty percent of body heat is lost from the head.

c. *Convection*—Air currents blow heat away from the body faster than it is produced.

d. *Evaporation*—Sweat (or other moisture) can moisten clothing and accelerate conduction.

e. *Respiration*—In a cold environment, cold air enters the body and leaves as warm air. The body loses heat by warming the colder air.

[PA.I.H.K1j; CAMI OK-06-033]

Chapter 5 **Human Factors**

35. What are the symptoms of hypothermia?

Body Temperature	Symptoms
99°–96°F	Intense shivering and impaired ability to perform complex tasks.
95°–91°F	Violent shivering, difficulty in speaking, sluggish thinking, amnesia.
90°–86°F	Shivering is replaced by muscular rigidity. Exposed skin is blue or puffy. Movements are jerky.

[PA.I.H.K1j; CAMI OK-06-033]

36. What is the first line of defense against hypothermia?

The first line of defense against hypothermia is shelter. The most readily available shelter at a pilot's disposal is the aircraft fuselage. Clothing is considered shelter, in the sense that it is your first immediate measure to retain body heat. An important fact to keep in mind is that when clothing becomes wet, it will lose its insulative quality. Wet clothing in wind will draw off body heat 200 times faster than wind alone.

[PA.I.H.K1j; CAMI OK-06-033]

37. What are several examples of optical illusions that may lead to landing errors?

Runway width illusion—A narrower-than-usual runway can create the illusion that the aircraft is at a higher altitude than it actually is. The pilot who does not recognize this illusion will fly a lower approach, with the risk of striking objects along the approach path or landing short. A wider-than-usual runway can have the opposite effect, with the risk of leveling out high and landing hard or overshooting the runway.

Runway and terrain slopes illusion—An upsloping runway, upsloping terrain, or both can create the illusion that the aircraft is at a higher altitude than it actually is. The pilot who does not recognize this illusion will fly a lower approach. A downsloping runway, downsloping approach terrain, or both, can have the opposite effect.

Featureless terrain illusion—An absence of ground features, as when landing over water, darkened areas, and terrain made

Private Pilot Oral Exam Guide   97

Chapter 5 **Human Factors**

featureless by snow, can create the illusion that the aircraft is at a higher altitude than it actually is. The pilot who does not recognize this illusion will fly a lower approach.

[PA.I.H.K1k; AIM 8-1-5]

38. Explain how rain on the windscreen (water refraction), haze, and fog can create optical illusions.

Water Refraction—Rain on the windscreen can create an illusion of being at a higher altitude due to the horizon appearing lower than it is. This can result in the pilot flying a lower approach.

Haze—Atmospheric haze can create an illusion of being at a greater distance and height from the runway. As a result, the pilot will have a tendency to be low on the approach.

Fog—Flying into fog can create an illusion of pitching up. Pilots who do not recognize this illusion will often steepen the approach quite abruptly.

[PA.I.H.K1k; FAA-H-8083-25]

39. Optical or visual illusions can increase the risk of an incident or accident occurring, even to the most experienced pilots. What can pilots do to mitigate that risk?

Pilots can take several proactive steps to mitigate the risk of incidents or accidents caused by visual illusions. Many illusions can be caused by conditions such as low visibility, nighttime operations, or when transitioning between visual and instrument flight environments.

Pilots should trust their flight instruments, especially when visual references are unreliable or absent. Instruments provide accurate information about the aircraft's attitude, altitude, and direction, counteracting misleading sensory perceptions. It is critical to maintain awareness of the environment. Study approach plates, terrain maps, and airport lighting systems before flight to anticipate potential visual challenges, such as sloping runways or featureless terrain. Fatigue can exacerbate the effects of visual illusions. Pilots should ensure they are well-rested and alert before flights, especially in conditions prone to illusions. Another tip is to be aware of flight deck lighting conditions. Ensure flight deck lighting is appropriate to maintain visibility without causing glare.

Chapter 5 **Human Factors**

Additionally, avoid staring at bright lights outside, as this can impair night vision and increase susceptibility to illusions like autokinesis.

[PA.I.H.K1k; FAA-H-8083-2]

40. Discuss the effects of nitrogen excesses from scuba diving upon a pilot or passenger in flight.

A pilot or passenger who intends to fly after scuba diving should allow the body sufficient time to rid itself of excess nitrogen absorbed during diving. If not, decompression sickness due to evolved gas can occur during exposure to low altitude and create a serious inflight emergency. The recommended waiting times before flight are as follows:

Flight altitudes up to 8,000 feet:

- Wait at least 12 hours after a dive that did not require a controlled ascent.
- Wait at least 24 hours after a dive in which a controlled ascent was required.

Flight altitudes above 8,000 feet:

- Wait at least 24 hours after any scuba dive.

Note: The recommended altitudes are actual flight altitudes above mean sea level and not pressurized cabin altitudes. This takes into consideration the risk of decompression of the aircraft during flight.

[PA.I.H.K1l; AIM 8-1-2]

41. What restrictions apply to pilots concerning the use of drugs and alcohol?

No person may act or attempt to act as a crewmember of a civil aircraft:

a. Within 8 hours after the consumption of any alcoholic beverage;

b. While under the influence of alcohol;

c. While using any drug that affects the person's faculties in any way contrary to safety; or

d. While having an alcohol concentration of 0.04 percent or more in a blood or breath specimen.

[PA.I.H.K2; 14 CFR 91.17]

Private Pilot Oral Exam Guide 99

Chapter 5 **Human Factors**

42. What regulations apply and what common sense should prevail concerning the use of alcohol?

The regulations prohibit pilots from performing crewmember duties within 8 hours after drinking any alcoholic beverage, while under the influence of alcohol, or having a blood alcohol concentration of 0.04 percent or more. Due to the slow destruction of alcohol in the bloodstream, a pilot may still be under influence, or over the 0.04 percent mark, 8 hours after drinking a moderate amount of alcohol. Therefore, an excellent rule is to allow at least 12 to 24 hours from "bottle to throttle," depending on the amount of alcoholic beverage consumed.

[PA.I.H.K2; 14 CFR 91.17, AIM 8-1-1]

43. Is it permissible for a pilot to allow a person on board an aircraft as a passenger if that person has had *any* alcohol?

The regulations require that a pilot not allow a person who "appears to be intoxicated or who demonstrates by manner or physical indications that the individual is under the influence of drugs (except a medical patient under proper care) to be carried in that aircraft." This does not indicate that the passenger may not have had *any* alcohol, but it is strongly encouraged for a pilot to know if a passenger has had alcohol and to consider additional aeromedical effects or potential behavioral concerns from a passenger who may be under the influence of alcohol.

[PA.I.H.K2; 14 CFR 91.17]

44. What aeromedical factors might a passenger who had consumed alcohol prior to flight be more susceptible to during a flight?

The consumption of alcohol may have behavioral and physiological effects that a pilot would want to be aware of for a passenger. The main effects may be reduced inhibitions that might cause the passenger to attempt to interfere with flight operations; alcohol's diuretic effects; and an increased susceptibility to hypoxia.

Alcohol consumption reduces inhibitions by impairing judgment and self-control, which can lead to reckless or disruptive behavior. In the confined, high-stress environment of an aircraft, these

100 Aviation Supplies & Academics

Chapter 5 **Human Factors**

effects may be exacerbated. Passengers under the influence might overestimate their abilities, ignore social norms, or misunderstand safety protocols. This diminished self-awareness and restraint can make them more likely to interfere with flight controls, either out of misguided curiosity or aggression. Such actions pose significant safety risks, as even minor disturbances in the flight deck can jeopardize the flight's operation.

Alcohol is a diuretic, meaning it increases urine production, leading to dehydration. For passengers on a plane, where cabin pressure and lower humidity levels already contribute to dehydration, consuming alcohol can exacerbate the effects. This may cause them to require a restroom more frequently than usual. Dehydration can affect overall physical comfort during the flight, making passengers more prone to irritability or disruptive behavior, which could further complicate flight operations and passenger safety.

Alcohol consumption can increase the effects of hypoxia, which is the reduced oxygen level experienced at higher altitudes. Alcohol impairs the body's ability to adapt to lower oxygen levels, making a passenger more susceptible to symptoms of hypoxia, such as confusion, dizziness, and fatigue. Even in a pressurized cabin of an aircraft where oxygen levels are maintained, they are still lower than at sea level, and alcohol exacerbates this effect. This combination can impair a passenger's judgment and reaction time, increasing the risk of them engaging in unsafe behavior or becoming incapacitated in an emergency situation.

[PA.I.H.K2; FAA-H-8083-25]

45. What might be considered best practices with regard to any passengers who have consumed any alcohol prior to flight but are not obviously under the influence of intoxicating liquors?

A pilot who has chosen to take a passenger who has consumed even minimal amounts of alcohol within a time near to flight departure should take extra care to manage that passenger. The pilot should monitor passengers for any signs of discomfort or unusual behavior, and if necessary, address the situation before it escalates. It is best to limit the passenger's access to any flight controls. Many pilots advise that passengers who have had any alcohol be placed in rear seats away from any flight controls.

Chapter 5 **Human Factors**

Another option may be to require another passenger to be seated with them or onboard to help manage any potential challenges that might be encountered during flight. A best practice is always to be conservative and not allow passengers who are even under minimal effects of alcohol consumption to be carried on board.

[PA.I.H.K2; FAA-H-8083-25]

46. Is it permissible for a pilot to allow a person who is obviously under the influence of intoxicating liquors or drugs to be carried aboard an aircraft?

No. Except in an emergency, no pilot of a civil aircraft may allow a person who appears to be intoxicated or who demonstrates by manner or physical indications that the individual is under the influence of drugs (except a medical patient under proper care) to be carried in that aircraft.

[PA.I.H.K2; 14 CFR 91.17]

47. For a pilot who has been taking an over-the-counter (OTC) cold medication, how do the various environmental factors the pilot is exposed to in flight affect the drug's physiological impact on them?

Drugs that cause no apparent side effects on the ground can create serious problems at relatively low altitudes. Even at typical general aviation altitudes, the changes in concentrations of atmospheric gases in the blood can enhance the effects of seemingly innocuous drugs and result in impaired judgment, decision-making, and performance.

[PA.I.H.K3; FAA-H-8083-25]

48. What regulations apply and what common sense should prevail concerning the use of drugs and medication?

Pilot performance can be seriously degraded by both prescribed and OTC medications, as well as by the medical conditions for which they are taken. The regulations prohibit pilots from performing crewmember duties while using any medication that affects their faculties in any way contrary to safety. The safest rule is not to fly as a crewmember while taking any medication, unless approved to do so by the FAA.

[PA.I.H.K3; AIM 8-1-1]

Chapter 5 **Human Factors**

49. **You recently experienced a bad cold and were treated by your personal physician. You continue to take the medications your physician prescribed, but you feel much better. Can you resume flying on your current medical certificate, or must you first see an FAA Aviation Medical Examiner (AME)?**

Anytime you experience an illness or an injury that you feel may affect your ability to safely fly an aircraft, you must self-ground until you feel better. 14 CFR §61.53 requires that all pilots voluntarily self-ground if one of the following is true:

a. They know or have reason to know of any medical condition that would make them unable to meet the requirements for the medical certificate necessary for the pilot operation.

b. They are taking medication or receiving other treatment for a medical condition that results in them being unable to meet the requirements for the medical certificate necessary for the pilot operation.

If in doubt about your condition or the medications you are taking, consult with an AME before resuming your flying activities.

[PA.I.H.K3; 14 CFR 61.53]

50. **Can you operate an aircraft while taking an OTC medication for an ongoing condition (allergies, hay fever, etc.)?**

Self-medication or taking medication in any form while you are flying can be extremely hazardous. Even simple home or over-the-counter remedies such as aspirin, laxatives, tranquilizers, and appetite suppressants may seriously impair the judgment and coordination needed while flying. The safest rule is to take no medication while flying, except with the advice of your Aviation Medical Examiner (AME). The FAA offers an "Over-The-Counter (OTC) Medications Reference Guide" that can be of assistance in making a decision (www.faa.gov/pilots/medical_certification /media/OTCMedicationsforPilots.pdf).

[PA.I.H.K3; FAA OTC Med Guide, FAA-P-8740-41]

Private Pilot Oral Exam Guide 103

Chapter 5 **Human Factors**

B. Single-Pilot Resource Management

1. Define the term *single-pilot resource management.*

Single-pilot resource management (SRM) is the art and science of managing all the resources (both on board the aircraft and from outside sources) available to a single pilot (prior to and during flight) to ensure that the successful outcome of the flight is never in doubt. SRM helps pilots learn to execute methods of gathering information, analyzing it, and making decisions.

[PA.I.H.K4; FAA-H-8083-9]

2. What are examples of the skills necessary for effective SRM?

SRM includes the concepts of aeronautical decision making (ADM), risk management (RM), task management (TM), automation management (AM), controlled flight into terrain (CFIT) awareness, and situational awareness (SA).

[PA.I.H.K4; FAA-H-8083-25]

3. What practical application provides a pilot with an effective method to practice SRM?

The **5P** checklist consists of the **P**lan, the **P**lane, the **P**ilot, the **P**assengers, and the **P**rogramming. It is based on the idea that the pilot essentially has five variables that impact their environment and that can cause the pilot to make a single critical decision, or several less critical decisions, that when added together can create a critical outcome.

[PA.I.H.K4; FAA-H-8083-9]

4. Explain the use of the 5P model to assess risk associated with each of the five factors.

At key decision points, application of the **5P** checklist should be performed by reviewing each of the critical variables:

Plan—Weather, route, publications, ATC reroutes/delays, fuel onboard/remaining.

Plane—Mechanical status, automation status, database currency, backup systems.

Pilot—Illness, medication, stress, alcohol, fatigue, eating (IMSAFE).

104 Aviation Supplies & Academics

Chapter 5 **Human Factors**

Passengers—Pilots/non-pilots, nervous or quiet, experienced or new, business or pleasure.

Programming—Autopilot, GPS, MFD/PFD; anticipate likely reroutes/clearances. Questions to ask: What is it doing? Why is it doing it? Did I do it?

[PA.I.H.K4; FAA-H-8083-2]

5. When is the use of the 5P checklist recommended?

The 5P concept relies on the pilot to adopt a scheduled review of the critical variables at points in the flight where decisions are most likely to be effective. These key decision points include preflight, pre-takeoff, hourly or at the midpoint of the flight, pre-descent, and just prior to the final approach fix (or, for VFR operations, just prior to entering the traffic pattern). They also should be used anytime an emergency situation arises.

[PA.I.H.K4; FAA-H-8083-9]

C. Aeronautical Decision Making

1. Define the term *aeronautical decision making* (ADM).

Aeronautical decision making (ADM) is a systematic approach to the mental process used by aircraft pilots to consistently determine the best course of action in response to a given set of circumstances.

[PA.I.H.K4; FAA-H-8083-9]

2. Explain the basic steps in the decision-making process.

a. Define the problem.
b. Choose a course of action.
c. Implement the decision.
d. Evaluate the outcome.

[PA.I.H.K4; FAA-H-8083-9]

3. What two models are commonly used when practicing aeronautical decision making?

The DECIDE model and the 3P model.

[PA.I.H.K4; FAA-H-8083-9]

Private Pilot Oral Exam Guide   105

Chapter 5 **Human Factors**

4. The DECIDE model of decision making involves which elements?

Remember: DECIDE

Detect a change needing attention.

Estimate the need to counter or react to a change.

Choose the most desirable outcome for the flight.

Identify actions to successfully control the change.

Do something to adapt to the change.

Evaluate the effect of the action countering the change.

[PA.I.H.K4; FAA-H-8083-2]

5. How is the 3P model different from the DECIDE model of ADM?

The 3P process (discussed in the "Risk Management" section later in this chapter) is a continuous loop of the pilot's handling of hazards. The DECIDE model and naturalistic decision-making focus on particular problems requiring resolution. Therefore, pilots exercise the 3P process continuously, while the DECIDE model and naturalistic decision-making result from the 3P process.

[PA.I.H.K4; FAA-H-8083-2]

6. Name five hazardous attitudes that can affect a pilot's ability to make sound decisions and properly exercise authority.

Attitude	Antidote
Anti-authority ("Don't tell me.")	Follow the rules—they are usually right.
Impulsivity ("Do it quickly.")	Think first—not so fast.
Invulnerability ("It won't happen to me.")	It could happen to me.
Macho ("I can do it.")	Taking chances is foolish.
Resignation ("What's the use?")	I can make a difference; I am not helpless.

[PA.I.H.R2; FAA-H-8083-9]

Chapter 5 **Human Factors**

7. What is the first step towards neutralizing a hazardous attitude?

Recognition of hazardous thoughts is the first step toward neutralizing them. After recognizing a thought as hazardous, the pilot should label it as hazardous and then state the corresponding antidote. Antidotes should be identified for each of the hazardous attitudes so they may be applied when needed.

[PA.I.H.R2; FAA-H-8083-25]

D. Risk Management

1. Define the term *risk management*.

Risk management is a decision-making process designed to systematically identify hazards, assess the degree of risk, and determine the best course of action. It is a logical process of weighing the potential costs of risks against the possible benefits of allowing those risks to stand uncontrolled.

[PA.II.A.R; FAA-H-8083-9]

2. What is the definition of a *hazard*?

A hazard is a present condition, event, object, or circumstance that could lead to or contribute to an unplanned or undesired event such as an accident.

[PA.II.A.R; FAA-H-8083-2]

3. What are several examples of aviation hazards?

a. A nick in the propeller blade.
b. Improper refueling of an aircraft.
c. Pilot fatigue.
d. Use of unapproved hardware on aircraft.
e. Weather.

[PA.II.A.R; FAA-H-8083-2]

4. What is the definition of *risk*?

Risk is the future impact of a hazard that is not controlled or eliminated.

[PA.II.A.R; FAA-H-8083-2]

Private Pilot Oral Exam Guide   107

Chapter 5 **Human Factors**

5. What are several factors that may contribute to a pilot's impaired performance?

According to the FAA *Aeronautical Information Manual* (*AIM*), paragraph 8-1-1 (Fitness for Flight), several factors can contribute to a pilot's impaired performance, potentially jeopardizing the safety of flight. These factors typically stem from physiological, psychological, and environmental conditions.

These factors may be related to medical certification, illness, medications, alcohol, fatigue, stress, and/or emotion. The *AIM* encourages pilots to use personal checklists and the IMSAFE checklist to determine if they are physically and mentally safe to fly and not impaired to do so.

[PA.I.H.R1; AIM 8-1-1]

6. How can the use of the PAVE checklist during flight planning help you to assess risk?

Use of the **PAVE** checklist provides pilots with a simple way to remember each category to examine for risk during flight planning. The pilot divides the risks of flight into four categories:

Pilot-In-command—General health, physical/mental/emotional state, proficiency, currency.

Aircraft—Airworthiness, equipment, performance capability.

enVironment—Weather hazards, terrain, airports/runways to be used, conditions.

External pressures—Meetings, people waiting at destination, desire to impress someone, etc.

[PA.II.A.R; FAA-H-8083-9]

7. Explain the use of a personal minimums checklist and how it can help a pilot control risk.

One of the most important concepts that safe pilots understand is the difference between what is *legal* in terms of the regulations, and what is *smart* or *safe* in terms of pilot experience and proficiency. One way a pilot can control the risks is to set personal minimums for items in each risk category. These are limits unique to that individual pilot's current level of experience and proficiency.

[PA.II.A.R; FAA-H-8083-9]

Chapter 5 **Human Factors**

8. What is one method you can use to control and manage risk?

One way a pilot can limit exposure to risks is to set personal minimums for items in each risk category, again using PAVE. These are limits unique to that individual pilot's current level of experience and proficiency:

Pilot—Experience/recency (takeoffs/landings, hours make/model), physical/mental condition (IMSAFE).

Aircraft—Fuel reserves VFR day/night, aircraft performance (weight and balance, density altitude, etc.), aircraft equipment (avionics familiarity, charts, survival gear).

enVironment—Airport conditions (runway condition/length), weather (winds, ceilings, visibilities).

External pressures—Allowance for delays, diversion, cancelation, alternate plans, personal equipment available for alternate plans (phone numbers, credit cards, medications).

[PA.II.A.R; FAA-H-8083-2]

9. Explain the use of a personal checklist such as "I'M SAFE" to determine personal risks.

Personal self-assessment checklists assist pilots in conducting preflight checks on themselves, reviewing their physical and emotional states that could have an effect on their performance. The "I'M SAFE" checklist reminds pilots to consider the following:

Illness—*Do I have any symptoms?*

Medication—*Have I been taking prescription or over-the-counter drugs?*

Stress—*Am I under psychological pressure from my job? Do I have money, family, or health problems?*

Alcohol—*Have I been drinking alcohol within 8 hours? Within 24 hours?*

Fatigue—*Am I tired and not adequately rested?*

Emotions—*Am I fully recovered from any extremely upsetting events?*

[PA.II.A.R; FAA-H-8083-9]

Private Pilot Oral Exam Guide 109

Chapter 5 **Human Factors**

10. Describe how the 3P model can be used for practical risk management.

The Perceive, Process, Perform (**3P**) model for risk management offers a simple, practical, and systematic approach that can be used during all phases of flight. To use it, pilots will:

Perceive the hazards for a flight, which are present events, objects, or circumstances that could contribute to an undesired future event. Think through circumstances related to the **PAVE** risk categories (**P**ilot, **A**ircraft, en**V**ironment, and **E**xternal pressures). The fundamental question to ask is, "What could hurt me, my passengers, or my aircraft?"

Process the hazards by evaluating their impact on flight safety. Think through the **C**onsequences of each hazard, **A**lternatives available, **R**eality of the situation, and **E**xternal pressures (**CARE**) that might influence their analysis.

Perform by implementing the best course of action. Remember the **TEAM** method: **T**ransfer (Can the risk decision be transferred to someone else? Can you consult someone?); **E**liminate (Is there a way to eliminate the hazard?); **A**ccept (Do the benefits of accepting risk outweigh the costs?); **M**itigate (What can you do to reduce the risk?).

[PA.II.A.R; FAA-H-8083-2]

11. Explain how often a pilot should use the 3P model of ADM throughout a flight.

Once a pilot has completed the 3P decision process and selected a course of action, the process begins again because the circumstances brought about by the course of action require analysis. The decision-making process is a continuous loop of perceiving, processing, and performing.

[PA.II.A.R; FAA-H-8083-9]

12. What is a risk assessment matrix?

A risk assessment matrix is a tool used to assess the likelihood of an event occurring and the severity or consequences of that event. The matrix assists a pilot in differentiating between low, medium, and high-risk flights.

[PA.II.A.S3; FAA-H-8083-2, FAA-H-8083-25]

110 Aviation Supplies & Academics

Chapter 5 **Human Factors**

13. What is a flight risk assessment tool (FRAT)?

A FRAT is a preflight planning tool that uses a series of questions in each of the major risk categories (PAVE) to help a pilot identify and quantify risk for a flight. The tool enables proactive hazard identification, is easy to use, and can visually depict risk. It is an invaluable tool in helping pilots make better go/no-go decisions and should be a part of every flight. A FRAT fact sheet is available at www.faa.gov/newsroom/safety-briefing/flight-risk-assessment-tools.

[PA.II.A.S3; FAA FRAT]

14. Most pilots are goal-oriented, which can sometimes result in a tendency to ignore established personal limitations in favor of completing a flight. How can a pilot mitigate the risk of this occurring to them?

Pilots with a goal-oriented mindset who may be tempted to ignore personal minimums can mitigate this risk through deliberate strategies aimed at reinforcing safety-first decision-making. It is important to develop conservative personal minimums for weather, fuel, and alternate planning based on skill level, experience, and current proficiency. Write these down and review them regularly to reinforce commitment. It can be hard to fight the risks of "get-there-itis," the dangerous tendency to prioritize reaching a destination over safe decision-making. Being aware of this bias can help pilots make more rational choices during flight.

Utilizing a preflight risk assessment tool to objectively evaluate flight conditions and ensure they align with personal minimums can be a good way to evaluate the information more objectively.

Always plan alternate routes, destinations, and clear decision points before departure. Knowing that options are available reduces pressure to press on.

Another good practice is developing a network of other pilots, mentors, or instructors with whom you share your proposed flight plans and personal minimums. Having someone to provide an external perspective encourages adherence to established limits.

It can also be helpful to reflect on past flights and decision-making processes to identify areas for improvement. Focus on long-term safety over short-term goals.

[PA.I.H.R2, PA.I.H.R4; FAA-H-8083-2]

Chapter 5 **Human Factors**

E. Task Management

1. Define the term *task management*.

Task management is the process by which pilots manage the many concurrent tasks that must be performed to safely and efficiently operate an aircraft.

[PA.I.H.R3; FAA-H-8083-9]

2. What are several factors that can reduce a pilot's ability to manage workload effectively?

Environmental conditions—Temperature and humidity extremes, noise, vibration, and lack of oxygen.

Physiological stress—Fatigue, lack of physical fitness, sleep loss, missed meals (leading to low blood sugar levels), and illness.

Psychological stress—Social or emotional factors, such as a death in the family, a divorce, a sick child, or a demotion at work. This type of stress may also be related to mental workload, such as analyzing a problem, navigating an aircraft, or making decisions.

[PA.I.H.R3; FAA-H-8083-25]

3. What are several options that a pilot can employ to decrease workload and avoid becoming overloaded?

Stop, think, slow down, and prioritize. Tasks such as locating an item on a chart or setting a radio frequency may be delegated to another pilot or passenger; an autopilot, if available, may be used; or ATC may be enlisted to provide assistance.

[PA.I.H.R3; FAA-H-8083-25]

4. What is one method of prioritizing tasks to avoid an overload situation?

During any situation, and especially in an emergency, remember the phrase, "Aviate, navigate, and communicate."

[PA.I.H.R3; FAA-H-8083-25]

5. How can tasks be completed in a timely manner without causing a distraction from flying?

By planning, prioritizing, and sequencing tasks, a potential work overload situation can be avoided. As experience is gained, a pilot

Chapter 5 **Human Factors**

learns to recognize future workload requirements and can prepare for high workload periods during times of low workload.

[PA.I.H.R3; FAA-H-8083-9]

6. Why are pilots encouraged to use checklists?

The checklist is an aid to the pilot's memory and helps to ensure that critical items necessary for the safe operation of aircraft are not overlooked or forgotten. They provide a standardized method for verifying aircraft configuration and a logical sequence for accomplishing tasks inside and outside the flight deck.

[PA.II.A.S1; FAA-H-8083-3]

7. What are two common methods of checklist usage?

a. *Do-Verify (DV) method*—Consists of the checklist being accomplished in a variable sequence without a preliminary challenge. After all of the action items on the checklist have been completed, the checklist is then read again while each item is verified. The DV method allows the pilot/flight crew to use flow patterns from memory to accomplish a series of actions quickly and efficiently.

b. *Challenge-Do-Verify (CDV) method*—Consists of a pilot/ crewmember making a challenge before an action is initiated, taking the action, and then verifying that the action item has been accomplished. The CDV method is most effective in two-pilot crews where one crewmember issues the challenge and the second crewmember takes the action and responds to the first crewmember, verifying that the action was taken.

[PA.II.A.S1; AC 120-71]

8. What are several examples of common errors that can occur when using a checklist?

a. Checklist items are missed because of distraction or interruption (by passengers, ATC, etc.).

b. Checklist items are incorrectly performed (hurrying checklist; reading item but not verifying or setting).

c. Failure to use the appropriate checklist for a specific phase of flight.

d. Too much time is spent with head down, reading the checklist and compromising safety.

(continued)

Private Pilot Oral Exam Guide   113

Chapter 5 **Human Factors**

    e. Checklist is not readily accessible in the flight deck.

    f. Emergency/abnormal procedures checklist is not readily available.

    g. Memory items are accomplished but not confirmed with the checklist.

[PA.II.A.S1; FAA-H-8083-3]

9. In what phases of flight should a prepared checklist be used?

    a. Preflight inspection
    b. Before engine start
    c. Engine starting
    d. Before taxiing
    e. Before takeoff
    f. After takeoff
    g. Cruise
    h. Descent
    i. Before landing
    j. After landing
    k. Engine shutdown and securing

[PA.II.A.S1; FAA-H-8083-3]

10. What are several recommended methods for managing checklist accomplishment?

    a. The pilot should touch/point at each control, display, or switch.

    b. Verbally state the desired status of the checklist item.

    c. When complete, announce that "___ checklist is complete."

[PA.II.A.S1; AC 120-71]

11. What are immediate action items?

An immediate action item is an action that must be accomplished so expeditiously (in order to avoid or stabilize a hazardous situation) that time is not available for the pilot/crewmember to refer to a manual or checklist. Once the emergency has been brought under control, the pilot refers to the actual checklist to verify that all action items were accomplished. Only after this is done should the remainder of the checklist be completed.

[PA.II.A.S1; AC 120-71]

114 Aviation Supplies & Academics

Chapter 5 **Human Factors**

F. Situational Awareness

1. Define the term *situational awareness*.

Situational awareness (SA) is the accurate perception and understanding of all the factors and conditions within the five fundamental risk elements (flight, pilot, aircraft, environment, external pressures) that affect safety before, during, and after the flight.

[PA.I.H.R3; FAA-H-8083-25]

2. What are some of the elements inside and outside the aircraft that a pilot must consider to maintain situational awareness?

Inside the aircraft—The status of aircraft systems, pilot, and passengers.

Outside the aircraft—Awareness of where the aircraft is in relation to terrain, traffic, weather, and airspace.

[PA.I.H.R3; FAA-H-8083-9]

3. What are several factors that reduce situational awareness?

Factors that reduce SA include fatigue, distractions, unusual or unexpected events, complacency, high workload, unfamiliar situations, and inoperative equipment.

[PA.II.A.S4; FAA-H-8083-15]

4. When flying a technically advanced aircraft (TAA), what are several procedures that help ensure that situational awareness is enhanced, not diminished, by the automation?

Two basic procedures are to always double-check the system and to use verbal callouts. At a minimum, ensure the presentation makes sense. Was the correct destination entered into the navigation system? Callouts, even for single-pilot operations, are an excellent way to maintain situational awareness as well as manage information.

[PA.II.B.S4; FAA-H-8083-25]

Private Pilot Oral Exam Guide 115

Chapter 5 **Human Factors**

5. **What additional procedures can be used for maintaining situational awareness in technically advanced aircraft?**

   a. Perform verification checks of all programming prior to departure.

   b. Check the flight routing; ensure all routing matches the planned route of flight.

   c. Always verify waypoints.

   d. Make use of all onboard navigation equipment; use VOR to backup GPS, and vice versa.

   e. Match the use of the automated system with pilot proficiency; stay within personal limitations.

   f. Plan a realistic flight route to maintain situational awareness; ATC doesn't always give you direct routing.

   g. Be ready to verify computer data entries; incorrect keystrokes can lead to loss of situational awareness.

   [PA.II.B.R1; FAA-H-8083-25]

6. **You have the proper charts, have planned your route of flight, and have a detailed navigation log. Once airborne, you decide that it's much easier to let the automation fly the airplane and manage the navigation. You will handle the communications and monitor the automation. Explain what the hazards are in this scenario.**

   Pilots should avoid relying solely on automation tools during a cross-country flight because overdependence can reduce situational awareness, degrade manual flying skills, and leave the pilot unprepared for equipment failures or unexpected situations.

   Automation tools, such as GPS and autopilot, enhance navigation and workload management but do not replace the pilot's responsibility to actively monitor flight progress. Blind reliance on automation can lead to missed deviations from the planned route, airspace violations, or proximity to terrain and other hazards.

   Automation systems can malfunction or provide incorrect information. Pilots must understand the limitations and failure modes of their systems and be ready to revert to traditional navigation and control methods if needed.

Chapter 5 **Human Factors**

Continuous monitoring of instruments, verifying autopilot actions, and cross-checking automation outputs against visual and other navigation cues ensure a balanced approach to flight management.

[PA.I.H.K4, PA.II.B.R1; FAA-H-8083-2]

G. CFIT Awareness

1. A majority of controlled flight into terrain (CFIT) accidents have been attributed to what factors?

a. Lack of pilot currency.

b. Loss of situational awareness.

c. Pilot distractions and breakdown of SRM.

d. Failure to comply with minimum safe altitudes.

e. Breakdown in effective ADM.

f. Insufficient planning, especially for the descent and arrival segments.

[PA.II.A.K4; AC 61-134]

2. A pilot can decrease the likelihood of a CFIT accident at the destination by identifying what risk factors prior to flight?

Factors such as airport location, runway lighting, weather/ daylight conditions, approach specifications, ATC capabilities and limitations, type of operation, departure procedures, controller/ pilot phraseology, and crew configuration should all be considered prior to flight.

[PA.II.A.K4; AC 61-134]

3. Describe several operational techniques that will help you avoid a CFIT accident.

a. Maintain situational awareness at all times.

b. Adhere to safe takeoff and departure procedures.

c. Familiarize yourself with surrounding terrain features and obstacles.

d. Adhere to published routes and minimum altitudes.

e. Fly a stabilized approach.

(continued)

Private Pilot Oral Exam Guide 117

Chapter 5 **Human Factors**

    f. Understand ATC clearances and instructions.

    g. Don't become complacent.

    h. Utilize onboard terrain awareness systems integrated with navigation systems for additional awareness of potential hazards.

[PA.II.A.K4; AC 61-134]

H. Automation Management

1. What does the term *automation management* refer to?

Automation management is the demonstrated ability to control and navigate an aircraft by means of the automated systems installed in the aircraft.

[PA.II.B.S3; FAA-H-8083-9]

2. In what three areas must a pilot be proficient when using advanced avionics or any automated system?

The pilot must know what to expect, know how to monitor the system for proper operation, and be prepared to promptly take appropriate action if the system does not perform as expected.

[PA.II.B.S3; FAA-H-8083-25]

3. What is the most important aspect of managing an autopilot/FMS?

Knowing at all times the modes that are engaged or armed to engage, and being capable of verifying that armed functions (e.g., navigation tracking or altitude capture) engage at the appropriate time.

[PA.II.B.S3; FAA-H-8083-9]

4. At a minimum, the pilot flying with advanced avionics must know how to manage which three primary items?

The course deviation indicator (CDI), the navigation source, and the autopilot.

[PA.II.B.S3; FAA-H-8083-25]

118   Aviation Supplies & Academics

Chapter 5 **Human Factors**

5. Automation management is a good place to practice the standard callout technique. What are standard callouts?

To assist in maintaining situational awareness, professional flight crews often use standard callouts. For example, the non-flying pilot may call 2,000 and 1,000 feet prior to reaching an assigned altitude. The callouts may be "two to go" and "one to go." Single-pilot operations can also benefit from this practice by adopting standard set callouts that can be used in the different segments of a flight. Examples of standard callouts are: "Power Set," "Airspeed Alive," "Rotate," "Positive Rate—Gear Up," "Localizer Alive," "Glideslope Alive," "Nav Source Verified," "Approach Mode Armed," "Approach Mode Active," and "Final Approach Fix."

[PA.II.B.S3; FAA-H-8083-16]

Private Pilot Oral Exam Guide   119

Aircraft Systems 6

Chapter 6 **Aircraft Systems**

Notice: Some of the following questions reference the systems of a Cessna 152. Be sure to review your aircraft's POH/AFM for specific information regarding the systems in your aircraft type.

A. Aircraft Flight Controls

1. What are the four main control surfaces and what are their functions?

Elevators—The elevators control the movement of the airplane about its lateral axis. This motion is called pitch.

Ailerons—The ailerons control the airplane's movement about its longitudinal axis. This motion is called roll.

Rudder—The rudder controls movement of the airplane about its vertical axis. This motion is called yaw.

Trim tabs—Trim tabs are small, adjustable, hinged surfaces on the aileron, rudder, or elevator control surfaces. They are labor-saving devices that enable the pilot to release manual pressure on the primary control.

[PA.I.G.K1a; FAA-H-8083-25]

2. How are the various flight controls operated?

The flight control surfaces are manually actuated through the use of either a rod or cable system. A control wheel actuates the ailerons and elevator, and rudder/brake pedals actuate the rudder.

[PA.I.G.K1a, PA.I.G.K1b; POH/AFM]

3. What are flaps and what is their function?

The wing flaps are movable panels on the inboard trailing edges of the wings. They are hinged so that they may be extended downward into the flow of air beneath the wings to increase both lift and drag. Their purpose is to permit a slower airspeed and a steeper angle of descent during a landing approach. In some cases, they may also be used to shorten the takeoff distance.

[PA.I.G.K1b; FAA-H-8083-25]

Chapter 6 **Aircraft Systems**

4. Describe the landing gear system on the airplane.

A pilot should be familiar with several key aspects of their aircraft's landing gear system to ensure safe operation during takeoff, landing, and taxiing.

a. Understand whether the aircraft has tricycle (nosewheel) or tailwheel (taildragger) landing gear, as this affects handling during taxi and landing, especially in crosswinds.

b. Understand and be able to inspect and describe any shock systems associated with the gear.

c. Be familiar with the maintenance schedule for the landing gear, including inspections of tires, struts, and actuators. Regular inspections ensure proper function and early detection of any issues.

For retractable gear:

a. Know whether the landing gear is manually or hydraulically/ electrically operated.

b. Be aware of the gear extension and retraction procedures, including checking that the gear is properly locked in place before takeoff and landing as well as any emergency procedures.

c. Be familiar with any gear position indicators and warning lights (e.g., gear unsafe, gear down) that confirm whether the landing gear is properly deployed or retracted.

d. Know any operational limitations of the gear retraction or deployment process.

[PA.I.G.K1d; POH/AFM]

5. How do brake systems work on most light general aviation aircraft?

Most light general aviation aircraft use a hydraulic brake system to provide reliable and efficient stopping power. These systems are typically operated via toe brakes located on the upper portion of the rudder pedals, and in some cases, a hand-operated brake lever may also be present.

When the pilot applies pressure to the brake pedals, the master cylinders generate hydraulic pressure by compressing brake fluid. The pressurized fluid travels through brake lines to the brake assemblies located at the main wheels. At the wheel, the fluid

Private Pilot Oral Exam Guide 123

Chapter 6 **Aircraft Systems**

pressure engages the brake pads or shoes, which press against a rotating disc (disc brakes) or drum (drum brakes), creating friction to slow or stop the aircraft.

Many aircraft allow independent control of left and right brakes, enabling differential braking, which assists with steering during ground operations, especially when the nose wheel is free-castering or in tight turns. The parking brake system, usually set via a separate lever, locks hydraulic pressure in the brake lines to hold the aircraft stationary. Proper maintenance of brake fluid levels and system components is essential for safe operation. Pilots should test the brakes during taxi to ensure functionality and remain aware that excessive or uneven application can cause wear, overheating, or skidding.

[PA.I.G.K1d; FAA-H-8083-25]

6. What type of hydraulic fluid does your aircraft use and what color is it?

Refer to your POH/AFM. A mineral-based hydraulic fluid (MIL-H-5606) is the most widely used type for small aircraft. It has an odor similar to penetrating oil and is dyed red. A newer, fire-resistant fluid (MIL-H-83282) is also used in small aircraft and is dyed red.

[PA.I.G.K1e; FAA-H-8083-25, FAA-H-8083-31]

7. How is steering accomplished on the ground?

Light airplanes are generally provided with nosewheel steering capabilities through a simple system of mechanical linkage connected to the rudder pedals. When a rudder pedal is depressed, a spring-loaded bungee (push-pull rod) connected to the pivotal portion of a nosewheel strut will turn the nose wheel.

[PA.I.G.K1; POH/AFM]

8. If the braking system is not working on your general aviation aircraft, will a parking brake still work?

If the main braking system on a general aviation aircraft fails, the parking brake may not provide an effective alternative, as its operation is typically dependent on the same hydraulic system as the primary brakes. In most aircraft, the parking brake works by locking the hydraulic pressure already applied to the main brakes.

124   Aviation Supplies & Academics

Chapter 6 **Aircraft Systems**

If there is a loss of hydraulic pressure due to a failure, the parking brake will likely be inoperative.

However, if the failure is isolated to a specific component, such as the brake pedals or a leak affecting only one wheel, the parking brake may still function temporarily, provided some hydraulic pressure remains. Pilots should not rely on the parking brake for stopping the aircraft during taxi, takeoff, or landing, as it is not designed for dynamic braking and this may result in further damage or unsafe conditions.

If braking is compromised, pilots should use alternative methods, such as reducing power, using aerodynamic braking (flaps and spoilers, if equipped), and steering into areas with soft ground or uphill slopes to slow the aircraft safely.

[PA.I.G.K1d; FAA-H-8083-25]

9. What is the primary difference between a free-castering nose wheel and a nose wheel that is interconnected on an airplane?

The primary difference between a free-castering nose wheel and an interconnected nose wheel lies in how the wheel is controlled for steering during ground operations.

A *free-castering nose wheel* pivots freely around its vertical axis and is not directly connected to the rudder pedals or any other control surface. Steering is achieved through differential braking (applying brakes to one main wheel while the other remains unbraked) and using engine thrust for directional control. This design is simpler and lighter, reducing maintenance complexity.

An *interconnected nose wheel* is mechanically or hydraulically linked to the rudder pedals, allowing direct steering input through pedal movements without having to apply brakes to make most turns. In these systems, the nose wheel moves in response to rudder pedal input.

Note: Know which of these your aircraft is equipped with, and some of the limitations and benefits of your particular system.

[PA.I.G.K1d; FAA-H-8083-25]

Chapter 6 **Aircraft Systems**

B. Engine System Components

1. What type of engine does your aircraft have?

Most general aviation aircraft have either carbureted or fuel-injected, normally aspirated, direct drive, air-cooled, horizontally opposed, four- or six-cylinder, overhead-valve engines. Know the manufacturer and horsepower of the engine in the aircraft you will be using, and know its general specifications.

[PA.I.G.K1c; POH/AFM]

2. What four strokes must occur in each cylinder of a typical four-stroke engine in order for it to produce full power?

The four strokes are:

Intake—Begins as the piston starts its downward travel, causing the intake valve to open and the air–fuel mixture to be drawn into the cylinder.

Compression—Begins when the intake valve closes, and the piston starts moving back to the top of the cylinder. This phase of the cycle is used to obtain a much greater power output from the air–fuel mixture once it is ignited.

Power—Begins when the air–fuel mixture is ignited, which causes a tremendous pressure increase in the cylinder and forces the piston downward away from the cylinder head, creating the power that turns the crankshaft.

Exhaust—Used to purge the cylinder of burned gases; begins when the exhaust valve opens and the piston starts to move toward the cylinder head once again.

[PA.I.G.K1c; FAA-H-8083-25]

3. What are the five basic functions of aircraft engine oil?

a. *Lubricates* the engine's moving parts.

b. *Cools* the engine by reducing friction.

c. *Removes* heat from the cylinders.

d. *Seals* provide a seal between the cylinder walls and pistons.

e. *Cleans* by carrying off metal and carbon particles and other oil contaminants.

[PA.I.G.K1c; FAA-H-8083-25]

126 Aviation Supplies & Academics

Chapter 6 **Aircraft Systems**

4. What is the purpose of a carburetor?

Carburetion may be defined as the process of mixing fuel and air in the correct proportions so as to form a combustible mixture. The carburetor vaporizes liquid fuel into small particles and then mixes it with air. It measures the airflow and meters fuel accordingly.

[PA.I.G.K1c; FAA-H-8083-25]

5. Explain how the carburetor heat system operates.

A carburetor heat valve, controlled by the pilot, allows unfiltered, heated air from a shroud located around an exhaust riser or muffler to be directed to the induction air manifold prior to the carburetor. Carburetor heat should be used anytime suspected or known carburetor icing conditions exist.

[PA.I.G.K1c; POH/AFM]

6. What change occurs to the air–fuel mixture when applying carburetor heat?

Normally, the introduction of heated air into the carburetor will result in a richer mixture. Warm air is less dense, resulting in less air for the same amount of fuel. Use of carburetor heat can cause a decrease in engine power of up to 15 percent.

[PA.I.G.K1c; FAA-H-8083-25]

7. What is the purpose of the throttle control?

The throttle allows the pilot to manually control the amount of air–fuel charge entering the cylinders. This in turn regulates the engine speed and power.

[PA.I.G.K1c; FAA-H-8083-25]

8. What is the purpose of the mixture control?

It regulates the air–fuel ratio. All airplane engines incorporate a device called a mixture control, by which the air–fuel ratio can be controlled by the pilot during flight. The purpose of a mixture control is to prevent the mixture from becoming too rich at high altitudes due to decreasing air density. It is also used to lean the mixture during cross-country flights to conserve fuel and provide optimum power.

[PA.I.G.K1c; FAA-H-8083-25]

Private Pilot Oral Exam Guide 127

Chapter 6 **Aircraft Systems**

9. Describe a fuel injection system installed in some aircraft.

A fuel-injection system injects fuel directly into the cylinders, or just ahead of the intake valve. It incorporates six basic components:

a. *Engine-driven fuel pump*—Provides fuel under pressure from the fuel tank to the air–fuel control unit.

b. *Air–fuel control unit*—Meters fuel based on the mixture control setting and sends it to the fuel manifold valve at a rate controlled by the throttle.

c. *Fuel manifold valve*—Distributes fuel to the individual fuel discharge nozzles.

d. *Discharge nozzles*—Located in each cylinder head, these inject the air–fuel mixture at the precise time for each cylinder directly into each cylinder intake port.

e. *Auxiliary fuel pump*—Provides fuel under pressure to air–fuel control unit for engine starting and/or emergency use.

f. *Fuel pressure/flow indicators*—Measures metered fuel pressure/flow.

[PA.I.G.K1c; FAA-H-8083-25]

10. What type of ignition system does your airplane have?

Engine ignition is provided by two engine-driven magnetos and two spark plugs per cylinder. The ignition system is completely independent of the aircraft electrical system. The magnetos are engine-driven, self-contained units supplying electrical current without using an external source of current. However, before they can produce current, the magnetos must be actuated, as the engine crankshaft is rotated by some other means. To accomplish this, the aircraft battery furnishes electrical power to operate a starter which, through a series of gears, rotates the engine crankshaft. This in turn actuates the armature of the magneto to produce the sparks for ignition of the fuel in each cylinder. After the engine starts, the starter system is disengaged, and the battery no longer contributes to the actual operation of the engine.

[PA.I.G.K1c; POH/AFM]

Chapter 6 **Aircraft Systems**

11. What are the two main advantages of a dual ignition system?

a. Increased safety in case one system fails; the engine may be operated on the other until a landing is safely made.

b. More complete and even combustion of the mixture, and consequently, improved engine performance, i.e., the air–fuel mixture will be ignited on each side of the combustion chamber and burn toward the center.

[PA.I.G.K1c; FAA-H-8083-25]

12. During the before takeoff magneto check, you notice that the right magneto is overly rough or experiences a drop outside of tolerances. Explain what the problem could be and what actions you will take next.

If a pilot notices that the right magneto is extremely rough during the before takeoff magneto check, it suggests a potential issue with the magneto or its associated components. Common causes for a rough running magneto include:

a. *Spark plug fouling*—The spark plugs on the right magneto may be fouled, preventing proper ignition. This can be caused by carbon buildup, moisture, or other contaminants.

b. *Faulty magneto*—A malfunction in the right magneto itself, such as a worn or defective component, could cause rough engine operation.

c. *Wiring or connector issues*—Loose or corroded wiring connections between the magneto and the engine could cause intermittent electrical contact, resulting in rough operation.

d. *Fuel or air distribution problem*—Uneven fuel distribution or air mixture issues may cause rough operation specific to one magneto

The pilot should try the following actions:

a. *Perform a full check*—Review engine gauges for abnormal readings and observe the behavior of the engine during the magneto check to determine if the roughness persists at both low and high RPM.

b. *Switch to both magnetos*—If the roughness disappears when switching back to both magnetos, it may indicate an issue isolated to the right magneto or a spark plug attached to it.

Private Pilot Oral Exam Guide 129

Chapter 6 **Aircraft Systems**

    c. *Leaning procedure*—A pilot may attempt to "lean" the engine out while running on the affected magneto. In some cases, the higher operating temperature may help clear some carbon buildup. This should only be done in accordance with manufacturer recommendations to avoid any potential engine damage by running it too lean.

    d. *Inspect the spark plugs*—If possible, inspect the spark plugs or request maintenance if the issue persists.

    e. *Consult with maintenance*—If troubleshooting doesn't resolve the issue, it is safest to contact maintenance before proceeding with the flight.

Roughness during the magneto check indicates a potential safety issue, and the pilot should not proceed with takeoff until it's resolved.

[PA.I.G.R1; FAA-H-8083-25, POH/AFM]

13. What causes carburetor icing, and what are the first indications of its presence?

The vaporization of fuel, combined with the expansion of air as it passes through the carburetor, causes a sudden cooling of the mixture. The temperature of the air passing through the carburetor may drop as much as 33°C (60°F) within a fraction of a second. Water vapor is squeezed out by this cooling, and if the temperature in the carburetor reaches 0°C (32°F) or below, the moisture will be deposited as frost or ice inside the carburetor. For airplanes with a fixed-pitch propeller, the first indication of carburetor icing is loss of RPM. For airplanes with controllable-pitch (constant-speed) propellers, the first indication is usually a drop in manifold pressure.

[PA.I.G.K1c; FAA-H-8083-25]

14. What method is used to determine that carburetor ice has been eliminated?

When heat is first applied, there will be a drop in RPM in airplanes equipped with a fixed-pitch propeller; there will be a drop in manifold pressure in airplanes equipped with a controllable-pitch propeller. If ice is present, there will be a rise in RPM or manifold pressure after the initial drop (often accompanied by intermittent engine roughness); and then, when the carburetor heat is turned

130 Aviation Supplies & Academics

Chapter 6 **Aircraft Systems**

off, the RPM or manifold pressure will rise to a setting greater than that before application of heat. The engine should run more smoothly after the ice has been removed.

[PA.I.G.K1c; FAA-H-8083-25]

15. What conditions are favorable for carburetor icing?

Carburetor ice is most likely to occur when temperatures are below 21°C (70°F) and the relative humidity is above 80 percent. However, due to the sudden cooling that takes place in the carburetor, icing can occur even with temperatures as high as 38°C (100°F) and humidity as low as 50 percent. This temperature drop can be as much as 33°C to 39°C (60°F to 70°F).

[PA.I.G.K1c; FAA-H-8083-25]

16. What is detonation?

Detonation is an uncontrolled, explosive ignition of the air–fuel mixture within the cylinder's combustion chamber. It causes excessive temperature and pressure which, if not corrected, can quickly lead to failure of the piston, cylinder, or valves. In less severe cases, detonation causes engine overheating, roughness, or loss of power. Detonation is characterized by high cylinder-head temperatures and is most likely to occur when operating at high power settings.

[PA.I.G.K1c; FAA-H-8083-25]

17. What are some of the most common operational causes of detonation?

a. Using a lower fuel grade than that specified by the aircraft manufacturer.

b. Operating with extremely high manifold pressures in conjunction with low RPM.

c. Operating the engine at high power settings with an excessively lean mixture.

d. Extended ground operations or steep climbs where cylinder cooling is reduced.

[PA.I.G.K1c; FAA-8083-25]

Private Pilot Oral Exam Guide   131

Chapter 6 **Aircraft Systems**

18. What action should be taken if detonation is suspected?

Detonation may be avoided by following these basic guidelines during the various phases of ground and flight operations:

a. Ensure that the proper grade of fuel is used.

b. Keep the cowl flaps (if available) in the full-open position while on the ground to provide the maximum airflow through the cowling.

c. Use an enriched fuel mixture, as well as a shallow climb angle, to increase cylinder cooling during takeoff and initial climb.

d. Avoid extended, high-power, steep climbs.

e. Develop the habit of monitoring the engine instruments to verify proper operation according to procedures established by the manufacturer.

[PA.I.G.K1c; FAA-H-8083-25]

19. What is preignition?

Preignition occurs when the air–fuel mixture ignites prior to the engine's normal ignition event, resulting in reduced engine power and high operating temperatures. Premature burning is usually caused by a residual hot spot in the combustion chamber, often created by a small carbon deposit on a spark plug, a cracked spark plug insulator, or other damage in the cylinder that causes a part to heat sufficiently to ignite the air–fuel charge. As with detonation, preignition may also cause severe engine damage, because the expanding gases exert excessive pressure on the piston while still on its compression stroke.

[PA.I.G.K1c; FAA-H-8083-25]

20. What action should be taken if preignition is suspected?

Corrective actions for preignition include any type of engine operation which would promote cooling such as:

a. Reduce power.
b. Reduce the climb rate for better cooling.
c. Enrich the air–fuel mixture.
d. Open cowl flaps if available.

[PA.I.G.K1c; FAA-H-8083-25]

132 Aviation Supplies & Academics

Chapter 6 **Aircraft Systems**

21. **During the before-takeoff runup, you switch the magnetos from the BOTH position to the RIGHT position and notice there is no RPM drop. What condition does this indicate?**

The left P-lead is not grounding, or the engine has been running only on the right magneto because the left magneto has totally failed.

[PA.I.G.R1; FAA-H-8083-25]

22. **During a cross-country flight, you notice that the oil pressure is low but the oil temperature is normal. What is the problem and what action should be taken?**

A low oil pressure in flight could be the result of any one of several problems, the most common being that of insufficient oil. If the oil temperature continues to remain normal, a clogged oil pressure relief valve or an oil pressure gauge malfunction could be the culprit. In any case, it is advisable to land at the nearest airport to check for the cause of the trouble.

[PA.I.G.K1e; FAA-H-8083-25]

23. **What procedures should be followed concerning a partial loss of power in flight?**

If a partial loss of power occurs, the first priority is to establish and maintain a suitable airspeed (best glide airspeed if necessary). Then, select an emergency landing area and remain within gliding distance. As time allows, attempt to determine the cause and correct it.

Complete the following checklist:

a. Check the carburetor heat.

b. Check the amount of fuel in each tank and switch fuel tanks if necessary.

c. Check the fuel selector valve's current position.

d. Check the mixture control.

e. Check that the primer control is all the way in and locked.

f. Check the operation of the magnetos in all three positions; both, left, and right.

[PA.I.G.K1c; POH/AFM]

Private Pilot Oral Exam Guide 133

Chapter 6 **Aircraft Systems**

24. What procedures should be followed if an engine fire develops in flight?

In the event of an engine fire in flight, the following procedures should be used:

a. Set the mixture control to Idle Cutoff.

b. Set the fuel selector valve to Off.

c. Turn the master switch to Off.

d. Set the cabin heat and air vents to Off; leave the overhead vents On.

e. Establish an airspeed of 100 KIAS and increase the descent, if necessary, to find an airspeed that will provide for an incombustible mixture.

f. Execute a forced landing procedures checklist.

[PA.I.G.K2; POH/AFM]

25. What procedures should be followed if an engine fire develops on the ground during starting?

Continue to attempt an engine start as a start will cause flames and excess fuel to be sucked back through the carburetor.

a. If the engine starts:

   • Increase the power to a higher RPM for a few moments; and

   • Shut down the engine and inspect it.

b. If the engine does not start:

   • Set the throttle to the Full position.

   • Set the mixture control to Idle Cutoff.

   • Continue to try an engine start in an attempt to put out the fire by vacuum.

c. If the fire continues:

   • Turn the ignition switch to Off.

   • Turn the master switch to Off.

   • Set the fuel selector to Off.

In all cases, evacuate the aircraft and obtain a fire extinguisher and/ or assistance.

[PA.I.G.K2; POH/AFM]

Chapter 6 **Aircraft Systems**

C. Fuel System

1. How does the fuel system in your aircraft deliver fuel to the engine?

This will depend on your particular aircraft. In most high-wing aircraft, fuel is transferred from the wing tanks to the engine by the gravity feed system. Low-wing aircraft do not have the benefit of gravity and will typically have a fuel pump used for priming or additional pressure and an engine-driven fuel pump.

From there, the fuel is mixed with air and then flows into the cylinders through the intake manifold tubes.

[PA.I.G.K1e; POH/AFM]

2. What is the purpose of the fuel tank vents?

As the fuel level in an aircraft fuel tank decreases, a vacuum would be created within the tank which would eventually result in a decreasing fuel flow and finally engine stoppage. Fuel system venting provides a way of replacing fuel with outside air, preventing formation of a vacuum.

[PA.I.G.K1e; POH/AFM]

3. Does your aircraft use a fuel pump?

This will depend on your particular aircraft. In most high-wing aircraft, fuel is transferred from the wing tanks to the engine by the gravity feed system. The gravity system does not require a fuel pump because the fuel is always under positive pressure. However, some aircraft (even high-wing aircraft) may have supplemental fuel pumps for priming or creating pressure during maneuvering or at higher altitudes. Low-wing aircraft do not have the benefit of gravity and will typically have a fuel pump used for priming or for additional pressure to supplement the engine-driven fuel pump, or to serve as a backup in case it fails.

[PA.I.G.K1e; POH/AFM]

4. What type of fuel does your aircraft require (minimum octane rating and color)?

Most aircraft use 100LL fuel that is blue in color. Some aircraft may also be approved to use "auto gas" or "recreational fuel." This would require a supplemental type certificate (STC). Additionally, some newer fuels are being developed that may be approved for

Private Pilot Oral Exam Guide 135

Chapter 6 **Aircraft Systems**

use in some aircraft. Refer to your POH/AFM and any STCs that may have been authorized for your particular aircraft.

[PA.I.G.K1e; POH/AFM]

5. Can other types of fuel be used if the specified grade is not available?

Airplane engines are designed to operate using a specific grade of fuel as recommended by the manufacturer. If the proper grade of fuel is not available, it is possible, but not desirable, to use the next higher grade as a substitute. Always reference the aircraft's POH/AFM. Auto gas should *never* be used in aircraft engines unless the aircraft has been modified with an FAA-issued supplemental type certificate (STC).

[PA.I.G.K1e; FAA-H-8083-25]

6. What color of dye is added to the following fuel grades: 80, 100, 100LL, and Jet A?

Grade	Color
80 (obsolete)	Red
100 (obsolete)	Green
100LL	Blue
Jet A	Colorless or straw

[PA.I.G.K1e; FAA-H-8083-25, FAA-P-8740-35]

7. If a non-turbine piston-engine-powered airplane is accidentally fueled with Jet A fuel, will it start?

Yes. Reciprocating engines may run briefly on jet fuel, but detonation and overheating will soon cause power failure. When an aircraft that requires avgas is inadvertently fueled with Jet A, there is usually a small amount of avgas remaining in the aircraft's fuel system (tanks, fuel lines, carburetor, etc.). This remaining fuel can enable an aircraft to taxi, perform an engine run-up, and possibly even take off before experiencing a catastrophic engine failure.

Note: Other than the kerosene smell and the oily feel when rubbed between the fingers, it can be very difficult to visually identify an accidental mixture of 100LL Avgas (blue) and Jet A (straw color).

[PA.I.G.K1e; FAA-H-8083-25, FAA-P-8740-35]

Chapter 6 **Aircraft Systems**

8. What are sustainable aviation fuels (SAF)?

Sustainable aviation fuels (SAF) are alternative fuels designed to reduce the environmental impact of aviation. SAF is produced from renewable resources, such as plant oils, waste materials, or agricultural byproducts, and is chemically similar to conventional jet fuel. Unlike traditional jet fuel, SAF can significantly lower carbon emissions and greenhouse gases when burned in aircraft engines.

SAF is considered a crucial part of efforts to reduce the aviation industry's carbon footprint and achieve climate goals. A goal of these fuels is to be used in current aircraft engines and infrastructure without modifications. Widespread availability of and implementation of these fuels has experienced challenges, but pilots should be aware that new fuel options are being provided that may or may not be usable in their particular aircraft.

Some aircraft have supplemental type certificate authorizations to use alternate fuels for their engines. Before using such a fuel, a pilot should refer to any approvals if present.

[PA.I.G.K1e; FAA Sustainability, POH/AFM]

9. If a pilot finds themselves at an airport that offers "aviation fuel" other than 100LL, such as 94UL or G100UL, may the pilot use that in their aircraft instead of the 100LL?

If a pilot encounters aviation fuel options like 94UL or G100UL at an airport, they must first verify that the fuel is approved for use in their specific aircraft. The most important consideration is whether the aircraft's engine and fuel system are certified for those particular fuels.

100LL (Low Lead) is the standard aviation fuel for piston-engine aircraft, and many aircraft are specifically designed to use this fuel. 94UL (Unleaded) and G100UL (a newer unleaded aviation fuel) are alternative fuels, but not all aircraft are approved to use them. Before using 94UL or G100UL, the pilot should check their airplane flight manual (AFM) or the aircraft's type certificate to determine if these fuels are listed as acceptable. If the aircraft is certified for alternative fuels, such as 94UL or G100UL, the pilot can use them as long as they meet the specified requirements.

(continued)

Private Pilot Oral Exam Guide   137

Chapter 6 **Aircraft Systems**

There may also be additional airworthiness directives (ADs), supplemental type certificates (STC), or other requirements to use these and other new alternate fuel types.

If the aircraft is not approved for those fuels, using them could lead to engine performance issues or damage and may void the aircraft's warranty or insurance.

[PA.I.G.K1e; POH/AFM]

10. What is the function of a manual primer, and how does it operate?

The primary function of a manual primer on an equipped aircraft is to provide assistance in starting the engine. The primer draws fuel from the fuel strainer and injects it directly into the cylinder intake ports. This usually results in a quicker, more efficient engine start.

[PA.I.G.K1e; POH/AFM]

D. Electrical System

1. Describe the electrical system on your aircraft.

Electrical energy is typically provided by a 14- or 28-volt, direct-current system powered by an engine-driven 60-amp alternator and a 12- or 24-volt battery. Some aircraft systems may still have generators instead of alternators.

[PA.I.G.K1f; POH/AFM]

2. How are the circuits for the various electrical accessories within the aircraft protected?

Most of the electrical circuits in an airplane are protected from an overload condition by either circuit breakers or fuses, or both. Circuit breakers perform the same function as fuses except that when an overload occurs, a circuit breaker can be reset.

[PA.I.G.K1f; POH/AFM]

3. The electrical system provides power for what equipment in the airplane?

Normally, the following:

a. Radio equipment
b. Turn coordinator
c. Fuel gauges

138 Aviation Supplies & Academics

Chapter 6 **Aircraft Systems**

    d. Pitot heat
    e. Landing light
    f. Taxi light
    g. Strobe lights
    h. Interior lights
    i. Instrument lights
    j. Position lights
    k. Flaps (maybe)
    l. Stall warning system (maybe)
    m. Oil temperature gauge
    n. Electric fuel pump (maybe)

[PA.I.G.K1g; POH/AFM]

4. What does the ammeter indicate?

The ammeter indicates the flow of current, in amperes, from the alternator to the battery or from the battery to the electrical system. With the engine running and master switch on, the ammeter will indicate the charging rate to the battery. If the alternator has gone offline and is no longer functioning, or the electrical load exceeds the output of the alternator, the ammeter indicates the discharge rate of the battery.

[PA.I.G.K1f; POH/AFM]

5. What is the function of the voltage regulator?

The voltage regulator is a device that monitors system voltage, detects changes, and makes the required adjustments in the output of the alternator to maintain a constant regulated system voltage. It must do this at low RPM, such as during taxi, as well as at high RPM in flight. In a 28-volt system, it will maintain 28 volts ± 0.5 volts.

[PA.I.G.K1f; POH/AFM]

6. Why is the generator/alternator voltage output slightly higher than the battery voltage?

The difference in voltage keeps the battery charged. For example, a 12-volt battery would be supplied with 14 volts.

[PA.I.G.K1f; FAA-H-8083-25]

Chapter 6 **Aircraft Systems**

7. Interpret the following ammeter indications.

a. Ammeter indicates a right deflection (positive).

- *After starting*—The power from the battery used for starting is being replenished by the alternator. Or, if a full-scale charge is indicated for more than 1 minute, the starter is still engaged, and a shutdown is indicated.
- *During flight*—A faulty voltage regulator is causing the alternator to overcharge the battery. Reset the system and if the condition continues, terminate the flight as soon as possible.

b. Ammeter indicates a left deflection (negative).

- *After starting*—It is normal during start. At other times this indicates the alternator is not functioning or an overload condition exists in the system. The battery is not receiving a charge.
- *During flight*—The alternator is not functioning, or an overload exists in the system. The battery is not receiving a charge. Possible causes: the master switch was accidentally shut off, or the alternator circuit breaker tripped.

[PA.I.G.K1i; FAA-H-8083-25]

8. What action should be taken if the ammeter indicates a continuous discharge while in flight?

The alternator has quit producing a charge, so the alternator circuit breaker should be checked and reset if necessary. If this does not correct the problem, the pilot should complete the following actions:

a. Turn off the alternator; pull the circuit breaker (the field circuit will continue to draw power from the battery).

b. Turn off all electrical equipment not essential to flight (the battery is now the only source of electrical power).

c. Terminate the flight and make a landing as soon as possible.

[PA.I.G.K1i; FAA-H-8083-25]

Chapter 6 **Aircraft Systems**

9. What action should be taken if the ammeter indicates a continuous charge while in flight (more than two needle widths)?

If a continuous excessive rate of charge were allowed for any extended period of time, the battery would overheat and evaporate the electrolyte at an excessive rate. A possible explosion of the battery could result. Also, electronic components in the electrical system would be adversely affected by higher-than-normal voltage. Protection is provided by an overvoltage sensor, which will shut the alternator down if an excessive voltage is detected. If this should occur, the following actions should be taken:

a. Turn off the alternator; pull the circuit breaker (the field circuit will continue to draw power from the battery).

b. Turn off all electrical equipment not essential to flight (the battery is now the only source of electrical power).

c. Terminate the flight and make a landing as soon as possible.

Exam Tip: Expect the examiner to test your knowledge of the aircraft's electrical system by asking several "what if" type questions, such as: What if your alternator failed in flight? What systems, instruments, and equipment would be operative/inoperative? After an alternator failure, what systems and equipment will the battery supply power to? How long will the battery supply power? When the battery finally dies, will the engine continue to operate? Ensure that you know your aircraft's electrical system well and can answer these types of questions.

[PA.I.G.K1i; FAA-H-8083-25]

10. If a pilot finds their aircraft has a dead battery for some reason (e.g., perhaps the master electrical switch was left on), how can they get the aircraft started? Can an external power source (jumping) be used?

If a pilot finds that their aircraft's battery is dead, such as from leaving the master switch on, there are ways to start the aircraft, including using an external power source. However, safety and proper procedures must be followed in accordance with any procedures outlined in the aircraft's AFM/POH.

Some aircraft allow external power sources to be used to "jump" an aircraft, while others do not. It is important to confirm any procedure for using external power and ensure compatibility with

Chapter 6 **Aircraft Systems**

the aircraft's electrical system. Some aircraft are 14-volt and some are 28-volt systems. Make sure to use a proper power source if utilizing external power.

It is also important to ensure that the GPU or power source is connected correctly and all switches are set as per the aircraft manual to prevent damage to avionics or electrical systems. Also, once the engine starts, the pilot should confirm that the alternator is functioning and charging the electrical system.

[PA.II.C.K2; FAA-H-8083-25]

11. If you cannot start your airplane due to a low battery, and you complete an external start using a ground power cart, what problems might still occur after the engine has started?

After an external start using a ground power cart, several issues may arise, especially if the battery remains weak or completely discharged. A low or dead battery may not have enough power to sustain critical electrical systems during flight, even if the engine-driven alternator is operating. This could result in failures of radios, navigation equipment, or lighting, particularly if the alternator fails. A depleted battery will demand a high charge rate from the alternator once the engine starts. This can overheat the alternator or cause it to fail prematurely, leading to a total electrical failure in flight. A weak battery may not stabilize electrical system voltage, causing potential damage to sensitive avionics or interruptions in their operation. If the battery cannot provide sufficient backup power to the ignition system in certain aircraft (e.g., electronic ignition systems), the engine may shut down if the alternator fails. A weak battery could also be an indicator of deeper problems, such as a failing alternator, damaged wiring, or poor battery maintenance, which may need to be addressed before flight.

A best practice is to charge the battery fully and test it prior to flight instead of just using an external power start to get the aircraft going (unless absolutely necessary).

[PA.II.C.K2; FAA-H-8083-25]

Chapter 6 **Aircraft Systems**

12. In the event of an electrical system failure, for what time duration can you reasonably expect electrical power from the battery?

In the event of an electrical system failure, such as an alternator malfunction, the duration of power available from the aircraft's battery depends on its capacity, charge level, and the electrical load at the time of failure.

For most general aviation aircraft, a fully charged battery can provide power for 15 to 30 minutes under typical loads. However, if nonessential systems such as cabin lighting, radios, and autopilot are turned off to conserve power (load shedding), this duration can be extended. Pilots should familiarize themselves with their aircraft's POH/AFM for specific guidance on managing electrical loads in an emergency.

Modern aircraft equipped with advanced avionics or glass cockpits may have a higher electrical demand, reducing battery endurance. In these cases, secondary alternators, backup battery systems, or standby instruments may provide additional operational time for critical systems.

[PA.IX.C.K2; FAA-H-8083-3]

13. What effect would positioning the master switch to the Off position have on aircraft systems while in flight?

Positioning the master switch to the Off position in flight would shut down the aircraft's electrical system by disconnecting both the battery and the alternator from the electrical bus. This action would result in all systems dependent on the electrical system—such as avionics, lights, and flaps (in electrically powered systems)—to immediately lose power. For aircraft with glass cockpits, displays may go dark unless a backup battery is available.

The engine will generally continue running, as most light aircraft use magneto-based ignition systems that operate independently of the electrical system. However, if the aircraft has electronic ignition or fuel-injection systems requiring electrical power, the engine may fail.

Radios, GPS, transponders, and other avionics systems would shut down, complicating communication with air traffic control and situational awareness.

(continued)

Private Pilot Oral Exam Guide 143

Chapter 6 **Aircraft Systems**

Aircraft with electrically operated landing gear or flaps may be unable to extend these systems without the master switch on, unless manual backup procedures are available.

[PA.I.G.K1f; FAA-H-8083-3]

E. Pitot/Static Flight Instruments

1. What instruments operate off the pitot/static system?

Altimeter, vertical speed indicator, and airspeed indicator.

[PA.I.G.K1h; FAA-H-8083-15]

2. How does an altimeter work?

A sensitive altimeter is an aneroid barometer that measures the absolute pressure of the ambient air and displays it in terms of feet above a selected pressure level. The sensitive element in a sensitive altimeter is a stack of evacuated, corrugated bronze aneroid capsules. The air pressure acting on these aneroids tries to compress them against their natural springiness, which tries to expand them. The result is that their thickness changes as the air pressure changes. Stacking several aneroids increases the dimension change as the pressure varies over the usable range of the instrument.

[PA.I.G.K1h; FAA-H-8083-15]

3. What are the limitations of a pressure altimeter?

Nonstandard pressure and temperature:

a. Temperature variations expand or contract the atmosphere and raise or lower pressure levels that the altimeter senses.

- *On a warm day*—The pressure level is higher than on a standard day. The altimeter indicates lower-than-actual altitude.
- *On a cold day*—The pressure level is lower than on a standard day. The altimeter indicates higher-than-actual altitude.

b. Changes in surface pressure also affect pressure levels at altitude:

- *Higher-than-standard pressure*—The pressure level is higher than on a standard day. The altimeter indicates lower-than-actual altitude.

144 Aviation Supplies & Academics

Chapter 6 **Aircraft Systems**

- *Lower-than-standard pressure*—The pressure level is lower than on a standard day. The altimeter indicates higher-than-actual altitude.

Remember: High to low or hot to cold, look out below!

[PA.I.G.K1h; FAA-H-8083-15]

4. Define and state how you would determine the following: absolute altitude, indicated altitude, pressure altitude, true altitude, and density altitude.

Absolute altitude—The vertical distance of an aircraft above the terrain.

Indicated altitude—The altitude read directly from the altimeter (uncorrected) after it is set to the current altimeter setting.

Pressure altitude—The altitude when the altimeter setting window is adjusted to 29.92. Pressure altitude is used for computer solutions to determine density altitude, true altitude, true airspeed, etc.

True altitude—The true vertical distance of the aircraft above sea level. Airport, terrain, and obstacle elevations found on aeronautical charts are true altitudes.

Density altitude—Pressure altitude corrected for nonstandard temperature variations. Directly related to an aircraft's takeoff, climb, and landing performance.

[PA.I.G.K1h; FAA-H-8083-25]

5. How does the airspeed indicator operate?

The airspeed indicator is a sensitive, differential pressure gauge which measures the difference between impact pressure from the pitot head and undisturbed atmospheric pressure from the static source. The difference is registered by the airspeed pointer on the face of the instrument.

[PA.I.G.K1h; FAA-H-8083-25]

6. What is the limitation of the airspeed indicator?

The airspeed indicator is subject to proper flow of air in the pitot/static system.

[PA.I.G.K1h; FAA-H-8083-15]

Private Pilot Oral Exam Guide 145

Chapter 6 **Aircraft Systems**

7. What are the errors of the airspeed indicator?

Position error—Caused by the static ports sensing erroneous static pressure; slipstream flow causes disturbances at the static port, preventing actual atmospheric pressure measurement. It varies with airspeed, altitude, and configuration, and may be a plus or minus value.

Density error—Changes in altitude and temperature are not compensated for by the instrument.

Compressibility error—Caused by the packing of air into the pitot tube at high airspeeds, resulting in higher-than-normal indications. It is usually not a factor at slower speeds.

[PA.I.G.K1h; FAA-H-8083-15]

8. What are the different types of aircraft speeds?

Indicated airspeed (IAS)—The speed of the airplane as observed on the airspeed indicator. It is the airspeed without correction for indicator, position (or installation), or compressibility errors.

Calibrated airspeed (CAS)—The airspeed indicator reading corrected for position (or installation) and instrument errors. CAS is equal to TAS at sea level in a standard atmosphere. The color-coding for various design speeds marked on airspeed indicators may be IAS or CAS.

Equivalent airspeed (EAS)—The airspeed indicator reading corrected for position (or installation) or instrument error, and for adiabatic compressible flow for the particular altitude. EAS is equal to CAS at sea level in a standard atmosphere.

True airspeed (TAS)—CAS corrected for altitude and nonstandard temperature; the speed of the airplane in relation to the air mass in which it is flying.

[PA.I.G.K1h; FAA-H-8083-25]

Chapter 6 **Aircraft Systems**

9. Name several important airspeed limitations not marked on the face of the airspeed indicator.

Design maneuvering speed (V_A)—The maximum speed at which the structural design's limit load can be imposed (either by gusts or full deflection of the control surfaces) without causing structural damage. *Note:* Operating at or below V_A does not provide structural protection against multiple full control inputs in one axis or full control inputs in more than one axis at the same time.

Landing gear operating speed (V_{LO})—The maximum speed for extending or retracting the landing gear if using aircraft equipped with retractable landing gear.

Best angle-of-climb speed (V_X)—Important when a short-field takeoff to clear an obstacle is required.

Best rate-of-climb speed (V_Y)—The airspeed that will give the pilot the most altitude in a given period of time.

[PA.I.G.K1h; FAA-H-8083-25]

10. What airspeed limitations apply to the color-coded marking system of the airspeed indicator?

Marking	Meaning
White arc	Flap operating range
Lower A/S limit white arc	V_{S0} (stall speed or minimum steady flight speed in landing configuration)
Upper A/S limit white arc	V_{FE} (maximum flap extension speed)
Green arc	Normal operating range
Lower A/S limit green arc	V_{S1} (stall speed clean or specified configuration)
Upper A/S limit green arc	V_{NO} (normal operations speed or maximum structural cruise speed)
Yellow arc	Caution range (operations in smooth air only)
Red line	V_{NE} (never exceed speed; above this speed, structural failure may occur.)

[PA.I.G.K1h; FAA-H-8083-25]

Private Pilot Oral Exam Guide   147

Chapter 6 **Aircraft Systems**

11. How does the vertical speed indicator work?

The vertical speed indicator is a pressure differential instrument. Inside the instrument case is an aneroid very much like the one in an airspeed indicator. Both the inside of this aneroid and the inside of the instrument case are vented to the static system, but the case is vented through a calibrated orifice that causes the pressure inside the case to change more slowly than the pressure inside the aneroid. As the aircraft ascends, the static pressure becomes lower and the pressure inside the case compresses the aneroid, moving the pointer upward, showing a climb and indicating the number of feet per minute the aircraft is ascending.

[PA.I.G.K1h; FAA-H-8083-15]

12. What are the limitations of the vertical speed indicator (VSI)?

The VSI is not accurate until the aircraft is stabilized. Because of the restriction in airflow to the static line, a 6 to 9 second lag is required to equalize or stabilize the pressures. Sudden or abrupt changes in aircraft attitude will cause erroneous instrument readings as airflow fluctuates over the static port. Both rough control technique and turbulent air result in unreliable needle indications.

[PA.I.G.K1h; FAA-H-8083-25]

13. What instruments are affected when the pitot tube freezes, becomes clogged, or is covered?

When the pitot tube freezes, becomes clogged, or is covered, the airspeed indicator (ASI) is directly affected, as it relies on the pitot tube to measure dynamic air pressure. The extent of the impact depends on whether the blockage occurs in the tube itself, the drain hole, or both. If only the pitot tube is blocked, the ASI will read zero because no dynamic pressure is being delivered to the system. Static pressure continues to equalize through the static ports, rendering the ASI inoperative. If both the pitot tube and the drain hole are blocked, the ASI may behave unpredictably and act like an altimeter. It will display higher airspeeds as altitude increases (due to trapped air expanding in the tube) and lower airspeeds as altitude decreases, which can lead to erroneous airspeed readings.

The altimeter and vertical speed indicator (VSI) rely solely on static pressure and are unaffected by pitot tube blockages unless the static port is also obstructed.

[PA.I.G.K1h; FAA-H-8083-25]

148 Aviation Supplies & Academics

Chapter 6 **Aircraft Systems**

14. What should a pilot do if they suspect their pitot tube has been affected by icing coverage?

If a pilot suspects the pitot tube is affected by icing, they should immediately activate the pitot heat (if installed) to melt the ice and restore normal operation. The airspeed indicator (ASI) will likely be the first instrument to display abnormal behavior, such as erratic or zero readings, signaling a potential pitot tube blockage.

If pitot heat is not available or does not resolve the issue, the pilot should treat the ASI as unreliable and rely on backup instruments or other performance cues, such as engine power settings, pitch attitude, and GPS ground speed, to maintain safe flight.

Additionally, the pilot should consider exiting the icing conditions by changing altitude or direction, following proper procedures. In extreme cases, they should declare an emergency if flight safety is compromised. Preventive use of pitot heat before entering visible moisture in cold conditions is critical to avoiding icing-related malfunctions.

[PA.I.G.K1h; FAA-H-8083-25]

15. What instruments are affected when the static port freezes, becomes clogged, or is covered?

When the static port freezes, becomes clogged, or is covered, the instruments that rely on static pressure—namely the altimeter, vertical speed indicator (VSI), and airspeed indicator (ASI)—will be affected. The specific effects depend on whether the blockage is partial or complete. If the static port is blocked, the altimeter will freeze at the altitude where the blockage occurred, as it can no longer measure changing atmospheric pressure. The VSI will become inoperative and remain at zero, as it cannot detect pressure changes that indicate rate of climb or descent.

The ASI will display erroneous readings. It may underread at lower altitudes and overread at higher altitudes, as it requires both static and dynamic pressures to function accurately. With a blocked static port, it cannot adjust for changes in altitude.

Exam Tip: Know if your aircraft has an alternate static port source, how to utilize it, and what potential errors it might induce compared to the aircraft's normal static port.

[PA.I.G.K1h; FAA-H-8083-25]

Private Pilot Oral Exam Guide 149

Chapter 6 **Aircraft Systems**

16. What is the purpose of the alternate static source?

The purpose of an alternate static source is to provide a backup source of static pressure for the aircraft's pitot-static instruments—altimeter, vertical speed indicator (VSI), and airspeed indicator (ASI)—in case the primary static port becomes blocked or inoperative.

When activated, the alternate static source typically draws air from inside the cabin, allowing the instruments to continue functioning. However, because cabin air pressure can differ slightly from external static pressure due to airflow and ventilation effects, the instruments may not display entirely accurate readings.

An altimeter may read slightly higher than actual altitude. Typically, a VSI will show a momentary deviation before stabilizing. Additionally, the ASI will typically read slightly higher than actual airspeed.

Using the alternate static source is critical during emergencies, such as icing or contamination that obstructs the primary static port. Pilots should follow the aircraft's POH/AFM for procedures to activate the alternate static source and compensate for any potential instrument errors.

[PA.I.G.K1h; FAA-H-8083-25]

17. If a pilot changes their altimeter setting up or down, what effects would they see? What change would a pilot see if they changed their altimeter setting from 29.15 to 29.85?

Changing the altimeter setting up or down directly affects the altitude displayed on the altimeter. The altimeter measures altitude based on atmospheric pressure and uses the setting to adjust for local barometric pressure changes.

When the setting is increased (e.g., from 29.80 to 30.00), the altimeter will show a higher altitude. This happens because the altimeter assumes higher atmospheric pressure at sea level, recalibrating the reading accordingly. When the setting is decreased (e.g., from 30.00 to 29.80), the altimeter will show a lower altitude. The reduced setting assumes lower atmospheric pressure at sea level, lowering the indicated altitude.

Chapter 6 **Aircraft Systems**

For every 0.01 inHg change in the altimeter setting, the altitude changes by 10 feet. For example, adjusting the setting by 0.10 inHg would result in a 100-foot change in the indicated altitude.

For example, if a pilot changes the altimeter setting from 29.15 to 29.85, they are increasing the pressure setting by 0.70 inches of mercury (inHg). This adjustment causes the altimeter to display a higher altitude because the altimeter is calibrated to indicate altitude based on atmospheric pressure.

A change of 0.70 inHg = 0.70 × 10 feet = 700 feet.

The altimeter will display an altitude 700 feet higher after changing the setting from 29.15 to 29.85.

[PA.I.G.K1h; FAA-H-8083-25]

F. Gyroscopic Flight Instruments

1. What instruments contain gyroscopes?

The most common gyroscopically driven instruments have historically been attitude indicators and heading indicators. Some turn coordinators may also be gyroscopic. Many modern aircraft no longer have vacuum-driven gyroscopic instruments, and a pilot should know which systems are in the aircraft they will be operating.

[PA.I.G.K1h; FAA-H-8083-25]

2. What are the two fundamental properties of a gyroscope?

Rigidity in space—A gyroscope remains in a fixed position in the plane in which it is spinning.

Precession—The tilting or turning of a gyro in response to a deflective force. The reaction to this force does not occur at the point where it was applied; rather, it occurs at a point that is 90° later in the direction of rotation. The rate at which the gyro precesses is inversely proportional to the speed of the rotor and proportional to the deflective force.

[PA.I.G.K1h; FAA-H-8083-25]

Chapter 6 **Aircraft Systems**

3. What are the various power sources that may be used to power the gyroscopic instruments in an airplane?

In some airplanes, all the gyros are vacuum, pressure, or electrically operated; in others, vacuum or pressure systems provide the power for the heading and attitude indicators, while the electrical system provides the power for the turn coordinator. Most airplanes have at least two sources of power to ensure at least one source of bank information if one power source fails.

[PA.I.G.K1h; FAA-H-8083-25]

4. How does the vacuum system operate?

An engine-driven vacuum pump provides suction which pulls air from the instrument case. Normal pressure entering the case is directed against rotor vanes to turn the rotor (gyro) at high speed, much like a water wheel or turbine operates. Air is drawn into the instrument through a filter from the flight deck and eventually vented outside. Vacuum values vary between manufacturers (usually between 4.5 and 5.5 inHg) but provide rotor speeds from 8,000 to 18,000 RPM.

[PA.I.G.K1h; FAA-H-8083-25]

5. How does the attitude indicator operate?

The gyro in the attitude indicator is mounted on a horizontal plane and depends upon rigidity in space for its operation. The horizon bar represents the true horizon. This bar is fixed to the gyro and remains in a horizontal plane as the airplane is pitched or banked about its lateral or longitudinal axis, indicating the attitude of the airplane relative to the true horizon.

[PA.I.G.K1h; FAA-H-8083-25]

6. What are the limitations of an attitude indicator?

The pitch and bank limits depend upon the make and model of the instrument. Limits in the banking plane are usually from 100° to 110°, and the pitch limits are usually from 60° to 70°. If either limit is exceeded, the instrument will tumble or spill and will give incorrect indications until reset. Some modern attitude indicators will not tumble.

[PA.I.G.K1h; FAA-H-8083-25]

152 Aviation Supplies & Academics

Chapter 6 **Aircraft Systems**

7. What are the errors of the attitude indicator?

Attitude indicators are free from most errors, but depending upon the speed with which the erection system functions, there may be a slight nose-up indication during a rapid acceleration and a nose-down indication during a rapid deceleration. There is also a possibility of a small bank angle and pitch error after a 180° turn. These inherent errors are small and correct themselves within a minute or so after returning to straight-and-level flight.

[PA.I.G.K1h; FAA-H-8083-15]

8. How does the heading indicator operate?

The operation of the heading indicator uses the principle of rigidity in space. The rotor turns in a vertical plane, and the compass card is fixed to the rotor. Since the rotor remains rigid in space, the points on the card hold the same position in space relative to the vertical plane. As the instrument case and the airplane revolve around the vertical axis, the card provides clear and accurate heading information.

[PA.I.G.K1h; FAA-H-8083-25]

9. What are the limitations of the heading indicator?

The bank and pitch limits of the heading indicator vary with the particular design and make of instrument. On some heading indicators found in light airplanes, the limits are approximately 55° of pitch and 55° of bank. When either of these attitude limits is exceeded, the instrument tumbles or spills and no longer gives the correct indication until reset. After spilling, it may be reset with the caging knob. Many of the modern instruments used are designed in such a manner that they will not tumble.

[PA.I.G.K1h; FAA-H-8083-25]

10. What error is the heading indicator subject to?

Because of precession, caused chiefly by friction, the heading indicator will creep or drift from a heading to which it is set. Among other factors, the amount of drift depends largely upon the condition of the instrument. The heading indicator may indicate as much as 15° error per every hour of operation.

[PA.I.G.K1h; FAA-H-8083-25]

Private Pilot Oral Exam Guide 153

Chapter 6 **Aircraft Systems**

11. How does the turn coordinator operate?

The turn part of the instrument uses precession to indicate direction and approximate rate of turn. A gyro reacts by trying to move in reaction to the force applied thus moving the needle or miniature aircraft in proportion to the rate of turn. The slip/skid indicator is a liquid-filled tube with a ball that reacts to centrifugal force and gravity.

[PA.I.G.K1g; FAA-H-8083-15]

12. What information does the turn coordinator provide?

The turn coordinator shows the yaw and roll of the aircraft around the vertical and longitudinal axes. The miniature airplane will indicate direction of the turn as well as rate of turn. When aligned with the turn index, it represents a standard rate of turn of 3° per second. The inclinometer of the turn coordinator indicates the coordination of aileron and rudder. The ball indicates whether the airplane is in coordinated flight or is in a slip or skid.

[PA.I.G.K1g; FAA-H-8083-25]

13. What will the turn indicator indicate when the aircraft is in a skidding or a slipping turn?

Slip—The ball in the tube will be on the inside of the turn; not enough rate of turn for the amount of bank.

Skid—The ball in the tube will be to the outside of the turn; too much rate of turn for the amount of bank.

[PA.I.G.K1g; FAA-H-8083-25]

G. Magnetic Compass

1. How does the magnetic compass operate?

Magnetized needles fastened to a float assembly, around which is mounted a compass card, align themselves parallel to the Earth's lines of magnetic force. The float assembly is housed in a bowl filled with acid-free white kerosene.

[PA.I.G.K1g; FAA-H-8083-25]

Chapter 6 **Aircraft Systems**

2. What limitations does the magnetic compass have?

The jewel-and-pivot type mounting allows the float freedom to rotate and tilt up to approximately 18° angle of bank. At steeper bank angles, the compass indications are erratic and unpredictable.

[PA.I.G.K1g; FAA-H-8083-15]

3. What are the various compass errors?

a. *Oscillation error*—Erratic movement of the compass card caused by turbulence or rough control technique.

b. *Deviation error*—Due to electrical and magnetic disturbances in the aircraft.

c. *Variation error*—Angular difference between true and magnetic north; reference isogonic lines of variation.

d. *Dip errors, which include:*
   • *Acceleration error*—On east or west headings, while accelerating, the magnetic compass shows a turn to the north, and when decelerating, it shows a turn to the south.
   Remember: ANDS
   Accelerate
   North
   Decelerate
   South
   • *Northerly turning error*—The compass leads in the south half of a turn, and lags in the north half of a turn.
   Remember: UNOS
   Undershoot
   North
   Overshoot
   South

[PA.I.G.K1g; FAA-H-8083-15]

Private Pilot Oral Exam Guide 155

Chapter 6 **Aircraft Systems**

H. Avionics Systems

Exam Tip: Be prepared to answer questions about any and all equipment installed in the aircraft (for example, if your aircraft has an autopilot, GPS system, how the audio panel works, etc.). Have an in-depth knowledge of all of the systems' operations, even if you rarely use them.

1. Describe the function of the following avionics equipment: AHRS, ADC, PFD, MFD, FD, FMS, INS, TAWS, and TIS.

AHRS—Attitude and heading reference system. Composed of three-axis sensors that provide heading, attitude, and yaw information for aircraft. AHRS are designed to replace traditional mechanical gyroscopic flight instruments and provide superior reliability and accuracy.

ADC—Air data computer. An aircraft computer that receives and processes pitot pressure, static pressure, and temperature to calculate precise altitude, indicated airspeed, true airspeed, vertical speed, and air temperature.

PFD—Primary flight display. A display that provides increased situational awareness to the pilot by replacing the traditional six instruments with an easy-to-scan display that shows the horizon, airspeed, altitude, vertical speed, trend, trim, rate of turn, and more.

MFD—Multi-function display. A flight deck display capable of presenting information (such as navigation data, moving maps, terrain awareness, etc.) to the pilot in configurable ways; often used in concert with the PFD.

FD—Flight director. An electronic flight computer that analyzes the navigation selections, signals, and aircraft parameters. It presents steering instructions on the flight display as command bars or crossbars for the pilot to position the nose of the aircraft over or follow.

FMS—Flight management system. A computer system containing a database for programming of routes, approaches, and departures that can supply navigation data to the flight director/autopilot from various sources, and can calculate flight data such as fuel consumption, time remaining, possible range, and other values.

156 Aviation Supplies & Academics

Chapter 6 **Aircraft Systems**

INS—Inertial navigation system. A computer-based navigation system that tracks the movement of an aircraft via signals produced by onboard accelerometers. The initial location of the aircraft is entered into the computer and all subsequent movement is then sensed and used to keep the aircraft's position updated.

TAWS—Terrain awareness and warning system. Uses the aircraft's GPS navigation signal and altimetry systems to compare the position and trajectory of the aircraft against a more detailed terrain and obstacle database. This database attempts to detail every obstruction that could pose a threat to an aircraft in flight.

TIS—Traffic Information Service is a ground-based advanced avionics traffic display system which receives transmissions on locations of nearby aircraft from radar-equipped air traffic control facilities and provides alerts and warnings to the pilot.

[PA.I.G.K1g; FAA-H-8083-25, DAT]

2. What is the function of a magnetometer?

A magnetometer is a device that measures the strength of the Earth's magnetic field to determine aircraft heading; it provides this information digitally to the AHRS, which then sends it to the PFD.

[PA.I.G.K1g; FAA-H-8083-25]

3. When powering up an aircraft with an FMS/RNAV unit installed, how will you verify the effective dates of the navigation database?

The effective dates for the navigation database are typically shown on a start-up screen that is displayed as the system cycles through its startup self-test.

[PA.I.G.K1g; POH/AFM]

4. Does an aircraft have to remain stationary during AHRS system initialization?

Some AHRSs must be initialized on the ground prior to departure. The initialization procedure allows the system to establish a reference attitude used as a benchmark for all future attitude changes. Other systems are capable of initialization while taxiing as well as in flight.

[PA.I.G.K1g; POH/AFM]

Private Pilot Oral Exam Guide 157

Chapter 6 **Aircraft Systems**

5. Which standby flight instruments are normally provided in an advanced avionics aircraft?

Every aircraft equipped with electronic flight instruments must also contain a minimal set of backup/standby instruments. Usually conventional round dial instruments, they typically include an attitude indicator, an airspeed indicator, and an altimeter.

[PA.I.G.K1g; POH/AFM]

6. If one display fails (PFD or MFD), what information will be presented on the remaining display?

In the event of a display failure, some systems offer a reversion capability to display the primary flight instruments and engine instruments on the remaining operative display.

[PA.I.G.K1g; POH/AFM]

7. When a display failure occurs, what other system components will be affected?

In some systems, failure of a display will also result in partial loss of navigation, communication, and GPS capability. Reference your specific POH/AFM.

[PA.I.G.K1g; POH/AFM]

8. What display information will be affected when an ADC failure occurs?

Inoperative airspeed, altitude, and vertical speed indicators, shown with red Xs on the PFD, indicate the failure of the air data computer.

[PA.I.G.K1g; POH/AFM]

9. What display information will be lost when an AHRS failure occurs?

An inoperative attitude indicator, shown with a red X on the PFD, indicates failure of the AHRS.

[PA.I.G.K1g; POH/AFM]

Chapter 6 **Aircraft Systems**

10. How will loss of a magnetometer affect the AHRS operation?

Heading information will be lost.

[PA.I.G.K1g; POH/AFM]

11. For aircraft with electronic flight instrumentation, what is the function of the standby battery?

The standby battery is held in reserve and kept charged in case of a failure of the charging system and a subsequent exhaustion of the main battery. The standby battery is brought online when the main battery voltage is depleted to a specific value, approximately 19 volts. Generally, the standby battery switch must be in the ARM position for this to occur, but pilots should refer to the aircraft flight manual (POH/AFM) for specifics on an aircraft's electrical system.

[PA.I.G.K1g; FAA-H-8083-15]

12. What are the two types of ADS-B equipment?

Automatic Dependent Surveillance–Broadcast Out (ADS-B Out)—Automatically broadcasts aircraft's GPS position, altitude, velocity, and other information out to ATC ground-based surveillance stations as well as directly to other aircraft. It is required in all airspace where transponders are required.

Automatic Dependent Surveillance–Broadcast In (ADS-B In)—The receipt, processing, and display of ADS-B transmissions. ADS-B In capability is necessary to receive ADS-B traffic and broadcast services (e.g., FIS-B and TIS-B).

[PA.I.G.K1g; AC 90-114]

13. Briefly describe Traffic Information Services–Broadcast (TIS-B).

TIS-B is the broadcast of ATC-derived traffic information to ADS-B equipped (1090ES or UAT) aircraft from ground radio stations. The source of this traffic information is derived from ground-based air traffic surveillance sensors. TIS-B service is available throughout the National Airspace System where there is both adequate surveillance coverage from ground sensors and adequate broadcast coverage from ADS-B ground radio stations.

(continued)

Private Pilot Oral Exam Guide   159

Chapter 6 **Aircraft Systems**

Note: TIS-B is not related to Traffic Information Service (TIS). TIS is only available at specific terminal Mode S radar sites. Though similar in some ways, TIS is not related to TIS-B. (See *AIM* 4-5-6.)

[PA.I.G.K1g; AIM 4-5-6, 4-5-8, AC 90-114]

14. Explain the limitations a pilot should be aware of when using TIS-B for situational awareness.

a. TIS-B is not intended to be used as a collision avoidance system and does not relieve the pilot's responsibility to see and avoid other aircraft, in accordance with 14 CFR §91.113(b).

b. A pilot may receive an intermittent TIS-B target of themselves, typically when maneuvering (e.g., climbing turns) due to the radar not tracking the aircraft as quickly as ADS-B.

c. The ADS-B-to-radar association process within the ground system may at times have difficulty correlating an ADS-B report with corresponding radar returns from the same aircraft. When this happens, the pilot may see duplicate traffic symbols (e.g., TIS-B shadows) on the flight deck display.

d. Updates of TIS-B traffic reports will occur less often than ADS-B traffic updates. TIS-B position updates will occur approximately once every 3 to 13 seconds depending on the type of radar system in use within the coverage area. In comparison, the update rate for ADS-B is nominally once per second.

e. The TIS-B system only uplinks data pertaining to transponder-equipped aircraft. Aircraft without a transponder will not be displayed as TIS-B traffic.

[PA.I.G.K1g; AIM 4-5-8, AC 90-114]

15. Automation in the flight deck has made aviation safer. Does total risk increase or decrease when passively monitoring an automated system for faults or abnormalities? How can you mitigate that risk?

While automation in the flight deck has certainly made aviation safer by reducing pilot workload, total risk can increase when pilots passively monitor automated systems for faults or abnormalities. This is because overreliance on automation can lead to decreased situational awareness and monitoring complacency,

160 Aviation Supplies & Academics

Chapter 6 **Aircraft Systems**

increasing the chances of missing crucial signs of malfunction or system errors.

If pilots are only passively monitoring automation, they may fail to notice subtle signs of issues, such as unexpected flight path deviations, abnormal instrument readings, or changes in performance, all of which could indicate a malfunction. Additionally, if a system does fail or behave unexpectedly, a pilot who is disengaged from manual flight could be slower to respond, increasing the risk of accidents or mishandling the situation.

To mitigate this risk, pilots should adopt a proactive approach:

a. Stay actively engaged with the flight by frequently cross-checking automated systems against other instruments and external cues.

b. Regularly practice manual flying skills to stay prepared to take control in case of an emergency.

c. Familiarize themselves with the aircraft's automation system to understand its behavior and potential failure modes.

d. Periodically verify system performance and make sure alerts or abnormal readings are addressed promptly.

e. Regularly switch tasks to ensure continuous situational awareness, preventing overreliance on automation.

By maintaining a balance between utilizing automation and staying engaged in flight monitoring, pilots can minimize the risks associated with overreliance and ensure safer operations.

[PA.I.G.R3; FAA-H-8083-2]

I. Anti-Icing and Deicing Systems

1. Define the terms *anti-icing equipment* and *deicing equipment* and state several examples of each.

Anti-icing equipment—Prevents ice from forming on certain protected surfaces. Examples are heated pitot tubes and static ports, carburetor heat, heated fuel vents, propeller blades with electrothermal boots, and heated windshields. It is normally actuated prior to flight into suspected icing conditions. Reference your POH/AFM.

(continued)

Private Pilot Oral Exam Guide 161

Chapter 6 **Aircraft Systems**

Deicing equipment—Removes ice that has already formed on protected surfaces. It is generally pneumatic boots on the wing and tail leading edges.

[PA.I.G.K1j; FAA-H-8083-3; FAA-H-8083-25]

2. Describe how an aircraft deicing system works.

Upon pilot actuation, boots attached to the wing leading edges inflate with air from a pneumatic pump(s) to break off accumulated ice. After a few seconds of inflation, they are deflated back to their normal position with vacuum assistance. The pilot monitors the buildup of ice and cycles the boots as directed in the POH/AFM.

[PA.I.G.K1j; FAA-H-8083-3]

3. If an airplane has anti-icing and/or deicing equipment installed, can it be flown into icing conditions?

Even though it may appear elaborate and complete, the presence of anti-icing and deicing equipment does not necessarily mean that an airplane is approved for flight in icing conditions. The POH/AFM, placards, and even the manufacturer should be consulted for specific determination of approvals and limitations. For an aircraft to be operated into known icing conditions, it will be certificated as capable of "flight into known icing (FIKI)."

[PA.I.G.K1j; FAA-H-8083-3]

4. What components must an aircraft have to be considered authorized for flight into known icing (FIKI)?

To be considered FIKI (flight into known icing) certificated, an aircraft must be equipped with specific components designed to safely operate in known icing conditions. These components are tested and approved as part of the aircraft's certification process by the FAA. The key components include the following ice protection systems:

a. *Wing and tail deicing boots*—Pneumatically operated inflatable boots that break off accumulated ice.

b. *Wing and tail anti-icing systems*—Heated leading edges (electrical or bleed air) to prevent ice buildup.

c. *Engine anti-icing/deicing*—Often includes heated engine inlets or a combination of air bleed systems and chemical additives to prevent ice on engine components.

162   Aviation Supplies & Academics

Chapter 6 **Aircraft Systems**

d. *Propeller deicing*—Uses a heated or chemical system to remove ice from the propeller blades.

e. *Pitot-static system anti-icing*—Pitot tubes and static ports must be heated to prevent them from freezing and ensuring accurate airspeed and altitude readings.

f. *Windshield anti-icing/deicing*—Heated windshields or other methods (e.g., chemical treatments) to prevent ice accumulation affecting the pilot's visibility.

Systems may be electrical, pneumatic, or chemical. Electrical systems will often be used for windshields and propellers, but in some cases deicing fluids may be used with other systems.

The aircraft must be tested for safe operation while these systems are active, with demonstrated capabilities to prevent or remove ice in conditions where it is known to occur. These systems and procedures ensure that a FIKI-certified aircraft can safely operate in known icing conditions without compromising safety.

[PA.I.G.K1j; FAA-H-8083-25]

J. Other Systems

1. How does the aircraft cabin heat system work on your aircraft?

In most light aircraft, heating is provided by fresh air that is heated by an exhaust shroud and directed into the cabin through a series of ducts.

[PA.I.G.K1i; POH/AFM]

2. How does the pilot control the temperature in the cabin?

Temperature is controlled by mixing outside air (cabin air control) with heated air (cabin heat control) in a manifold near the cabin firewall. This air is then ducted to vents located on the cabin floor.

[PA.I.G.K1i; POH/AFM]

3. When flying an aircraft equipped with airbags or airbags in the seat belts, what does the pilot need to know?

If an aircraft is equipped with airbags or airbag seat belts, the pilot must understand their purpose, operation, and limitations to ensure safety in case of an emergency. Airbags in aircraft are designed to enhance occupant safety during a crash or impact, similar to

Private Pilot Oral Exam Guide   163

Chapter 6 **Aircraft Systems**

their use in automobiles. They help reduce the risk of head, neck, and chest injuries by cushioning the occupant during a sudden deceleration or impact.

Airbags are typically located in the seat belt system or in side panels. The airbags will only deploy during specific, high-impact events. Pilots should know that the deployment is generally triggered by forces above a certain threshold, such as a hard landing or collision. The pilot should ensure that the airbags and seat belts are properly installed and the system is in good condition. Always check for any warning lights or indicators that the airbag system is malfunctioning.

Airbag-equipped seat belts may have slightly different adjustments than traditional seat belts. Ensure the belt is properly adjusted for comfort and safety, as airbags can cause additional pressure on the body during deployment.

Understanding the operation and limitations of airbags in the seat belts helps pilots ensure the safety of themselves and passengers during flight and in the event of an emergency.

[PA.IX.D.S2; AFM/POH]

4. What does a pilot need to know about if their aircraft is equipped with an aircraft ballistic parachute system?

If an aircraft is equipped with an aircraft ballistic parachute system, the pilot should understand its purpose, activation procedures, and limitations to ensure effective use in an emergency. There will likely be manufacturer recommendations the pilot should be familiar with regarding usage and best practices.

These systems are designed to provide an emergency recovery option in the event of a catastrophic failure, such as engine failure, structural damage, or other emergencies that make controlled flight impossible. They are intended to slow the descent of the entire aircraft, potentially saving the lives of the occupants and the pilot.

Pilots must be familiar with the deployment handle location, typically in the flight deck, and understand how to activate the system. Pulling the handle deploys the parachute, which then slows the descent of the aircraft. Some systems may require the pilot to release control of the aircraft or may automatically deploy at certain altitudes.

Chapter 6 **Aircraft Systems**

These systems are designed to be used at specific altitudes. Most systems recommend activation above a minimum safe altitude to ensure the parachute has time to deploy and slow the aircraft to a safe landing speed. The pilot must understand the system's weight limits, airspeed restrictions, and aircraft type compatibility. It's important to know that the parachute system may not work effectively in all situations (e.g., severe turbulence or high-speed flight).

These systems require regular inspections and maintenance to ensure they remain functional in the event of an emergency. The pilot should verify that the system is inspected and properly maintained according to the manufacturer's recommendations. Some of them have AD compliance periods that must be met.

[PA.IX.D.R2, PA.IX.D.S3; AFM/POH]

Private Pilot Oral Exam Guide   165

Performance
and Limitations   **7**

Chapter 7 **Performance and Limitations**

A. Aerodynamics

1. What are the four dynamic forces that act on an airplane during all maneuvers?

Lift—The upward-acting force.

Gravity (or weight)—The downward-acting force.

Thrust—The forward-acting force.

Drag—The backward-acting force.

[PA.I.F.K3; FAA-H-8083-25]

2. What flight condition will result in the sum of the opposing forces being equal?

In steady-state, straight-and-level, unaccelerated flight, the sum of the opposing forces is equal to zero. There can be no unbalanced forces in steady, straight flight (Newton's Third Law). This is true whether flying level or when climbing or descending. It does not mean the four forces are equal. It means the opposing forces are equal to, and thereby cancel the effects of, each other.

[PA.I.F.K3; FAA-H-8083-25]

3. What aerodynamic forces are working on an aircraft during a climb?

During a climb, several aerodynamic forces act on an aircraft, influencing its performance and behavior:

a. *Lift*—The upward force generated by the wings. During a climb, the aircraft continues to generate lift to counteract its weight, but the angle of attack typically increases to maintain sufficient lift for the climb.

b. *Weight*—The force pulling the aircraft downward due to gravity. In a climb, weight must be overcome by the vertical component of lift for the aircraft to gain altitude.

c. *Thrust*—The forward force provided by the engines. In a climb, the engines must produce enough thrust to counteract drag and maintain a positive climb rate.

d. *Drag*—The resistance force that opposes the aircraft's motion through the air. During a climb, drag increases with airspeed, but the aircraft needs to overcome this to continue gaining altitude. The components of drag include parasite drag and induced drag.

168 Aviation Supplies & Academics

Chapter 7 **Performance and Limitations**

During a climb, the aircraft's engine power, angle of attack, and aerodynamics work together to provide the necessary forces for upward flight. The balance between these forces determines the climb rate and efficiency.

[PA.I.F.K3; FAA-H-8083-25]

4. What aerodynamic forces are working on an aircraft during a descent?

During a descent, several aerodynamic forces interact to influence the aircraft's flight path:

a. *Lift*—Lift still acts upward, but during a descent, the aircraft's angle of attack is typically reduced, and lift becomes less than the weight. The difference between lift and weight allows the aircraft to descend.

b. *Weight*—Weight, caused by gravity, is the force pulling the aircraft downward. It works to accelerate the descent, and in most cases, weight exceeds lift during a descent, causing the aircraft to lose altitude.

c. *Thrust*—Thrust is provided by the engines and is used to overcome drag and maintain airspeed. During a descent, thrust is often reduced to prevent excessive speed buildup, allowing gravity to assist the descent.

d. *Drag*—Drag opposes the aircraft's motion and increases with airspeed. During a descent, drag helps to slow the aircraft and control its speed. Induced drag (from lift) and parasite drag (from the aircraft's shape) both play a role in the descent process.

In a descent, the aircraft's balance of these forces is adjusted to control the rate of descent, airspeed, and overall descent profile.

[PA.I.F.K3; FAA-H-8083-25]

5. What is an airfoil? State some examples.

An airfoil is a device that gets a useful reaction (namely *lift*) from air moving over its surface. Wings, horizontal tail surfaces, vertical tail surfaces, and propellers are examples of airfoils.

[PA.I.F.K3; FAA-H-8083-25]

Chapter 7 **Performance and Limitations**

6. What is the angle of incidence?

The angle of incidence is the angle formed by the longitudinal axis of the airplane and the chord of the wing. It is measured by the angle at which the wing is attached to the fuselage. The angle of incidence is fixed and cannot be changed by the pilot.

[PA.I.F.K3; FAA-H-8083-25]

7. What is a relative wind?

The relative wind is the direction of the airflow with respect to the wing. When a wing is moving forward and downward, the relative wind moves backward and upward. The flight path and relative wind are always parallel but travel in opposite directions.

[PA.I.F.K3; FAA-H-8083-25]

8. What is the angle of attack?

The angle of attack is the angle between the wing chord line and the direction of the relative wind; it can be changed by the pilot.

[PA.I.F.K3; FAA-H-8083-25]

9. What is Bernoulli's Principle?

Bernoulli's Principle states that the pressure of a fluid (liquid or gas) decreases at points where the speed of the fluid increases. In the case of airflow, high-speed flow is associated with low pressure and low-speed flow with high pressure. The airfoil of an aircraft is designed to increase the velocity of the airflow above its surface, thereby decreasing pressure above the airfoil. Simultaneously, the impact of the air on the lower surface of the airfoil increases the pressure below. This combination of pressure decrease above and pressure increase below produces lift.

[PA.I.F.K3; FAA-H-8083-25]

10. What are several factors that will affect both lift and drag?

Wing area—Lift and drag acting on a wing are roughly proportional to the wing area. A pilot can change wing area by using certain types of flaps (e.g., Fowler flaps).

Shape of the airfoil—As the upper curvature of an airfoil is increased (up to a certain point), the lift produced increases. Lowering an aileron or flap device can accomplish this. Also, ice

170 Aviation Supplies & Academics

Chapter 7 **Performance and Limitations**

or frost on a wing can disturb normal airflow, changing its camber and disrupting its lifting capability.

Angle of attack—As angle of attack is increased, both lift and drag are increased, up to a certain point.

Velocity of the air—An increase in the velocity of the air passing over the wing increases lift and drag.

Air density—Lift and drag vary directly with the density of the air. As air density increases, lift and drag increase. As air density decreases, lift and drag decrease. The factors that affect air density are pressure, temperature, and humidity.

[PA.I.F.K3; FAA-H-8083-25]

11. What is torque effect?

Torque effect involves Newton's Third Law of Physics: For every action, there is an equal and opposite reaction. Applied to the airplane, this means that as the internal engine parts and the propeller are revolving in one direction, an equal force is trying to rotate the airplane in the opposite direction. Torque effect is greatest when at low airspeeds with high power settings and a high angle of attack.

[PA.I.F.K3; FAA-H-8083-25]

12. What effect does torque reaction have on an airplane on the ground and in flight?

In flight—Torque reaction is acting around the longitudinal axis, tending to make the airplane roll. To compensate, some of the older airplanes are rigged in a manner to create more lift on the wing that is being forced downward. The more modern airplanes are designed with the engine offset to counteract this effect of torque.

On the ground—During the takeoff roll, an additional turning moment around the vertical axis is induced by torque reaction. As the left side of the airplane is being forced down by torque reaction, more weight is being placed on the left main landing gear. This results in more ground friction, or drag, on the left tire than on the right, causing a further turning moment to the left.

[PA.I.F.K3; FAA-H-8083-25]

Private Pilot Oral Exam Guide 171

Chapter 7 **Performance and Limitations**

13. What are the four factors that contribute to torque effect?

Torque reaction of the engine and propeller—For every action, there is an equal and opposite reaction. The rotation of the propeller (from the flight deck) to the right tends to roll or bank the airplane to the left.

Gyroscopic effect of the propeller—Gyroscopic precession applies here: the resultant action or deflection of a spinning object when a force is applied to the outer rim of its rotational mass. If the axis of a propeller is tilted, the resulting force will be exerted 90° ahead in the direction of rotation and in the same direction as the applied force. It is most noticeable on takeoffs in taildraggers when the tail is raised.

Corkscrewing effect of the propeller slipstream—High-speed rotation of an airplane propeller results in a corkscrewing rotation to the slipstream as it moves rearward. At high propeller speeds and low forward speeds (as in a takeoff), the slipstream strikes the vertical tail surface on the left side, pushing the tail to the right and yawing the airplane to the left.

Asymmetrical loading of the propeller (P-Factor)—When an airplane is flying with a high angle of attack, the bite of the downward-moving propeller blade is greater than the bite of the upward-moving blade. This is due to the downward-moving blade meeting the oncoming relative wind at a greater angle of attack than the upward-moving blade. Consequently, there is greater thrust on the downward-moving blade on the right side, and this forces the airplane to yaw to the left.

[PA.I.F.K3; FAA-H-8083-25]

14. What forces cause an airplane to turn?

An airplane turns due to the horizontal component of lift, which acts as the centripetal force pulling the aircraft toward the center of the turn. When the pilot banks the airplane using the ailerons, the total lift generated by the wings tilts from pointing straight upward to an angled direction. This creates two components of lift: a vertical component (counteracting weight) and a horizontal component, which causes the airplane to move in a curved path.

For a coordinated turn, the pilot must also use the rudder to counteract adverse yaw. Adverse yaw occurs because the

172 Aviation Supplies & Academics

Chapter 7 **Performance and Limitations**

downward-deflected aileron on the rising wing produces more lift and drag than the upward-deflected aileron on the opposite wing. The rudder prevents the nose from yawing opposite to the direction of the turn, keeping the turn smooth and aligned.

Additionally, turning introduces increased load factor on the aircraft because the total lift must also support the airplane's weight. To maintain altitude during a turn, the pilot must increase the angle of attack by pulling back on the yoke or stick. Failure to do so can result in a descent.

[PA.I.F.K3; FAA-H-8083-25]

15. What causes an airplane (except a T-tail) to pitch nose down when power is reduced and controls are not adjusted?

When power is reduced and the controls are not adjusted, an airplane will pitch nose-down due to several key aerodynamic factors:

a. *Decrease in lift*—Reducing power lowers the airflow over the wings, which decreases the amount of lift generated. As lift decreases, the aircraft's nose tends to drop because the lift vector is no longer strong enough to counteract the aircraft's weight.

b. *Change in center of pressure*—As power is reduced, the angle of attack may decrease, which shifts the center of pressure rearward. This change causes a moment that pitches the aircraft's nose down.

c. *Thrust line effect*—In most aircraft, the engine's thrust is slightly above or below the center of gravity. When power is reduced, the loss of forward thrust results in a nose-down pitching moment because the engine's thrust line is no longer opposing the aircraft's natural tendency to pitch.

d. *Trim change*—When power is reduced, the aircraft may require a different trim setting to maintain level flight. Without adjusting the trim, the airplane can pitch down as a result of the imbalance between the lift and the forces.

[PA.I.F.K3; FAA-H-8083-25]

Private Pilot Oral Exam Guide   173

Chapter 7 **Performance and Limitations**

16. What is centrifugal force?

Centrifugal force is the equal and opposite reaction of the airplane to the change in direction, and it acts equal and opposite to the horizontal component of lift.

[PA.I.F.K3; FAA-H-8083-25]

17. What is load factor?

Load factor is the ratio of the total load supported by the airplane's wing to the actual weight of the airplane and its contents. In other words, it is the actual load supported by the wings divided by the total weight of the airplane. It can also be expressed as the ratio of a given load to the pull of gravity, e.g., to refer to a load factor of three as 3 Gs. In this case, the weight of the airplane is equal to 1 G, and if a load of three times the actual weight of the airplane were imposed upon the wing due to curved flight, the load factor would be equal to 3 Gs.

[PA.I.F.K2e; FAA-H-8083-25]

18. For what two reasons is load factor important to pilots?

a. Because of the obviously dangerous overload that is possible for a pilot to impose on the aircraft structure.

b. Because an increased load factor increases the stalling speed and makes stalls possible at seemingly safe flight speeds.

[PA.I.F.K2e; FAA-H-8083-25]

19. What situations may result in load factors reaching the maximum or being exceeded?

Level turns—The load factor increases at a terrific rate after a bank has reached 45° or 50°. The load factor in a 60° banked turn is 2 Gs. The load factor in an 80° banked turn is 5.76 Gs. The wing must produce lift equal to these load factors if altitude is to be maintained.

Turbulence—Severe vertical gusts cause a sudden increase in angle of attack, resulting in large loads that are resisted by the inertia of the airplane.

Speed—The amount of excess load that can be imposed upon the wing depends on how fast the airplane is flying. At speeds below maneuvering speed, the airplane will stall before the load factor

Chapter 7 **Performance and Limitations**

can become excessive. At speeds above maneuvering speed, the limit load factor for which an airplane is stressed can be exceeded by abrupt or excessive application of the controls or by strong turbulence.

[PA.I.F.K2e; FAA-H-8083-25]

20. What aerodynamic effects should a pilot be aware of during a steep turn?

During a steep turn, several aerodynamic effects can impact the aircraft's performance and handling:

a. *Increased load factor*—As the bank angle increases, the load factor (G-forces) also increases. In a steep turn (greater than 45° of bank), the load factor can double or more. This means the aircraft experiences greater stress on the wings and structure, and pilots may need to apply more back pressure on the control yoke to maintain altitude.

b. *Increased stall speed*—With higher G-forces, the stall speed increases during a steep turn. This means the aircraft must maintain a higher airspeed to prevent a stall, and the pilot must ensure the airspeed remains within the safe range.

c. *Increased induced drag*—The steeper the bank, the more induced drag is created due to the increased angle of attack needed to maintain level flight. This can affect engine performance and climb rate.

d. *Possible adverse yaw*—Steep turns can cause adverse yaw, where the aircraft's nose tends to yaw in the opposite direction of the roll. This requires additional coordination with the rudder to maintain smooth, coordinated flight.

[PA.I.F.K3; FAA-H-8083-25]

21. The amount of excess load that can be imposed on the structure of an airplane is dependent on what factor?

The amount of excess load that can be imposed on an airplane's structure primarily depends on the speed of the airplane and the angle of attack. These factors determine the amount of lift generated by the wings, which in turn affects the load factor.

At lower speeds, the wing must be at a higher angle of attack to generate sufficient lift. However, as speed increases, the wings can produce much more lift for the same angle of attack. This means

Private Pilot Oral Exam Guide 175

Chapter 7 **Performance and Limitations**

that at higher speeds, even small control inputs or turbulence can create significant loads on the aircraft structure.

The design limits of the airplane, outlined in the limit load factor and published in the pilot's operating handbook (POH), also play a critical role. Load factors are measured in Gs (multiples of gravity), and typical light aircraft are certified for a maximum of 3.8 Gs in normal category operations. Exceeding these limits can cause structural damage or failure.

Pilots must also be aware of the maneuvering speed (V_A), which is the maximum speed at which the aircraft can handle abrupt control inputs without exceeding structural limits. Below this speed, the airplane will stall before structural damage occurs due to excess load. Above this speed, the risk of overstressing the aircraft increases significantly.

Understanding how speed and angle of attack influence excess load is essential for safe operation, particularly during steep turns, turbulence, or abrupt maneuvers.

[PA.I.F.K2e; FAA-H-8083-25]

22. What are the different operational categories for aircraft, and within which category does your aircraft fall?

The maximum safe load factors (limit load factors) determine the operational category specified for airplanes. The various categories are as follows:

Category	Limit load factor
Normal	+3.8 to −1.52
Utility (mild aerobatics including spins)	+4.4 to −1.76
Aerobatic	+6.0 to −3.00

[PA.I.F.K2e; FAA-H-8083-25]

23. What effect does an increase in load factor have on stalling speed?

As load factor increases, stalling speed increases. Any airplane can be stalled at any airspeed within the limits of its structure and the strength of the pilot. At a given airspeed, the load factor increases as angle of attack increases, and the wing stalls because the angle of attack has been increased to a certain angle. Therefore, there is a direct relationship between the load factor imposed upon the wing

176 Aviation Supplies & Academics

Chapter 7 **Performance and Limitations**

and its stalling characteristics. A rule for determining the speed at which a wing will stall is that the stalling speed increases in proportion to the square root of the load factor.

[PA.I.F.K2e; FAA-H-8083-25]

24. Will the indicated airspeed at which an aircraft stalls change as altitude is increased?

The indicated airspeed (IAS) at which an aircraft stalls does not change with altitude. Stall speed, as displayed on the airspeed indicator, is determined by the angle of attack at which the wing reaches its critical angle and can no longer generate sufficient lift. This critical angle of attack remains constant regardless of altitude, so the stall speed shown on the instrument is consistent at all altitudes.

However, the true airspeed (TAS) at which the aircraft stalls will increase with altitude. This is because the air density decreases as altitude increases, reducing the number of air molecules flowing over the wings. To generate the same amount of lift, the aircraft must move through the thinner air at a higher TAS. The airspeed indicator, calibrated for sea-level conditions, does not account for this change in air density, so it continues to display the same IAS at which the stall will occur.

For pilots, this means the IAS to monitor for a stall remains constant at all altitudes, but the TAS (and the potential ground speed) at stall will be higher at higher altitudes. Pilots must understand this relationship, particularly when flying in high-altitude environments where thinner air can affect performance.

[PA.I.F.K3; FAA-H-8083-25]

25. Define the term *maneuvering speed*.

Maneuvering speed is the maximum speed at which the limit load can be imposed (either by gusts or full deflection of the control surfaces) without causing structural damage. It is the speed below which the pilot can, in smooth air, move a single flight control one time, to its full deflection, for one axis of airplane rotation only (pitch, roll, or yaw) without risk of damage to the airplane. Speeds up to but not exceeding the maneuvering speed allow an aircraft to stall prior to experiencing an increase in load factor that would exceed the limit load of the aircraft.

(continued)

Private Pilot Oral Exam Guide 177

Chapter 7 **Performance and Limitations**

Note: Operating at or below maneuvering speed does not provide structural protection against multiple full control inputs in one axis or full control inputs in more than one axis at the same time.

[PA.I.F.K3; FAA-H-8083-25, SAIB CE-11-17]

26. Discuss the effect on maneuvering speed of an increase or decrease in weight.

Maneuvering speed increases with an increase in weight and decreases with a decrease in weight. An aircraft operating at a reduced weight is more vulnerable to rapid accelerations encountered during flight through turbulence or gusts. Design limit load factors could be exceeded if a reduction in maneuvering speed is not accomplished. An aircraft operating at or near gross weight in turbulent air is much less likely to exceed design limit load factors and may be operated at the published maneuvering speed for gross weight if necessary.

[PA.I.F.K3; FAA-H-8083-25]

27. Define *loss of control in-flight* (LOC-I) and describe several situations that might increase the risk of an LOC-I accident occurring.

LOC-I is defined as a significant deviation of an aircraft from the intended flight path, and it often results from an airplane upset. Maneuvering is the most common phase of flight for LOC-I accidents to occur; however, LOC-I accidents occur in all phases of flight. Situations that increase the risk of this include uncoordinated flight, equipment malfunctions, pilot complacency, distraction, turbulence, and poor risk management, such as attempting to fly in IMC when the pilot is not qualified or proficient in it.

[PA.VII.A.K1; FAA-H-8083-3]

28. What causes an airplane to stall?

The direct cause of every stall is an excessive angle of attack. Each airplane has a particular angle of attack at which the airflow separates from the upper surface of the wing and the stall occurs. This critical angle of attack varies from 16° to 20° depending on the airplane's design, but each airplane has only one specific angle of attack where the stall occurs, regardless of airspeed, weight, load factor, or density altitude.

[PA.VII.A.K1; FAA-H-8083-25]

178 Aviation Supplies & Academics

Chapter 7 **Performance and Limitations**

29. What is a spin?

A spin in a small airplane or glider is a controlled (recoverable) or uncontrolled (possibly unrecoverable) maneuver in which the airplane or glider descends in a helical path while flying at an angle of attack greater than the critical angle of attack. Spins result from aggravated stalls in either a slip or a skid. If a stall does not occur, a spin cannot occur.

[PA.VII.D.K1; AC 61-67]

30. What causes a spin?

The primary cause of an inadvertent spin is exceeding the critical angle of attack while applying excessive or insufficient rudder, and to a lesser extent, aileron.

[PA.VII.D.K2; AC 61-67]

31. When are spins most likely to occur?

A stall/spin situation can occur in any phase of flight but is most likely to occur in the following situations:

a. *Engine failure on takeoff during climbout*—Pilot tries to stretch glide to landing area by increasing back pressure or makes an uncoordinated turn back to departure runway at a relatively low airspeed.

b. *Crossed-control turn from base to final (slipping or skidding turn)*—Pilot overshoots final (possibly due to a crosswind) and makes uncoordinated turn at a low airspeed.

c. *Engine failure on approach to landing*—Pilot tries to stretch glide to runway by increasing back pressure.

d. *Go-around with full nose-up trim*—Pilot applies power with full flaps and nose-up trim combined with uncoordinated use of rudder.

e. *Go-around with improper flap retraction*—Pilot applies power and retracts flaps rapidly, resulting in a rapid sink rate followed by an instinctive increase in back pressure.

[PA.VII.D.K1; AC 61-67]

Private Pilot Oral Exam Guide   179

Chapter 7 **Performance and Limitations**

32. What procedure should be used to recover from an inadvertent spin?

a. Close the throttle (if not already accomplished).

b. Neutralize the ailerons.

c. Apply full opposite rudder.

d. Briskly move the elevator control forward to approximately the neutral position. (Some aircraft require merely a relaxation of back pressure; others require full forward elevator pressure).

e. Once the stall is broken the spinning will stop. Neutralize the rudder when the spinning stops.

f. When the rudder is neutralized, gradually apply enough aft elevator pressure to return to level flight.

Remember: PARE

Power—Reduce to idle.

Ailerons—Position to neutral.

Rudder—Apply full opposite against rotation.

Elevator—Apply positive, forward of neutral, movement to break stall.

Once the spin rotation stops, neutralize the rudder, and begin applying back pressure to return to level flight.

Note: Always reference your airplane's POH/AFM for the appropriate spin recovery procedure.

[PA.VII.D.K3; AC 61-67]

33. What does the term *dynamic stability* refer to with regard to aircraft aerodynamics?

Dynamic stability refers to an aircraft's response over time to a disturbance from its equilibrium flight path. It is a measure of how the oscillations (or movements) caused by the disturbance behave as the aircraft tries to return to steady flight.

An aircraft with *positive dynamic stability* will experience oscillations that decrease in magnitude over time, eventually returning to its original flight condition. For example, if the nose pitches up due to turbulence, a dynamically stable aircraft will oscillate less and less with each cycle until it stabilizes.

180 Aviation Supplies & Academics

Chapter 7 **Performance and Limitations**

An aircraft with *neutral dynamic stability* will continue to oscillate at the same amplitude without returning to equilibrium or diverging further.

An aircraft with *negative dynamic stability* will have oscillations that increase in magnitude over time, potentially leading to a loss of control.

Dynamic stability is influenced by factors such as the aircraft's design, center of gravity, and control system. It works in conjunction with static stability, which describes the initial tendency of the aircraft to return to equilibrium.

[PA.I.F.K3; FAA-H-8083-25]

34. What does the term *static stability* refer to with regard to aircraft aerodynamics?

Static stability refers to an aircraft's initial tendency to return to its original flight condition after a small disturbance. It describes the aircraft's response right after the disturbance, without considering how it behaves over time. There are three types of static stability: positive, neutral, and negative.

Positive static stability—The aircraft will return to its original position after being displaced. For example, if the nose pitches up, a positively stable aircraft will naturally try to pitch back down to level flight.

Neutral static stability—The aircraft will stay at its new position after a disturbance without returning to the original attitude or diverging. For instance, if the nose pitches up, it will remain there without further motion.

Negative static stability—The aircraft will tend to move further away from its original position after a disturbance. For example, if the nose pitches up, it will continue to climb uncontrollably.

Static stability is crucial for aircraft design, ensuring that the aircraft remains controllable after disturbances. It is influenced by factors like the center of gravity and the configuration of the wings and tail. Pilots must understand static stability to ensure safe flight and anticipate the aircraft's behavior under various conditions.

[PA.I.F.K3; FAA-H-8083-25]

Private Pilot Oral Exam Guide   181

Chapter 7 **Performance and Limitations**

35. What causes adverse yaw?

Adverse yaw is a phenomenon in which the airplane heading changes in a direction opposite to that commanded by a roll control input. For example, when turning an airplane to the left, the downward deflected aileron on the right produces more lift on the right wing. Since the downward deflected right aileron produces more lift, it also produces more drag, while the opposite left aileron has less lift and less drag. This added drag attempts to pull or veer the airplane's nose in the direction of the raised wing (right); that is, it tries to turn the airplane in the direction opposite to that desired. This undesired veering is referred to as adverse yaw.

[PA.I.F.K3; FAA-H-8083-25]

36. What is ground effect?

Ground effect is a condition of improved performance that an airplane experiences when it is operating near the ground. A change occurs in the three-dimensional flow pattern around the airplane because the airflow around the wing is restricted by the ground surface. This reduces the wing's upwash, downwash, and wingtip vortices. In order for ground effect to be of a significant magnitude, the wing must be quite close to the ground.

[PA.IV.C.K4; FAA-H-8083-3]

37. What major problems can be caused by ground effect?

During landing—At a height of approximately one-tenth of a wingspan above the surface, drag may be 50 percent less than when the airplane is operating out of ground effect. Therefore, any excess speed during the landing phase may result in a significant float distance. In such cases, if care is not exercised, the pilot may run out of runway and options at the same time.

During takeoff—Due to the reduced drag in ground effect, the aircraft may seem capable of takeoff well below the recommended speed. However, as the airplane rises out of ground effect with a deficiency of speed, the greater induced drag may result in very marginal climb performance, or the inability of the airplane to fly at all. In extreme conditions, such as high temperature, high gross weight, and high density altitude, the airplane may become initially airborne with a deficiency of speed and then settle back to the runway.

[PA.IV.C.K4; FAA-H-8083-3]

Chapter 7 **Performance and Limitations**

B. Weight and Balance

1. Define the following: *empty weight, gross weight, useful load, arm, moment, center of gravity,* and *datum*.

Empty weight—The weight of the airframe, engines, all permanently installed equipment, and unusable fuel. Depending on the FARs under which the aircraft was certificated, either the undrainable oil or full reservoir of oil is included.

Gross weight—The maximum allowable weight of both the airplane and its contents.

Useful load—The weight of the pilot, copilot, passengers, baggage, usable fuel, and drainable oil.

Arm—The horizontal distance in inches from the reference datum line to the center of gravity of the item.

Moment—The product of the weight of an item multiplied by its arm. Moments are expressed in pound-inches.

Center of gravity—The point about which an aircraft would balance if it were possible to suspend it at that point. Expressed in inches from datum.

Datum—An imaginary vertical plane or line from which all measurements of arm are taken. Established by the manufacturer.

[PA.I.F.K2f; FAA-H-8083-1, FAA-H-8083-25]

2. What basic equation is used in all weight and balance problems to find the center of gravity location of an airplane and/or its components?

Weight × Arm = Moment

By rearrangement of this equation to the following forms, with any two known values, the third value can be found:

Weight = Moment ÷ Arm

Arm (CG) = (Total) Moment ÷ (Total) Weight

Remember: WAM (**W**eight × **A**rm = **M**oment)

[PA.I.F.K2f; FAA-H-8083-25]

Private Pilot Oral Exam Guide   183

Chapter 7 **Performance and Limitations**

3. When shifting weight from one location to another on an airplane (forward or aft), what happens to the total moments?

When weight is shifted from one location to another, the total weight of the aircraft is unchanged. The total moments, however, do change in relation and proportion to the direction and distance the weight is moved. When weight is moved forward, the total moments decrease; when weight is moved aft, total moments increase. The moment change is proportional to the amount of weight moved.

[PA.I.F.K2f; FAA-H-8083-25]

4. What is the formula for a weight shift?

$$\frac{\text{Weight shifted}}{\text{Total weight}} = \frac{\text{Change in CG}}{\text{Distance weight is shifted}}$$

[PA.I.F.K2f; FAA-H-8083-25]

5. What performance characteristics will be adversely affected when an aircraft has been overloaded?

a. Higher takeoff speed
b. Longer takeoff run
c. Reduced rate and angle of climb
d. Lower maximum altitude
e. Shorter range
f. Reduced cruising speed
g. Reduced maneuverability
h. Higher stalling speed
i. Higher landing speed
j. Longer landing roll
k. Excessive weight on the nose wheel

[PA.I.F.K2f; FAA-H-8083-1]

184 Aviation Supplies & Academics

Chapter 7 **Performance and Limitations**

6. What effect does a forward center of gravity have on an aircraft's flight characteristics?

Higher stall speed—Stalling angle of attack is reached at a higher speed due to increased wing loading.

Slower cruise speed—Increased drag; greater angle of attack is required to maintain altitude.

More stable—The center of gravity is farther forward from the center of pressure, which increases longitudinal stability.

Greater back elevator pressure required—Longer takeoff roll; higher approach speeds and problems with landing flare.

[PA.I.F.K2f; FAA-H-8083-1]

7. What effect does a rearward center of gravity have on an aircraft's flight characteristics?

Lower stall speed—Less wing loading.

Higher cruise speed—Reduced drag; smaller angle of attack is required to maintain altitude.

Less stable—Stall and spin recovery are more difficult; the center of gravity is closer to the center of pressure, causing longitudinal instability.

[PA.I.F.K2f; FAA-H-8083-1]

8. What are the standard weights assumed for the following when calculating weight and balance problems: crew and passengers; fuel (avgas and Jet A); oil; and water?

Crew and passengers	190 lb each
Avgas Jet A	6 lb/US gal 6.75 lb/US gal
Oil	7.50 lb/US gal
Water	8.35 lb/US gal

[PA.I.F.K2f; FAA-H-8083-25, AC 120-27]

Private Pilot Oral Exam Guide   185

Chapter 7 **Performance and Limitations**

9. **The rental aircraft you normally fly has just returned from the avionics shop with newer, lighter-weight avionics. When reviewing the aircraft weight and balance record, you don't see an A&P entry reflecting this change. Is this normal? Why?**

No. Changes of fixed equipment may have a major effect upon the weight of the aircraft. Many aircraft are overloaded by the installation of extra radios or instruments. Fortunately, the replacement of older, heavy electronic equipment with newer, lighter types results in a weight reduction. This weight change, however helpful, can cause the CG to shift, which must be computed and annotated in the weight and balance record. It is the responsibility of the A&P mechanic or technician making any repair or alteration to know the weight and location of these changes, and to compute the CG and record the new empty weight and empty weight center of gravity (EWCG) in the aircraft weight and balance record.

Exam Tip: When reviewing your weight and balance computations, the examiner may ask to see the aircraft document you referenced to obtain the aircraft's actual weight and balance data (empty weight, moment, etc.) for the aircraft (make, model, serial number) used for the test. Make sure that you have that information readily available and that it represents the aircraft's most recent/current weight and balance data.

[PA.I.F.K2f, PA.I.B.K1b; FAA-H-8083-1]

10. **While en route, will the CG of your aircraft change as it uses fuel?**

Most general aviation aircraft have their fuel tanks located at or very close to the center of gravity by design to avoid major changes in center of gravity (CG) based on fuel burn. If the fuel tanks are located near the CG, such as wing tanks, the shift in CG as fuel is burned will be minimal because the weight reduction occurs close to the aircraft's balance point.

However, if the aircraft is equipped with additional or supplemental fuel tanks, the pilot must be aware of the positioning of the fuel and how it will affect the CG position as fuel is burned. For fuel tanks that are ahead of the CG, the center of gravity will shift aft as the fuel is burned. For tanks that are located behind the CG, the CG will shift forward as fuel is burned.

Chapter 7 **Performance and Limitations**

Pilots must account for this potential shift during flight planning, particularly in aircraft with limited CG ranges. An excessive CG shift could lead to instability, reduced control effectiveness, or difficulty maintaining desired pitch attitudes.

A POH/AFM or any supplemental type certificate information for changes to the aircraft fuel system will provide guidance on how CG changes with fuel usage.

A best practice for the pilot is to compute a weight and balance at takeoff and at an expected landing fuel condition to determine if the aircraft will remain within the CG range throughout the flight.

[PA.I.F.K2f; FAA-H-8083-25]

11. You are considering using your four-seat aircraft for a summer camping trip. Could you remove the back seats to make more room for your camping gear and gain a little extra weight capacity from removing their weight from the aircraft?

Removing seats from the aircraft would change the center of gravity position of the aircraft prior to loading. While it may be physically done, this would require preparation of an updated weight and balance document to determine the empty weight center of gravity, after which a pilot could consider their loading. Without this extra step, this would not be allowed. Some owners do choose to have multiple weight and balances prepared and documented by their mechanic for different aircraft configurations (such as removing seats).

[PA.I.F.K2f; FAA-H-8083-25]

C. Aircraft Performance

1. What are some of the main elements of aircraft performance?

a. Takeoff and landing distance
b. Rate of climb
c. Ceiling
d. Payload
e. Range
f. Speed

(continued)

Private Pilot Oral Exam Guide   187

Chapter 7 **Performance and Limitations**

    g. Fuel economy
    h. Maneuverability
    i.   Stability
    j.   Glide distance

[PA.I.F.R1; FAA-H-8083-25]

2. What factors affect the performance of an aircraft during takeoffs and landings?

    a. Air density (density altitude)
    b. Surface wind
    c. Runway surface
    d. Upslope or downslope of runway
    e. Weight
    f.   Powerplant thrust

[PA.I.F.K2a; FAA-H-8083-25]

3. What effect does wind have on aircraft performance?

Takeoff—The effect of a headwind is that it allows the aircraft to reach the lift-off speed at a lower ground speed, which will increase airplane performance by shortening the takeoff distance and increasing the angle of climb. The effect of a tailwind is that the aircraft will need to achieve greater ground speed to get to lift-off speed. This decreases aircraft performance by increasing takeoff distance and reducing the angle of climb.

Landing—The effect of wind on landing distance is identical to its effect on takeoff distance. A headwind will lower ground speed and increase airplane performance by steepening the approach angle and reducing the landing distance. A tailwind will increase ground speed and decrease performance by decreasing the approach angle and increasing the landing distance.

Cruise flight—Winds aloft have a somewhat opposite effect on airplane performance. A headwind will decrease performance by reducing ground speed, which in turn increases the fuel requirement for the flight. A tailwind will increase performance by increasing the ground speed, which in turn reduces the fuel requirement for the flight.

[PA.I.F.K2a; FAA-H-8083-25]

188 Aviation Supplies & Academics

Chapter 7 **Performance and Limitations**

4. How does weight affect takeoff and landing performance?

Increased gross weight can significantly affect both takeoff and landing performance of an aircraft, as increased weight directly impacts the forces required for flight and the available safety margins. It directly results in the following during takeoff:

a. Higher liftoff speed.

b. Greater mass to accelerate (slow acceleration).

c. Increased retarding force (drag and ground friction).

d. Longer takeoff distance.

e. Reduced climb performance leading to shallower climb angles and lower climb rates.

When landing, an increased weight has the following effects:

a. *Longer landing roll*—Heavier aircraft carry more momentum, requiring more runway distance to decelerate to a full stop.

b. *Higher approach speed*—A heavier aircraft requires a higher speed to avoid stalling during landing, increasing touchdown speed.

c. *Greater braking force*—More weight demands greater braking effort, which can increase the risk of brake overheating or runway overrun.

The effect of gross weight on landing distance is that the airplane will require a greater speed to support the airplane at the landing angle of attack and lift coefficient, resulting in an increased landing distance.

Operating at or near maximum weight limits reduces performance margins and leaves less room for error during critical phases of flight.

[PA.I.F.K2f; FAA-H-8083-25]

5. Define the term *maximum landing weight* and describe how it might affect a pilot's planning for a flight.

The maximum landing weight is the highest weight at which an aircraft is certified to safely land. This limit is established by the manufacturer and considers the structural integrity of the landing gear, airframe, and braking system, as well as performance factors such as landing distance and control responsiveness. Exceeding the

Private Pilot Oral Exam Guide   189

Chapter 7 **Performance and Limitations**

maximum landing weight during landing can result in structural damage, reduced braking efficiency, or a longer landing roll, potentially leading to a runway overrun.

A maximum landing weight in many aircraft is less than the maximum gross weight.

Pilots should ensure their landings will be at a weight condition that is less than the maximum landing weight. If a pilot takes off at a weight higher than this, and needs to land sooner than expected, they may need to consider flying for a period of time to reduce fuel weight to get the aircraft under a maximum landing weight prior to landing. Most general aviation aircraft do not have a way to dump fuel or otherwise safely reduce loads. If it's necessary to complete a landing over the maximum landing weight for emergency reasons, a pilot should have maintenance determine if the aircraft has experienced any adverse effects that might affect airworthiness.

[PA.I.F.R2; AFM/POH]

6. What effect does an increase in density altitude have on takeoff and landing performance?

An increase in density altitude results in:

a. Increased takeoff distance (greater takeoff TAS required).

b. Reduced rate of climb (decreased thrust and reduced acceleration).

c. Increased true airspeed on approach and landing (same IAS).

d. Increased landing roll distance.

[PA.I.F.K2a; FAA-P-8740-2]

7. Define the term *density altitude*.

Density altitude is pressure altitude corrected for nonstandard temperature. Under standard atmospheric conditions, air at each level in the atmosphere has a specific density, and under standard conditions, pressure altitude and density altitude identify the same level. Therefore, density altitude is the vertical distance above sea level in the standard atmosphere at which a given density is found.

[PA.I.F.K2a; FAA-H-8083-25]

Chapter 7 **Performance and Limitations**

8. How does air density affect aircraft performance?

The density of the air has a direct effect on:

a. Lift produced by the wings;
b. Power output of the engine;
c. Propeller efficiency; and
d. Drag forces.

[PA.I.F.K2a; FAA-H-8083-25]

9. What factors affect air density?

Altitude—The higher the altitude, the less dense the air.

Temperature—The warmer the air, the less dense it is.

Humidity—More humid air is less dense.

[PA.I.F.K2a; FAA-P-8740-2]

10. How do temperature, altitude, and humidity affect density altitude?

a. Density altitude will increase (low air density) when one or more of the following occurs:
  • High air temperature
  • High altitude
  • High humidity

b. Density altitude will decrease (high air density) when one or more of the following occurs:
  • Low air temperature
  • Low altitude
  • Low humidity

[PA.I.F.K2a; FAA-P-8740-2]

11. You're planning a VFR departure from Durango, Colorado (KDRO), elevation 6,689 feet MSL, in a Cessna 172. Explain the potential hazards that exist when departing KDRO compared to departing from Los Angeles (KLAX), elevation 127 feet MSL. Is there anything you can do to mitigate the risk?

Departing from an airport at a higher elevation, such as Durango, Colorado, at 6,689 feet MSL, presents unique hazards compared to departing from an airport at sea level due to the effects of

Private Pilot Oral Exam Guide 191

Chapter 7 **Performance and Limitations**

density altitude. As elevation increases, the air becomes less dense, meaning there is less oxygen and lower atmospheric pressure. This reduces engine performance, propeller efficiency, and the aircraft's lift capabilities.

At a higher elevation, the takeoff distance required may be longer due to reduced engine power and lift. The aircraft may also experience a reduced climb rate since the engines cannot produce as much power in thinner air, and the wings produce less lift. In the event of an engine failure shortly after takeoff, a higher elevation makes it more difficult to glide to a suitable landing area due to the lack of sufficient climb performance.

In contrast, at lower elevations like near sea level, the aircraft's performance is closer to its optimal levels, with more available power, better climb rates, and shorter takeoff distances. This makes departures from lower-altitude airports generally safer and easier to manage. Thus, higher-altitude departures require more careful planning, including adjusting for reduced aircraft performance.

[PA.I.F.K2a; FAA-H-8083-2]

12. What is the difference between a service ceiling and an absolute ceiling?

The service ceiling and absolute ceiling are both performance limits related to an aircraft's ability to climb, but they differ in definition and operational significance.

The *service ceiling* is the maximum altitude at which an aircraft can maintain a steady rate of climb of 100 feet per minute (fpm) under standard atmospheric conditions at maximum weight. Beyond this altitude, the aircraft's climb performance diminishes significantly, making further ascent impractical. The service ceiling represents the point where the aircraft still has enough excess power and lift to sustain a minimal climb rate.

The *absolute ceiling*, on the other hand, is the maximum altitude the aircraft can reach under the same conditions. At this altitude, the aircraft's maximum lift equals its weight, and the maximum engine power equals the drag, resulting in a climb rate of zero. In other words, the aircraft cannot climb any higher because it lacks the performance to overcome these aerodynamic and power limitations.

Chapter 7 **Performance and Limitations**

In practical terms, the service ceiling is the highest altitude at which pilots typically operate the aircraft with reasonable climb performance, while the absolute ceiling is a theoretical limit where the aircraft can barely maintain level flight. Operating near the absolute ceiling is generally unsafe due to minimal performance margins, making it impractical for normal operations. Understanding these limits is critical for safe flight planning and avoiding scenarios where climb performance becomes a safety concern.

[PA.I.F.K1; FAA-H-8083-25]

13. Define the following airplane performance speeds: V_{S0}, V_{S1}, V_Y, V_X, V_{LE}, V_{LO}, V_{FE}, V_A, V_{NO}, V_{NE}.

Note: Ensure that you know these speeds for your particular airplane.

V_{S0}—Stall speed in landing configuration; the calibrated power-off stalling speed or the minimum steady flight speed at which the airplane is controllable in the landing configuration.

V_{S1}—Stall speed clean or in specified configuration; the calibrated power-off stalling speed or the minimum steady flight speed at which the airplane is controllable in a specified configuration.

V_Y—Best rate-of-climb speed; the calibrated airspeed at which the airplane will obtain the maximum increase in altitude per unit of time. This best rate-of-climb speed normally decreases slightly with altitude.

V_X—Best angle-of-climb speed; the calibrated airspeed at which the airplane will obtain the highest altitude in a given horizontal distance. This best angle-of-climb speed normally increases with altitude.

V_{LE}—Maximum landing gear extension speed; the maximum calibrated airspeed at which the airplane can be safely flown with the landing gear extended. This is a problem involving stability and controllability.

V_{LO}—Maximum landing gear operating speed; the maximum calibrated airspeed at which the landing gear can be safely extended or retracted. This is a problem involving the air loads imposed on the operating mechanism during extension or retraction of the gear.

(continued)

Private Pilot Oral Exam Guide   193

Chapter 7 **Performance and Limitations**

V_{FE}—Maximum flap extension speed; the highest calibrated airspeed permissible with the wing flaps in a prescribed extended position. This is a problem involving the air loads imposed on the structure of the flaps.

V_A—Maneuvering speed; the calibrated design maneuvering airspeed. This is the maximum speed at which the limit load can be imposed (either by gusts or full deflection of the control surfaces) without causing structural damage.

V_{NO}—Normal operating speed; the maximum calibrated airspeed for normal operation or the maximum structural cruise speed. This is the speed above which exceeding the limit load factor may cause permanent deformation of the airplane structure.

V_{NE}—Never exceed speed; the calibrated airspeed which should never be exceeded. If flight is attempted above this speed, structural damage or structural failure may result.

[PA.I.F.R2; AFM/POH]

14. Explain the difference between best glide speed and minimum sink speed.

Best glide speed—The speed and configuration that provides the greatest forward distance for a given loss of altitude. In most airplanes, best glide airspeed will be roughly halfway between V_X (best angle of climb speed) and V_Y (best rate of climb speed).

Minimum sink speed—Used to maximize the time that the airplane remains in flight. Use of minimum sink speed results in the airplane losing altitude at the lowest rate. It is important that pilots realize that flight at the minimum sink airspeed results in less distance traveled and is useful in flight situations where time in flight is more important than distance flown (e.g., more time to fix problem, ditching at sea). Minimum sink speed is not an often-published airspeed but generally is a few knots less than best glide speed.

[PA.I.F.R1; FAA-H-8083-3]

194 Aviation Supplies & Academics

Chapter 7 **Performance and Limitations**

15. How many miles can you glide in your aircraft per 1,000 feet of altitude lost?

A rule of thumb for Cessna 152s and 172s is 1.5 NM per 1,000 feet of altitude lost above ground level. Reference your aircraft's POH/AFM and also consider experimenting to determine how far your aircraft can glide. This glide distance may differ based on aircraft weight conditions.

[PA.I.F.R1; POH/AFM]

16. During flight planning, explain how to determine the time, fuel, and distance to climb for the departure leg of the flight plan.

The chart to check for climb performance is the time, fuel, and distance-to-climb chart in your aircraft's POH/AFM. This chart will give the time it will take to accomplish the climb, the fuel amount used during the climb, and the ground distance that will be covered during the climb. To use this chart, obtain the information for the departing airport and for the cruise altitude.

[PA.I.F.R1; FAA-H-8083-25]

17. During flight planning, explain how to determine the planned TAS and fuel burn (gallons per hour) during cruise flight.

The aircraft's POH/AFM provides cruise and range performance charts which are designed to give TAS, fuel consumption, endurance in hours, and range in miles at specific cruise configurations and under the specified conditions. Select the pressure altitude and temperature that is closest to the planned altitude and expected temperature. Choose the planned engine speed to obtain power, true airspeed, and cruise fuel flow numbers.

[PA.I.F.R1; FAA-H-8083-25]

18. Explain the factors that affect the airplane's rate of fuel consumption.

The rate of fuel consumption depends on many factors: condition of the engine, propeller RPM, richness of the mixture, and the percentage of horsepower used for flight at cruising speed.

[PA.I.F.R1; FAA-H-8083-25]

Private Pilot Oral Exam Guide 195

Chapter 7 **Performance and Limitations**

19. **What information can you obtain from the following charts: takeoff charts, crosswind and headwind component chart, landing charts, and stall speed performance charts?**

    a. *Takeoff charts*—These allow you to compute the takeoff distance of the airplane with no flaps or with a specific flap configuration. You can also compute distances for a no-flap takeoff over a 50-foot obstacle scenario as well as with flaps over a 50-foot obstacle. The takeoff distance chart provides for various airplane weights, altitudes, temperatures, winds, and obstacle heights.

    b. *Crosswind and headwind component chart*—This allows for figuring the headwind and crosswind component for any given wind direction and velocity.

    c. *Landing charts*—Provide normal landing distance as well as landing distance over a 50-foot obstacle.

    d. *Stall speed performance charts*—These are designed to give an understanding of the speed at which the airplane will stall in a given configuration. It will typically take into account the angle of bank, the position of the gear and flaps, and the throttle position.

    [PA.I.F.R1; FAA-H-8083-25]

20. **The performance chart numbers for your aircraft are based on test flights conducted in a new aircraft. What best practices are recommended for pilots to minimize risk when using the charts to make performance calculations for takeoff, enroute cruise, and landing?**

    Since performance data that is provided offers absolute best case performance conditions, pilots are encouraged to add extra safety margins to any calculations that are completed. For example, when calculating a takeoff distance, a pilot might choose to compute the number based on the chart and then add an extra 50 percent for a safety margin. If a pilot calculates that 1,000 feet of runway would be required for takeoff, they might add an additional 50 percent (500 feet) to this, and not allow themselves to takeoff with a runway available of less than 1,500 feet.

    Building personal minimums in addition to using provided minimum performance data charts can enhance safety. It is

196   Aviation Supplies & Academics

Chapter 7 **Performance and Limitations**

generally a good practice for a pilot to build in more safety margins when flying in aircraft they are less familiar with, at airports they are not familiar with, or in more demanding performance conditions such as higher elevation airports. A pilot's personal minimums may be continuously changing based on conditions, external pressures, and/or the operating environment. Few safety-minded pilots are willing to operate at the absolute minimums provided in performance chart calculations.

[PA.I.F.R1; FAA-H-8083-25]

21. Define the term *pressure altitude*, and state why it is important.

Pressure altitude—The altitude indicated when the altimeter setting window (barometric scale) is adjusted to 29.92 inHg. This is the altitude above the standard datum plane, a theoretical plane where air pressure (corrected to 15°C) equals 29.92 inHg. Pressure altitude is used to compute density altitude, true altitude, true airspeed, and other performance data.

[PA.I.F.K2a; FAA-H-8083-3]

22. The following questions are designed to provide pilots with a general review of the basic information they should know about their specific airplane before taking a flight check or review.

1. *What is the normal climb-out speed?*
2. *What is the best rate-of-climb speed?*
3. *What is the best angle-of-climb speed?*
4. *What is the maximum flap extension speed?*
5. *What is the maximum gear extension speed?*
6. *What is the stall speed in the normal landing configuration?*
7. *What is the stall speed in the clean configuration?*
8. *What is the normal approach-to-land speed?*
9. *What is maneuvering speed?*
10. *What is red-line speed?*
11. *What engine-out glide speed will give you maximum range?*
12. *What is the make and horsepower of the engine?*
13. *How many usable gallons of fuel can you carry?*

Private Pilot Oral Exam Guide 197

Chapter 7 **Performance and Limitations**

14. *Where are the fuel tanks located, and what are their capacities?*

15. *Where are the fuel vents for your aircraft?*

16. *What is the octane rating of the fuel used by your aircraft?*

17. *Where are the fuel sumps located on your aircraft? When should you drain them?*

18. *What are the minimum and maximum oil capacities?*

19. *What weight of oil is being used?*

20. *What is the maximum oil temperature and pressure?*

21. *Do the aircraft avionics have any limitations placed on them?*

22. *What limitations does the autopilot have?*

23. *What are the nose wheel turning limitations for your aircraft?*

24. *What is the maximum allowable/demonstrated crosswind component for the aircraft?*

25. *How many people will this aircraft carry safely with a full fuel load?*

26. *What is the maximum allowable weight the aircraft can carry with baggage in the baggage compartment?*

27. *What takeoff distance is required for a takeoff made from a sea level pressure altitude?*

28. *What is your maximum allowable useful load?*

29. *Solve a weight and balance problem for the flight you plan to make with one passenger who weighs 170 pounds.*

    a. *Does your load fall within the weight and balance envelope?*

    b. *What is the final gross weight?*

    c. *How much fuel can be carried?*

    d. *How much baggage can be carried with full fuel?*

30. *Know the function of the various types of antennae on your aircraft.*

Exam Tip: Make sure to perform a weight and balance calculation for both departure and arrival fuel weights to ensure the aircraft remains within the CG envelope for the entire flight.

[PA.I.F.R2]

Chapter 7 **Performance and Limitations**

23. Why are some aircraft not allowed to perform forward slips with flaps extended?

Some aircraft are restricted from performing forward slips with flaps extended because of the potential for aerodynamic instability or airflow disruption that can affect the control or safety of the aircraft. These restrictions are typically noted in the aircraft's pilot's operating handbook (POH) or airplane flight manual (AFM) and are based on the design and flight characteristics of the specific model.

A forward slip is a maneuver used to increase descent rate without increasing airspeed, often during an approach to landing. It involves crossing the controls by applying opposite aileron and rudder. In some aircraft, extending the flaps changes the airflow over the wings and tail surfaces in ways that can create undesirable handling characteristics during a forward slip.

Extended flaps may alter the aerodynamic forces on the tail, reducing elevator or rudder effectiveness during the slip and causing loss of control authority. The disturbed airflow caused by the flaps can lead to buffeting or unpredictable behavior. Additionally, the increased aerodynamic loads during a slip could exceed the design limits of the extended flaps in some cases.

Pilots should always consult the limitations section of their POH/AFM and any placards in the aircraft to ensure compliance with operating restrictions. If a forward slip is necessary, it's important to verify whether it is permitted with flaps extended to ensure safe operation.

[PA.I.F.R2; POH/AFM]

Private Pilot Oral Exam Guide 199

Airport Operations

8

Chapter 8 **Airport Operations**

A. Communications, Light Signals, and Runway Lighting Systems

1. Explain where a pilot would look for radio communication frequencies and other airport data.

Communication frequencies and airport data may be found in the following:

a. Aeronautical charts (on the chart tab)

b. The *Chart Supplement*

c. Notices to Airmen (NOTAMs)

d. Automated Terminal Information Service (ATIS) broadcasts

e. GPS navigation databases and charting apps

[PA.III.A.K1; FAA-H-8083-25]

2. Explain the phraseology a pilot should use on initial contact with an ATC facility.

Use the following format:

a. Name of the facility being called.

b. Your full aircraft identification.

c. If on the ground, your position; if in the air, your location.

d. Your request, if it is short.

Example: "Columbia Ground, Cessna Three One Six Zero Foxtrot, south ramp, ready to taxi, with information Bravo."

[PA.III.A.K2, PA.III.A.R4; AIM 4-2-3]

3. When used to acknowledge time-critical ATC instructions, explain the meaning of the following words: Wilco, Roger, Affirmative, and Negative.

Wilco means: "I will comply."

Roger means: "I have received and understood your last transmission."

Affirmative means: "Yes."

Negative means: "No."

[PA.III.A.K2; FAA-P-8740-47]

Chapter 8 **Airport Operations**

4. Is it acceptable to abbreviate your call sign on an initial contact with an ATC facility?

It is very important to ensure use of correct call signs. Aircraft with similar call signs may be on the same frequency, and improper use of call signs can result in one pilot executing a clearance intended for another aircraft. To avoid this problem, never abbreviate your call sign on an initial contact, or at any time when other aircraft call signs you hear on the frequency have similar numbers/sounds or identical letters/numbers to those of your own aircraft (e.g., Cessna 6132F, Cessna 1622F, Baron 123F, Cherokee 7732F, etc.).

[PA.III.A.K2, PA.III.A.R4; FAA-P-8740-47]

5. What is the most common type of communication radio equipment installed in general aviation aircraft? How many channels are available?

In general aviation, the most common types of radios are VHF. A VHF radio operates on frequencies between 118.0 and 136.975 MHz and is classified as 720 or 760 depending on the number of channels it can accommodate. The 720 and 760 use 0.025 spacing (118.025, 118.050, etc.) with the 720 having a frequency range up to 135.975 and the 760 going up to 136.975.

[PA.III.A.K2; FAA-H-8083-25]

6. What frequencies are used for ground control?

The majority of ground control frequencies are 121.6 to 121.9 MHz.

[PA.III.A.K1; AIM 4-3-14]

7. What is a Common Traffic Advisory Frequency (CTAF)?

A CTAF is a frequency designated for the purpose of carrying out airport advisory practices while operating to or from an airport without an operating control tower. The CTAF may be a UNICOM, MULTICOM, FSS, or TOWER frequency and is identified in appropriate aeronautical publications.

[PA.III.A.K1; AIM 4-1-9]

Private Pilot Oral Exam Guide   203

Chapter 8 **Airport Operations**

8. What is UNICOM, and what frequencies are designated for its use?

UNICOM is a nongovernment communication facility which may provide airport information at certain airports. Airports other than those with a control tower/FSS on airport will normally use 122.700, 122.725, 122.800, 122.975, 123.000, 123.050, and 123.075 MHz. Airports with a control tower or an FSS on airport will normally use 122.950 MHz.

[PA.III.A.K2; AIM 4-1-9, 4-1-11]

9. What does ATIS mean?

Automatic Terminal Information Service (ATIS) is the continuous broadcast of recorded noncontrol information in selected high-activity terminal areas. Its purpose is to improve controller effectiveness and to relieve frequency congestion by automating the repetitive transmission of essential but routine information.

[PA.III.A.K2; AIM 4-1-13]

10. What is an RCO?

A remote communications outlet (RCO) is an unmanned communications facility remotely controlled by ATC personnel, established for the purpose of providing ground-to-ground communication between ATC and pilots located at satellite airports. ATC may use the RCO to deliver enroute clearances and departure authorizations, and to acknowledge IFR cancellations or departure/landing times. As a secondary function, RCOs may be used for advisory purposes whenever the aircraft is below the coverage of the primary air/ground frequency.

[PA.III.A.K2; P/CG]

11. If operating into an airport without an operating control tower, FSS, or UNICOM, what procedure should be followed?

Where there is no tower, FSS, or UNICOM station on the airport, use MULTICOM frequency 122.9 for self-announce procedures. MULTICOM is a mobile service not open to public use; it is used to provide communications essential to conduct the activities being performed by or directed from private aircraft.

[PA.III.A.S1; AIM 4-1-9, P/CG]

204 Aviation Supplies & Academics

Chapter 8 **Airport Operations**

12. **What would be an indication that a microphone/PTT switch is stuck in the transmit position in your airplane? What would you do?**

One indication would be a lack of sounds from the receiver. Some aircraft transmitters will indicate that they're transmitting by displaying a "T" on the display. Check your volume, recheck your frequency, and make sure that your microphone/push-to-talk (PTT) button is not stuck in the transmit position. Depending on the airplane, other possible actions would be unplugging the microphone/PTT, unplugging a headset, etc.

[PA.III.A.K5; AIM 4-2-2]

13. **If operating into an airport *without* an operating control tower that is located within the Class D airspace of an airport with an operating control tower, is it always necessary to communicate with the tower?**

Yes, operations to or from an airport in Class D airspace (airport traffic area) require communication with the tower even when operating to/from a satellite airport.

[PA.III.A.K2; 14 CFR 91.129]

14. **When conducting flight operations into an airport with an operating control tower, when should initial contact be established?**

When operating at an airport where traffic control is being exercised by a control tower, pilots are required to maintain two-way radio contact with the tower while operating within Class B, Class C, and Class D surface areas, unless the tower authorizes otherwise. Initial call-up should be made about 15 miles from the airport. Also, not all airports with an operating control tower will have Class D airspace. These airports do not have weather reporting, which is a requirement for surface-based controlled airspace. Pilots are expected to use good operating practices and communicate with the control tower.

[PA.III.A.K2; AIM 4-3-2]

Private Pilot Oral Exam Guide 205

Chapter 8 **Airport Operations**

15. When departing a Class D surface area, what communications procedures are recommended?

Unless there is good reason to leave the tower frequency before exiting the Class B, Class C, and Class D surface areas, it is good operating practice to remain on the tower frequency for the purpose of receiving traffic information. In the interest of reducing tower frequency congestion, pilots are reminded that it is not necessary to request permission to leave the tower frequency once outside of Class B, Class C, and Class D surface areas.

[PA.III.A.K2; AIM 4-3-2]

16. Arrange the following radio facilities in the order they would be used when operating into or out of a tower-controlled airport within Class B, C, or D airspace: Approach Control, ATIS, Ground Control, Control Tower, Clearance Delivery, Departure Control

Arriving Aircraft: ATIS, Approach Control, Control Tower, Ground Control.

Departing Aircraft: ATIS, Clearance Delivery (if required for the surrounding airspace, i.e., Class B, C or D airspace), Ground Control, Control Tower, Departure Control.

[PA.III.A.K2; AIM 4-3-2]

17. What does the operation of an airport rotating beacon during the hours of daylight indicate?

In Class B, Class C, Class D, and Class E surface areas, operation of the airport beacon during the hours of daylight often indicates that the ground visibility is less than 3 miles and/or the ceiling is less than 1,000 feet. ATC clearance in accordance with 14 CFR Part 91 is required for landing, takeoff, and flight in the traffic pattern. Pilots should not rely solely on the operation of the airport beacon to indicate if weather conditions are IFR or VFR. There is no regulatory requirement for daylight operation, and it is the pilot's responsibility to comply with proper preflight planning as required by Part 91.

[PA.III.A.K3; AIM 2-1-9]

Chapter 8 **Airport Operations**

18. When may a pilot intentionally deviate from an ATC clearance or instruction?

No pilot may deviate from an ATC clearance unless:

a. An amended clearance has been obtained;

b. An emergency exists; or

c. In response to a traffic and collision avoidance system resolution advisory.

[PA.III.A.S3; 14 CFR 91.123]

19. As pilot-in-command, what action, if any, is required of you if you deviate from an ATC instruction and priority is given?

Two actions are required of you as PIC:

a. Each pilot-in-command who, in an emergency or in response to a traffic alert and collision avoidance system resolution advisory, deviates from an ATC clearance or instruction must notify ATC of that deviation as soon as possible.

b. Each pilot-in-command who is given priority by ATC in an emergency shall submit a detailed report of that emergency within 48 hours to the manager of that ATC facility, if requested by ATC (on-the-ground responsibility).

[PA.III.A.K2; 14 CFR 91.123]

20. The acronym LAHSO refers to what specific air traffic control procedure?

LAHSO stands for Land and Hold Short Operations, which is an air traffic control procedure used to increase efficiency at airports by allowing aircraft to land on a runway and then hold short of another runway or taxiway intersection. This procedure allows multiple aircraft to use the same runway space more effectively, particularly in busy airports, by having one aircraft land and then hold short of an intersection while another aircraft may take off or land on the same runway.

Pilots need to be aware of the specific LAHSO clearance issued by air traffic control, which includes the landing instructions, the point where they should hold short, and the runway or taxiway where the aircraft should stop. When accepting a LAHSO clearance, the pilot must be able to stop the aircraft before reaching the hold-short

Private Pilot Oral Exam Guide 207

Chapter 8 **Airport Operations**

point, so sufficient runway length must be available for a safe landing and stop.

The pilot-in-command has the final authority to accept or decline any land and hold short clearance. The safety and operation of the aircraft remain the responsibility of the pilot. Pilots are expected to decline a LAHSO clearance if they determine it will compromise safety.

[PA.III.B.K1; AIM 4-3-11]

21. ATC has instructed you to line up and wait on the departure runway due to crossing traffic on an intersecting taxiway. What is considered a reasonable amount of time to wait for a takeoff clearance before calling ATC?

When instructed to "line up and wait" on the departure runway, a pilot should remain alert and ready for takeoff clearance. However, if no clearance or further instructions are received within approximately 90 seconds, or if there is uncertainty about the situation (e.g., no visible crossing traffic), the pilot should contact ATC to confirm the clearance status.

[PA.III.A.R1; AIM 5-2-5, SAFO 11004]

22. Where can available landing distance (ALD) data be found?

Available landing distance (ALD) data are published in the *Chart Supplement* and in the *U.S. Terminal Procedures Publications*.

[PA.III.B.K1; AIM 4-3-11]

Chapter 8 **Airport Operations**

23. In the event of radio failure while operating an aircraft to, from, through, or on an airport having an operational tower, what are the different types and meanings of light gun signals you might receive from an ATC tower?

Type	Color	Meaning on ground	Meaning in flight
Steady	Green	Cleared for takeoff	Cleared to land
Steady	Red	Stop	Give way/circle
Flashing	Green	Cleared to taxi	Return for landing
Flashing	Red	Taxi clear of landing area	Airport unsafe; Do not land
Flashing	White	Return to starting point	*(Not applicable)*
Alternating	Red/green	Use extreme caution	Use extreme caution

[PA.III.A.K5, PA.III.A.K3; 14 CFR 91.125]

24. Explain when transponder and ADS-B Out equipment should be operated while on the ground.

Civil and military aircraft should operate with the transponder in the altitude reporting mode and ADS-B Out transmissions enabled at all airports, any time the aircraft is positioned on any portion of the airport movement area. This includes all defined taxiways and runways. Pilots must pay particular attention to ATIS and airport diagram notations, General Notes (included on airport charts), and comply with directions pertaining to transponder and ADS-B usage.

[PA.III.A.K4; AIM 4-1-20]

25. If the aircraft radio fails in flight under VFR while operating into a tower-controlled airport, what conditions must be met before a landing may be made at that airport?

a. Weather conditions must be at or above basic VFR weather minimums;

b. Visual contact with the tower is maintained; and

c. A clearance to land is received.

[PA.III.A.K5; 14 CFR 91.126, 91.127, 91.129]

Private Pilot Oral Exam Guide 209

Chapter 8 **Airport Operations**

26. What procedures should be used when attempting communications with a tower when the aircraft transmitter or receiver (or both) are inoperative?

Arriving aircraft receiver inoperative:

a. Remain outside or above Class D surface area.

b. Determine direction and flow of traffic.

c. Advise tower of aircraft type, position, altitude, and intention to land. Request to be controlled by light signals.

d. At 3 to 5 miles, advise tower of position and join traffic pattern.

e. Watch tower for light gun signals.

Arriving aircraft transmitter inoperative:

a. Remain outside or above Class D surface area.

b. Determine direction and flow of traffic.

c. Monitor frequency for landing or traffic information.

d. Join the traffic pattern and watch for light gun signals.

e. Daytime, acknowledge by rocking wings. Nighttime, acknowledge by flashing landing light or navigation lights.

Arriving aircraft transmitter and receiver inoperative:

a. Remain outside or above Class D surface area.

b. Determine direction and flow of traffic.

c. Join the traffic pattern and watch for light gun signals.

d. Acknowledge light signals as noted above.

Note: When an aircraft with a coded radar beacon transponder experiences a loss of two-way radio capability, the pilot should adjust the transponder to reply on Mode A/3, Code 7600. The pilot should understand that the aircraft may not be in an area of radar coverage.

[PA.III.A.K5; AIM 4-2-13, 6-4-2]

27. Describe the type of information provided when receiving VFR radar assistance from ATC.

Radar-equipped ATC facilities provide radar assistance to aircraft on instrument flight plans and to VFR aircraft, provided the aircraft can communicate with the facility and are within radar coverage. This basic service includes safety alerts, traffic advisories, limited vectoring when requested, and sequencing at locations where this

210 Aviation Supplies & Academics

Chapter 8 **Airport Operations**

procedure has been established. ATC issues traffic advisories based on observed radar targets. This service is not intended to relieve the pilot of the responsibility to see and avoid other aircraft.

[PA.III.A.K7; FAA-H-8083-25, AIM 4-1-17]

28. Describe the various types of terminal radar services available for VFR aircraft.

Basic radar service—Safety alerts, traffic advisories, limited radar vectoring (on a workload-permitting basis), and sequencing at locations where procedures have been established for this purpose and/or when covered by a letter of agreement.

TRSA service—Radar sequencing and separation service for participating VFR aircraft in a terminal radar service area (TRSA).

Class C service—In addition to basic radar service, provides approved separation between IFR and VFR aircraft and sequencing of VFR arrivals to the primary airport.

Class B service—In addition to basic radar service, provides approved separation of aircraft based on IFR, VFR, and/or weight, and sequencing of VFR arrivals to the primary airport(s).

[PA.III.A.K7; AIM 4-1-18]

29. When is immediate notification to the NTSB required?

The operator of an aircraft shall immediately, and by the most expeditious means available, notify the nearest National Transportation Safety Board (NTSB) office when an aircraft accident or any of the following listed serious incidents occur:

a. Flight control system malfunction.

b. Crewmember unable to perform normal duties.

c. Inflight fire.

d. Aircraft collision inflight.

e. Property damage, other than aircraft, estimated to exceed $25,000.

f. Overdue aircraft (believed to be in accident).

g. Release of all or a portion of a propeller blade from an aircraft.

h. Complete loss of information (excluding flickering), from more than 50 percent of an aircraft's EFIS flight deck displays.

[PA.III.A.K8; 49 CFR 830.5]

Private Pilot Oral Exam Guide 211

Chapter 8 **Airport Operations**

30. Explain the difference between an aircraft incident and an aircraft accident.

Aircraft incident means an occurrence other than an accident associated with the operation of an aircraft, which affects or could affect the safety of operations.

Aircraft accident means an occurrence associated with the operation of an aircraft which takes place between the time any person boards the aircraft with the intention of flight and all such persons have disembarked, and in which any person suffers death or serious injury, or in which the aircraft receives substantial damage.

[PA.III.A.K8; 49 CFR 830.2]

31. Define the term *serious injury*.

Serious injury means any injury that:

a. Requires hospitalization for more than 48 hours, commencing within 7 days from the date the injury was received;

b. Results in a fracture of any bone (except simple fractures of fingers, toes, or nose);

c. Causes severe hemorrhages, nerve, muscle, or tendon damage;

d. Involves any internal organ; or

e. Involves second- or third-degree burns, or any burns affecting more than 5% of the body surface.

[PA.III.A.K8; 49 CFR 830.2]

32. Define the term *substantial damage*.

Substantial damage means damage or failure which adversely affects the structural strength, performance or flight characteristics of the aircraft and which would normally require major repair or replacement of the affected component. Engine failure or damage limited to an engine if only one engine fails or is damaged; bent fairings or cowling; dented skin; small punctured holes in the skin or fabric; ground damage to rotor or propeller blades; and damage to landing gear, wheels, tires, flaps, engine accessories, brakes, or wing tips are not considered substantial damage for the purpose of 49 CFR Part 830.

[PA.III.A.K8; 49 CFR 830.2]

212 Aviation Supplies & Academics

Chapter 8 **Airport Operations**

33. Will notification to the NTSB always be necessary in any aircraft accident even if there were no injuries?

Refer to the definition of accident. An aircraft accident can involve substantial damage and/or injuries, and the NTSB always requires a report if this is the case.

[PA.III.A.K8; 49 CFR Part 830]

34. Where are accident or incident reports filed?

The operator of an aircraft shall file any report with the field office of the Board nearest the accident or incident.

[PA.III.A.K8; 49 CFR Part 830]

35. After an accident or incident has occurred, how soon must a report be filed with the NTSB?

The operator shall file a report on NTSB Form 6120.1/2, available from NTSB field offices, the NTSB in Washington D.C., or the FAA Flight Standards District Office:

a. Within 10 days after an accident.

b. When, after 7 days, an overdue aircraft is still missing.

Note: A report on an incident for which notification is required as described shall be filed only as requested by an authorized representative of the NTSB.

[PA.III.A.K8; 49 CFR Part 830]

36. What is the Aviation Safety Reporting System (ASRS)?

The Aviation Safety Reporting System (ASRS) is a voluntary program managed by the FAA that allows pilots, air traffic controllers, and other aviation professionals to report safety-related incidents or hazards without the risk of legal repercussions. It is designed to help identify and analyze safety trends, improve aviation safety, and reduce accidents.

Reports submitted to the ASRS can involve issues like near-miss incidents, operational errors, or mechanical failures and are reviewed by a team of safety experts. The information is anonymized to protect the identity of those who submit reports, and the findings are used to improve training, procedures, and regulations.

(continued)

Private Pilot Oral Exam Guide   213

Chapter 8 **Airport Operations**

The ASRS provides valuable data that can be shared with aviation professionals to promote awareness and prevent similar incidents in the future. Additionally, the program offers educational resources for pilots, such as monthly newsletters and safety bulletins, which highlight common issues and solutions.

Participation in ASRS can be an effective way for pilots to contribute to aviation safety while protecting themselves from penalties, as long as the report is submitted before an investigation begins or enforcement action is taken. This system helps create a culture of safety and encourages reporting, ultimately enhancing the safety of the aviation industry.

[PA.III.A.K8; FAA-H-8083-19, AC 00-46]

37. Can the FAA use ASRS reports submitted to NASA for enforcement purposes?

Pilots, air traffic controllers, flight attendants, mechanics, ground personnel, and others involved in aviation operations submit reports to the ASRS when they are involved in, or observe, an incident or situation in which aviation safety may have been compromised. All submissions are voluntary.

Reports sent to the ASRS are held in strict confidence. More than one million reports have been submitted to date and no reporter's identity has ever been breached by the ASRS. ASRS de-identifies reports before entering them into the incident database. All personal and organizational names are removed. Dates, times, and related information, which could be used to infer an identity, are either generalized or eliminated.

The FAA offers ASRS reporters further guarantees and incentives to report. It has committed itself not to use ASRS information against reporters in enforcement actions. It has also chosen to waive fines and penalties, subject to certain limitations, for unintentional violations of federal aviation statutes and regulations that are reported to ASRS. The FAA's initiation and continued support of the ASRS program and its willingness to waive penalties in qualifying cases is a measure of the value it places on the safety information gathered, and the products made possible, through incident reporting to the ASRS.

[PA.III.A.K8; 14 CFR 91.25, AC 00-46]

214 Aviation Supplies & Academics

Chapter 8 **Airport Operations**

38. An airport diagram indicates the letters "RWSL." Explain what these letters indicate.

Runway status lights system (RWSL) is a system of runway and taxiway lighting to provide pilots with increased situational awareness by illuminating runway entry lights (REL) when the runway is unsafe for entry or crossing, and take-off hold lights (THL) when the runway is unsafe for departure. The lights automatically turn red when other traffic makes it dangerous to enter, cross, or begin takeoff.

[PA.III.A.K9; AIM 2-1-6, P/CG]

39. When approaching or operating on a ramp, what should pilots know and be prepared to recognize regarding hand signals from a lineman?

The FAA *AIM* paragraph 4-3-26 outlines standard hand signals used by ground personnel to communicate with pilots during ground operations. These signals are crucial for maintaining safety and coordination when verbal communication or radio use is impractical, such as during taxiing, parking, or pushback.

Pilots should familiarize themselves with the standardized hand signals provided in the *AIM* to understand instructions given by marshallers. Common signals include those for engine start, stop, brake set/release, and directional movements like turn left, turn right, or proceed straight. Other signals indicate emergencies, such as cutting the engine or fire on the aircraft. Additionally, pilots should note that some signals may vary slightly by location or operator. However, the *AIM*'s standardized signals are widely used and provide a reliable baseline.

Some good signals you should be able to recognize and/or signal yourself include:

a. All clear (OK)
b. Start engine
c. Pull chocks
d. Proceed straight ahead
e. Left turn
f. Right turn
g. Slow down
h. Stop

(continued)

Private Pilot Oral Exam Guide 215

Chapter 8 **Airport Operations**

    i. Insert chocks

    j. Cut engines

    k. Emergency stop

[PA.III.A.R1; AIM 4-3-26]

B. Traffic Patterns

1. What are the two main categories of airports?

Towered airport—Pilots are required to maintain two-way radio communication with ATC and to acknowledge and comply with their instructions.

Non-towered airport—Two-way radio communications are not required, although it is a good operating practice for pilots to transmit their intentions on the specified frequency for the benefit of other traffic in the area.

Note: These two types of airports can be further subdivided into civil airports, military/federal government airports, and private airports.

[PA.III.B.K1; FAA-H-8083-25]

2. Explain the purpose of an airport traffic pattern.

An airport traffic pattern is the traffic flow or pattern that is prescribed for aircraft landing at, taxiing on, or taking off from the airport. To ensure that air traffic flows into and out of an airport in an orderly manner, a traffic pattern is established based on the local conditions, to include the direction and altitude of the pattern and the procedures for entering and leaving the pattern.

[PA.III.B.K2; FAA-H-8083-3]

3. What are the basic components of an airport traffic pattern?

a. *Upwind leg*—A flight path parallel to the landing runway in the direction of landing.

b. *Crosswind leg*—A flight path at right angles to the landing runway off its upwind end.

c. *Downwind leg*—A flight path parallel to the landing runway in the direction opposite to landing. The downwind leg normally extends between the crosswind leg and the base leg.

216 Aviation Supplies & Academics

Chapter 8 **Airport Operations**

d. *Base leg*—A flight path at right angles to the landing runway off its approach end. The base leg normally extends from the downwind leg to the intersection of the extended runway centerline.

e. *Final approach*—A flight path in the direction of landing along the extended runway centerline. The final approach normally extends from the base leg to the runway. An aircraft making a straight-in approach VFR is also considered to be on final approach.

[PA.III.B.K2; FAA-H-8083-3]

4. When approaching an airport with an operating control tower, when should initial contact be made with the ATC tower?

Initial call-up should be made about 15 miles from the airport.

[PA.III.B.K1; AIM 4-3-2]

5. When landing at a non-towered airport, how should a pilot choose the runway on which to land?

Landing and takeoff should be accomplished on the operating runway most nearly aligned into the wind. However, if a secondary runway is used (e.g., for length limitations), pilots using the secondary runway should avoid the flow of traffic to the runway most nearly aligned into the wind.

[PA.III.B.K2; AC 90-66]

6. Explain the general rules that apply when conducting traffic pattern operations at a non-towered airport within Class E or G airspace.

Each person operating an aircraft to or from an airport without an operating control tower shall:

a. in the case of an airplane approaching to land, make all turns of that airplane to the left unless the airport displays approved light signals or visual markings indicating that turns should be made to the right, in which case the pilot shall make all turns to the right.

b. in the case of an aircraft departing an airport, comply with any traffic patterns established for that airport in 14 CFR Part 93.

[PA.III.B.K2; 14 CFR 91.126, 91.127]

Private Pilot Oral Exam Guide 217

Chapter 8 **Airport Operations**

7. Does the FAA mandate that traffic patterns be left traffic?

The FAA does not regulate traffic pattern entry, only traffic pattern flow. However, FAA regulations applying to non-towered airports (14 CFR §91.126) indicate that "Each pilot of an airplane must make all turns of that airplane to the left unless the airport displays approved light signals or visual markings indicating that turns should be made to the right, in which case the pilot must make all turns to the right."

This means that when entering the traffic pattern at an airport without an operating control tower, inbound pilots are expected to observe other aircraft already in the pattern and to conform to the traffic pattern in use. If there are no other aircraft present, the pilot should check traffic indicators on the ground and wind indicators to determine which runway and traffic pattern direction to use. For example, an aircraft on an instrument approach flying on the final approach course to land would follow the requirements dictated by the approach procedure. Further, to mitigate the risk of a midair collision at a non-towered airport in other-than-instrument conditions, the FAA does not recommend that the pilot execute a straight-in approach for landing when other aircraft are in the traffic pattern. The straight-in approach may cause a conflict with aircraft in the traffic pattern and on base to final and increase the risk of a midair collision.

[PA.III.B.K1; 14 CFR 91.126, 91.127]

8. What does the FAA recommend with regard to traffic pattern entry at a non-towered airport?

Arriving aircraft should enter the airport's traffic pattern at traffic pattern altitude and avoid straight-in approaches for landing to mitigate the risk of a midair collision. The FAA discourages VFR straight-in approaches to landings due to increased risk of a midair collision. However, if a pilot chooses to execute a straight-in approach for landing without entering the airport traffic pattern, the pilot should self-announce their position on the designated CTAF when they are approximately 8–10 miles from the airport, and coordinate their straight-in approach and landing with other airport traffic. Pilots choosing to execute a straight-in approach do not have a particular priority over other aircraft in the traffic pattern and must comply with the provisions of 14 CFR §91.113(g).

218 Aviation Supplies & Academics

Chapter 8 **Airport Operations**

Entries into traffic patterns while descending may create collision hazards and should be avoided. Entry to the downwind leg should be at a 45-degree angle abeam the midpoint of the runway to be used for landing. Aircraft should always enter the pattern at pattern altitude, especially when flying over midfield and entering the downwind directly.

[PA.III.B.K2; AC 90-66]

9. How would a pilot know if an airport had non-standard, right traffic patterns for any or all runways?

A pilot can determine if an airport has non-standard, right traffic patterns for any or all runways by consulting the *Chart Supplement*, sectional charts, and airport diagrams. Airports with right traffic patterns will have this information noted to ensure pilots are aware of the deviation from the standard left-hand traffic pattern.

On sectional charts, right traffic patterns are indicated by an "RP" followed by the runway number (e.g., "RP 18" for Runway 18). If all runways at the airport require right traffic, it will typically state RP ALL. These annotations are found near the airport symbol on the chart.

In the *Chart Supplement*, the traffic pattern section provides detailed information about traffic flow, including any non-standard patterns, altitudes, and noise abatement procedures.

[PA.III.B.K1; AC 90-66]

10. What should a pilot know about back-taxi operations?

At non-towered airports, the FAA discourages back-taxi operations because they increase the risk of a surface collision with landing aircraft. Remember, at towered airports, ATC authorizes a back-taxi and provides collision avoidance for this operation.

[PA.III.B.K1; AC 90-66]

11. What is the recommended traffic advisory practice for pilots approaching a non-towered airport?

Approximately 10 miles from the destination airport, monitor the CTAF for other traffic and self-announce your position, altitude, and intention. Also, all traffic within a 10-mile radius of a non-towered airport, or a part-time-towered airport when the

Private Pilot Oral Exam Guide 219

Chapter 8 **Airport Operations**

control tower is not operating, should monitor and communicate their intentions on the designated CTAF as they approach to enter the traffic pattern to avoid a traffic conflict. For IFR-arriving aircraft, in addition to communicating with ATC, the pilot/crew is advised to monitor the airport's CTAF to obtain traffic volume.

[PA.III.B.K1; AC 90-66]

12. What communication should a pilot make prior to taking off at a non-towered airport?

On the airport's CTAF, you should communicate and coordinate your takeoff intention with aircraft inbound and in the traffic pattern and announce the runway to be used, the direction of flight on departure, or whether you intend to remain in the traffic pattern. This action will reduce the risk of a surface or midair collision during takeoff. Also, coordinate the takeoff with other traffic in the traffic pattern, traffic inbound for landing, or traffic on a straight-in approach to any of the airport's runways.

[PA.III.B.K1; AIM 4-1-9, AC 90-66, AC 90-48]

13. Whose responsibility is it to ensure collision avoidance during operations at non-towered airports?

The pilot-in-command (PIC) has the primary responsibility to see and avoid other aircraft and to help other aircraft see and avoid their aircraft. You should keep lights and strobes on. The use of any traffic pattern procedure does not alter the responsibility of each pilot to see and avoid other aircraft. Pilots are also encouraged to participate in Operation Lights On, a voluntary pilot safety program that is designed to improve the see-and-avoid capabilities.

[PA.III.B.R1; AC 90-66]

14. When operating in Class D airspace, what procedure should be used when approaching to land on a runway with a visual approach slope indicator?

Aircraft approaching to land on a runway served by a visual approach slope indicator (VASI) shall maintain an altitude at or above the glide slope until a lower altitude is necessary for a safe landing.

[PA.III.B.K1; 14 CFR 91.129]

Chapter 8 **Airport Operations**

15. Explain the recommended traffic pattern entry procedure at a non-towered airport.

Arriving aircraft should be at traffic pattern altitude and allow for sufficient time to view the entire traffic pattern before entering. Entries into traffic patterns while descending may create collision hazards and should be avoided. Entry to the downwind leg should be at a 45-degree angle abeam the midpoint of the runway to be used for landing. The pilot may use discretion to choose an alternate type of entry, especially when intending to cross over midfield, based upon the traffic and communication at the time of arrival.

[PA.III.B.K2; AC 90-66, AIM 4-3-3]

16. Explain the recommended traffic pattern departure procedure at a non-towered airport.

When departing the traffic pattern, airplanes should continue straight out or exit with a 45-degree left turn (right turn for right traffic pattern) beyond the departure end of the runway after reaching pattern altitude. Pilots need to be aware of any traffic entering the traffic pattern prior to commencing a turn.

[PA.III.B.K2; AC 90-66, AIM 4-3-3]

17. What is considered standard for a traffic pattern altitude?

Unless otherwise required by the applicable distance from cloud criteria (14 CFR §91.155):

a. Propeller-driven aircraft enter the traffic pattern at 1,000 feet AGL.

b. Large and turbine-powered aircraft enter the traffic pattern at an altitude of not less than 1,500 feet AGL or 500 feet above the established pattern altitude.

c. Helicopters operating in the traffic pattern may fly a pattern similar to the fixed-wing aircraft pattern, but at a lower altitude (500 feet AGL) and closer to the runway. This pattern may be on the opposite side of the runway from fixed-wing traffic when airspeed requires or for practice power-off landings (autorotation) and if local policy permits. Landings not to the runway must avoid the flow of fixed wing traffic.

(continued)

Private Pilot Oral Exam Guide   221

Chapter 8 **Airport Operations**

Note: Specific airport traffic pattern altitude information and any additional remarks may be found in the *Chart Supplement*.

[PA.III.B.K1; AIM 4-3-3]

18. How might a pilot know if an airport has a standard or non-standard traffic pattern altitude?

Traffic pattern altitudes if other than standard will be noted in the *Chart Supplement* data for the airport. Pilots are strongly encouraged to review the *Chart Supplement* data for any airports they visit prior to arrival.

[PA.III.B.K1; AC 90-66]

19. Explain the different methods a pilot may use to determine the proper runway and traffic pattern in use at an airport without an operating control tower.

a. At an airport with a full or part-time UNICOM station in operation, an advisory may be obtained which will usually include wind direction and velocity, favored or designated runway, right or left traffic, altimeter setting, known traffic, NOTAMs, etc.

b. Many airports are now providing completely automated weather, radio check capability, and airport advisory information on an automated UNICOM system. Availability of the automated UNICOM will be published in the *Chart Supplement* and approach charts.

c. At those airports where these services are not available, a segmented circle visual indicator system, if installed, is designed to provide traffic pattern information. The segmented circle system consists of the following components:

- The segmented circle
- The wind direction indicator (wind sock, cone, or tee)
- The landing direction indicator (a tetrahedron)
- Landing strip indicators
- Traffic pattern indicators

[PA.III.B.K1; AC 90-66, AIM 4-1-9, 4-3-4]

Chapter 8 **Airport Operations**

20. State the required action in a confrontation between aircraft of the same category for each of the following situations: converging, approaching head-on, or overtaking.

Converging—Aircraft to the right has the right-of-way.

Approaching head-on—Both aircraft shall alter course to the right.

Overtaking—The aircraft being overtaken has the right-of-way; the pilot of the overtaking aircraft shall alter course to the right.

[PA.III.B.K3; 14 CFR 91.113]

21. Explain the right-of-way rules that apply when two or more aircraft are approaching an airport for the purpose of landing.

Aircraft on final approach to land or while landing have the right-of-way over aircraft in flight or operating on the surface, except that they shall not take advantage of this rule to force an aircraft off the runway surface which has already landed and is attempting to make way for an aircraft on final approach. When two or more aircraft are approaching an airport for the purpose of landing, the aircraft at the lower altitude has the right-of-way, but it shall not take advantage of this rule to cut in front of another which is on final approach to land or to overtake that aircraft.

[PA.III.B.K3; 14 CFR 91.113, AC 90-66]

22. What are some recommended collision avoidance procedures and considerations while flying near airports and in traffic patterns?

Collision avoidance is a critical skill for pilots and involves both proactive measures and adherence to established procedures. Pilots should regularly scan the sky using an effective visual scan technique, such as dividing the field of vision into sectors and focusing on each for a few seconds. Avoid fixating on one area for too long. Before turning, climbing, or descending, clear the area by visually checking for traffic in all directions. It helps to maintain steady headings and altitudes unless deviation is required, avoiding sudden, unpredictable maneuvers.

It is advised that pilots monitor the Common Traffic Advisory Frequency (CTAF) at uncontrolled airports and listen for position reports. At towered airports, follow ATC instructions and stay

Private Pilot Oral Exam Guide 223

Chapter 8 **Airport Operations**

aware of other traffic. If equipped, monitor TCAS or ADS-B In for traffic advisories. These systems provide additional situational awareness of nearby aircraft.

Pilots should know and apply FAA right-of-way rules, such as yielding to aircraft on the right or giving way to landing traffic.

It is generally a good practice for a pilot to turn on landing or position lights when in areas of high-traffic density, such as approaching airports, traffic patterns, or busy airspace such as a training alert area, to increase their visibility to other pilots.

[PA.III.B.R1; AIM 4-4-15]

23. What is the order of right-of-way as applied to the different categories of aircraft?

Balloons
Gliders
Airships
Airplanes
Rotorcraft
Uncrewed aircraft systems

Aircraft towing or refueling other aircraft have the right-of-way over all other engine-driven aircraft.

Remember: BGAARU; Powered-lift aircraft follow airplane right-of-way rules.

Small uncrewed aircraft must yield the right of way to all aircraft, airborne vehicles, and launch and reentry vehicles.

[PA.III.B.K3; 14 CFR 91.113, 107.37]

24. When would an aircraft have the right-of-way over all other air traffic?

An aircraft in distress has the right-of-way over all other air traffic.

[PA.III.B.K3; 14 CFR 91.113]

25. Pilots should be aware that UAS (drones) are allowed to operate in what areas?

Small uncrewed aircraft may not be operated in Class B, Class C, or Class D airspace or within the lateral boundaries of the surface area of Class E airspace designated for an airport unless that person

Chapter 8 **Airport Operations**

has prior authorization from ATC. Additionally, no person may operate a small uncrewed aircraft in a manner that interferes with operations and traffic patterns at any airport, heliport, or seaplane base.

Small UAS may not be operated higher than 400 feet above ground level, unless the small uncrewed aircraft is flown within a 400-foot radius of a structure and does not fly higher than 400 feet above the structure's immediate uppermost limit. Some drones may be flown higher with ATC authorization for which a NOTAM is issued to notify pilots.

[PA.I.E.K1; AIM 7-6-6, AC 107-2, 14 CFR Part 107]

26. Identify several hazards that a pilot should consider when operating in an airport traffic pattern.

a. Collision hazards.

b. Distractions, task prioritization, loss of situational awareness, or disorientation.

c. Windshear and wake turbulence.

[PA.III.B.R1, PA.III.B.R2, PA.III.B.R3; FAA-S-ACS-6]

27. Explain how a pilot can mitigate the risk of an inflight collision when operating in the traffic pattern at a non-towered airport.

a. Be conspicuous. Use landing lights and strobes.

b. Announce your positions and intentions on the CTAF.

c. Be aware of possible no-radio aircraft.

d. Don't assert right-of-way if it will result in a collision hazard.

e. If there is an unresolved conflict, break off the approach and go around to the non-pattern side of the runway.

[PA.III.B.R1, PA.III.B.R2, PA.III.B.R3; FAA-H-8083-3]

28. Define the term *wake turbulence*.

Every aircraft generates wake turbulence while in flight. Wake turbulence is a function of an aircraft producing lift, resulting in the formation of two counterrotating vortices trailing behind the aircraft.

[PA.III.B.R3; AIM 7-4-1]

Private Pilot Oral Exam Guide   225

Chapter 8 **Airport Operations**

29. Explain how wake vortices are created.

The creation of a pressure differential over the wing surface generates lift. The lowest pressure occurs over the upper wing surface and the highest pressure under the wing. This pressure differential triggers the roll up of the airflow at the rear of the wing, resulting in swirling air masses trailing downstream of the wing tips. After the roll up is completed, the wake consists of two counterrotating cylindrical vortices.

[PA.III.B.R3; AIM 7-4-2]

30. What factors govern the strength of a vortex generated by an aircraft?

Weight, speed, wingspan, and shape of the generating aircraft's wing all govern the strength of the vortex. The vortex characteristics of any given aircraft can also be changed by extension of flaps or other wing configuring devices. However, the vortex strength from an aircraft increases proportionately to an increase in operating weight or a decrease in aircraft speed. Since the turbulence from a "dirty" aircraft configuration hastens wake decay, the greatest vortex strength occurs when the generating aircraft is *heavy*, *clean*, and *slow*.

[PA.III.B.R3; AIM 7-4-3]

31. Where is an encounter with wake turbulence likely to occur?

Pilot should avoid the area below and behind the wake-generating aircraft, especially at low altitude where even a momentary wake encounter could be catastrophic. Pilots should also be particularly alert in calm wind conditions and situations where the vortices could:

a. Remain in the touchdown area.

b. Drift from aircraft operating on a nearby runway.

c. Sink into the takeoff or landing path from a crossing runway.

d. Sink into the traffic pattern from other airport operations.

e. Sink into the flight path of VFR aircraft operating on the hemispheric altitude 500 feet below.

[PA.III.B.R3; AIM 7-4-5]

Chapter 8 **Airport Operations**

32. What kind of aircraft conditions or configurations make the worst kind of wake turbulence, which a pilot should be aware of and mitigate the risks of by adjusting their arrival timing?

Since the turbulence from a dirty aircraft configuration, with flaps and landing gear extended, hastens wake decay, the greatest vortex strength occurs when the generating aircraft is *heavy*, *clean*, and *slow*. Be alert to the wake turbulence you could be generating to smaller aircraft.

[PA.III.B.R3; AC 90-66]

33. Explain the operational procedures that should be followed when wake vortices are suspected to exist.

a. *Landing behind a larger aircraft on the same runway*—Stay at or above the larger aircraft's final approach flight path. Note its touchdown point and land beyond it.

b. *Landing behind a larger aircraft, when parallel runway is closer than 2,500 feet*—Consider possible drift to your runway. Stay at or above the larger aircraft's final approach flight path, and note its touchdown point.

c. *Landing behind a larger aircraft, crossing runway*—Cross above the larger aircraft's flight path.

d. *Landing behind a departing larger aircraft on the same runway*—Note the larger aircraft's rotation point, and land well prior to rotation point.

e. *Landing behind a departing larger aircraft, crossing runway*—Note the larger aircraft's rotation point. If past the intersection, continue the approach, and land prior to the intersection. If the larger aircraft rotates prior to the intersection, avoid flight below the larger aircraft's flight path. Abandon the approach unless a landing is ensured well before reaching the intersection.

f. *Departing behind a large aircraft*—Note the larger aircraft's rotation point and rotate prior to the larger aircraft's rotation point. Continue climbing above the larger aircraft's climb path until turning clear of the larger aircraft's wake. Avoid subsequent headings that will cross below and behind a larger aircraft.

(continued)

Private Pilot Oral Exam Guide 227

Chapter 8 **Airport Operations**

g. *Intersection takeoffs, same runway*—Be alert to adjacent larger aircraft operations, especially of your runway. If intersection takeoff clearance is received, avoid subsequent heading which will cross below a larger aircraft's path.

h. *Departing or landing after a larger aircraft executing a low approach, missed approach or touch-and-go landing*—Vortices settle and move laterally near the ground. Because of this, the vortex hazard may exist along the runway and in your flight path after a larger aircraft has executed a low approach, missed approach, or a touch-and-go landing, particularly in light quartering wind conditions. You should ensure that an interval of at least 2 minutes has elapsed before your takeoff or landing.

i. *En route VFR (thousand-foot altitude plus 500 feet)*—Avoid flight below and behind a large aircraft's path. If a larger aircraft is observed above or on the same track (meeting or overtaking) adjust your position laterally, preferably upwind.

Remember: Acceptance of instructions from ATC is an acknowledgment that the pilot will ensure safe takeoff and landing intervals and accept the responsibility for providing wake turbulence separation.

[PA.III.B.R3; AIM 7-4-6]

34. What type of automated weather is provided at most controlled airports?

The Automated Terminal Information Service (ATIS) is a recording of the local weather conditions and other pertinent non-control information broadcast on a local frequency in a looped format. It is normally updated once per hour but is updated more often when changing local conditions warrant. Important information is broadcast on ATIS including weather, runways in use, specific ATC procedures, and any airport construction activity that could affect taxi planning.

[PA.III.B.K4; AIM 4-1-13]

Chapter 8 **Airport Operations**

35. What type of automated weather is available at uncontrolled airports?

Many airports throughout the National Airspace System are equipped with either Automated Surface Observing System (ASOS) or Automated Weather Observing System (AWOS). At uncontrolled airports that are equipped with ASOS/AWOS with ground-to-air broadcast capability, the one-minute updated airport weather should be available to you within approximately 25 NM of the airport below 10,000 feet. The frequency for the weather broadcast will be published on sectional charts and in the *Chart Supplement*.

[PA.III.B.K4; AIM 4-3-27]

Private Pilot Oral Exam Guide   229

National Airspace System 9

Chapter 9 **National Airspace System**

A. General

1. What are the two categories of airspace in the National Airspace System?

Regulatory and non-regulatory.

[PA.I.E.K1; FAA-H-8083-25]

2. Within the two categories of airspace in the NAS, what are the four types of airspace?

a. Controlled airspace
b. Uncontrolled airspace
c. Special use airspace
d. Other airspace

[PA.I.E.K1; FAA-H-8083-25]

3. Explain the factors that determine the category and type of airspace an area will have.

The categories and types of airspace are dictated by the complexity or density of aircraft movements, nature of the operations conducted within the airspace, level of safety required, and national and public interest.

Exam Tip: Be prepared to explain the type of airspace your planned route of flight will take you through from departure to arrival at your destination. Know the required visibility, cloud clearance, and communication requirements at any point and altitude along your route of flight. Also, expect "what if you're here" questions concerning special use airspace, special VFR clearances, etc.

[PA.I.E.K1; FAA-H-8083-25]

4. Briefly describe the terms *controlled airspace* and *uncontrolled airspace*.

Controlled airspace—A generic term that covers the different classifications of airspace and defined dimensions within which air traffic control (ATC) service is provided in accordance with the airspace classification. Controlled airspace consists of Class A, Class B, Class C, Class D, and Class E.

Uncontrolled airspace—Or Class G airspace, is the portion of the airspace that has not been designated as Class A, B, C, D, or E. It is therefore designated uncontrolled airspace. Class G

232 Aviation Supplies & Academics

Chapter 9 **National Airspace System**

airspace extends from the surface to the base of the overlying Class
E airspace. Although ATC has no authority or responsibility to
control air traffic, pilots should remember there are visual flight
rules (VFR) minimums that apply to Class G airspace.

[PA.I.E.K1; FAA-H-8083-25]

B. Controlled Airspace

1. What is Class A airspace?

Generally, that airspace from 18,000 feet MSL up to and including
FL600, including that airspace overlying the waters within 12
NM of the coast of the 48 contiguous states and Alaska; and
designated international airspace beyond 12 NM off the coast
of the 48 contiguous states and Alaska within areas of domestic
radio navigational signal or ATC radar coverage, and within which
domestic procedures are applied.

[PA.I.E.K1; AIM 3-2-2]

2. Can a flight under VFR be conducted within Class A airspace?

No, unless otherwise authorized by ATC, each person operating
an aircraft in Class A airspace must operate that aircraft under
instrument flight rules (IFR).

[PA.I.E.K1; 14 CFR 91.135, AIM 3-2-2]

3. What is the minimum pilot certification for operations conducted within Class A airspace?

The pilot must hold at least a Private Pilot Certificate with an
Instrument Rating.

[PA.I.E.K1; 14 CFR 91.135]

4. What minimum equipment is required for flight operations within Class A airspace?

a. A two-way radio capable of communicating with ATC on the
frequency assigned.

b. A Mode C altitude encoding transponder.

c. ADS-B and TIS-B equipment operating on 1090 MHz ES
frequency.

(continued)

Private Pilot Oral Exam Guide   233

Chapter 9 **National Airspace System**

d. Equipped with instruments and equipment required for IFR operations.

[PA.I.E.K1; 14 CFR 91.135, 91.215, 91.225]

5. How is Class A airspace depicted on navigational charts?

Class A airspace is not specifically charted.

[PA.I.E.K2; AIM 3-2-2]

6. What is the definition of Class B airspace?

Generally, that airspace from the surface to 10,000 feet MSL surrounding the nation's busiest airports in terms of IFR operations or passenger enplanements. The configuration of each Class B airspace area is individually tailored and consists of a surface area and two or more layers (some Class B airspace areas resemble upside-down wedding cakes) and is designed to contain all published instrument procedures once an aircraft enters the airspace.

[PA.I.E.K1; AIM 3-2-3]

7. What minimum pilot certification is required to operate an aircraft within Class B airspace?

No person may take off or land a civil aircraft at an airport within a Class B airspace area or operate a civil aircraft within a Class B airspace area unless:

a. The pilot-in-command holds at least a Private Pilot Certificate;

b. The pilot-in-command holds a Recreational Pilot Certificate and has met the requirements of 14 CFR §61.101(d); or the requirements for a student pilot seeking a Recreational Pilot Certificate in 14 CFR §61.94;

c. The pilot-in-command holds a Sport Pilot Certificate and has met the requirements of 14 CFR §61.325; or the requirements for a student pilot seeking a Recreational Pilot Certificate in 14 CFR §61.94; or

d. The aircraft is operated by a student pilot who has met the requirements of 14 CFR §61.94 or §61.95 of this chapter, as applicable.

Chapter 9 **National Airspace System**

Note: Certain Class B airspace areas do not allow pilot operations to be conducted to or from the primary airport unless the pilot-in-command holds at least a Private Pilot Certificate (example: Dallas/ Fort Worth International).

[PA.I.E.K1; 14 CFR 91.131]

8. What is the minimum equipment required for operations of an aircraft within Class B airspace?

a. An operable two-way radio capable of communications with ATC on the appropriate frequencies for that area.

b. A Mode C altitude encoding transponder.

c. ADS-B Out equipment—operating on UAT 978 MHz or 1090 MHz ES frequency.

d. If IFR, an operable VOR or TACAN receiver or an operable and suitable RNAV system.

[PA.I.E.K1; 14 CFR 91.131, 91.215, 91.225]

9. Before operating an aircraft into Class B airspace, what basic requirement must be met?

Arriving aircraft must obtain an ATC clearance from the ATC facility having jurisdiction for that area prior to operating an aircraft in that area.

[PA.I.E.K1; 14 CFR 91.131]

10. What minimum weather conditions are required when conducting VFR flight operations within Class B airspace?

VFR flight operations must be conducted clear of clouds with at least 3 SM flight visibility.

[PA.I.E.K1; 14 CFR 91.155]

11. How is Class B airspace depicted on navigational charts?

Class B airspace is charted on Sectional Charts, IFR enroute low altitude charts, and Terminal Area Charts. A solid, shaded blue line depicts the lateral limits of Class B airspace. Numbers indicate the base and top, e.g., 100/25, 100/SFC.

[PA.I.E.K2; AIM 3-2-3]

Private Pilot Oral Exam Guide 235

Chapter 9 **National Airspace System**

12. What basic ATC services are provided to all aircraft operating within Class B airspace?

VFR pilots will be provided sequencing and separation from other aircraft while operating within Class B airspace.

[PA.I.E.K1; AIM 3-2-3]

13. It becomes apparent that wake turbulence may be encountered while ATC is providing sequencing and separation services in Class B airspace. Whose responsibility is it to avoid this turbulence?

The pilot-in-command is responsible. The services provided by ATC do not relieve pilots of their responsibilities to see and avoid other traffic operating in basic VFR weather conditions, to adjust their operations and flight path as necessary to preclude serious wake turbulence encounters, to maintain appropriate terrain and obstruction clearance, or to remain in weather conditions equal to or better than the minimums required by 14 CFR §91.155.

[PA.I.E.K1; AIM 3-2-3]

14. What is the maximum speed allowed when operating inside Class B airspace, under 10,000 feet and within a Class D surface area?

Unless otherwise authorized or required by ATC, no person may operate an aircraft at or below 2,500 feet above the surface within 4 NM of the primary airport of a Class C or Class D airspace area at an indicated airspeed of more than 200 knots. This restriction does not apply to operations conducted within a Class B airspace area. Such operations shall comply with the below 10,000 feet MSL restriction: "No person shall operate an aircraft below 10,000 feet MSL, at an indicated airspeed of more than 250 knots."

[PA.I.E.K1; 14 CFR 91.117]

15. When operating beneath the lateral limits of Class B airspace, or in a VFR corridor designated through Class B airspace, what maximum speed is authorized?

No person may operate an aircraft in the airspace underlying a Class B airspace area designated for an airport or in a VFR corridor designated through such a Class B airspace area, at an indicated airspeed of more than 200 knots (230 mph).

[PA.I.E.K1; 14 CFR 91.117]

Chapter 9 **National Airspace System**

16. What is a VFR corridor?

A VFR corridor is a designated airspace route that allows pilots flying under visual flight rules (VFR) to safely navigate through or around busy areas, typically around airports with controlled airspace, without needing direct clearance from ATC. These corridors are, in effect, a hole through Class B airspace. They are often established in high-traffic areas, such as near large airports or busy metropolitan areas, to help separate VFR traffic from IFR traffic, reducing the risk of midair collisions.

VFR corridors are usually marked on sectional charts and provide pilots with a structured route that keeps them within VFR conditions while transiting through or near controlled airspace, such as Class B, C, or D. The routes are designed to ensure safe separation between different types of air traffic.

Pilots flying through a VFR corridor must adhere to the specified altitudes and procedures outlined in the charts. While pilots may not require an ATC clearance to fly through the corridor, they are still responsible for maintaining communication with ATC and adhering to any instructions or advisories provided.

[PA.I.E.K3; AIM 3-5-5]

17. How may a pilot use published VFR routes, or VFR flyways, to help them transition Class B airspace without an ATC clearance or communication with air traffic control?

A pilot may use published VFR routes or VFR flyways to help transition Class B airspace without an ATC clearance or communication by following these designated routes that provide a safe, structured path through busy airspace. These routes are published in VFR navigation charts (VNCs) and are designed for pilots flying VFR to navigate through or around Class B airspace while avoiding conflicts with other air traffic.

VFR routes are typically designed to help pilots stay clear of congested airspace or minimize the need for direct communication with ATC. However, it is important to note that even on these routes, pilots must remain outside (typically below the shelf) of Class B airspace unless they have explicit permission to enter, which usually requires ATC communication.

By using these routes, pilots can maintain separation from higher-density traffic, especially around major airports, while still

Private Pilot Oral Exam Guide 237

Chapter 9 **National Airspace System**

complying with airspace regulations. It is important to check for specific route details, such as altitudes and restrictions, before planning to use a VFR route. Pilots should also be aware that VFR flyways may only be available in certain areas or times, so preflight planning and checking current charts is essential.

[PA.I.E.K3; AIM 3-5-5]

18. What is Class C airspace?

Generally, Class C airspace is that airspace from the surface to 4,000 feet above the airport elevation (charted in MSL) surrounding those airports that have an operational control tower, are serviced by a radar approach control, and have a certain number of IFR operations or passenger enplanements.

[PA.I.E.K1; AIM 3-2-4]

19. What are the basic dimensions of Class C airspace?

Although the configuration of each Class C airspace area is individually tailored, the airspace usually consists of a 5 NM radius core surface area that extends from the surface up to 4,000 feet above the airport elevation, and a 10 NM radius shelf area that extends from 1,200 feet to 4,000 feet above the airport elevation. The outer area radius will be 20 NM, with some variations based on site specific requirements. The outer area extends outward from the primary airport and extends from the lower limits of radar/radio coverage up to the ceiling of the approach control airspace.

[PA.I.E.K1; AIM 3-2-4]

20. What minimum pilot certification is required to operate an aircraft within Class C airspace?

Any pilot with a Student Pilot Certificate or higher certificate level may operate in Class C airspace.

[PA.I.E.K1; AIM 3-2-4]

21. What minimum equipment is required to operate an aircraft within Class C airspace?

Unless otherwise authorized by the ATC having jurisdiction over the Class C airspace area, no person may operate an aircraft within a Class C airspace area designated for an airport unless that aircraft is equipped with the following:

238 Aviation Supplies & Academics

Chapter 9 **National Airspace System**

a. A two-way radio.

b. Automatic pressure altitude reporting equipment with Mode C capability.

c. ADS-B Out equipment—operating on UAT 978 MHz or 1090 MHz ES frequency.

[PA.I.E.K1; 14 CFR 91.130, 91.215, 91.225]

22. When operating an aircraft through Class C airspace or to an airport within Class C airspace, what basic requirement must be met?

Each person must establish two-way radio communications with the ATC facilities providing air traffic services prior to entering that airspace and thereafter maintain those communications while within that airspace.

[PA.I.E.K1; 14 CFR 91.130]

23. Define what is meant by *established* in this context: "Two-way radio communications must be established prior to entering Class C airspace."

If a controller responds to a radio call with, "(aircraft call sign) standby," radio communications have been established. It is important to understand that if the controller responds to the initial radio call *without* using the aircraft identification, radio communications have *not* been established and the pilot may not enter the Class C airspace.

[PA.I.E.K1; AIM 3-2-4]

24. When departing a satellite airport without an operative control tower located within Class C airspace, what requirement must be met?

Each person must establish and maintain two-way radio communications with the ATC facilities having jurisdiction over the Class C airspace area as soon as practicable after departing.

[PA.I.E.K1; 14 CFR 91.130]

Private Pilot Oral Exam Guide 239

Chapter 9 **National Airspace System**

25. What minimum weather conditions are required when conducting VFR flight operations within Class C airspace?

VFR flight operations within Class C airspace require 3 SM flight visibility and cloud clearances of at least 500 feet below, 1,000 feet above, and 2,000 feet horizontal to clouds.

[PA.I.E.K1; 14 CFR 91.155]

26. How is Class C airspace depicted on navigational charts?

A solid magenta line is used to depict Class C airspace. Class C airspace is charted on Sectional Charts, IFR enroute low altitude charts, and Terminal Area Charts where appropriate.

[PA.I.E.K2; AIM 3-2-4]

27. What type of air traffic control services are provided when operating within Class C airspace?

When two-way radio communications and radar contact are established, all VFR aircraft are:

a. Sequenced to the primary airport.

b. Provided Class C services within the Class C airspace and the outer area.

c. Provided basic radar services beyond the outer area on a workload permitting basis. This can be terminated by the controller if workload dictates.

[PA.I.E.K1; AIM 3-2-4]

28. Where is Mode C transponder and ADS-B Out equipment required?

In general, the regulations require aircraft to be equipped with an operable Mode C transponder and ADS-B Out equipment when operating:

a. In Class A, Class B, or Class C airspace areas.

b. Above the ceiling and within the lateral boundaries of Class B or Class C airspace up to 10,000 feet MSL.

c. Class E airspace at and above 10,000 feet MSL within the 48 contiguous states and the District of Columbia, excluding the airspace at and below 2,500 feet AGL.

240 Aviation Supplies & Academics

Chapter 9 **National Airspace System**

d. Within 30 miles of a Class B airspace primary airport, below 10,000 feet MSL (Mode C Veil).

e. For ADS-B Out: Class E airspace at and above 3,000 feet MSL over the Gulf of Mexico from the coastline of the United States out to 12 nautical miles.

f. All aircraft flying into, within, or across the contiguous United States ADIZ.

Note: Civil and military aircraft should operate with the transponder in the altitude reporting mode and ADS-B Out transmissions enabled (if equipped) at all airports, any time the aircraft is positioned on any portion of an airport movement area. This includes all defined taxiways and runways.

[PA.I.E.K1; AIM 4-1-20, 14 CFR 91.215, 91.225, 99.13]

29. If your Mode C transponder/ADS-B Out equipment fails while en route, can you continue flight into Class B or Class C airspace?

If your Mode C transponder or ADS-B Out equipment fails en route, continuing flight into Class B or Class C airspace depends on certain conditions. According to FAA regulations, these airspaces require a functioning Mode C transponder and ADS-B Out equipment. However, if the equipment fails after departure and you're already en route, you must notify ATC as soon as possible and request permission to continue.

ATC may allow you to proceed through Class B or Class C airspace at their discretion, provided it is operationally safe. Without ATC authorization, entering these airspaces is prohibited. If the equipment fails before departure and the flight plan includes operating in Class B or Class C airspace, you must obtain a deviation authorization from ATC before takeoff.

[PA.I.E.K1; AIM 4-1-20]

30. Is Mode C transponder/ADS-B Out equipment required for flight over Class C airspace if operating below 10,000 feet MSL?

Yes, Mode C transponder and ADS-B Out equipment are required for flight over Class C airspace, even if operating below 10,000 feet MSL. According to FAA regulations, ADS-B Out equipment is mandatory within a 30 NM radius of the primary airport in Class B

Private Pilot Oral Exam Guide 241

Chapter 9 **National Airspace System**

airspace (Mode C Veil) and above the ceiling of Class C airspace up to 10,000 feet MSL.

[PA.I.E.K1; AIM 4-1-20]

31. What is the maximum speed an aircraft may be operated within Class C airspace?

Unless otherwise authorized or required by ATC, no person may operate an aircraft at or below 2,500 feet above the surface within 4 NM of the primary airport of a Class C airspace area at an indicated speed of more than 200 knots (230 mph).

[PA.I.E.K1; AIM 3-2-4]

32. What is Class D airspace?

Generally, Class D airspace extends upward from the surface to 2,500 feet above the airport elevation (charted in MSL) surrounding those airports that have an operational control tower. The configuration of each Class D airspace area is individually tailored and when instrument procedures are published, the airspace will normally be designed to contain those procedures.

[PA.I.E.K1; AIM 3-2-5]

33. When operating an aircraft through Class D airspace or to an airport within Class D airspace, what requirement must be met?

Each person must establish two-way radio communications with the ATC facilities providing air traffic services prior to entering that airspace and thereafter maintain those communications while within that airspace.

Note: ADS-B Out equipment is not required in Class D airspace provided that the Class D airspace is not located within a 30 NM Mode C Veil.

[PA.I.E.K1; 14 CFR 91.129]

Chapter 9 **National Airspace System**

34. When departing a satellite airport without an operative control tower located within Class D airspace, what requirement must be met?

Each person must establish and maintain two-way radio communications with the ATC facility having jurisdiction over the Class D airspace area as soon as practicable after departing.

[PA.I.E.K1; 14 CFR 91.129]

35. Is an ATC clearance required if flight operations are conducted through a Class E surface area arrival extension?

Class E airspace may be designated as extensions to Class B, Class C, Class D, and Class E surface areas. Class E airspace extensions begin at the surface and extend up to the overlying controlled airspace. The extensions provide controlled airspace to contain standard instrument approach procedures without imposing a communications requirement on pilots operating under VFR. Surface area arrival extensions become part of the surface area and are in effect during the same times as the surface area.

[PA.I.E.K1; AIM 3-2-5, 3-2-6]

36. What minimum weather conditions are required when conducting VFR flight operations within Class D airspace?

VFR flight operations within Class D airspace require 3 SM flight visibility and cloud clearances of at least 500 feet below, 1,000 feet above and 2,000 feet horizontal to clouds.

[PA.I.E.K1; 14 CFR 91.155]

37. How is Class D airspace depicted on navigational charts?

Class D airspace areas are depicted on Sectional and Terminal Area Charts with blue segmented lines, and on IFR enroute low altitude charts with a boxed [D].

[PA.I.E.K2; AIM 3-2-5]

Private Pilot Oral Exam Guide   243

Chapter 9 **National Airspace System**

38. What type of air traffic control services are provided when operating within Class D airspace?

No separation services are provided to VFR aircraft. When meteorological conditions permit, regardless of the type of flight plan or whether or not under the control of a radar facility, the pilot is responsible to see and avoid other traffic, terrain, or obstacles. A controller, on a workload permitting basis, will provide radar traffic information, safety alerts, and traffic information for sequencing purposes.

[PA.I.E.K1; AIM 3-2-5, 5-5-8, 5-5-10]

39. What is the maximum speed an aircraft may be operated within Class D airspace?

Unless otherwise authorized or required by ATC, no person may operate an aircraft at or below 2,500 feet above the surface within 4 NM of the primary airport of a Class D airspace area at an indicated airspeed of more than 200 knots (230 mph).

[PA.I.E.K1; AIM 3-2-5]

40. When a control tower located at an airport within Class D airspace ceases operation for the day, what happens to the lower limit of the controlled airspace?

During the hours the tower is not in operation, Class E surface area rules, or a combination of Class E rules down to 700 feet AGL and Class G rules to the surface, will become applicable. Check the *Chart Supplement* for specifics.

[PA.I.E.K1; AIM 3-2-5]

41. Will all airports with an operating control tower always have Class D airspace surrounding them?

No; some airports do not have the required weather reporting capability necessary for surface-based controlled airspace. The controlled airspace over these airports normally begins at 700 feet or 1,200 feet AGL and can be determined from visual aeronautical charts.

[PA.I.E.K1; AIM 4-3-2]

Chapter 9 **National Airspace System**

42. What is the definition of *controlled airspace*?

Controlled airspace is airspace of defined dimensions within which air traffic control service is provided to IFR flights and to VFR flights in accordance with the airspace classification. Controlled airspace is a generic term that covers Class A, Class B, Class C, Class D, and Class E airspace.

[PA.I.E.K1; P/CG]

43. What are some different examples of Class E airspace?

a. *Surface area designated for an airport where a control tower is not in operation*—Class E surface areas extend upward from the surface to a designated altitude or to the adjacent or overlying controlled airspace and are configured to contain all instrument procedures.

b. *Extension to a surface area*—Class E airspace may be designated as extensions to Class B, Class C, Class D, and Class E surface areas. Class E airspace extensions begin at the surface and extend up to the overlying controlled airspace. The extensions provide controlled airspace to contain standard instrument approach procedures without imposing a communications requirement on pilots operating under VFR.

c. *Airspace used for transition*—Class E airspace areas may be designated for transitioning aircraft to/from the terminal or enroute environment. They extend upward from either 700 feet AGL or 1,200 feet AGL and are designated for airports with an approved instrument procedure. The 700 feet/1,200 feet AGL Class E airspace transition areas remain in effect continuously, regardless of airport operating hours or surface area status.

d. *Enroute domestic areas*—Class E airspace areas that extend upward from a specified altitude and provide controlled airspace in those areas where there is a requirement to provide IFR enroute ATC services, but the Federal airway system is inadequate.

e. *Federal airways and low-altitude RNAV routes*—Federal airways and low-altitude RNAV routes are Class E airspace areas and, unless otherwise specified, extend upward from 1,200 feet AGL to, but not including 18,000 feet MSL.

f. *Offshore airspace areas*—Class E airspace areas that extend upward from a specified altitude to, but not including, 18,000

Private Pilot Oral Exam Guide 245

Chapter 9 **National Airspace System**

feet MSL. These areas provide controlled airspace beyond 12 miles from the coast of the United States in those areas where there is a requirement to provide IFR enroute ATC services, and within which the US is applying domestic procedures.

g. *Unless designated at a lower altitude*—Class E airspace in the US consists of the airspace extending upward from 14,500 feet MSL to, but not including, 18,000 feet MSL overlying the 48 contiguous states, the District of Columbia, and Alaska, including the waters within 12 NM from the coast of the 48 contiguous states and Alaska.

h. *The airspace above FL 600 is Class E airspace.*

[PA.I.E.K1; AIM 3-2-6]

44. What are the operating rules and pilot/equipment requirements to operate within Class E airspace?

a. *Pilot certification*—Student Pilot Certificate.

b. *Equipment:*

i. An operable radar beacon transponder with automatic altitude reporting capability and operable ADS-B Out equipment is required at and above 10,000 feet MSL within the 48 contiguous states and the District of Columbia, excluding the airspace at and below 2,500 feet above the surface; and

ii. Operable ADS-B Out equipment at and above 3,000 feet MSL over the Gulf of Mexico from the coastline of the United States out to 12 NM offshore.

[PA.I.E.K1; AIM 3-2-6]

45. Unless otherwise authorized or required by ATC, what is the maximum indicated airspeed at which a person may operate an aircraft below 10,000 feet MSL?

No person may operate an aircraft below 10,000 feet MSL at an indicated airspeed of more than 250 knots (288 mph).

[PA.I.E.K1; 14 CFR 91.117]

Chapter 9 **National Airspace System**

46. When a Class C or Class D surface area is not in effect continuously (for example, where a control tower only operates part-time), what will happen to the surface area airspace when the tower closes?

The surface area airspace will change to either a Class E surface area or Class G airspace. In such cases, the "Airspace" entry for the airport in the *Chart Supplement* will state "other times Class E" or "other times Class G." When a part-time surface area changes to Class E airspace, the Class E arrival extensions will remain in effect as Class E airspace. If a part-time Class C, Class D, or Class E surface area becomes Class G airspace, the arrival extensions will change to Class G at the same time.

[PA.I.E.K1; AIM 3-2-6]

47. Explain the purpose of Class E transition areas.

Class E transition areas extend upward from either 700 feet AGL (magenta vignette) or 1,200 feet AGL (blue vignette) and are designated for airports with an approved instrument procedure. Class E transition areas exist to help separate (via cloud clearance) arriving and departing IFR traffic from VFR aircraft operating in the vicinity.

Note: Do not confuse the 700-foot and 1,200-foot Class E transition areas with surface areas or surface area extensions. Class E Surface (SFC) Airspace is symbolized with a magenta dashed line.

[PA.I.E.K1; AIM 3-2-6]

48. Are you required to establish communications with a control tower located within Class E airspace?

Yes, unless otherwise authorized or required by ATC, no person may operate an aircraft to, from, through, or on an airport having an operational control tower unless two-way communications are maintained between that aircraft and the control tower. Communications must be established prior to 4 NM from the airport, up to and including 2,500 feet AGL.

Note: This is not a mistake, but they are not very common. In some limited cases airports have an operating control tower but are not Class D airspace. The lack of Class D airspace does not preclude the requirement to contact the control tower if it is in operation.

[PA.I.E.K1; 14 CFR 91.127]

Private Pilot Oral Exam Guide 247

Chapter 9 **National Airspace System**

49. How is Class E airspace depicted on navigational charts?

Class E airspace below 14,500 feet MSL is charted on sectional, terminal, and IFR enroute low altitude charts. The lateral and vertical limits of all Class E controlled airspace up to but not including 18,000 feet are shown by narrow bands of vignette on sectional and terminal area charts. Controlled airspace floors of 700 feet AGL are defined by a magenta vignette; floors other than 700 feet that abut uncontrolled airspace are defined by a blue vignette; differing floors greater than 700 feet AGL are annotated by a symbol and a number indicating the floor. If the ceiling is less than 18,000 feet MSL, the value (prefixed by the word "ceiling") is shown along the limits of the controlled airspace.

[PA.I.E.K2; AIM 3-2-6, FAA CUG]

50. How are Class E surface extension areas depicted on navigational charts?

Class E airspace areas that serve as extensions to Class B, Class C, and Class D airspace are depicted by a magenta segmented line.

[PA.I.E.K2; FAA CUG]

51. What minimum flight visibility and clearance from clouds are required for VFR flight in the following situations?

Class C, D, or E Airspace

Less than 10,000 feet MSL:
- Visibility—3 SM.
- Cloud clearance—500 feet below, 1,000 feet above, 2,000 feet horizontal.

At or above 10,000 feet MSL:
- Visibility—5 SM.
- Cloud clearance—1,000 feet below, 1,000 feet above, 1 SM horizontal.

Class G Airspace

1,200 feet or less above the surface (regardless of MSL altitude):
Day:
- Visibility—1 SM.
- Cloud clearance—Clear of clouds.

Night:
- Visibility—3 SM.
- Cloud clearance—500 feet below, 1,000 feet above, 2,000 feet horizontal.

Chapter 9 **National Airspace System**

More than 1,200 feet above the surface but less than 10,000 feet MSL:

Day:
- Visibility—1 SM.
- Cloud clearance—500 feet below, 1,000 feet above, 2,000 feet horizontal.

Night:
- Visibility—3 SM.
- Cloud clearance—500 feet below, 1,000 feet above, 2,000 feet horizontal.

More than 1,200 feet above the surface and at or above 10,000 feet MSL:

- Visibility—5 SM.
- Cloud clearance—1,000 feet below, 1,000 feet above, 1 SM horizontal.

Exam Tip: An airplane traveling at 100 knots will travel 2,000 feet in 12 seconds. To be more than 2,000 feet laterally from a cloud, you would have to be at least 12 seconds away from it in level flight at this speed. This would additionally mean that between clouds, you would have to be able to fly 24 seconds. If you are closer than this to a cloud, you are not meeting VFR lateral cloud clearances in many airspaces. Be aware of this on your practical test; *many* applicants have been issued disapprovals for failure to maintain cloud clearances!

[PA.I.E.K1; 14 CFR 91.155]

52. What are the basic VFR weather minimums required for operation of an aircraft into Class B, Class C, Class D, or Class E airspace?

1,000-foot ceiling and 3 miles visibility. Except as provided in 14 CFR §91.157 (special VFR), no person may:

a. Operate an aircraft beneath the ceiling under VFR within the lateral boundaries of controlled airspace designated to the surface for an airport when the ceiling is less than 1,000 feet.

b. Take off or land an aircraft, or enter the traffic pattern of an airport, under VFR, within the lateral boundaries of the surface areas of Class B, Class C, Class D, or Class E airspace designated for an airport unless ground visibility at that airport

Private Pilot Oral Exam Guide 249

Chapter 9 **National Airspace System**

is at least 3 SM or, if ground visibility is not reported, unless flight visibility during landing or takeoff or while operating in the traffic pattern is at least 3 SM.

[PA.I.E.K1; 14 CFR 91.155]

53. Why do the Class E airspace cloud clearance and visibility requirements change above 10,000 feet?

This is because of the increased speeds and potential traffic at higher altitudes. Aircraft operating at and above 10,000 feet often travel faster and require greater time and distance to detect and avoid other aircraft.

Below 10,000 feet, the requirements are 3 statute miles visibility, with clearance of 500 feet below, 1,000 feet above, and 2,000 feet horizontally from clouds. This provides sufficient separation for slower-moving aircraft commonly found at lower altitudes.

Above 10,000 feet, the requirements increase to 5 statute miles visibility, with 1,000 feet below, 1,000 feet above, and 1 SM horizontally from clouds. The greater distances account for the faster speeds of high-performance aircraft typically operating at these altitudes. These increased requirements improve safety by giving pilots more time to visually detect and avoid other traffic or obstructions, especially when visibility is reduced or when flying near clouds that could obscure other aircraft.

[PA.I.E.K1; FAA Safety ALC-25]

54. If VFR flight minimums cannot be maintained, can a VFR flight be made into Class B, C, D, or E airspace?

No, with one exception. A "special VFR clearance" may be obtained from ATC prior to operating within a Class B, Class C, Class D, or Class E surface area provided the flight can remain clear of clouds with at least 1 SM ground visibility if taking off or landing, or 1 SM flight visibility for operations within Class B, Class C, Class D, and Class E surface areas.

[PA.I.E.K4; AIM 4-4-6]

250   Aviation Supplies & Academics

Chapter 9 **National Airspace System**

55. Are special VFR clearances always available to pilots in all classes of airspace?

A VFR pilot may request and be given a clearance to enter, leave, or operate within most Class D and Class E surface areas and some Class B and Class C surface areas, traffic permitting, and providing such flight will not delay IFR operations.

Note: Special VFR operations by fixed-wing aircraft are prohibited in some Class B and Class C surface areas due to the volume of IFR traffic. A list of these Class B and Class C surface areas is contained in 14 CFR Part 91. They are also depicted on Sectional Aeronautical Charts.

[PA.I.E.K4; AIM 4-4-6]

56. If it becomes apparent that a special VFR clearance will be necessary, what facility should the pilot contact in order to obtain one?

When a control tower is located within a Class B, Class C, or Class D surface area, requests for clearances should be made to the tower. In a Class E surface area, clearance may be obtained from the nearest tower, FSS, or center.

[PA.I.E.K4; AIM 4-4-6]

57. Can a special VFR clearance be obtained into or out of Class B, C, D, or E airspace at night?

Special VFR operations by fixed-wing aircraft are prohibited between sunset and sunrise unless the pilot is instrument-rated and the aircraft is equipped for IFR flight.

[PA.I.E.K4; AIM 4-4-6]

C. Uncontrolled Airspace

1. What is the definition of Class G airspace?

Uncontrolled airspace, or Class G airspace, is the portion of the airspace that has not been designated as Class A, B, C, D, or E. It is therefore designated uncontrolled airspace. Class G airspace extends from the surface to the base of the overlying Class E airspace. Although ATC has no authority or responsibility to control air traffic, pilots should remember there are visual flight rules (VFR) minimums that apply to Class G airspace.

[PA.I.E.K1; FAA-H-8083-25, AIM 3-3-1]

Private Pilot Oral Exam Guide   251

Chapter 9 **National Airspace System**

2. Are you required to establish communications with a tower located within Class G airspace?

Yes; unless otherwise authorized or required by ATC, no person may operate an aircraft to, from, through, or on an airport having an operational control tower unless two-way communications are maintained between that aircraft and the control tower. Communications must be established prior to 4 NM from the airport, up to and including 2,500 feet AGL.

[PA.I.E.K1; 14 CFR 91.126]

3. What are the vertical limits of Class G airspace?

Class G airspace begins at the surface and continues up to the overlying controlled (Class E) airspace, not to exceed 14,500 feet MSL.

[PA.I.E.K1; FAA-H-8083-25]

4. What is the minimum cloud clearance and visibility required when conducting flight operations in a traffic pattern at night in Class G airspace below 1,200 feet AGL?

When the visibility is less than 3 statute miles (SM) but not less than 1 SM during night hours, an airplane may be operated clear of clouds if operated in an airport traffic pattern within one-half mile of the runway.

[PA.I.E.K1; 14 CFR 91.155]

D. Special Use Airspace

1. What is a prohibited area?

Prohibited areas contain certain airspace of defined dimensions identified by an area on the surface of the earth within which flight of aircraft is prohibited. Such areas are established for security or other reasons associated with national welfare.

[PA.I.E.K3; AIM 3-4-2]

2. What is a restricted area?

Restricted areas contain airspace identified by an area on the surface of the earth within which the flight of aircraft, while not wholly prohibited, is subject to restrictions. These areas denote the existence of unusual, often invisible, hazards to aircraft, such as

252 Aviation Supplies & Academics

Chapter 9 **National Airspace System**

artillery firing, aerial gunnery, or guided missiles. Penetration of restricted areas without authorization from the using or controlling agency may be extremely hazardous to the aircraft and its occupants.

[PA.I.E.K3; AIM 3-4-3]

3. Under what conditions, if any, may pilots enter restricted or prohibited areas?

No person may operate an aircraft within a restricted area contrary to the restrictions imposed, or within a prohibited area, unless that person has the permission of the using or controlling agency. Normally *no* operations are permitted within a prohibited area, and *prior* permission must always be obtained before operating within a restricted area.

[PA.I.E.K3; 14 CFR 91.133]

4. Your cross-country route of flight takes you through a restricted area. Will you have to fly around it?

Flying through a restricted area is only allowed when the area is not active or when the pilot has received specific authorization from the controlling agency. The activity status of restricted areas is typically published in the Notices to Airmen (NOTAMs) or indicated on aeronautical charts. Additionally, pilots can confirm the status in real time by contacting the controlling agency or air traffic control.

If the restricted area is active, pilots must avoid it, planning a route that keeps them out of it laterally or based on the altitude at which they will fly. For example, a restricted area may be active from 10,000 feet to 26,000 feet, and a pilot could fly their cross-country route at a lower altitude, such as cruising at 8,000 feet.

[PA.I.E.K3; AIM 3-4-3, 14 CFR 91.133]

5. What is a warning area?

A warning area is airspace of defined dimensions extending from 3 NM outward from the coast of the United States, containing activity that may be hazardous to nonparticipating aircraft. The purpose of such an area is to warn nonparticipating pilots of the potential danger. A warning area may be located over domestic or international waters, or both.

[PA.I.E.K3; AIM 3-4-4]

Private Pilot Oral Exam Guide   253

Chapter 9 **National Airspace System**

6. What is a military operations area (MOA)?

A MOA consists of airspace of defined vertical and lateral limits established for the purpose of separating certain military training activities from IFR traffic. Pilots operating under VFR should exercise extreme caution while flying within an MOA when military activity is being conducted. The activity status (active/inactive) of MOAs may change frequently. Therefore, pilots should contact any FSS within 100 miles of the area to obtain accurate real-time information concerning the MOA hours of operation. Prior to entering an active MOA, pilots should contact the controlling agency for traffic advisories.

[PA.I.E.K3; AIM 3-4-5]

7. How can a pilot determine the vertical limits of a military operations area (MOA)?

MOAs are depicted on sectional charts with the letters "MOA" followed by a number. The vertical limits are listed on the chart, typically in feet above mean sea level (MSL). These limits show the altitude range where military operations occur. NOTAMs will also provide up-to-date information about the MOA's active hours, altitude ranges, and any changes to the area's vertical or lateral boundaries. The *Chart Supplement* additionally often contains additional details about MOAs, including specific vertical limits, when needed for clarity. If a pilot is unsure or needs confirmation during flight, contacting ATC is another reliable way to verify the vertical limits of an active MOA.

[PA.I.E.K3; FAA CUG, Sectional Chart Legend]

8. Your cross-country route of flight takes you through a military operations area. Will you have to fly around it?

A pilot is allowed to fly through a military operations area (MOA); however, caution is necessary. MOAs are designated airspace where military training activities, such as high-speed maneuvers or aerial combat exercises, occur. While operations in MOAs do not require prior authorization for civilian pilots, safety considerations are critical.

Pilots should check for active MOAs during preflight planning by consulting aeronautical charts and NOTAMs or contacting Flight Service. Real-time activity status can also be obtained from ATC.

Chapter 9 **National Airspace System**

If the MOA is active, the pilot may still transit through it, but there is a potential risk of encountering military aircraft performing fast, unpredictable maneuvers.

For added safety, pilots are encouraged to contact ATC when flying through an active MOA, especially if under visual flight rules (VFR). While ATC cannot deny entry, they can provide traffic advisories, helping pilots avoid conflicts with military operations.

If the MOA is not active, it operates as uncontrolled airspace, and normal VFR or IFR rules apply. Pilots should always maintain situational awareness and exercise vigilance when flying through MOAs to ensure a safe flight.

[PA.I.E.K3; AIM 3-4-3, 14 CFR 91.133]

9. What is an alert area?

Alert areas are depicted on aeronautical charts to inform nonparticipating pilots of areas that may contain a high volume of pilot training or an unusual type of aerial activity. Pilots should be particularly alert when flying in these areas. All activity within an alert area shall be conducted in accordance with regulations, without waiver, and pilots of participating aircraft as well as pilots transiting the area shall be equally responsible for collision avoidance.

[PA.I.E.K3; AIM 3-4-6]

10. Are there any restrictions when flying through an alert area? Can you fly through one at any time?

Yes, pilots can fly through an alert area at any time, but there are important considerations. Alert areas are designated airspace sections where unusual or high-density flight activities, such as military training, aerobatic maneuvers, or glider operations, occur. These areas are marked on sectional charts with the letter "A" followed by a number (e.g., A-123).

While there are no specific restrictions prohibiting flight through an alert area, pilots must exercise extreme caution and maintain heightened vigilance. The activities within these areas may involve rapid maneuvering, high-speed operations, or non-standard flight patterns, increasing the risk of midair collisions.

It is a good practice to avoid alert areas when possible or plan to transit at altitudes that minimize interaction with the activities.

Chapter 9 **National Airspace System**

Pilots should also closely monitor the appropriate radio frequency for situational awareness and broadcast their intentions to help avoid conflicts.

Before flying through an alert area, review chart notes for operational details and consider contacting nearby air traffic control facilities for more information.

[PA.I.E.K3; AIM 3-4-6]

11. What is a controlled firing area (CFA)?

CFAs contain activities that, if not conducted in a controlled environment, could be hazardous to nonparticipating aircraft. The distinguishing feature of the CFA, as compared to other special use airspace, is that its activities are suspended immediately when spotter aircraft, radar, or ground lookout positions indicate an aircraft might be approaching the area. CFAs are not charted.

[PA.I.E.K3; AIM 3-4-7]

12. What is a National Security Area (NSA)?

NSAs consist of airspace of defined vertical and lateral dimensions established at locations where there is a requirement for increased security and safety of ground facilities. Pilots are requested to voluntarily avoid flying through the depicted NSA. When it is necessary to provide a greater level of security and safety, flight in NSAs may be temporarily prohibited by regulation under the provisions of 14 CFR §99.7.

[PA.I.E.K3; AIM 3-4-8]

13. Where can information on special use airspace be found?

The frequency for the controlling agency is tabulated in the margins of the applicable IFR and VFR charts. Permanent SUAs (except CFAs) are charted on Sectional Aeronautical Charts, VFR Terminal Area Charts, and applicable enroute charts, and include the hours of operation, altitudes, and the controlling agency. For temporary restricted areas and MOAs, pilots should review the Domestic Notices found on the Federal NOTAM System website at notams.aim.faa.gov/notamSearch or the FAA SUA website at sua.faa.gov.

[PA.I.E.K3; AIM 3-4-1, 3-4-9]

256 Aviation Supplies & Academics

Chapter 9 **National Airspace System**

E. Other Airspace Areas

1. What are examples of "other" airspace areas?

Other airspace areas is a general term referring to the majority of the remaining airspace. It includes:

- Local airport advisory
- Military Training Route (MTR)
- Temporary Flight Restriction (TFR)
- Parachute jump aircraft operations
- Published VFR routes
- Terminal radar service area (TRSA)
- Special Air Traffic Rules (SATR) and Special Flight Rules Area (SFRA)

[PA.I.E.K3; AIM 3-5-1 to 3-5-7]

2. What are Military Training Routes?

Military Training Routes (MTRs) are developed for use by the military for the purpose of conducting low-altitude, high speed training. The routes above 1,500 feet AGL are developed to be flown, to the maximum extent possible, under IFR. The routes at 1,500 feet AGL and below are generally developed to be flown under VFR. Routes below 1,500 feet AGL use four-digit identifiers (e.g., IR 1004, VR 1008). Routes above 1,500 feet AGL use three-digit identifiers (e.g., IR 003, VR 004). IR is for IFR routes and VR is for VFR routes.

[PA.I.E.K3; AIM 3-5-2]

3. What is a Temporary Flight Restriction (TFR)?

A TFR is a regulatory action issued via the US NOTAM system to restrict certain aircraft from operating within a defined area, on a temporary basis, to protect persons or property in the air or on the ground. They may be issued due to a hazardous condition, a special event, or as a general warning for the entire FAA airspace. TFR information can be obtained from an FSS or at tfr.faa.gov.

[PA.I.E.K3; AC 91-63, AIM 3-5-3]

Private Pilot Oral Exam Guide 257

Chapter 9 **National Airspace System**

4. How far away must a pilot stay from a major sporting event?

For a flight-restricted area for a major sporting event, the amount of airspace needed to protect persons and property on the surface or in the air, to maintain air safety and efficiency, or to prevent the unsafe congestion of aircraft will vary depending on the size of the event and the factors listed in 14 CFR §91.145(b). The restricted airspace will normally be limited to a 3 NM radius from the center of the event and 2,500 feet above the surface but will not be greater than the minimum airspace necessary for the management of aircraft operations in the vicinity of the specified area.

[PA.I.E.K3; 14 CFR 91.145]

5. Where can a pilot find information on parachute jump aircraft operations?

Procedures relating to parachute jump areas are contained in 14 CFR Part 105. Parachute jump aircraft operations are published in the *Chart Supplement*, and jump sites that are used frequently are depicted on sectional charts. Frequently, NOTAMs describe active parachute jumping locations and times.

[PA.I.E.K3; AIM 3-5-4, FAA-H-8083-25]

6. What is the purpose of Published VFR routes?

Published VFR routes are for transitioning around, under, and through some complex airspace. Terms such as VFR flyway, VFR corridor, Class B airspace VFR transition route, and terminal area VFR route have been applied to such routes. These routes are generally found on VFR terminal area planning charts.

[PA.I.E.K3; AIM 3-5-5, FAA-H-8083-25]

7. Where can a pilot find information on VFR flyways, VFR corridors, and Class B airspace transition routes used to transition busy terminal airspace?

Information will normally be depicted on the reverse side of VFR Terminal Area Charts, commonly referred to as Class B airspace charts.

[PA.I.E.K3; AIM 3-5-5]

258 Aviation Supplies & Academics

Chapter 9 **National Airspace System**

8. What is a Terminal Radar Service Area (TRSA)?

A TRSA consists of airspace surrounding designated airports wherein ATC provides radar vectoring, sequencing, and separation on a full-time basis for all IFR and participating VFR aircraft. Pilot participation is urged but not mandatory.

[PA.I.E.K3; AIM 3-5-6, P/CG]

9. What class of airspace is a TRSA?

TRSAs do not fit into any of the US airspace classes, are not contained in Part 71, and there are not any operating rules in Part 91. The primary airport(s) within the TRSA become Class D airspace. The remaining portion of a TRSA overlies other controlled airspace, which is normally Class E airspace beginning at 700 or 1,200 feet and established to transition to/from the enroute/terminal environment. TRSAs will continue to be an airspace area where participating pilots can receive additional radar services that have been redefined as TRSA service.

[PA.I.E.K3; AIM 3-5-6]

10. How are TRSAs depicted on navigational charts?

TRSAs are depicted on VFR Sectional and Terminal Area Charts with a solid black line and altitudes for each segment. The Class D portion is charted with a blue segmented line.

[PA.I.E.K2; AIM 3-5-6]

11. Are you required to have an ATC clearance when operating within the lateral boundaries of a TRSA?

A pilot is not required to have an ATC clearance when operating within the lateral boundaries of a Terminal Radar Service Area. TRSAs are established around some airports to provide optional radar services for VFR aircraft, enhancing traffic separation and situational awareness.

While participation in TRSA services is voluntary for VFR pilots, it is highly recommended. By contacting ATC and accepting their radar services, pilots gain added safety through traffic advisories, sequencing, and potential conflict avoidance with other aircraft. However, if a pilot chooses not to participate, they must comply with basic VFR rules and exercise heightened vigilance for other traffic.

[PA.I.E.K3; AIM 3-5-6]

Private Pilot Oral Exam Guide   259

Chapter 9 **National Airspace System**

12. What is a FAA-Recognized Identification Area (FRIA)?

A FAA-Recognized Identification Area (FRIA) is a designated airspace area where certain uncrewed aircraft systems (UAS), such as drones, can operate without the requirement for remote identification (Remote ID). In these areas, UAS operations are allowed to fly without broadcasting identification signals, provided the operation is within the specific boundaries of the FRIA.

FRIAs are typically found at locations like FAA-approved UAS test sites or certain public-use airports that have been designated by the FAA. The idea behind FRIAs is to provide a safe operating environment for drones, especially for educational, research, or hobbyist purposes, without the need for Remote ID technology in areas where there is low risk to crewed aviation or the public.

These areas are important for fostering safe integration of UAS into the National Airspace System while maintaining safety for both manned and unmanned aircraft. Pilots should be aware that FRIAs are distinct from other types of airspace and that drones operating outside of these areas are subject to Remote ID requirements.

[PA.I.E.K3; AC 89-3]

13. If a pilot determines there is a NOTAM for UAS operations within 3 NM of a location and up to 3,000 feet AGL, does that mean the pilot may not fly in that area?

This does not necessarily mean a pilot cannot fly in that area, but it does indicate a restriction or advisory for manned aircraft operations. The NOTAM serves as a warning that UAS operations may be taking place, and pilots must exercise caution.

Pilots should review the specific NOTAM details to understand the exact restrictions or recommended procedures. For example, the NOTAM may provide hours of operation, the type of UAS activity, or any required coordination with ATC.

If the NOTAM specifies restrictions, such as temporary flight restrictions (TFRs), pilots must comply. However, if the NOTAM is informational, pilots should remain vigilant, maintain situational awareness, and ensure they are clear of UAS operations when flying through or near the area. In some cases, contacting ATC for

Chapter 9 **National Airspace System**

clarification or to request a clearance could be advisable. Many of these UAS NOTAM advisories are not TFRs.

[PA.I.E.K3; 14 CFR Part 107]

14. Explain the requirements to operate an aircraft within airspace designated as a SATR area or SFRA.

Special Air Traffic Rules (SATR)—Rules that govern procedures for conducting flights in certain areas listed in 14 CFR Part 93. The term SATR is used in the United States to describe the rules for operations in specific areas designated in the Code of Federal Regulations.

Special Flight Rules Area (SFRA)—Airspace of defined dimensions, above land areas or territorial waters, within which the flight of aircraft is subject to the rules set forth in 14 CFR Part 93, unless otherwise authorized by ATC. Not all areas listed in Part 93 are designated SFRA, but special air traffic rules apply to all areas described in Part 93.

Note: Procedures, nature of operations, configuration, size, and density of traffic vary among the identified areas.

[PA.I.E.K3; AIM 3-5-7]

15. What should a pilot know if they were planning to fly into an airport in the Washington, DC, Special Flight Rules Area (SFRA)?

A pilot planning to fly into an airport within the Washington DC SFRA must be aware of several important requirements to ensure compliance and safety. The SFRA is a restricted airspace designed to protect the DC area from potential security threats.

SFRA training—Pilots must complete an online training course provided by the FAA. This course covers the special procedures, rules, and regulations for flying into and within the SFRA and includes topics such as VFR routes, flight plan filing, transponder requirements, and specific communication procedures with ATC.

Knowledge of VFR corridors—Pilots must be familiar with the specific VFR corridors and routes designated for use when flying through the SFRA. These routes are designed to ensure safe and efficient transit through controlled airspace.

(continued)

Private Pilot Oral Exam Guide   261

Chapter 9 **National Airspace System**

Certification—Pilots must hold at least a Private Pilot Certificate to operate within the SFRA. Additionally, they must have a current medical certificate and meet the appropriate flight review and currency requirements.

Flight plan filing—For VFR operations in the SFRA, pilots are required to file a flight plan and maintain two-way radio communication with ATC before entering and while within the SFRA.

Transponder requirements—Aircraft must be equipped with a Mode C transponder and ADS-B out when flying in the SFRA, and pilots must be familiar with the transponder codes and operations.

Pilots can complete the required training through the FAA's website and must carry the training completion certificate. Only after meeting these training and procedural requirements can a pilot legally fly in the Washington DC SFRA.

[PA.I.E.K3; AIM 3-5-8]

16. What would a pilot need to do to fly into one of the few airports inside the Washington DC Flight Restricted Zone (FRZ), the inner ring inside of the Washington, DC SFRA?

To fly into one of the airports in the Flight Restricted Zone (FRZ), a pilot conducting any type of flight operation in the Washington DC SFRA/FRZ must comply with the requirements in:

a. 14 CFR §93.339—Requirements for operating in the DC SFRA, including the DC FRZ.

b. 14 CFR §91.161—Special awareness training required for pilots flying under visual flight rules within a 60-nautical mile radius of the Washington, DC VOR/DME; also located on the FAA website at www.faasafety.gov.

c. Any 14 CFR §99.7 special security instructions for the DC SFRA/FRZ published via NOTAM by FAA in the interest of national security.

This is additional training and authorization that results in the pilot being issued a special pin number after background checking is done. A flight plan in this area may not be filed online or via a third-party service.

[PA.I.E.K3; AIM 3-5-8]

262 Aviation Supplies & Academics

Chapter 9 **National Airspace System**

17. What is an ADIZ, and where are they located?

An Air Defense Identification Zone (ADIZ) is an area of airspace over land or water in which the ready identification, location, and control of all aircraft (except Department of Defense and law enforcement aircraft) are required in the interest of national security.

[PA.I.E.K3; FAA CUG, P/CG]

18. What requirements must be satisfied prior to operations into, within, or across an ADIZ?

Operational requirements for aircraft operations associated with an ADIZ are as follows:

Flight plan—An IFR or DVFR flight plan must be filed and activated with the appropriate aeronautical facility.

Two-way radio—An operating two-way radio is required.

Transponder—Aircraft must be equipped with an operable radar beacon transponder having altitude reporting (Mode C) capabilities. The transponder must be turned on and set to the assigned ATC code.

Position reports—For IFR flights, normal position reporting. For DVFR flights, an estimated time of ADIZ penetration must be filed at least 15 minutes prior to entry.

Land-based ADIZ are activated and deactivated over US metropolitan areas as needed, with dimensions, activation dates, etc., disseminated via NOTAM. Pilots unable to comply with all NOTAM requirements must remain clear of land-based ADIZ. Pilots entering a land-based ADIZ without authorization or who fail to follow all requirements risk interception by military fighter aircraft.

[PA.I.E.K3; AIM 5-6-4, 14 CFR Part 99]

19. What is a Weather Reconnaissance Area (WRA)?

Airspace with defined dimensions and published by a NOTAM, which is established to support weather reconnaissance/research flights. ATC services are not provided within WRAs. Only participating weather reconnaissance/research aircraft from the 53rd WRS and NOAA AOC are permitted to operate within a

Private Pilot Oral Exam Guide   263

Chapter 9 **National Airspace System**

WRA. A WRA may only be established in airspace within US Flight Information Regions (FIR) outside of US territorial airspace.

Hurricane Hunters from the US Air Force Reserve 53rd Weather Reconnaissance Squadron (WRS) and the National Oceanic and Atmospheric Administration (NOAA) Aircraft Operations Center (AOC) operate weather reconnaissance/research aircraft missions, in support of the National Hurricane Operations Plan (NHOP), to gather meteorological data on hurricanes and tropical cyclones. 53rd WRS and NOAA AOC aircraft normally conduct these missions in airspace identified in a published WRA NOTAM.

[PA.I.E.K3; AIM 3-5-9]

F. Airspace Classification Summary

The following section summarizes the requirements for operations within the various airspace classes.

1. Discuss Class A airspace.

Vertical dimensions	18,000 ft MSL up to and including FL600
Operations permitted	IFR
Entry prerequisites	ATC clearance
Minimum pilot qualifications	Instrument Rating
Two-way radio communications	Yes
VFR minimum visibility	N/A
VFR minimum distance from clouds	N/A
Aircraft separation	All
Conflict resolution	N/A
Traffic advisories	N/A
Safety advisories	Yes

[PA.I.E.K1; AIM 3-2-2, 14 CFR 91.135]

264 Aviation Supplies & Academics

Chapter 9 **National Airspace System**

2. Discuss Class B airspace.

Vertical dimensions	Surface to 10,000 ft MSL
Operations permitted	IFR and VFR
Entry prerequisites	ATC clearance
Minimum pilot qualifications	Private/Student Pilot Certificate
Two-way radio communications	Yes
VFR minimum visibility	3 SM
VFR minimum distance from clouds	Clear of clouds
Aircraft separation	All
Conflict resolution	Yes
Traffic advisories	Yes
Safety advisories	Yes

[PA.I.E.K1; AIM 3-2-3, 14 CFR 91.131]

3. Discuss Class C airspace.

Vertical dimensions	Surface to 4,000 ft AGL (charted MSL)
Operations permitted	IFR and VFR
Entry prerequisites	ATC clearance for IFR; radio contact for all
Minimum pilot qualifications	Student Pilot Certificate
Two-way radio communications	Yes
VFR minimum visibility	3 SM
VFR minimum distance from clouds	500 ft below, 1,000 ft above, and 2,000 ft horizontal
Aircraft separation	IFR, SVFR, and runway operations
Conflict resolution	Between IFR and VFR operations
Traffic advisories	Yes
Safety advisories	Yes

[PA.I.E.K1; AIM 3-2-4, 14 CFR 91.130]

Private Pilot Oral Exam Guide 265

Chapter 9 **National Airspace System**

4. Discuss Class D airspace.

Vertical dimensions	Surface to 2,500 ft AGL (charted MSL)
Operations permitted	IFR and VFR
Entry prerequisites	ATC clearance for IFR; radio contact for all
Minimum pilot qualifications	Student Pilot Certificate
Two-way radio communications	Yes
VFR minimum visibility	3 SM
VFR minimum distance from clouds	500 ft below, 1,000 ft above, and 2,000 ft horizontal
Aircraft separation	IFR, SVFR, and runway operations
Conflict resolution	No
Traffic advisories	Workload permitting
Safety advisories	Yes

[PA.I.E.K1; AIM 3-2-5, 14 CFR 91.129]

5. Discuss Class E airspace.

Vertical dimensions	Except for 18,000 feet MSL, no defined vertical limit. Extends upward from either the surface or a designated altitude to the overlying or adjacent controlled airspace.
Operations permitted	IFR and VFR
Entry prerequisites	ATC clearance for IFR
Minimum pilot qualifications	Student Pilot Certificate
Two-way radio communications	Yes for IFR
VFR minimum visibility	3 SM*
VFR minimum distance from clouds	500 ft below, 1,000 ft above, and 2,000 ft horizontal*
Aircraft separation	IFR and SVFR
Conflict resolution	No
Traffic advisories	Workload permitting
Safety advisories	Yes

[PA.I.E.K1; AIM 3-2-6, 14 CFR 91.127]

266 Aviation Supplies & Academics

Chapter 9 **National Airspace System**

6. Discuss Class G airspace.

Vertical dimensions	Surface up to the overlying controlled (Class E) airspace, not to exceed 14,500 ft MSL
Operations permitted	IFR and VFR
Entry prerequisites	None
Minimum pilot qualifications	Student Pilot Certificate
Two-way radio communications	No
VFR minimum visibility	1 SM*
VFR minimum distance from clouds	500 ft below, 1,000 ft above, and 2,000 ft horizontal*
Aircraft separation	None
Conflict resolution	No
Traffic advisories	Workload permitting
Safety advisories	Yes

[PA.I.E.K1; AIM 3-3-1, 14 CFR 91.126, 91.155]

Different visibility minima and distance from cloud requirements exist for night operations, operations above 10,000 feet MSL, and operations below 1,200 feet AGL.

Private Pilot Oral Exam Guide   267

Weather Information

10

Chapter 10 **Weather Information**

A. Weather Sources

1. What service does the FAA provide for pilots to obtain a weather briefing?

The FAA provides the Flight Service program, which provides weather briefings to pilots through its Flight Service Stations (FSS) by phone (1-800-WX-BRIEF) and online at 1800wxbrief.com (contracted through Leidos Flight Service).

[PA.I.C.K1; AIM 7-1-2]

2. What are the three main categories of FAA-approved sources of aviation weather information?

Federal government—The FAA and National Weather Service (NWS) collect weather observations. The NWS analyzes the observations and produces forecasts and the FAA and NWS disseminate observations, analyses, and forecasts through a variety of systems. The federal government is the only approval authority for sources of weather observations (e.g., contract towers and airport operators).

Enhanced Weather Information System (EWINS)—An EWINS is an FAA-authorized, proprietary system for tracking, evaluating, reporting, and forecasting the presence or lack of adverse weather phenomena. The FAA authorizes a certificate holder to use an EWINS to produce flight movement forecasts, adverse weather phenomena forecasts, and other meteorological advisories.

Commercial weather information providers—These entitites repackage proprietary weather products based on NWS information with formatting and layout modifications but make no material changes to the weather information. Other commercial providers produce forecasts, analyses, and other proprietary weather products that may substantially differ from the information contained in NWS products.

[PA.I.C.K1; FAA-H-8083-28, AIM 7-1-3]

3. You're planning a cross-country flight. Does the weather data provided by commercial and/or third-party vendors satisfy the preflight action required by 14 CFR §91.103?

Pilots and operators should be aware that weather services provided by entities other than the FAA, NWS, or their contractors may not meet FAA/NWS quality control standards. All operators

270 Aviation Supplies & Academics

Chapter 10 **Weather Information**

and pilots contemplating using such services should request and/ or review an appropriate description of services and provider disclosure. Pilots and operators should be cautious when using unfamiliar products or products not supported by FAA/NWS technical specifications. When in doubt, consult with an FAA Flight Service Specialist.

[PA.I.C.K2; AIM 7-1-3]

4. Does the FAA consider weather self-briefings compliant with the regulations?

For many general aviation (GA) pilots, Flight Service remains an important source of comprehensive weather and aeronautical information. However, most pilots have become more accustomed to performing a self-briefing than calling Flight Service. According to the FAA, a self-briefing may be compliant with current Federal Aviation Regulations. By self-briefing, pilots can often improve their knowledge of weather and aeronautical information. Flight Service personnel are available should a pilot need assistance.

[PA.I.C.S1; AC 91-92]

5. Describe some ways a pilot can conduct a preflight self-briefing on the weather, NOTAMs, ATC delays, etc.

A preflight self-briefing ensures a pilot gathers all relevant information to safely plan and execute a flight. When self-briefing, a pilot should refer to as many information resources that pertain to their route of flight and the airports that will or may be used. Some key points to this can include:

a. *Weather*—Start by reviewing METARs, TAFs, and area forecasts for departure, enroute, and destination conditions. Check for adverse weather such as thunderstorms, icing, turbulence, and visibility restrictions. Use charts like surface analysis, prog charts, and winds aloft for broader weather patterns. Look at SIGMETs, AIRMETs, and convective outlooks for hazardous weather.

b. *NOTAMs*—Review Notices to Airmen (NOTAMs) for closed runways, unserviceable NAVAIDs, TFRs, or special procedures affecting your route.

(continued)

Private Pilot Oral Exam Guide   271

Chapter 10 **Weather Information**

   c. *ATC delays and airspace restrictions*—Check for anticipated ATC delays, flow restrictions, or special use airspace (SUA) activity.

   d. *Fuel requirements and alternates*—Ensure weather and NOTAMs are acceptable at your destination and alternate airports, considering fuel reserves.

   e. *Performance considerations*—Account for weather, elevation, weight, and winds in takeoff, climb, and landing performance.

   f. *Tools and resources*—Use tools like 1800WXBRIEF, an aviation EFB with data sources, aviationweather.gov, or other FAA resources for a comprehensive briefing.

[PA.I.C.K2; AC 91-92]

6. What types of weather briefings are available from an AFSS/FSS briefer?

Standard briefing—Request when you are planning a flight and you have not received a previous briefing or have not received preliminary information through online resources.

Abbreviated briefing—Request when you need information to supplement mass-disseminated data, update a previous briefing, or when you need only one or two items.

Outlook briefing—Request whenever your proposed time of departure is six or more hours from the time of the briefing, for planning purposes only.

Inflight briefing—Request when needed to update a preflight briefing.

[PA.I.C.K2; AIM 7-1-5]

7. What pertinent information should a weather briefing include?

For a standard briefing, the briefer will automatically provide the following information in the following sequence: adverse conditions, VFR flight not recommended, synopsis, current conditions, enroute forecast, destination forecast, winds aloft, Notices to Airmen (NOTAMs), ATC delays, and any additional information upon request.

[PA.I.C.K2; AIM 7-1-5]

272 Aviation Supplies & Academics

Chapter 10 **Weather Information**

8. What does it mean when a briefing includes the wording "VFR Flight Not Recommended?"

When VFR flight is proposed and sky conditions or visibilities are present or forecast (surface or aloft) that in the briefer's judgment would make flight under VFR doubtful, the briefer will describe the conditions, describe the affected locations, and use the phrase "VFR flight not recommended." This recommendation is advisory in nature. The final decision as to whether the flight can be conducted safely rests solely with the pilot. Upon receiving a "VFR flight not recommended" statement, the non-IFR rated pilot will need to make a go or no-go decision.

[PA.I.C.S3; AIM 7-1-5]

9. When planning a cross-country flight, how can a pilot mitigate the risk of inadvertent flight into IMC?

Some strategies a pilot might use to avoid flight into inadvertent IMC include thorough preflight briefing and planning, planning for alternate routes and airports if unexpected weather is encountered, and continuing to monitor weather en route using onboard and radio-based weather information services. Pilots can establish personal minimums that are greater than minimum weather restrictions to help avoid flying into degrading weather. Pilots should be aware of pressures related to "get-there-itis" and a desire to complete a flight; this is critical to being willing to stop a flight, divert, or delay a flight to another time to avoid flying into weather for which a pilot is not prepared. An instrument-rated pilot could also mitigate some of the risk by either filing an IFR flight plan and operating on IFR procedures even in VFR conditions or being prepared to do so if the weather conditions change en route and it is warranted. All pilots should be familiar with basic instrument procedures such as a 180-degree turn to get out of conditions experienced, ATC services available to them, and basic climb or descent procedures using aircraft instruments. Pilots are highly encouraged to be familiar with and capable of using aircraft automation tools such as an autopilot to help manage workload and improve aircraft stability during any maneuvering.

[PA.I.C.K3; FAA-H-8083-25]

Private Pilot Oral Exam Guide 273

Chapter 10 **Weather Information**

10. What is a Flight Information Service–Broadcast (FIS-B)?

Flight Information Service–Broadcast (FIS-B) is a ground-based broadcast service provided through the Automatic Dependent Surveillance–Broadcast (ADS-B) Universal Access Transceiver (UAT) network. The service provides users with a 978 MHz data link capability when operating within range and line-of-sight of a transmitting ground station. FIS-B enables users of properly equipped aircraft to receive and display a suite of broadcast weather and aeronautical information products.

[PA.I.C.K2g; FAA-H-8083-25, AIM 7-1-9]

11. Can onboard datalink weather (FIS-B) be useful in navigating an aircraft safely around an area of thunderstorms?

FIS aviation weather products (for example, graphical ground-based radar precipitation depictions) are not appropriate for tactical (typical timeframe of less than 3 minutes) avoidance of severe weather such as negotiating a path through a weather hazard area. FIS supports strategic (typical timeframe of 20 minutes or more) weather decision-making, such as route selection to avoid a weather hazard area in its entirety. The misuse of information beyond its applicability may place the pilot and aircraft in jeopardy. In addition, FIS should never be used in lieu of an individual preflight weather and flight planning briefing.

[PA.I.C.K2g; FAA-H-8083-28, AIM 7-1-9]

12. While en route, how can a pilot obtain updated weather information?

a. Flight Service on 122.2 MHz and appropriate remote communication outlet (RCO) frequencies.

b. Automated Terminal Information Service (ATIS), Automated Surface Observing System (ASOS), or Automated Weather Observing Systems (AWOS) broadcasts along your route of flight.

c. Listen to Air Route Traffic Control Center (ARTCC) broadcasts—Aviation Watch Notification Messages (formerly AWWs), convective Significant Meteorological Information (SIGMETs), SIGMETs, Airmen's Meteorological Information (AIRMET), urgent pilot weather reports (PIREPs), or Center

274 Aviation Supplies & Academics

Chapter 10 **Weather Information**

Weather Advisory (CWA) alerts are broadcast once on all frequencies, except emergency.

d. Datalink weather—Flight deck display of FIS-B information.

e. Air traffic control (ATC) (workload permitting).

Exam Tip: Be prepared to demonstrate how you would obtain in-flight weather advisories and updates, and how you would communicate with a FSS while en route.

[PA.I.C.K2g; FAA-H-8083-25]

B. Weather Products

Observations

1. What is a METAR and what are the two types?

A METAR (aviation routine weather report) is an hourly surface observation of conditions observed at an airport. There are two types of METAR reports: a routine METAR report transmitted every hour and an aviation selected special weather report (SPECI). This is a special report that can be given at any time to update the METAR for rapidly changing weather conditions, aircraft mishaps, or other critical information.

[PA.I.C.K2a; FAA-H-8083-28, FAA-H-8083-28]

2. Describe the basic elements of a METAR.

A METAR report contains the following elements in order as presented:

a. *Type of reports*—The METAR, and the SPECI (aviation special weather report).

b. *ICAO station identifier*—A four-letter station identifier from the International Civil Aviation Organization (ICAO); in the contiguous United States (CONUS), the three-letter identifier is prefixed with K.

c. *Date and time of report*—A six-digit date/time group appended with Z (UTC; Coordinated Universal Time). The first two digits are the date, then two for the hour, and two for minutes.

d. *Modifier (as required)*—If used, the modifier AUTO identifies the report as an automated weather report with no human intervention. If AUTO is shown in the body of the report, AO1

Private Pilot Oral Exam Guide   275

Chapter 10 **Weather Information**

or AO2 will be encoded in the remarks section to indicate the type of precipitation sensor used at the station.

e. *Wind*—Five-digit group (six digits if speed is over 99 knots); first three digits = wind direction, in tens of degrees referenced to true north. Directions less than 100 degrees are preceded with a zero; the next two digits are the average speed in knots, measured or estimated (or, if over 99 knots, the next three digits).

f. *Visibility*—Surface visibility in statute miles, space, fractions of statute miles (as needed), and the letters SM.

g. *Runway visual range (RVR)*—As required.

h. *Weather phenomena*—Broken into two categories: qualifiers and weather phenomena.

i. *Sky condition*—Amount/height/type (as required) or indefinite ceiling/height (vertical visibility). Heights are recorded in feet AGL.

j. *Temperature/dew point group*—Two-digit format in whole degrees Celsius, separated by a solidus (/). Temperatures below zero are prefixed with M.

k. *Altimeter*—Four-digit format representing tens, units, tenths, and hundredths of inches of mercury prefixed with A. The decimal point is not reported or stated.

l. *Remarks (RMK) (as required)*—Operationally significant weather phenomena, location of phenomena, beginning and ending times, and/or direction of movement.

Example: METAR KLAX 140651Z AUTO 00000KT 1SM R35L/4500V6000FT -RA BR BKN030 10/10 A2990 RMK AO2

[PA.I.C.K2a; FAA-H-8083-28, FAA-H-8083-28]

3. Describe several types of weather observing programs available.

a. *Manual observations*—With only a few exceptions, these reports are from airport locations staffed by FAA personnel who manually observe, perform calculations, and enter their observations into the communication system.

b. *AWOS*—Automated Weather Observing System; consists of various sensors, a processor, a computer-generated voice subsystem, and a transmitter to broadcast local,

276 Aviation Supplies & Academics

Chapter 10 **Weather Information**

minute-by-minute weather data directly to the pilot. Observations will include the prefix "AUTO" in data.

c. *AWOS broadcasts*—Computer-generated voice is used to automate the broadcast of minute-by-minute weather observations.

d. *ASOS/AWOS*—Automated Surface Observing System/ Automated Weather Observing System; the primary US surface weather observing systems. Both systems provide continuous minute-by-minute observations that generate METARs and other aviation weather information. Transmitted over a discrete VHF radio frequency or the voice portion of a local NAVAID, and receivable to a maximum of 25 NM from the station and a maximum altitude of 10,000 feet AGL. Observations made without human intervention will include the modifier "AUTO" in the report data. A maintenance indicator ($) is coded when an automated system detects that maintenance is needed on the system.

[PA.I.C.K2a; AIM 7-1-10]

4. What are PIREPs (UA), and where are they usually found?

A pilot report (PIREP) provides valuable information regarding the conditions as they actually exist in the air, which cannot be gathered from any other source. Pilots can confirm the height of bases and tops of clouds, locations of wind shear and turbulence, and the location of inflight icing. There are two types of PIREPs: routine (UA) and urgent (UUA). PIREPs should be given to the ground facility with which communications are established (i.e., FSS, ARTCC, or terminal ATC). Altitudes are MSL (mean sea level), visibilities SM (statute miles), and distances in NM (nautical miles). PIREPs are available from ATC, FSS, and online at aviationweather.gov/data/pirep.

[PA.I.C.K2a; FAA-H-8083-28]

Private Pilot Oral Exam Guide 277

Chapter 10 **Weather Information**

5. Decode the following pilot weather report (PIREP): KCMH UA/OV KAPE 230010/TM 1516/FL085/TP BE20/SK BKN 065/WX FV03SM HZ FU/TA 20/TB LGT

Here's the decoded version of the pilot weather report:

KCMH	The originating station is Columbus, Ohio (KCMH).
UA	This is an urgent weather report, indicating significant weather.
OV KAPE	The aircraft is reporting at or near the KAPE VOR (a navigation aid).
230010	The position is at 23 degrees 0 minutes (latitude), 10 nautical miles (distance from a reporting point).
TM 1516	The report was issued at 1516 UTC (Coordinated Universal Tme).
FL085	The flight level is 8,500 feet above sea level (FL085).
TP BE20	The type of aircraft is a Beechcraft Super King Air (BE20).
SK BKN 065	The sky condition is broken clouds at 6,500 feet above ground level (AGL).
WX FV03SM HZ FU	The weather is visibility 3 statute miles with haze and smoke (FU indicates smoke).
TA 20	The air temperature is 20°C.
TB LGT	Light turbulence (TB LGT) is reported.

This report indicates that the pilot is flying a Beechcraft Super King Air at 8,500 feet with light turbulence and broken clouds at 6,500 feet. The visibility is restricted to 3 miles due to haze and smoke, and the air temperature is 20°C.

[PA.I.C.K2a; AIM 7-1-18]

278 Aviation Supplies & Academics

Chapter 10 **Weather Information**

Aviation Weather Forecasts

1. What is a Terminal Aerodrome Forecast (TAF)?

It is a concise statement of the expected meteorological conditions significant to aviation for a specified time period within 5 SM of the center of the airport's runway complex (terminal). TAFs use the same weather codes found in METAR weather reports, in the following format:

a. *Type of reports*—A routine forecast (TAF), an amended forecast (TAF AMD), or a corrected forecast (TAF COR).

b. *ICAO station identifier*—A four-letter station identifier.

c. *Date and time of origin*—The date/time of forecast follows the terminal's location identifier. It contains the day of the month in two digits and time in four digits when the forecast is completed and ready for transmission, appended with a Z to denote UTC. *Example:* 061737Z (this TAF was issued on the 6th day of the month at 1737 UTC).

d. *Valid period date and time*—The first two digits are the day of the month for the start of the TAF, followed by two digits indicating the starting hour (UTC). The next two digits indicate the day of the month for the end of the TAF, and the last two digits are the ending hour (UTC) of the valid period. Scheduled 24- and 30-hour TAFs are issued four times per day, at 0000, 0600, 1200, and 1800Z. *Example:* A 00Z TAF issued on the 9th of the month and valid for 24 hours would have a valid period of 0900/0924.

e. *Forecasts*—Wind, visibility, significant and vicinity weather, cloud and vertical obscuration, nonconvective low-level wind shear, forecast change indicators (FM, TEMPO, and PROB).

[PA.I.C.K2c; FAA-H-8083-28]

2. How big of an area is a Terminal Aerodrome Forecast (TAF) valid for?

A TAF is valid for an area within a 5 statute mile radius from the center of the airport's runway complex. While TAFs are highly localized, pilots should remember that weather conditions can change significantly beyond the 5 SM radius, especially in regions with complex terrain or rapidly changing weather.

[PA.I.C.K2c; FAA-H-8083-28]

Private Pilot Oral Exam Guide   279

Chapter 10 **Weather Information**

3. If your destination has no terminal forecast, which primary source of information should be referenced for forecasted weather at the estimated time of arrival?

If your destination has no Terminal Aerodrome Forecast (TAF), the Graphical Forecasts for Aviation (GFA) tool should be referenced for forecasted weather at the estimated time of arrival. This source provides a broader overview of weather conditions over larger regions, including cloud coverage, visibility, and weather phenomena.

[PA.I.C.K2d; FAA-H-8083-28]

4. Define aviation area forecast (FA).

FAs are issued for the Gulf of Mexico, the Caribbean Sea, and Alaska. An FA is an abbreviated plain language forecast concerning the occurrence or expected occurrence of specified enroute weather phenomena. The FA (in conjunction with AIRMETs, SIGMETs, convective SIGMETs, CWAs, etc.) is used to determine forecast enroute weather over a specified geographic region. FAs cover an 18- to 24-hour period, depending on the region, and are issued three to four times daily, depending on the region, and are updated as needed.

[PA.I.C.K2d; FAA-H-8083-28]

5. From which primary source should information be obtained regarding expected weather at the estimated time of arrival (ETA) if your destination airport does not have a TAF?

The Graphical Forecasts for Aviation (GFA).

[PA.I.C.K2d; FAA-H-8083-28]

6. Describe the Graphical Forecasts for Aviation (GFA).

The GFA is a set of web-based graphics that provide observations, forecasts, and warnings that can be viewed from 18 hours in the past to 18 hours in the future. The GFA covers the CONUS from the surface up to FL480. Wind, icing, and turbulence forecasts are available in 3,000-foot increments from the surface up to 30,000 feet MSL, and in 6,000-foot increments from 30,000 feet MSL to 48,000 feet MSL. Turbulence forecasts are also broken into LO

Chapter 10 **Weather Information**

(below FL180) and HI (at or above 18,000 feet MSL) graphics. A maximum icing graphic and maximum wind velocity graphic (regardless of altitude) are also available. The GFA interactive web tool can be viewed at aviationweather.gov/gfa.

[PA.I.C.K2d; AIM 7-1-4, FAA-H-8083-28, AWC]

7. What type of aviation forecasts are available in the Forecast section of the GFA?

The Forecast section will provide gridded displays of various weather parameters as well as NWS textual weather observations, forecasts, and warnings out to 18 hours. Icing, turbulence, and wind gridded products are three-dimensional. Other gridded products are two-dimensional and may represent a composite of a three-dimensional weather phenomenon or a surface weather variable, such as horizontal visibility. The following GFA forecasts are available:

a. Ceiling & visibility (CIG/VIS)
b. Clouds
c. Precipitation/weather (PCPN/WX)
d. Thunderstorm (TS)
e. Temperature
f. Winds
g. Turbulence
h. Icing

[PA.I.C.K2d; AIM 7-1-4, AWC]

8. Describe some of the weather products available on the GFA.

Selecting the "Products" menu gives you the option to display weather data for the current time and the previous 18 hours (rounded to the nearest hour) and will provide the following:

a. SIGMET
b. G-AIRMET
c. Center Weather Adv
d. Prog charts
e. TAF map
f. Forecast discussions
g. METAR data

(continued)

Private Pilot Oral Exam Guide   281

Chapter 10 **Weather Information**

    h. TAF data

    i. PIREP data (pilot reports)

    j. Wind/temp data

    k. ITWS data

    l. WAFS grids

    m. SigWx charts

    n. TFM convective forecasts

[PA.I.C.K2d; AIM 7-1-4, AWC]

9. Using the Graphical Forecasts for Aviation (GFA) tool, what may a pilot determine about icing probability?

The GFA tool on the Aviation Weather Center (aviationweather.gov /gfa) allows a pilot to select altitudes and times up to 18 hours in the future to analyze icing probability and severity in geographic areas.

Exam Tip: Be prepared to interpret and discuss current and forecast weather along your planned route of flight. The evaluator will want you to demonstrate that you can interpret the various aviation weather reports, forecasts, and charts/graphics and make an assessment of how the weather will affect your planned flight. Also, expect the evaluator to place emphasis on your knowledge of weather phenomena such as thunderstorms, turbulence, icing, and visibility that are of particular concern to all pilots.

[PA.I.C.K2d; FAA-H-8083-28]

10. What are the four types of Inflight Aviation Weather Advisories?

Inflight Aviation Weather Advisories are forecasts to advise enroute aircraft of the development of potentially hazardous weather in four types: the SIGMET (WS), the convective SIGMET (WST), the AIRMET (WA; text or graphical product), and the Center Weather Advisory (CWA). All heights are referenced MSL, except in the case of ceilings (CIG) which indicate AGL.

[PA.I.C.K2g; AIM 7-1-6, FAA-H-8083-28]

Chapter 10 **Weather Information**

11. What is a Convective SIGMET?

A convective SIGMET (WST) implies severe or greater turbulence, severe icing, and low-level wind shear. They may be issued for any convective situation that the forecaster feels is hazardous to all categories of aircraft. Convective SIGMET bulletins are issued for the eastern (E), central (C) and western (W) United States. (Convective SIGMETs are not issued for Alaska or Hawaii.) Bulletins are issued hourly (at H+55). Special bulletins are issued at any time as required and updated at H+55. The text of the bulletin consists of either an observation and a forecast, or just a forecast. The forecast is valid for up to 2 hours and may include information regarding:

a. Severe thunderstorm due to:
   - Surface winds greater than or equal to 50 knots.
   - Hail at the surface greater than or equal to ¾ inches in diameter.
   - Tornadoes.

b. Embedded thunderstorms.

c. A line of thunderstorms.

d. Thunderstorms producing greater than or equal to heavy precipitation affecting 40 percent or more of an area of at least 3,000 square miles.

[PA.I.C.K2g; FAA-H-8083-28]

12. What is a SIGMET (WS)?

A SIGMET (WS) advises of weather that is potentially hazardous to all aircraft. SIGMETs are unscheduled products that are valid for 4 hours; SIGMETs associated with tropical cyclones and volcanic ash clouds are valid for 6 hours. Unscheduled updates and corrections are issued, as necessary. In the CONUS, SIGMETs are issued when the following phenomena occur or are expected to occur:

a. Severe icing not associated with thunderstorms.

b. Severe or extreme turbulence or clear air turbulence (CAT) not associated with thunderstorms.

c. Widespread dust storms or sandstorms lowering surface visibilities to below 3 miles.

d. Volcanic ash.

[PA.I.C.K2g; AIM 7-1-6]

Private Pilot Oral Exam Guide 283

Chapter 10 **Weather Information**

13. What is a G-AIRMET?

A G-AIRMET is a graphical advisory of weather that may be hazardous to aircraft but is less severe than a SIGMET. They are only valid at specific time snapshots. G-AIRMETs are issued at discrete times 3 hours apart for a period of up to 12 hours into the future (00, 03, 06, 09, and 12 hours). They are issued at 03:00, 09:00, 15:00 and 21:00 UTC (with updates issued as necessary). AIRMETs are issued by the Aviation Weather Center (AWC) for the contiguous 48 states and adjacent coastal waters. G-AIRMETs provide a higher forecast resolution than text AIRMET products. The aviation hazards depicted in a G-AIRMET are IFR conditions, mountain obscuration, icing, freezing level, turbulence, low-level wind shear (LLWS), and strong surface winds.

[PA.I.C.K2g; FAA-H-8083-28, AIM 7-1-6]

14. What is an AIRMET (WA)?

An AIRMET is a textual advisory of significant weather phenomena that describes conditions at intensities lower than those that require the issuance of SIGMETs. They are issued every 6 hours beginning at 0245 UTC. Pilots should use AIRMETs in the preflight and enroute phases of flight to enhance safety. Unscheduled updates and corrections are issued, as necessary. AIRMETs contain details about IFR conditions, mountain obscuration, icing, freezing level, turbulence, low-level wind shear (LLWS), and strong surface winds.

[PA.I.C.K2g; FAA-H-8083-28, AIM 7-1-6]

15. What are the different types of AIRMETs?

There are three types of AIRMETs: Sierra, Tango, and Zulu:

a. AIRMET Sierra describes IFR conditions and/or extensive mountain obscurations.

b. AIRMET Tango describes moderate turbulence, sustained surface winds of 30 knots or greater, and/or nonconvective low-level wind shear.

c. AIRMET Zulu describes moderate icing and provides freezing level heights.

[PA.I.C.K2g; AIM 7-1-6]

284 Aviation Supplies & Academics

Chapter 10 **Weather Information**

16. What is a winds and temperatures aloft forecast (FB)?

Winds and temperatures aloft are forecast for specific locations in the CONUS and also for a network of locations in Alaska and Hawaii. These forecasts, called FBs, are issued four times daily. In an FB, a four-digit code group shows wind direction, in reference to true north, and wind speed in knots, with an additional two-digit code group showing forecast temperatures in degrees Celsius. Wind forecasts are not issued for altitudes within 1,500 feet of a location's elevation.

Some of the features of FBs are:

a. Product header includes date and time observations collected, forecast valid date and time, and the time period during which the forecast is to be used.

b. Altitudes up to 15,000 feet are referenced to MSL; altitudes at or above 18,000 feet are referenced to flight levels (FL).

c. Temperatures are indicated in degrees Celsius (two digits) for the levels from 6,000 through 24,000 feet. Above 24,000 feet, the minus sign is omitted since temperatures are always negative at those altitudes. Temperature forecasts are not issued for altitudes within 2,500 feet of a location's elevation. Forecasts for intermediate levels are determined by interpolation.

d. Wind direction is indicated in tens of degrees (two digits) with reference to true north, and wind speed is given in knots (two digits). Light and variable wind or wind speeds of less than 5 knots are expressed by 9900. Forecast wind speeds of 100 through 199 knots are indicated by subtracting 100 from the speed and adding 50 to the coded direction. For example, a forecast of 250 degrees, 145 knots, is encoded as 7545. Forecast wind speeds of 200 knots or greater are indicated as a forecast speed of 199 knots. For example, 7799 is decoded as 270 degrees at 199 knots or greater.

Note: The AWC's website provides a graphical depiction of the FB Winds/Temps forecasts as well as a text version at aviationweather.gov/data/windtemp.

[PA.I.C.K2e; FAA-H-8083-28]

Private Pilot Oral Exam Guide 285

Chapter 10 **Weather Information**

17. What valuable information can be determined from winds and temperatures aloft forecasts (FB)?

Most favorable altitude—Based on winds and direction of flight.

Areas of possible icing—By noting air temperatures of +2°C to −20°C.

Temperature inversions—Temperature increases with altitude instead of decreasing.

Turbulence—By observing abrupt changes in wind direction and speed at different altitudes.

[PA.I.C.K2e; FAA-H-8083-28]

18. What are Center Weather Advisories?

A Center Weather Advisory (CWA) is an aviation warning for use by aircrews to anticipate and avoid adverse weather conditions in the enroute and terminal environments. The CWA is not a flight planning product; instead, it reflects current conditions expected at the time of issuance and/or is a short-range forecast for conditions expected to begin within two hours of issuance. CWAs are valid for a maximum of two hours. If conditions are expected to continue beyond the two-hour valid period, a statement will be included in the CWA.

[PA.I.C.K2g; FAA-H-8083-28]

19. What is a Convective Outlook (AC)?

A Convective Outlook (AC) is a narrative and graphical outlook of the potential for severe (tornado, wind gusts 50 knots or greater, or hail 1 inch or greater in diameter) and non-severe (general) convection and specific severe weather threats during the following 8 days. It defines areas of marginal risk (MRGL), slight risk (SLGT), enhanced risk (ENH), moderate risk (MDT), or high risk (HIGH) of severe weather based on a percentage probability.

[PA.I.C.K2f; FAA-H-8083-28]

286 Aviation Supplies & Academics

Chapter 10 **Weather Information**

Aviation Weather Charts

1. Give some examples of the various NWS weather charts you will use during preflight planning.

a. Surface analysis chart

b. Weather depiction chart

c. Short-range surface prognostic chart

d. Significant weather prognostic chart

e. Convective outlook chart

f. Constant pressure analysis chart

g. Freezing level graphics

[PA.I.C.K1; FAA-H-8083-28]

2. What is a surface analysis chart?

A surface analysis chart is an analyzed chart of surface weather observations. It depicts the distribution of multiple items including sea level pressure; the positions of highs, lows, ridges, and troughs; the location and character of fronts; and various boundaries such as drylines, outflow boundaries, sea-breeze fronts, and convergence lines. The chart is produced eight times daily.

[PA.I.C.K2b; FAA-H-8083-28]

3. What symbols are used to depict the following frontal systems on surface analysis charts: cold, warm, stationary, and occluded.

On surface analysis charts, the following symbols are used to depict frontal systems:

a. *Cold front*—A solid blue line with blue triangles pointing in the direction the front is moving.

b. *Warm front*—A solid red line with red semicircles pointing in the direction the front is moving.

c. *Stationary front*—An alternating red and blue line with red semicircles on one side and blue triangles on the opposite side, indicating the front is not moving significantly.

d. *Occluded front*—A solid purple line with alternating purple semicircles and triangles pointing in the direction the front is moving.

[PA.I.C.S1; FAA-H-8083-28]

Private Pilot Oral Exam Guide   287

Chapter 10 **Weather Information**

4. Define the following terms: *LIFR, IFR, MVFR,* and *VFR.*

LIFR—Low instrument flight rules (IFR); ceiling less than 500 feet and/or visibility less than 1 mile.

IFR—Ceiling 500 to less than 1,000 feet and/or visibility 1 to less than 3 miles.

MVFR—Marginal visual flight rules (VFR); ceiling 1,000 to 3,000 feet and/or visibility 3 to 5 miles inclusive.

VFR—Ceiling greater than 3,000 feet and visibility greater than 5 miles; includes sky clear.

[PA.I.C.K3; AIM 7-1-7]

5. Define the term *ceiling.*

The term *ceiling* refers to the height above the ground of the lowest cloud layer that is reported as broken, overcast, or obscuration (such as a layer of fog or smoke) and is not classified as "thin" or "partial." Ceiling is an important factor in aviation as it directly impacts a pilot's ability to operate under visual flight rules (VFR).

For VFR flights, certain minimum ceiling and visibility requirements must be met to ensure safe navigation and obstacle avoidance. A low ceiling may require a pilot to consider alternative routing, delay the flight, or transition to instrument flight rules (IFR) if appropriately rated and equipped.

[PA.I.C.K3f; FAA-H-8083-28]

6. What are short-range surface prognostic charts?

Short-range surface prognostic (prog) charts provide a forecast of surface pressure systems, fronts, and precipitation for a 2½-day period. They cover a forecast area of the 48 contiguous states and coastal waters and are prepared by the NWS Weather Prediction Center (and available on the AWC website). Predicted conditions are divided into five forecast periods: 12, 24, 36, 48 and 60 hours. Each chart depicts a snapshot of weather elements expected at the specified valid time. Charts are updated every three hours plus 12 and 24 hour forecasts updated four times a day and a 36 and 48 hour forecast updated twice a day.

[PA.I.C.K2; FAA-H-8083-28]

288 Aviation Supplies & Academics

Chapter 10 **Weather Information**

7. Describe a US low-level significant weather prog chart.

The low-level significant weather (SigWx) charts provide a forecast of aviation weather hazards primarily intended to be used as guidance products for preflight briefings. The forecast domain covers the CONUS and the coastal waters for altitudes Flight Level 240 (FL240) and below. Each depicts a snapshot of weather expected at the specified valid time. The charts depict weather flying categories, turbulence, and freezing levels, and are issued four times per day in two types: a 12-hour and a 24-hour prog.

[PA.I.C.K2; FAA-H-8083-28]

8. Describe a mid-level significant weather (SigWx) chart.

The mid-level significant weather chart provides a forecast and an overview of significant enroute weather phenomena over a range of flight levels from 10,000 feet MSL to FL450, and associated surface weather features. The chart is a snapshot of weather expected at the specified valid time and depicts numerous weather elements that can be hazardous to aviation. The AWC issues the 24-hour mid-level significant weather chart four times daily.

[PA.I.C.K2g; FAA-H-8083-28]

9. What is a convective outlook chart?

The convective outlook (AC) chart depicts areas forecast to have the potential for severe (tornado, wind gusts 50 knots or greater, or hail with a diameter of 1 inch or greater) and nonsevere (general) convection and specific severe weather threats during the following 8 days. The chart defines areas of marginal risk (MRGL), slight risk (SLGT), enhanced risk (ENH), moderate risk (MDT), or high risk (HIGH) of severe weather based on percentage probability, which varies for time periods from 1 day to 3 days, and then two probabilistic thresholds for days 4 through 8. The day 1, day 2, and day 3 ACs also depict areas of general thunderstorms (TSTM).

[PA.I.C.K2f; FAA-H-8083-28]

Private Pilot Oral Exam Guide 289

Chapter 10 **Weather Information**

10. What are some charts a pilot could refer to for determining the potential for and location of thunderstorms along an intended route of flight?

Pilots can refer to several charts to determine the potential for and location of thunderstorms along their intended route:

a. *Convective outlook (AC)*—Issued by the Storm Prediction Center (SPC), this chart identifies areas of expected thunderstorm activity, including the severity and probability of severe weather, for periods up to eight days in advance.

b. *Significant weather prognostic charts*—These charts provide a graphical depiction of forecasted weather conditions, including areas of convective activity and associated hazards like turbulence or icing. The low-level chart (up to FL240) is particularly useful for most general aviation flights.

c. *Radar summary charts*—These show current precipitation and thunderstorm activity, including the intensity, coverage, and movement of storms.

d. *Satellite imagery*—Infrared and visible satellite images help identify areas of developing thunderstorms by showing cloud formations and convective activity.

[PA.I.C.K3h; FAA-H-8083-28]

11. What are constant pressure level forecasts?

Constant pressure level forecasts are a computer model depiction of select weather (e.g., wind) at a specified constant pressure level (e.g., 300 mb), along with the altitudes (in meters) of the specified constant pressure level. They are used to provide an overview of weather patterns at specified times and pressure altitudes and are the source for winds and temperatures aloft forecasts. Pressure patterns cause and characterize much of the weather.

Typically, lows and troughs are associated with clouds and precipitation while highs and ridges are associated with fair weather, except in winter when valley fog may occur. The location and strength of the jet stream can be viewed at the 300 mb, 250 mb, and 200 mb levels:

925 mb — 2,500 ft
850 mb — 5,000 ft
700 mb — 10,000 ft

Chapter 10 **Weather Information**

500 mb — 18,000 ft
300 mb — 30,000 ft
250 mb — 34,000 ft
200 mb — 39,000 ft

[PA.I.C.K3a; FAA-H-8083-28]

12. What information does a freezing level graphics chart provide?

Freezing level graphics are used to assess the lowest freezing level heights and their values relative to flight paths. The chart uses colors to represent the height in hundreds of feet above mean sea level (MSL) of the lowest freezing level(s). The initial analysis and 3-hour forecast graphics are updated hourly. The 6-, 9-, and 12-hour forecast graphics are updated every three hours.

[PA.I.C.K3i; FAA-H-8083-28]

* * *

Exam Tip: Be prepared to interpret and discuss current and forecast weather along your planned route of flight. The evaluator will want you to demonstrate that you can interpret the various aviation weather reports, forecasts, and charts/graphics and make an assessment of how weather will affect your planned flight.

C. Meteorology

1. Briefly describe the composition of the Earth's atmosphere.

The Earth's atmosphere consists of numerous gases with nitrogen, oxygen, argon, and carbon dioxide making up 99.998 percent of all gases.

[PA.I.C.K3a; FAA-H-8083-28]

2. Most of the Earth's weather occurs in what region of the atmosphere?

Most of the Earth's weather occurs in the troposphere, which begins at the Earth's surface and extends up to approximately 36,000 feet. As the gases in this layer decrease with height, the air becomes thinner and the temperature decreases from about 15°C (59°F) to −56.5°C (−70°F).

[PA.I.C.K3a; FAA-H-8083-28]

Private Pilot Oral Exam Guide 291

Chapter 10 **Weather Information**

3. What are standard atmosphere temperature and pressure lapse rates?

A standard temperature lapse rate is one in which the temperature decreases at the rate of approximately 2°C (3.5°F) per 1,000 feet up to 36,000 feet. Above this point, the temperature is considered constant up to 80,000 feet. A standard pressure lapse rate is one in which pressure decreases at a rate of approximately 1 inHg per 1,000 feet of altitude gain to 10,000 feet.

[PA.I.C.K3a; FAA-H-8083-25]

4. If a standard temperature lapse rate is present, and the temperature on the surface is 8°C, where would a pilot expect the freezing level to be?

A standard temperature lapse rate decreases by 2°C per 1,000 feet of altitude. Starting at a surface temperature of 8°C, the freezing level (0 degrees Celsius) would be approximately 4,000 feet above the surface. This is calculated by dividing the 8-degree temperature difference by the 2-degree lapse rate per 1,000 feet.

[PA.I.C.K3a; FAA-H-8083-25]

5. What is a temperature inversion?

An inversion is an increase in temperature with height—a reversal of the normal decrease with height. An inversion aloft permits warm rain to fall through cold air below. The temperature in the cold air can be critical to icing. A ground-based inversion favors poor visibility by trapping fog, smoke, and other restrictions in low levels of the atmosphere. The air is stable, with little or no turbulence.

[PA.I.C.K3c; FAA-H-8083-28]

6. Explain the difference between a stable atmosphere and an unstable atmosphere. Why is the stability of the atmosphere important?

The stability of the atmosphere depends on its ability to resist vertical motion. A stable atmosphere makes vertical movement difficult, and small vertical disturbances dampen out and disappear. In an unstable atmosphere, small vertical air movements tend to become larger, resulting in turbulent airflow and convective activity. Instability can lead to significant turbulence, extensive vertical clouds, and severe weather.

[PA.I.C.K3a; FAA-H-8083-28]

292 Aviation Supplies & Academics

Chapter 10 **Weather Information**

7. How can you determine the stability of the atmosphere?

When temperature decreases uniformly and rapidly as you climb (approaching 3°C per 1,000 feet), you have an indication of unstable air. If the temperature remains unchanged or decreases only slightly with altitude, the air tends to be stable. When air near the surface is warm and moist, suspect instability.

[PA.I.C.K3a; FAA-H-8083-28]

8. List the effects of stable and unstable air on clouds, turbulence, precipitation, and visibility.

	Stable air	Unstable air
Clouds	Stratiform	Cumuliform
Turbulence	Smooth	Rough
Precipitation	Steady	Showery
Visibility	Fair to poor	Good

[PA.I.C.K3a; FAA-H-8083-28]

9. What causes the wind?

Differences in air density caused by changes in temperature result in a change in pressure. This, in turn, creates motion in the atmosphere, both vertically and horizontally, in the form of wind and convective currents.

[PA.I.C.K3b; FAA-H-8083-25]

10. What are the three forces that affect the wind?

Pressure gradient force (PGF), Coriolis force, and friction.

[PA.I.C.K3b; FAA-H-8083-28]

11. What are isobars?

An isobar is a line on a weather chart that connects areas of equal or constant barometric pressure.

[PA.I.C.K3a; FAA-H-8083-28]

Private Pilot Oral Exam Guide 293

Chapter 10 **Weather Information**

12. Explain how the pressure gradient force affects the wind.

Wind is driven by pressure differences that create a force called the *pressure gradient force* (PGF). Whenever a pressure difference develops over an area, the PGF makes the wind blow in an attempt to equalize pressure differences. This force is identified by height contour gradients on constant pressure charts and by isobar gradients on surface charts. PGF is directed from higher height/pressure to lower height/pressure and is perpendicular to contours/isobars. Whenever a pressure difference develops over an area, the PGF begins moving the air directly across the contours/isobars.

[PA.I.C.K3b; FAA-H-8083-28]

13. If the isobars are relatively close together on a surface weather chart or a constant pressure chart, what information does this provide?

The spacing of isobars on these charts defines how steep or shallow a pressure gradient is. When isobars are spaced very close together, a steep pressure gradient exists, which indicates higher wind speeds. A shallow pressure gradient (isobars not close together) usually means wind speeds will be slower.

[PA.I.C.K3a; FAA-H-8083-28]

14. What is the name of the force that deflects winds to the right in the northern hemisphere and left in the southern hemisphere?

The Coriolis force. It is at a right angle to wind direction and is directly proportional to wind speed.

[PA.I.C.K3b; FAA-H-8083-28]

15. What are several examples of local winds that may affect an aircraft in flight?

Local winds include a sea breeze, land breeze, lake breeze, lake effect, valley breeze, mountain-plains wind circulation, and mountain breeze.

[PA.I.C.K3b; FAA-H-8083-28]

Chapter 10 **Weather Information**

16. Explain the term *wind shear* and state the areas it is likely to occur.

Wind shear is the sudden, drastic change in wind speed and/or direction over a small area, from one level or point to another, usually in the vertical. Wind shear occurs in all directions, but for convenience, it is measured along vertical and horizontal axes, thus becoming horizontal and vertical wind shear. Wind shear can affect any flight at any altitude (e.g., at upper levels near jet streams or near the ground due to convection).

[PA.I.C.K3b; FAA-H-8083-28]

17. What types of weather information will you examine to determine if wind shear conditions might affect your flight?

a. *Terminal forecasts*—Any mention of low-level wind shear (LLWS) or the possibility of severe thunderstorms, heavy rain showers, hail, and wind gusts suggest the potential for LLWS and microbursts.

b. *METARs*—Inspect for any indication of thunderstorms, rain showers, or blowing dust. Additional signs, such as warming trends, gusty winds, cumulonimbus clouds, etc., should be noted.

c. *Severe weather watch reports, SIGMETs, and convective SIGMETs*—Severe convective weather is a prime source for wind shear and microbursts.

d. *LLWAS (low level windshear alert system) reports*—Installed at 110 airports in the US; designed to detect wind shifts between outlying stations and a reference centerfield station.

e. *PIREPs*—Reports of sudden airspeed changes on departure or approach and landing corridors provide a real-time indication of the presence of wind shear.

[PA.I.C.K3g; FAA-H-8083-28]

Chapter 10 **Weather Information**

18. While on a cross-country flight, you notice a lens-shaped cloud over a mountainous area along your route of flight. What does the presence of this type of cloud indicate?

It indicates the presence of a mountain wave, which is an atmospheric wave disturbance formed when stable air flow passes over a mountain or mountain ridge. Mountain waves are a form of mechanical turbulence that develop above and downwind of mountains and frequently produce severe to extreme turbulence. When sufficient moisture is present in the upstream flow, mountain waves produce cloud formations, including cap clouds, cirrocumulus standing lenticular (CCSL) clouds, altocumulus standing lenticular (ACSL) clouds, and rotor clouds. These clouds provide visual proof that mountain waves exist; however, the clouds may be absent if the air is too dry.

[PA.I.C.K3f; FAA-H-8083-28]

19. The amount of moisture in the air is dependent on what factor?

The temperature of the air. Every 11°C (20°F) increase in temperature doubles the amount of moisture the air can hold. Conversely, a decrease of 11°C (20°F) cuts the capacity in half.

[PA.I.C.K3d; FAA-H-8083-28]

20. Define the terms *relative humidity* and *dew point*.

Relative humidity—The ratio, usually expressed as a percentage, of water vapor actually in the air parcel compared to the amount of water vapor the air parcel could hold at a particular temperature and pressure.

Dew point—The temperature to which an air parcel must be cooled at constant pressure and constant water vapor pressure to allow the water vapor in the parcel to condense into water (dew).

[PA.I.C.K3d; FAA-H-8083-28]

21. What are the different precipitation types?

Precipitation types include drizzle, rain, freezing rain, freezing drizzle, snow, snow grains, ice crystals, ice pellets, hail, and small hail and/or snow pellets.

[PA.I.C.K3d; FAA-H-8083-28]

Chapter 10 **Weather Information**

22. What are the three ingredients necessary for precipitation to form?

Precipitation formation requires three ingredients: water vapor, sufficient lift to condense the water vapor into clouds, and a growth process that allows cloud droplets to grow large and heavy enough to fall as precipitation. Significant precipitation usually requires clouds to be at least 4,000 feet thick.

[PA.I.C.K3d; FAA-H-8083-28]

23. Explain the general characteristics in regard to the flow of air around high-pressure and low-pressure systems in the Northern Hemisphere.

Low pressure—inward, upward, and counterclockwise

High pressure—outward, downward, and clockwise

[PA.I.C.K3a; FAA-H-8083-28]

24. If your route of flight takes you toward a low-pressure system, in general what kind of weather can you expect? What if you were flying toward a high-pressure system?

A low-pressure system is characterized by rising air, which is conducive to cloudiness, precipitation, and bad weather. A high-pressure system is an area of descending air, which tends to favor dissipation of cloudiness and good weather.

[PA.I.C.K3a; FAA-H-8083-28]

25. Describe the different types of fronts.

Cold front—Occurs when a mass of cold, dense, and stable air advances and replaces a body of warmer air.

Occluded front—A frontal occlusion occurs when a fast-moving cold front catches up with a slow-moving warm front. The two types are the cold front occlusion and warm front occlusion.

Warm front—The boundary area formed when a warm air mass contacts and flows over a colder air mass.

Stationary front—When the forces of two air masses are relatively equal, the boundary or front that separates them remains stationary and influences the local weather for days. The weather is typically a mixture of both warm and cold fronts.

[PA.I.C.K3a; FAA-H-8083-28]

Private Pilot Oral Exam Guide 297

Chapter 10 **Weather Information**

26. What are the general characteristics of the weather a pilot would encounter when operating near a cold front? A warm front?

Cold front—As the front passes, expected weather can include towering cumulus or cumulonimbus clouds; heavy rain accompanied by lightning, thunder, and/or hail; tornadoes possible; poor visibility; winds variable and gusting; temperature/dew point and barometric pressure drop rapidly.

Warm front—As the front passes, expected weather can include stratiform clouds, drizzle, low ceilings and poor visibility, variable winds, and a rise in temperature.

Note: The weather associated with a front depends on the amount of moisture available, the degree of stability of the air that is forced upward, the slope of the front, the speed of frontal movement, and the upper wind flow.

[PA.I.C.K3a; FAA-H-8083-28]

27. What is a trough?

A trough (also called a trough line) is an elongated area of relatively low atmospheric pressure. At the surface, when air converges into a low, it cannot go outward against the pressure gradient, and it cannot go downward into the ground; it must go upward. Therefore, a low or trough is an area of rising air. Rising air is conducive to cloudiness and precipitation; hence, the general association of low pressure and bad weather.

[PA.I.C.K3a; FAA-H-8083-28]

28. What is a ridge?

A ridge (also called a ridge line) is an elongated area of relatively high atmospheric pressure. Moving out of a high or ridge depletes the quantity of air; therefore, these are areas of descending air. Descending air favors dissipation of cloudiness; hence the association of high pressure and good weather.

[PA.I.C.K3a; FAA-H-8083-28]

29. What does a cloud consist of, and why do clouds form?

A cloud is a visible aggregate of minute water droplets and/or ice particles in the atmosphere above the Earth's surface. Clouds form in the atmosphere as a result of condensation of water vapor

Chapter 10 **Weather Information**

in rising currents of air or by the evaporation of the lowest layer of fog. Rising currents of air are necessary for the formation of vertically deep clouds capable of producing precipitation heavier than light intensity.

[PA.I.C.K3f; FAA-H-8083-28]

30. What factor primarily determines the type and vertical extent of clouds?

The stability of the atmosphere.

[PA.I.C.K3f; FAA-H-8083-28]

31. Describe the four basic cloud forms observed in the Earth's atmosphere.

Cirri-form—High-level clouds that form above 20,000 feet, are usually composed of ice crystals, and are typically thin and white in appearance.

Nimbo-form—Nimbus is Latin meaning "rain." These clouds form between 7,000 and 15,000 feet and bring steady precipitation. As clouds thicken and precipitation begins, the cloud bases tend to lower toward the ground.

Cumuli-form—Clouds that show the vertical motion or thermal uplift of air taking place in the atmosphere. The height of the cloud base depends on the humidity of the rising air. The more humid the air, the lower the cloud base. The tops of these clouds can reach over 60,000 feet.

Strati-form—Stratus is Latin for "layer" or "blanket." These clouds consist of a featureless lower layer that can cover the entire sky like a blanket. The cloud bases are usually only a few hundred feet above the ground.

[PA.I.C.K3f; FAA-H-8083-28]

32. What are the three primary causes of turbulence?

a. Convective currents (called convective turbulence)

b. Obstructions in the wind flow (called mechanical turbulence)

c. Wind shear

[PA.I.C.K3g; FAA-H-803-28]

Private Pilot Oral Exam Guide 299

Chapter 10 **Weather Information**

33. What are the four intensity levels of turbulence?

Light—Causes slight, erratic changes in altitude and/or attitude (pitch, roll, or yaw).

Moderate—Changes in altitude and/or attitude occur, but the aircraft remains in positive control at all times. It usually causes variations in indicated airspeed.

Severe—Causes large, abrupt changes in altitude and/or attitude. It usually causes large variations in indicated airspeed. Aircraft may be momentarily out of control.

Extreme—The aircraft is violently tossed about and is practically impossible to control. It may cause structural damage.

[PA.I.C.K3g; FAA-H-8083-28]

34. Define the term *clear air turbulence*.

Clear air turbulence (CAT) is defined as sudden severe turbulence occurring in cloudless regions that causes violent buffeting of aircraft. CAT is a higher altitude turbulence (normally above 15,000 feet) particularly between the core of a jet stream and the surrounding air. CAT is especially troublesome because it is often encountered unexpectedly and frequently without visual clues to warn pilots of the hazard. The best available information on the location of CAT comes from pilots via PIREPs.

[PA.I.C.K3g; FAA-H-8083-28]

35. What are the factors necessary for a thunderstorm to form and what are the three stages of thunderstorm development?

For a thunderstorm to form, the air must have sufficient water vapor, an unstable lapse rate, and an initial upward boost (lifting) to start the storm process in motion. During its lifecycle, a thunderstorm cell progresses through three stages:

a. *Cumulus*—Characterized by a strong updraft.

b. *Mature*—Precipitation beginning to fall from the cloud base signals that a downdraft has developed, and a cell has entered the mature stage.

c. *Dissipating*—Downdrafts characterize the dissipating stage, and the storm dies rapidly.

[PA.I.C.K3h; FAA-H-8083-28]

300 Aviation Supplies & Academics

Chapter 10 **Weather Information**

36. What are the three principal types of thunderstorms?

Single cell—Also called ordinary cell thunderstorms, this type consists of only one cell; they are easily circumnavigated except at night or when embedded in other clouds. Single-cell thunderstorms are rare, as almost all thunderstorms are multi-celled.

Multicell (cluster and line)—Consists of a cluster of cells at different stages of their life cycles. As the first cell matures, it is carried downwind, and a new cell forms upwind to take its place. A multicell may have a lifetime of several hours (or more), which makes it tougher to circumnavigate than a single-cell thunderstorm. Supercells may be embedded within them.

Supercell—Consists primarily of a single, quasi-steady rotating updraft that persists for an extended period of time. Updraft speeds may reach 9,000 fpm (100 knots). They may persist for many hours (or longer), and their size and persistence make them tough to circumnavigate.

[PA.I.C.K3h; FAA-H-8083-28]

37. What are microbursts?

Microbursts are small-scale, intense downdrafts that, on reaching the surface, spread outward in all directions from the downdraft center. This causes the presence of both vertical and horizontal wind shears that can be extremely hazardous to all types and categories of aircraft, especially at low altitudes. Due to their small size, short life span, and the fact that they can occur over areas without surface precipitation, microbursts are not easily detectable using conventional weather radar or wind shear alert systems.

[PA.I.C.K3h; AIM 7-1-24]

38. Where are microbursts most likely to occur?

Microbursts can be found almost anywhere there is convective activity. They may be embedded in heavy rain associated with a thunderstorm or in light rain in benign-appearing virga. When little or no precipitation accompanies the microburst at the surface, a ring of blowing dust may be the only visual clue of its existence.

[PA.I.C.K3h; AIM 7-1-24]

Chapter 10 **Weather Information**

39. What are the main types of icing an aircraft may encounter?

Structural, induction system, and instrument icing.

[PA.I.C.K3i; FAA-H-8083-28]

40. Name the three types of structural ice that may occur in flight.

Clear icing, or glaze ice, is a glossy, clear, or translucent ice formed by the relatively slow freezing of large, supercooled water droplets. Clear icing conditions exist more often in an environment with warmer temperatures, higher liquid water contents, and larger droplets. It forms when only a small portion of the drop freezes immediately while the remaining unfrozen portion flows or smears over the aircraft surface and gradually freezes.

Rime icing is rough, milky, and opaque ice formed by the instantaneous freezing of small, supercooled water droplets after they strike the aircraft. It is the most frequently reported icing type. Rime icing formation favors colder temperatures, lower liquid water content, and small droplets.

Mixed icing is a mixture of clear ice and rime ice that forms as an airplane collects both rime and clear ice due to small-scale variations in liquid water content, temperature, and droplet sizes.

Note: In general, rime icing tends to occur at temperatures colder than −15°C, clear ice when the temperature is warmer than −10°C, and mixed ice at temperatures in between. This is only general guidance. The type of icing will vary depending on the liquid water content, droplet size, and aircraft-specific variables.

[PA.I.C.K3i; FAA-H-8083-28]

41. What is the definition of the term *freezing level*, and how can you determine where that level is?

The freezing level is the lowest altitude in the atmosphere over a given location at which the air temperature reaches 0°C. It is possible to have multiple freezing layers when a temperature inversion occurs above the defined freezing level. A pilot can use current icing products (CIP) and forecast icing products (FIP), as well as the freezing level graphics chart to determine the approximate freezing level. Other potential sources of icing information are GFAs, PIREPs, AIRMETs, SIGMETs, surface

302 Aviation Supplies & Academics

Chapter 10 **Weather Information**

analysis charts, low-level significant weather charts, and winds and temperatures aloft (for air temperature at altitude).

[PA.I.C.K3i; FAA-H-8083-28]

42. What action is recommended if you inadvertently encounter icing conditions?

When icing is detected, a pilot should do one of two things, particularly if the aircraft is not equipped with deicing equipment: leave the area of precipitation, or go to an altitude where the temperature is above freezing. If neither option is available, consider an immediate landing at the nearest suitable airport.

[PA.I.C.K3i; FAA-H-8083-15]

43. When planning a flight, what are some pieces of meteorological information a pilot should be aware of with respect to icing?

When planning a flight, pilots should review meteorological information to assess the risk of icing. Key pieces of information include:

a. *Freezing levels and charts*—Determine the altitude where the temperature is at or below freezing. Knowing the freezing level helps plan a route to avoid or safely exit icing conditions. Winds aloft charts and freezing level charts are good resources for this information.

b. *Weather reports and forecasts*—METARs and TAFs provide current and predicted conditions, including temperature, dew point, and precipitation, which can indicate icing potential. A pilot could use this data to calculate an expected freezing level under standard temperature lapse rate conditions.

c. *AIRMETs and SIGMETs*—These advisories highlight areas of known or forecasted icing conditions. AIRMET Zulu is specifically issued for moderate icing and freezing levels.

d. *PIREPs*—Pilot reports offer real-time accounts of icing conditions encountered by other pilots, including location, altitude, and severity.

e. *Cloud coverage charts*—The presence of visible moisture (e.g., clouds or precipitation) combined with subfreezing temperatures increases icing risks. Determining where clouds

Private Pilot Oral Exam Guide   303

Chapter 10 **Weather Information**

will occur will help a pilot determine when they might encounter icing.

f. *Forecast Icing Potential (FIP)*—This graphical tool shows areas with the likelihood and severity of icing, helping pilots avoid hazardous routes.

[PA.I.C.K3i; FAA-H-8083-28]

44. What is a sea breeze, and why do they occur?

A sea breeze is a local wind that flows from a body of water (such as an ocean or lake) toward the land. It occurs due to differences in heating rates between land and water. During the day, the land heats up faster than the water, causing the air above the land to rise as it becomes warmer and less dense. The cooler, denser air over the water moves in to replace the rising warm air, creating a breeze from the water to the land.

Sea breezes typically bring cooler, moist air inland and can influence local weather by increasing humidity, cloud formation, or even thunderstorms near coastal areas. Understanding sea breezes helps pilots anticipate wind changes and weather conditions during takeoff, landing, or low-altitude flight near coastal airports.

[PA.I.C.K3c; FAA-H-8083-28]

45. How does fog form?

Fog forms when the temperature and dew point of the air become identical (or nearly so). This may occur through cooling of the air to a little beyond its dew point (producing radiation fog, advection fog, or upslope fog) or by the addition of moisture elevating the dew point (producing frontal fog or steam fog).

[PA.I.C.K3j; FAA-H-8083-28]

46. Name and describe several types of fog.

a. *Radiation fog*—Favorable conditions are clear skies, little or no wind, and small temperature-dew point spread (high relative humidity). This fog forms almost exclusively at night or near daybreak.

b. *Advection fog*—Forms when moist air moves over colder ground or water. It is most common along coastal areas but often develops deep in continental areas. It may occur with

Chapter 10 **Weather Information**

winds, cloudy skies, over a wide geographic area, and at any time of the day or night.

c. *Upslope fog*—Forms as a result of moist, stable air being cooled adiabatically as it moves up sloping terrain. Once the upslope wind ceases, the fog dissipates.

d. *Frontal fog or precipitation-induced fog*—When warm, moist air is lifted over a front, clouds and precipitation may form. If the cold air below is near its dew point, evaporation (or sublimation) from the precipitation may saturate the cold air and form fog.

e. *Steam fog*—When very cold air moves across relatively warm water, enough moisture may evaporate from the water surface to produce saturation. As the rising water vapor meets the cold air, it immediately recondenses and rises with the air that is being warmed from below.

f. *Freezing fog*—Occurs when the temperature falls to 0°C (32°F) or below. Tiny, supercooled liquid water droplets in fog can freeze instantly on exposed surfaces when surface temperatures are at or below freezing.

[PA.I.C.K3j; FAA-H-8083-28]

47. What is frost, and what conditions are conducive to its formation?

Frost is ice crystal deposits formed by sublimation when the temperature and dew point are below freezing. Frost can form on an airplane sitting outside on a clear night when moisture is present in the air and the airplane's skin temperature falls below freezing due to radiation cooling.

[PA.I.C.K3k; FAA-H-8083-25]

48. Why is it more likely that a pilot would need to be concerned about the formation of fog when flying to an airport near a large body of water?

A pilot should be more concerned about fog formation near a large body of water because water retains heat longer than land, creating temperature and moisture differences. In the evening or early morning, the land cools quickly, while the water remains relatively warm. This contrast can cause the air over the land to reach its

Private Pilot Oral Exam Guide 305

Chapter 10 **Weather Information**

dew point, especially if there is moisture in the air, leading to fog formation.

The moisture from the nearby water body enhances the likelihood of radiation fog or advection fog. Radiation fog occurs when the ground cools the air above it, while advection fog happens when warm, moist air moves over cooler surfaces. Both can significantly reduce visibility, making navigation and landing challenging.

[PA.I.C.K3k; FAA-H-8083-25]

49. Is frost considered to be hazardous to flight? Why or why not?

Yes, because while frost does not change the basic aerodynamic shape of the wing, the roughness of its surface spoils the smooth flow of air, thus causing a slowing of airflow. This slowing of the air causes early airflow separation, resulting in a loss of lift. Even a small amount of frost on airfoils may prevent an aircraft from becoming airborne at normal takeoff speed. It is also possible that, once airborne, an aircraft could have an insufficient margin of airspeed above stall, so that moderate gusts or turning flight could produce incipient or complete stalling.

[PA.I.C.K3k; FAA-H-8083-28]

50. Does a pilot need to get *all* ice or frost off of an aircraft to be able to fly safely?

Yes. Any amount of frost or ice on the wings or body of the aircraft can affect airflow and lift. While an aircraft "may fly" with some on it, a pilot has no way of knowing what effects there will be on lift and drag and how it will affect performance or stall speeds. It is strongly encouraged that all icing and/or frost is removed from an aircraft surface prior to flight.

[PA.I.C.K3k; FAA-H-8083-28]

51. What are some ways a pilot could safely remove frost off their aircraft to then proceed with a flight?

When working to remove frost from an aircraft, the easiest way to do so likely is to put the aircraft in a warm hangar and allow the frost to melt and dry. A pilot may choose to help remove the frost as it warms up by using soft cloths to absorb the water and dry it more quickly, especially if the aircraft will be taken out of

Chapter 10 **Weather Information**

the hangar back into below-freezing temperatures. Some deicing fluids may also be sprayed or wiped on the surfaces to remove ice or frost. The use of any rough cloths or scrapers is discouraged, as they can do damage to paint and surface materials. Warm water dumped onto the aircraft is discouraged, especially in below-freezing temperatures, because it can refreeze and may end up flowing into areas and systems other than just on the surface of the aircraft. Another more time-consuming option is to wait for sun heating to warm up the aircraft surfaces or for the day to warm up, delaying a flight until the ice or frost can melt naturally.

[PA.I.C.K3k; FAA-H-8083-28]

52. Describe several additional types of obstructions to visibility that may occur in the atmosphere.

Weather and obstructions to visibility include fog, mist, haze, smoke, precipitation, blowing snow, dust storm, sandstorm, and volcanic ash.

[PA.I.C.K3l; FAA-H-8083-28]

Private Pilot Oral Exam Guide 307

Cross-Country Flight Planning

11

Chapter 11 **Cross-Country Flight Planning**

A. Flight Planning

1. Preflight action as required by regulation for all flights away from the vicinity of the departure airport shall include a review of what specific information?

For a flight under IFR or a flight not in the vicinity of an airport:

NOTAMs

Weather reports and forecasts

Known ATC traffic delays

Runway lengths at airports of intended use

Alternatives available if the planned flight cannot be completed

Fuel requirements

Takeoff and landing distance data

Remember: NW KRAFT

[PA.I.D.K1; 14 CFR 91.103]

2. What are the three types of VFR aeronautical charts commonly used by pilots?

a. *Sectional Aeronautical Charts*—Designed for visual navigation of slow to medium-speed aircraft. One inch equals 6.86 nautical miles (NM). They are revised every 56 days.

b. *VFR Terminal Area Charts (TAC)*—TACs depict the Class B airspace. While similar to sectional charts, TACs have more detail because the scale is larger. One inch equals 3.43 NM. Charts are revised every 56 days.

c. *VFR flyway planning charts*—This chart is printed on the reverse side of selected TAC charts. The coverage is the same as the associated TAC. They depict flight paths and altitudes recommended for use to bypass high-traffic areas. One inch equals 3.43 NM.

Exam Tip: Prior to your checkride, plan on studying the FAA's *Aeronautical Chart User's Guide* (CUG) for a thorough, in-depth review of all the chart terms and symbols provided on all of the FAA's aeronautical charts and publications.

[PA.I.D.S2; FAA-H-8083-25, AIM 9-1-4]

310 Aviation Supplies & Academics

Chapter 11 **Cross-Country Flight Planning**

3. How can a pilot determine that their printed aeronautical charts are current?

Aeronautical information changes rapidly, so it is important that pilots check the effective dates on each aeronautical chart and publication. To confirm that a chart or publication is current, refer to the next scheduled effective date printed on the cover. Pilots should also check NOTAMs for important updates between chart and publication cycles that are essential for safe flight.

[PA.I.D.S2; FAA CUG]

4. Are electronic flight bags (EFBs) approved for use as a replacement for paper reference material (POH and supplements, charts, etc.) in the flight deck?

Yes. EFBs can be used during all phases of flight operations in lieu of paper reference material when the information displayed is the functional equivalent of the paper reference material replaced and is current, up-to-date, and valid. It is recommended that a secondary or back-up source of aeronautical information necessary for the flight be available.

[PA.I.D.K1a; AC 91-78]

5. What publication provides pilots with updates to visual charts between edition dates?

The *Chart Supplement,* Sectional Aeronautical Charts, and VFR Terminal Area Charts are updated every 56 days. Safety alerts and charting notices are also available for free download at the FAA Aeronautical Information Services (AIS) website at www.faa.gov/air_traffic/flight_info/aeronav/.

[PA.I.D.S2; AIM 9-1-4]

6. Describe the type of information a pilot should review in the *Chart Supplement* prior to flight.

A pilot should review information about each airport at which a landing is intended. This includes the location, elevation, runway and lighting facilities, available services, UNICOM availability, types of fuel available (use to decide on refueling stops), control tower and ground control frequencies, traffic information, remarks, and other pertinent information.

[PA.I.D.S2; FAA-H-8083-25]

Private Pilot Oral Exam Guide 311

Chapter 11 **Cross-Country Flight Planning**

7. What are NOTAMs?

The Notice to Airmen (NOTAM) system provides pilots with time-critical aeronautical information that is temporary, information to be published on aeronautical charts at a later date, or information from another operational publication. The NOTAM is canceled when the information in the NOTAM is published on the chart or when the temporary condition is returned to normal status. NOTAMs may be disseminated up to 7 days before the start of activity. Pilots can access NOTAM information online via FNS NOTAM Search at notams.aim.faa.gov/notamSearch/ or from an FSS.

[PA.I.D.S2; AIM 5-1-3]

8. Describe the following classes of NOTAMs: Domestic NOTAM (D), FDC NOTAM, International NOTAM, and Military NOTAM.

a. *Domestic NOTAM (D)*—Information disseminated for all navigational facilities that are part of the NAS, all public-use aerodromes, seaplane bases, and heliports listed in the *Chart Supplement*. NOTAM (D) information includes taxiway closures, personnel and equipment near or crossing runways, and airport lighting aids that do not affect instrument approach criteria (e.g., VGSI).

b. *FDC NOTAMs*—Issued when it is necessary to disseminate regulatory information. FDC NOTAMs include amendments to published IAPs and other current aeronautical charts; TFRs; high barometric pressure warnings; laser light activity; ADS-B, TIS-B, and FIS-B service availability; satellite-based systems such as WAAS or GPS; and special notices. Additionally, US Domestic Security NOTAMs are FDC NOTAMs that inform pilots of certain US security activities or requirements.

c. *International NOTAMs*—Published in ICAO format per Annex 15, International NOTAMs are distributed to multiple countries. International NOTAMs basically duplicate data found in a US NOTAM. International NOTAMs received by the FAA from other countries are stored in the US NOTAM System.

d. *Military NOTAMs*—Originated by the US Air Force, Army, Marine, or Navy, Military NOTAMs pertain to military or joint-use navigational aids/airports that are part of the NAS.

312 Aviation Supplies & Academics

Chapter 11 **Cross-Country Flight Planning**

Military NOTAMs are published in the International NOTAM format and should be reviewed by users of a military or joint-use facility.

[PA.I.D.S2; AIM 5-1-3]

9. Where can NOTAM information be found?

a. Call Flight Service at 1-800-WX-BRIEF.

b. NOTAM Search at notams.aim.faa.gov/notamSearch.

c. Flight Service briefing website at 1800wxbrief.com.

d. In flight, FIS-B via ADS-B In.

Note: The NOTAM (D) and FDC NOTAM products broadcast via FIS-B are limited to those issued or effective within the past 30 days. Except for TFRs, NOTAMs older than 30 days are not provided.

[PA.I.D.S2; AIM 5-1-3]

10. How can a pilot determine if there are any known ATC delays for a cross-country flight?

Pilots can determine if there are any known ATC delays for a cross-country flight by checking Notices to Airmen (NOTAMs) and consulting the FAA's Traffic Management Program (TMP) resources. Specific delay information, such as ground delay programs (GDPs) or enroute restrictions, can be found through Flight Service briefings, either by calling Flight Service (1-800-WX-BRIEF) or using online tools like 1800wxbrief. com. Additionally, pilots can access delay information via FAA's Operational Status webpage or ATIS (Automatic Terminal Information Service) broadcasts at affected airports. Many electronic flight planning tools and apps also display ATC delay notifications as part of their briefing services. Always verify delay information prior to departure to ensure an accurate flight plan.

[PA.VIII.F.K1; AIM 7-1-5]

Private Pilot Oral Exam Guide 313

Chapter 11 **Cross-Country Flight Planning**

B. Pilotage and Dead Reckoning

1. What are three common ways to navigate?

To navigate successfully, pilots must know their approximate position at all times or be able to determine it whenever they wish. Position may be determined by:

a. Pilotage (by reference to visible landmarks);

b. Dead reckoning (by computing direction and distance from a known position); or

c. Radio navigation (by use of radio aids).

[PA.VI.A.K; FAA-H-8083-25]

2. Explain how a pilot navigates using pilotage.

Pilotage is navigation by reference to landmarks or checkpoints. It is a method of navigation that can be used on any course that has adequate checkpoints, but it is more commonly used in conjunction with dead reckoning and VFR radio navigation. The pilot visually identifies landmarks outside the aircraft and compares their position with their position on a chart relative to the plotted course line.

[PA.VI.A.K1; FAA-H-8083-25]

3. Define the term *dead reckoning*.

Dead reckoning is navigation solely by means of computations based on time, airspeed, distance, and direction. The products derived from these variables, when adjusted by wind speed and velocity, are heading and ground speed (GS). The predicted heading takes the aircraft along the intended path, and the GS establishes the time to arrive at each checkpoint and the destination. Except for flights over water, dead reckoning is usually used with pilotage for cross-country flying.

[PA.VI.A.K1; FAA-H-8083-25]

4. Explain what type of landmarks will make good checkpoints.

Appropriate checkpoints should be selected along the route and noted in some way. These should be easy-to-locate points, such as large towns, large lakes and rivers, or combinations of recognizable points such as towns with an airport, with a network of highways, or with railroads entering and departing. Normally, choose only

314 Aviation Supplies & Academics

Chapter 11 **Cross-Country Flight Planning**

towns indicated by splashes of yellow on the chart. Do not choose towns represented by a small circle—these may turn out to be only a half-dozen houses. (In isolated areas, however, towns represented by a small circle can be prominent checkpoints.)

[PA.VI.A.K4c; FAA-H-8083-25]

5. Explain the factors you considered when selecting the landmarks that you used for your checkpoints on your cross-country flight plan.

When planning a cross-country flight, selecting appropriate landmarks is crucial for effective navigation. Some good factors to consider could include the following:

a. *Visibility and size*—Choose landmarks that are large, distinct, and easy to identify from the air, such as rivers, lakes, highways, towns, or prominent terrain features. Avoid relying on small or obscure landmarks that may blend into the surroundings.

b. *Contrast and uniqueness*—Select features that contrast with the surrounding environment. For example, a bright blue lake in a forested area or a large industrial complex in a rural landscape is easier to spot.

c. *Distance and spacing*—Landmarks should be spaced appropriately to maintain situational awareness. Select points within a manageable distance, typically every 10–20 minutes of flight time, depending on your aircraft's speed.

d. *Redundancy*—Choose multiple landmarks along your route to cross-check your position. This can be especially important in areas with sparse or repetitive features, such as deserts or plains.

e. *Backup for navigation aids*—Identify visual landmarks near key waypoints or navigation fixes in case GPS or other navigation aids fail.

f. *Lighting and weather*—Consider how weather conditions, time of day, or lighting might affect the visibility of landmarks. Some features may be obscured at night or in hazy conditions.

g. *Safety considerations*—Select landmarks near alternate airports or emergency landing sites to provide options in case of an unplanned diversion.

(continued)

Private Pilot Oral Exam Guide   315

Chapter 11 **Cross-Country Flight Planning**

Thorough preflight planning with reliable and visible landmarks ensures safer and more confident navigation during cross-country flights.

[PA.VI.A.K4c; FAA-H-8083-25]

6. What are some ways a pilot can confirm that they are over the correct checkpoints and landmarks when flying a cross-country flight?

a. *Visual references*—Pilots can identify landmarks, such as roads, rivers, towns, and distinctive terrain features, by comparing them to the route on a sectional chart or GPS. This helps verify position.

b. *GPS and flight planning tools*—Many pilots use GPS to compare their current position to the planned route. The GPS will show the distance and direction to the next waypoint, helping confirm that the aircraft is on track.

c. *VOR or VORTAC stations*—By tuning into VOR or VORTAC stations, pilots can confirm their location using the aircraft's navigation system to verify their distance and bearing from the station.

d. *ATC communication*—Pilots can request position reports or verify their location with air traffic control, especially when in controlled airspace or near large airports.

e. *Time and distance*—Pilots can use time checks and estimated distances between checkpoints to calculate their position based on the aircraft's speed.

By combining these methods, a pilot can ensure they are on course and properly navigating during their cross-country flight.

[PA.VI.A.K4c; FAA-H-8083-25]

7. Describe several factors a pilot should consider when planning the route of flight for a VFR cross-country flight.

a. *Airspace*—Various classes of airspace and requirements to operate within; avoidance of certain special use airspace such as restricted areas, alert areas, CFAs, TFRs, and active MOAs.

316 Aviation Supplies & Academics

Chapter 11 **Cross-Country Flight Planning**

b. *Airports*—Availability of airports or suitable landing areas in case of an emergency or need for diversion; availability of fuel and services.

c. *Terrain and obstacle clearance*—Can the aircraft safely overfly, or must it divert around it? Also, avoidance of rugged or hostile terrain.

d. *Navigation/communication capability*—Availability of landmarks; VOR signal reception if using VOR navigation; communication availability for contacting Flight Service, ATC, etc.

[PA.I.D.K1; FAA-H-8083-25]

8. Describe several factors a pilot should consider when selecting the cruise altitude for a VFR cross-country flight.

a. *Trip length*—Longer distances make higher altitudes more desirable for better fuel consumption; shorter distances make lower altitudes more desirable; less time in climb results in faster ground speed, less fuel used.

b. *Winds aloft*—Headwinds and tailwinds significantly affect time en route and fuel used.

c. *Aircraft performance*—Time to climb; optimum TAS/fuel consumption; airplane altitude limitations.

d. *Terrain and obstacles*—Mountainous and rising terrain; antenna towers.

e. *Gliding distance*—Higher altitudes provide longer glides in case of an emergency.

f. *VFR cruising altitude*—Hemispheric rule applies if operating above 3,000 feet AGL.

g. *Airspace*—Fly above rather than through Class B, C, or D airspace.

h. *Weather*—Turbulence level, cloud bases, freezing level.

[PA.I.D.K2; FAA-H-8083-25]

Private Pilot Oral Exam Guide 317

Chapter 11 **Cross-Country Flight Planning**

9. Explain what maximum elevation figures depicted on VFR sectional charts indicate. Is a MEF stated in AGL or MSL?

The maximum elevation figure (MEF) represents the highest elevation, including terrain and other vertical obstacles (towers, trees, etc.), within a quadrant. MEF figures are depicted to the nearest 100-foot value. The last two digits of the number are not shown. Elevations are indicated in thousands and hundreds of feet above mean sea level.

[PA.I.D.S2; FAA CUG]

10. What is the lowest altitude an aircraft may be operated over an area designated as a US Wildlife Refuge, National Park, or Forest Service Area?

All aircraft are requested to maintain a minimum altitude of 2,000 feet above the surface.

[PA.I.D.S2; AIM 7-5-6]

11. Explain what the lines of latitude and longitude found on charts indicate.

Latitude—Also known as parallels, latitudes are a measurement north or south of the equator in degrees, minutes, and seconds.

Longitude—Also known as meridians, longitudes are a measurement east or west of the Prime Meridian in degrees, minutes, and seconds. The Prime Meridian is 0° longitude and runs through Greenwich, England.

[PA.I.D.S2; FAA-H-8083-25]

12. How do you convert from standard time to Coordinated Universal Time (UTC)?

You should take the local time (converted to military time) and add the time differential to convert to UTC.

Eastern Standard Time—add 5 hours
Central Standard Time—add 6 hours
Mountain Standard Time—add 7 hours
Pacific Standard Time—add 8 hours
Alaska Standard Time—add 9 hours
Hawaii Standard Time—add 10 hours

Note: For Daylight Savings Time, subtract 1 hour from the above.

[PA.I.D.K3b; AIM 4-2-12]

318 Aviation Supplies & Academics

Chapter 11 **Cross-Country Flight Planning**

13. **Determine the ETA at your destination airport given the following information: Your aircraft departs an airport in the Central Standard Time Zone at 0830 CST for a 2-hour flight to an airport located in the Mountain Standard Time Zone. At what Coordinated Universal Time (UTC) will you land at your destination?**

    - Convert departure time to UTC by adding 6 hours:
      0830 + 6:00 = 1430.
    - Add flight time of 2 hours to find arrival time.
      1430 + 2 = 1630Z.

    [PA.I.D.K3b; AIM 4-2-12]

14. **Explain how to measure direction on a sectional chart.**

    By using the meridians, direction from one point to another can be measured in degrees, in a clockwise direction from true north. To indicate a course to be followed in flight, draw a line on the chart from the point of departure to the destination and measure the angle that this line forms with a meridian.

    [PA.I.D.S2; FAA-H-8083-25]

15. **Which meridian along the course line should be used to measure the true course? Why?**

    Because meridians converge toward the poles, course measurement should be taken at a meridian near the midpoint of the course rather than at the point of departure. The course measured on the chart is known as the true course (TC). This is the direction measured by reference to a meridian or true north (TN). It is the direction of intended flight as measured in degrees clockwise from TN.

    [PA.I.D.S2; FAA-H-8083-25]

16. **Explain the difference between a course and a heading.**

    A course is the intended path of an aircraft over the Earth. A heading is the direction in which the airplane's nose is pointing during flight. The heading has the wind correction angle (WCA) applied to the course.

    [PA.VI.A.K5a; FAA-H-8083-25]

Private Pilot Oral Exam Guide   319

Chapter 11 **Cross-Country Flight Planning**

17. What is magnetic variation?

Variation is the compass error caused by the difference in the physical locations of the magnetic north pole and the geographic north pole. It is expressed as east variation or west variation depending upon whether magnetic north (MN) is to the east or west of true north (TN), respectively.

[PA.VI.A.K2; FAA-H-8083-25]

18. What is an isogonic line?

Shown on most aeronautical charts as broken magenta lines, isogonic lines connect points of equal magnetic variation. They show the amount and direction of magnetic variation, which from time to time may vary.

[PA.I.D.S2; FAA-H-8083-25]

19. How do you convert a true course or heading to a magnetic course or heading?

To convert true course or heading to magnetic course or heading, note the variation shown by the nearest isogonic line. If variation is west, add; if east, subtract.

Remember: East is Least (subtract), West is Best (add)

[PA.VI.A.K5a; FAA-H-8083-25]

20. What is magnetic deviation?

Because of magnetic influences within the airplane itself (electrical circuits, radios, lights, tools, engine, magnetized metal parts, etc.), the compass needle is frequently deflected from its normal reading. This deflection is called deviation. Deviation is different for each airplane and also varies for different headings of the same airplane. The deviation value may be found on a deviation card located in the airplane.

[PA.VI.A.K2; FAA-H-8083-25]

Chapter 11 **Cross-Country Flight Planning**

21. Explain how you would determine the following: true course, magnetic course, magnetic heading, true heading, variation, deviation, and compass heading.

True course (TC)—The course measured on the aeronautical chart. It is measured clockwise in degrees from TN on the mid-meridian.

Magnetic course (MC)—The true course with variation applied.

Magnetic heading (MH)—Magnetic course with wind correction angle (WCA) applied. It is the direction in which the nose of the aircraft points during the flight relative to magnetic north.

True heading (TH)—The true course with the wind correction angle (WCA) applied. It is the direction in which the nose of the aircraft points during the flight relative to true north.

Variation—Obtained from the isogonic line on the chart (added if West; subtracted if East).

Deviation—Obtained from the deviation card in the aircraft (added or subtracted from MH, as indicated).

Compass heading (CH)—The magnetic heading corrected for deviation.

[PA.VI.A.K5; FAA-H-8083-25]

22. What is the formula for determining the final compass heading?

$TC \pm WCA = TH \pm V = MH \pm D = CH$

[PA.VI.A.K5; FAA-H-8083-25]

23. Explain how to obtain a preflight briefing, complete a flight log, and file a simulated flight plan.

a. Call 1-800-WX-BRIEF for a briefing consisting of the latest/most current weather, airport, and enroute NAVAID information. Also, self-brief using online automated weather resources.

b. Draw course lines and mark checkpoints on the chart.

c. Enter checkpoints on the log. Measure distances between checkpoints and total leg length.

d. Enter NAVAIDs on the log.

e. Enter VOR courses on the log.

(continued)

Private Pilot Oral Exam Guide   321

Chapter 11 **Cross-Country Flight Planning**

f. Enter altitude on the log—consider hemispherical rule, winds aloft, airspace, terrain elevation etc.

g. Enter the wind (direction/velocity) and temperature on the log.

h. Measure the true course on the chart and enter it on the log.

i. Compute the true airspeed and enter it on the log.

j. Compute the WCA and ground speed and enter them on the log.

k. Determine variation from chart and enter it on the log.

l. Determine deviation from compass correction card and enter it on the log.

m. Enter compass heading on the log.

n. Measure distances on the chart and enter them on the log.

o. Figure ETE and ETA and enter them on the log.

p. Calculate fuel burn and usage; enter them on the log.

q. Compute weight and balance. (Ensure use of current W&B data from your aircraft's POH/AFM.)

r. Compute takeoff and landing performance.

s. Complete a Flight Plan form.

t. File the Flight Plan with Flight Service.

Exam Tip: Be sure to either print or save your weather briefing so that the information used for flight planning is available on the day of the checkride. Highlighting pertinent NOTAMs, information, etc., will make a favorable impression on the examiner. If required, updated weather can be obtained via computer, EFB, etc., on the actual day of the checkride.

[PA.I.D.K5; FAA-H-8083-25]

24. What are some ways a pilot can obtain an inflight weather update for their specific route of flight?

Pilots can obtain inflight weather updates through several methods to ensure safe and informed decision-making during their route of flight:

a. *Flight Service (FSS)*—Contact Flight Service on 122.2 MHz or other published frequencies to speak with a briefer for real-time updates, including METARs, TAFs, PIREPs, and SIGMETs.

322 Aviation Supplies & Academics

Chapter 11 **Cross-Country Flight Planning**

b. *Air traffic control (ATC)*—ATC can provide basic weather information, such as reported conditions, and relay significant changes or hazards along the route.

c. *Automatic weather sources*—Use automated systems like AWOS (Automated Weather Observing System) and ASOS (Automated Surface Observing System) via published frequencies or ATIS at nearby airports.

d. *Datalink weather*—Pilots with onboard ADS-B In or satellite subscription-based systems can access graphical weather data, including radar, METARs, TAFs, and winds aloft.

e. *Onboard radar and lightning detection*—Aircraft equipped with weather radar or storm scopes can provide real-time data about precipitation, thunderstorms, and lightning.

f. *PIREPs (pilot reports)*—Monitor reports from other pilots to stay informed about actual conditions, icing, or turbulence along the route.

g. *Electronic flight bags (EFBs)*—App-based programs, when connected to inflight connectivity, can deliver real-time weather updates.

[PA.I.C.K2g; FAA-H-8083-25]

25. While studying the sectional chart about your destination airport, you notice a small blue star after the control tower frequency. What is the significance of the blue star?

On a sectional chart, a small blue star following the control tower frequency for an airport indicates that the airport has a rotating beacon that operates from sunset to sunrise or during periods of reduced visibility. This beacon helps pilots visually identify the airport at night or in marginal weather conditions.

The rotating beacon alternates between green and white flashes for a civilian land airport. For a military airport, the flashes alternate white and green but include a second white flash in the sequence (white-green-white). The presence of the blue star is a reminder to pilots that they can use the beacon as a visual aid when locating the airport during nighttime or low-visibility operations.

[PA.I.E.K2; FAA CUG]

Chapter 11 **Cross-Country Flight Planning**

C. Basic Calculations

Review the following time, speed, distance, and fuel consumption problems. Several ground speed/true heading problems are also included.

[PA.I.D.K3]

Time, Speed, and Distance Problems

1. **If time equals 25 minutes and distance equals 47 NM, what will ground speed be?**

    113 knots

2. **If distance equals 84 NM and ground speed equals 139 knots, what will time be?**

    36 minutes

3. **If ground speed is 85 knots and time is 51 minutes, what will the distance be?**

    72 NM

Fuel Consumption Problems

4. **If gallons-per-hour is 9.3 and time is 1 hour, 27 minutes, how many gallons will be consumed?**

    13.5 gallons

5. **If the time is 2 hours, 13 minutes and gallons consumed is 32, what will the gallons-per-hour be?**

    14.4 gph

6. **If gallons consumed is 38, and gallons-per-hour is 10.8, what will the time be?**

    3 hours, 31 minutes

True Airspeed Problems

7. **If altitude is 10,000 feet, temperature is 0°C, and IAS is 115 knots, what will the TAS be?**

    135 knots TAS

324 Aviation Supplies & Academics

Chapter 11 **Cross-Country Flight Planning**

8. **If IAS is 103 knots, altitude is 6,000 feet, and the temperature is –10°C, what will the TAS be?**

   110 knots TAS

9. **If the temperature is 40°F, the IAS is 115 knots, and the altitude is 11,000 feet, what will the TAS be?**

   139 knots TAS

Density Altitude Problems

10. **If pressure altitude is 1,500 feet and the temperature is 35°C, what will the density altitude be?**

    4,100 feet

11. **If pressure altitude is 5,000 feet and the temperature is –10°C, what will the density altitude be?**

    3,150 feet

12. **If the pressure altitude is 2,000 feet and the temperature is 30°C, what will the density altitude be?**

    4,160 feet

Conversion Problems

13. **100 nautical miles = _____ statute miles**

    115 SM

14. **12 quarts oil = _____ pounds**

    22.5 pounds

15. **45 gallons fuel = _____ pounds**

    270 pounds

16. **80°F = _____ °C**

    27°C

17. **20 knots = _____ miles per hour**

    23 mph

Private Pilot Oral Exam Guide 325

Chapter 11 **Cross-Country Flight Planning**

Ground Speed/True Heading Problems

18. If wind direction is 220, wind speed is 030, true course is 146, and TAS is 135, what will ground speed and true heading be?

Ground speed is 124 knots, true heading is 158°.

19. If wind direction is 240, wind speed is 025, true course is 283 and TAS is 165, what will ground speed and true heading be?

Ground speed is 146 knots, true heading is 277°.

20. If wind direction is 060, wind speed is 030, true course is 036 and TAS is 140, what will ground speed and true heading be?

Ground speed is 112 knots, true heading is 041°.

D. VFR Flight Plan

1. What information is required by regulation in a VFR flight plan?

Unless otherwise authorized by ATC, each person filing a VFR flight plan shall include in it the following information:

a. The aircraft identification number and, if necessary, its radio call sign.

b. The type of the aircraft or, in the case of a formation flight, the type of each aircraft and the number of aircraft in the formation.

c. The full name and address of the pilot-in-command or, in the case of a formation flight, the formation commander.

d. The point and proposed time of departure.

e. The proposed route, cruising altitude (or flight level), and true airspeed at that altitude.

f. The point of first intended landing and the estimated elapsed time until over that point.

g. The amount of fuel on board (in hours).

h. The number of persons in the aircraft, except where that information is otherwise readily available to the FAA.

i. Any other information the pilot-in-command or ATC believes is necessary for ATC purposes.

[PA.I.D.K4; 14 CFR 91.153]

326 Aviation Supplies & Academics

Chapter 11 **Cross-Country Flight Planning**

2. How can a pilot file a VFR flight plan? Will an ATC tower automatically activate a VFR flight plan?

It is strongly recommended that a VFR flight plan be filed with a Flight Service Station or equivalent flight plan filing service. Pilots are responsible for activating flight plans with a Flight Service Station. Control tower personnel do not automatically activate VFR flight plans.

[PA.I.D.K5; AIM 5-1-5]

3. When are VFR flight plans required to be filed?

The requirements for the filing and activation of VFR flight plans can vary depending on in which airspace the flight is operating. Within the continental United States, a VFR flight plan is not normally required. VFR flights (except for DOD and law enforcement flights) into an air defense identification zone (ADIZ) are required to file DVFR flight plans. Flights within the Washington, DC Special Flight Rules Area (DC SFRA) have additional requirements that must be met. VFR flight to an international destination requires a filed and activated flight plan.

[PA.I.D.K5; AIM 5-1-5]

4. What is a DVFR flight plan?

Defense VFR; VFR flights (except for DOD and law enforcement flights) into an ADIZ are required to file DVFR flight plans for security purposes. The IFR or DVFR aircraft must depart within 5 minutes of the estimated departure time contained in the flight plan. DVFR flight plans must be filed using FAA Form 7233-4 or DD Form 1801.

[PA.I.D.K5; AIM 5-1-8]

5. How can a flight plan that has been filed with Flight Service be activated?

Pilots are encouraged to activate their VFR flight plans with Flight Service by the most expeditious means possible. This may be via radio or other electronic means. Pilots may also activate a VFR flight plan by using an assumed departure time. This assumed departure time will cause the flight plan to become active at the designated time. VFR flight plan proposals are normally retained for two hours following the proposed time of departure.

(continued)

Private Pilot Oral Exam Guide   327

Chapter 11 **Cross-Country Flight Planning**

Note: A pilot can call 1-800-WX-BRIEF on the ground and have them activate at ETD or call Flight Service in the air on a designated frequency and activate.

[PA.I.D.K5; AIM 5-1-5]

6. How can a pilot determine what frequency is appropriate for activating a VFR flight plan once airborne?

Two ways:

a. Ask the FSS briefer during the preflight weather briefing.

b. Consult the communications section under flight service for the airport of departure in the *Chart Supplement.*

[PA.I.D.K5; FAA-H-8083-25]

7. When you land at an airport with an ATC tower in operation, will the tower automatically close your flight plan?

Control towers do not automatically close VFR or DVFR flight plans, since they do not know if a particular VFR aircraft is on a flight plan. A pilot is responsible for ensuring that their VFR or DVFR flight plan is canceled. You should close your flight plan with the nearest FSS, or if one is not available, you may request any ATC facility to relay your cancellation.

[PA.I.D.K5; AIM 5-1-14]

8. If your flight is behind schedule, and you do not report the delay, or you forget to close your flight plan, how much time from the ETA does the FSS allow before search and rescue efforts are begun?

If you fail to report or cancel your flight plan within one-half hour after your ETA, search and rescue procedures are started.

[PA.I.D.K5; AIM 5-1-14]

9. What is the minimum safe altitude that an aircraft may be operated over a congested area of a city?

Except when necessary for takeoff or landing, no person may operate an aircraft over a congested area of a city, town, or settlement, or over any open-air assembly of persons, below an

328 Aviation Supplies & Academics

Chapter 11 **Cross-Country Flight Planning**

altitude of 1,000 feet above the highest obstacle within a horizontal radius of 2,000 feet of the aircraft.

[PA.I.D.K2; 14 CFR 91.119]

10. In areas other than congested areas, what minimum safe altitudes shall be used?

Except when necessary for takeoff or landing, an aircraft shall be operated no lower than 500 feet above the surface, except over open water or sparsely populated areas. In those cases, the aircraft may not be operated closer than 500 feet to any person, vessel, vehicle, or structure.

[PA.I.D.K2; 14 CFR 91.119]

11. Define *minimum safe altitude*.

An altitude allowing, if a power unit fails, an emergency landing without undue hazard to persons or property on the surface.

[PA.I.D.K2; 14 CFR 91.119]

12. When flying below 18,000 feet MSL, cruising altitude must be maintained by reference to an altimeter set using what procedure?

When the barometric pressure is 31.00 inHg or less, each person operating an aircraft must maintain the cruising altitude of that aircraft by reference to an altimeter that is set to the current reported altimeter setting of a station along the route and within 100 NM of the aircraft. If there is no station within this area, the current reported altimeter setting of an available station may be used. If the barometric pressure exceeds 31.00 inHg, consult the *Aeronautical Information Manual* for correct procedures.

[PA.I.E.K1; 14 CFR 91.121]

13. If an altimeter setting is not available before flight, what procedure should be used?

Use the same procedure as in the case of an aircraft not equipped with a radio: The elevation of the departure airport or an appropriate altimeter setting available before departure should be used.

[PA.I.F.K2a; 14 CFR 91.121]

Private Pilot Oral Exam Guide 329

Chapter 11 **Cross-Country Flight Planning**

14. What is the fuel requirement for VFR flight during the day?

During the day, you must be able to fly to the first point of intended landing and, assuming normal cruising speed, to fly after that for at least 30 minutes.

[PA.I.D.K3c; 14 CFR 91.151]

15. What is the fuel requirement for VFR flight at night?

At night, no person may begin a flight in an airplane under VFR conditions unless (considering wind and forecast weather conditions) there is enough fuel to fly to the first point of intended landing and, assuming normal cruising speed, to fly after that for at least 45 minutes.

[PA.I.D.K3c; 14 CFR 91.151]

16. When operating an aircraft under VFR in level cruising flight at an altitude of more than 3,000 feet above the surface, what rules apply concerning specific altitudes flown?

When operating above 3,000 feet AGL but less than 18,000 feet MSL on a *magnetic course* of 0° to 179°, fly at an odd-thousand-foot MSL altitude plus 500 feet. When on a *magnetic course* of 180° to 359°, fly at an even-thousand-foot MSL altitude plus 500 feet.

[PA.I.D.K2; 14 CFR 91.159]

E. Navigation Systems and Radar Services

1. Name several types of navigational aids.

a. VOR (Very High Frequency Omnidirectional Range)

b. VORTAC (VHF Omnidirectional Range/Tactical Air Navigation)

c. DME (Distance Measuring Equipment)

d. RNAV (Area Navigation) includes INS, VOR/DME-referenced, and GPS.

e. PBN (performance-based navigation) includes RNP (Required Navigation Performance).

[PA.VI.B.K1; AIM 1-1-3 to 1-1-7, 1-1-17]

Chapter 11 **Cross-Country Flight Planning**

2. What is a VOR or VORTAC?

VORs are VHF radio stations that project radials in all directions
(360°) from the station, like spokes from the hub of a wheel. Each
of these radials is denoted by its outbound magnetic direction.
Almost all VOR stations will also be VORTACs. A VORTAC
(VOR Tactical Air Navigation) provides the standard bearing
information of a VOR plus distance information to pilots of
airplanes that have distance measuring equipment (DME).

[PA.VI.B.K1; FAA-H-8083-25]

3. Within what frequency range do VORs operate?

Transmitting frequencies of omnirange stations are in the VHF
(very high frequency) band between 108 and 117.95 MHz, which
are immediately below aviation communication frequencies.

[PA.VI.B.K1; FAA-H-8083-25]

4. What is a VOR radial?

A radial is defined as a line of magnetic bearing extending from an
omnidirectional range (VOR). A VOR projects 360 radials from
the station. These radials are always identified by their direction
from the station. Regardless of heading, an aircraft on the 360°
radial will always be located north of the station.

[PA.VI.B.K1; FAA-H-8083-25]

5. How are VOR NAVAIDs designated?

VORs are designated by their standard service volumes (SSV). The
three legacy SSV designations are Terminal (T), Low (L), and High
(H). The two new SSV are VOR Low (VL) and VOR High (VH).

[PA.VI.B.K1; AIM 1-1-8]

6. What are the normal usable distances for the various classes of VOR stations?

A NAVAID will have service volume restrictions if it does not
conform to signal strength and course quality standards throughout
the published SSV. Service volume restrictions are first published
in Notices to Airmen (NOTAMs) and then with the alphabetical
listing of the NAVAIDs in the *Chart Supplement*. Service volume
restrictions do not generally apply to published instrument
procedures or routes unless published in NOTAMs for the affected
instrument procedure or route.

Private Pilot Oral Exam Guide 331

Chapter 11 Cross-Country Flight Planning

SSV Class Designator	Altitude and Range Boundaries
T (Terminal)	From 1,000 feet above the transmitter height (ATH) up to and including 12,000 feet ATH at radial distances out to 25 NM.
L (Low-altitude)	From 1,000 feet ATH up to and including 18,000 feet ATH at radial distances out to 40 NM.
H (High-altitude)	From 1,000 feet ATH up to and including 14,500 feet ATH at radial distances out to 40 NM. From 14,500 ATH up to and including 60,000 feet at radial distances out to 100 NM. From 18,000 feet ATH up to and including 45,000 feet ATH at radial distances out to 130 NM.
VL (VOR Low)	From 1,000 feet ATH up to but not including 5,000 feet ATH at radial distances out to 40 NM. From 5,000 feet ATH up to but not including 18,000 feet ATH at radial distances out to 70 NM.
VH (VOR High)	From 1,000 feet ATH up to but not including 5,000 feet ATH at radial distances out to 40 NM. From 5,000 feet ATH up to but not including 14,500 feet ATH at radial distances out to 70 NM. From 14,500 ATH up to and including 60,000 feet at radial distances out to 100 NM. From 18,000 feet ATH up to and including 45,000 feet ATH at radial distances out to 130 NM.
DL (DME Low)	For altitudes up to 12,900 feet ATH at a radial distance corresponding to the LOS to the NAVAID. From 12,900 feet ATH up to but not including 18,000 feet ATH at radial distances out to 130 NM.
DH (DME High)	For altitudes up to 12,900 feet ATH at a radial distance corresponding to the LOS to the NAVAID. From 12,900 ATH up to and including 60,000 feet at radial distances out to 100 NM. From 12,900 feet ATH up to and including 45,000 feet ATH at radial distances out to 130 NM.

[PA.VI.B.K1; AIM 1-1-8]

Chapter 11 **Cross-Country Flight Planning**

7. What limitations, if any, apply to VOR reception distances?

VORs are subject to line-of-sight restrictions, and the range varies proportionally to the altitude of the receiving equipment.

[PA.VI.B.K1; AIM 1-1-3]

8. What are the different methods for checking the accuracy of VOR receiver equipment?

a. *VOT check*—plus or minus 4°

b. *Ground checkpoint*—plus or minus 4°

c. *Airborne checkpoint*—plus or minus 6°

d. *Dual VOR check*—4° between each other

e. *Selected radial over a known ground point*—plus or minus 6°

Note: Locations of airborne check points, ground check points, and VOTs are published in the *Chart Supplement.*

[PA.VI.B.K1; AIM 1-1-4, 14 CFR 91.171]

9. What is DME?

Distance measuring equipment (DME) is an ultra-high frequency (UHF) navigational aid present with VOR/DMEs and VORTACs. It measures, in nautical miles (NM), the slant range distance of an airplane from a VOR/DME or VORTAC (both hereafter referred to as a VORTAC). DME operates on frequencies in the UHF spectrum between 960 MHz and 1215 MHz. Reliable signals may be received at distances up to 199 NM at line-of-sight altitude.

[PA.VI.B.K1; FAA-H-8083-25]

10. What is the VOR Minimum Operational Network?

The VOR Minimum Operational Network (MON) is a backup system for navigation in the event of a GPS outage. The FAA has retained a limited number of VOR stations as part of this network to ensure pilots can still navigate using VOR signals. The MON provides coverage across the continental United States, allowing aircraft to navigate to an airport within 100 nautical miles that has an instrument approach procedure not reliant on GPS. It is designed primarily for aircraft operating at or above 5,000 feet AGL. The MON ensures basic navigation capabilities for pilots in non-GPS environments, supporting safety and continuity of

Private Pilot Oral Exam Guide 333

Chapter 11 **Cross-Country Flight Planning**

operations. Pilots should consult aeronautical charts and FAA publications to identify MON-designated VORs.

[PA.VI.B.K1; AIM 1-1-3]

11. What does reverse sensing refer to with regard to VOR navigation?

Reverse sensing occurs when a pilot incorrectly interprets the VOR indications due to improper setup or usage. It happens when the aircraft's course deviation indicator (CDI) shows the opposite direction of correction needed to stay on course.

This typically occurs if the pilot selects the reciprocal course (the opposite of the intended course) on the VOR receiver and fails to set the course appropriately when using a TO/FROM indication.

For example, if flying toward a VOR with the "FROM" course set, or away with the "TO" course set, the CDI will indicate in reverse, leading the pilot to correct in the wrong direction.

To avoid reverse sensing, ensure the correct course is dialed on the VOR receiver based on the desired TO or FROM direction. Modern systems like horizontal situation indicators (HSI) eliminate reverse sensing entirely by providing proper indications regardless of course selection.

[PA.VI.B.K1; FAA-H-8083-25]

12. When referencing a sectional chart, explain why the 360-degree radial on a VORTAC compass rose is not pointing toward the top of the chart.

When referencing a sectional chart, the 360-degree radial on a VORTAC (VHF Omnidirectional Range and Tactical Air Navigation) compass rose does not point toward the top of the chart because sectional charts are oriented to magnetic north, not true north. This means that the chart is designed to reflect the magnetic variation in the area.

Magnetic variation (or declination) is the difference between true north and magnetic north, which varies depending on the location. The radial on a VORTAC compass rose is oriented to the magnetic north referenced by the VORTAC itself, which is specific to the location of the VOR station.

As the sectional chart is designed to show the layout of navigational aids (such as VORs, VORTACs, and airways), it

334 Aviation Supplies & Academics

Chapter 11 **Cross-Country Flight Planning**

aligns the radial with the magnetic north of that specific VOR station. Therefore, when navigating, pilots should account for the variation in magnetic direction and be aware of how it differs from true north to avoid navigational errors.

[PA.VI.B.K1; FAA-H-8083-25]

13. Where can a pilot find information on the location of the nearest VOT testing station?

Pilots can find information on the location of the nearest VOT (VOR test facility) testing station in several key resources. The most reliable source is the *Chart Supplement*, which lists VOT frequencies and associated locations for airports or enroute facilities. Additionally, VOT testing station details, including frequencies and operational notes, can be found in FAA publications or on the FAA website. Some electronic flight planning tools and avionics databases also provide this information. Pilots should reference these sources before flight to confirm the availability and location of VOT stations for performing accurate VOR equipment checks as required by regulations.

[PA.VI.B.K1; AIM 1-1-4]

14. Will all VOR stations have the capability of providing distance information to aircraft equipped with DME?

No, aircraft receiving equipment that provides for automatic DME selection assures reception of azimuth and distance information from a common source, only when designated VOR/DME, VORTAC, ILS/DME, and LOC/DME are selected.

[PA.VI.B.K1; AIM 1-1-7]

15. Give a brief explanation of the Global Positioning System (GPS).

GPS is a satellite-based radio navigation system that broadcasts a signal used by receivers to determine a precise position anywhere in the world. The receiver tracks multiple satellites and determines a pseudo-range measurement that is then used to determine the user's location.

[PA.VI.B.K2; AIM 1-1-17]

Private Pilot Oral Exam Guide 335

Chapter 11 **Cross-Country Flight Planning**

16. What are the different types of GPS receivers available for use?

GPS receivers used for VFR navigation vary from fully integrated IFR/VFR installations used to support VFR operations, to handheld devices. Pilots must understand the limitations of the receivers prior to using them in flight to avoid misusing navigation information.

[PA.VI.B.K2; AIM 1-1-17]

17. What is the purpose of RAIM?

Receiver autonomous integrity monitoring (RAIM) is a self-monitoring function performed by a GPS receiver to ensure that adequate GPS signals are being received from the satellites at all times. This function requires adequate simultaneous reception of at least five GPS satellites for IFR navigation reliability, works independently, and notifies the pilot when there is a problem with GPS signal reception.

[PA.VI.B.K2; FAA-H-8083-25, AIM 1-1-17]

18. Where can a pilot obtain RAIM availability information?

Pilots may obtain GPS RAIM availability information by using a manufacturer-supplied RAIM prediction tool or using the Service Availability Prediction Tool (SAPT) on the FAA enroute and terminal RAIM prediction website. Pilots can also request GPS RAIM aeronautical information from an FSS during preflight briefings.

[PA.VI.B.K2; AIM 1-1-17]

19. If RAIM capability is lost in flight, can you continue to use GPS for navigation?

Without RAIM capability, the pilot has no assurance of the accuracy of the GPS position. VFR GPS panel-mount receivers and handheld units have no RAIM alerting capability. This prevents the pilot from being alerted to the loss of the required number of satellites in view or the detection of a position error.

[PA.VI.B.K2; FAA-H-8083-25, AIM 1-1-17]

336 Aviation Supplies & Academics

Chapter 11 **Cross-Country Flight Planning**

20. Before conducting a flight using GPS equipment for navigation, what basic preflight checks should be made?

a. Verify that the GPS equipment is properly installed and certified for the planned operation.

b. Verify that the databases (navigation, terrain, obstacle, etc.) have not expired.

c. Review GPS NOTAM/RAIM information related to the planned route of flight.

d. Review the operational status of ground-based NAVAIDs and related aircraft equipment (e.g., 30-day VOR check) appropriate to the route of flight.

e. Determine that the GPS receiver operation manual or airplane flight manual supplement is on board and available for use.

[PA.VI.B.K2; FAA-H-8083-16]

21. How can a pilot determine what type of operation a GPS receiver is approved for?

The pilot should reference the POH/AFM and supplements to determine the limitations and operating procedures for the particular GPS equipment installed. Most systems require that the avionics operations manual/handbook be on board as a limitation of use.

[PA.VI.B.K2; POH/AFM]

22. Where can a pilot obtain current GPS NOTAMs?

The Federal NOTAM System (FNS) website (notams.aim.faa .gov/notamSearch) provides a single, authoritative source for all NOTAMs including current GPS NOTAMs.

[PA.VI.B.R3; AIM 1-1-17]

23. How many satellites does a GPS receiver require to compute its position?

3 satellites—yields a latitude and longitude position only (2D)

4 satellites—yields latitude, longitude, and altitude position (3D)

5 satellites—3D and RAIM

6 satellites—3D and RAIM (isolates corrupt signal and removes from navigation solution)

[PA.VI.B.K2; FAA-H-8083-15]

Private Pilot Oral Exam Guide 337

Chapter 11 **Cross-Country Flight Planning**

24. What is WAAS?

The Wide Area Augmentation System (WAAS) is a ground and satellite integrated navigational error correction system that provides accuracy enhancements to signals received from the Global Positioning System. WAAS provides extremely accurate lateral and vertical navigation signals to aircraft equipped with GPS/WAAS-enabled certified (TSO C-146) equipment.

[PA.VI.B.K2; FAA-H-8083-15, AIM 1-1-18]

25. What limitations should you be aware of when using a panel-mount VFR GPS or a handheld VFR GPS system for navigation?

a. *RAIM capability*—Many VFR GPS receivers and all handheld units have no RAIM alerting capability. Loss of the required number of satellites in view, or the detection of a position error, cannot be displayed to the pilot by such receivers.

b. *Database currency*—In many receivers, an updatable database is used for navigation fixes, airports, and instrument procedures. These databases must be maintained to the current update for IFR operation, but no such requirement exists for VFR use.

c. *Antenna location*—In many VFR installations of GPS receivers, antenna location is more a matter of convenience than performance. Handheld GPS receiver antenna location is limited to the flight deck or cabin only and is rarely optimized to provide a clear view of available satellites. Loss of signal, coupled with a lack of RAIM capability, could present erroneous position and navigation information with no warning to the pilot.

[PA.VI.B.K2; AIM 1-1-17]

26. What are VFR waypoints?

VFR waypoints provide pilots with a supplementary tool to assist with position awareness while navigating visually in aircraft equipped with area navigation receivers (such as GPS). They provide navigational aids for pilots unfamiliar with an area, waypoint definition of existing reporting points, and enhanced navigation in and around Class B and Class C airspace and around special use airspace. VFR waypoint names consist of a five-letter identifier beginning with "VP" and are retrievable from navigation

338 Aviation Supplies & Academics

Chapter 11 **Cross-Country Flight Planning**

databases; they should be used only when operating under VFR conditions.

[PA.VI.A.K4c; FAA-H-8083-25]

27. What is ADS-B?

Automatic Dependent Surveillance–Broadcast (ADS-B) is a surveillance system in which an aircraft to be detected is fitted with cooperative equipment in the form of a data link transmitter. The aircraft broadcasts its GPS-derived position and other information such as position, altitude, and velocity over the data link, which is received by a ground-based transmitter/receiver (transceiver) for processing and display at an ATC facility. In addition, aircraft equipped with ADS-B In capability can also receive these broadcasts and display the information to improve the pilot's situational awareness of other traffic. ADS-B is automatic because no external interrogation is required. It is dependent because it relies on onboard position sources and broadcast transmission systems to provide surveillance information to ATC and other users.

[PA.VI.B.K4; P/CG]

28. Explain how a transponder operates.

A transponder is the airborne radar beacon receiver/transmitter portion of the Air Traffic Control Radar Beacon System (ATCRBS) which automatically receives radio signals from interrogators on the ground, and selectively replies with a specific reply pulse or pulse group only to those interrogations being received on the mode to which it is set to respond.

[PA.VI.B.K4; P/CG, FAA-H-8083-25]

29. Explain the difference between Mode A, Mode C, and Mode S transponders.

Mode A transmits position as a 4-digit identifying code only.

Mode C transmits position and pressure altitude information automatically.

Mode S transmits position, pressure altitude information and permits data exchange.

[PA.VI.B.K4; AC 90-114, FAA-H-8083-25]

Private Pilot Oral Exam Guide 339

Chapter 11 **Cross-Country Flight Planning**

30. Identify the following transponder codes: 1200, 7500, 7600, and 7700.

1200—VFR operations
7500—Hijack
7600—Communications failure
7700—Emergency

Note: ADS-B systems integrated with the transponder will automatically set the applicable emergency status when 7500, 7600, or 7700 are entered into the transponder. ADS-B systems not integrated with the transponder, or systems with optional emergency codes, will require that the appropriate emergency code is entered through a pilot interface.

[PA.VI.B.K4; AIM 4-1-20, 4-5-7, 6-2-2, 6-3-4, 6-4-2]

F. Diversion and Lost Procedures

1. While en route on a cross-country flight, the weather has deteriorated, and it has become necessary to divert to an alternate airport. Assuming no GPS or DME capability, describe how a pilot can navigate to an alternate airport.

- After selecting a nearby alternate, the pilot will approximate the magnetic course to the alternate using a straight edge and a compass rose from a nearby VOR or an airway that closely parallels their direction to the alternate.
- The pilot can use the straight edge and scale at the bottom of the chart to approximate a distance to the alternate. This course and distance can be fine-tuned later, as time permits, with a plotter.
- If time permits, the pilot will start their diversion over a prominent ground feature. However, in an emergency, they should divert promptly toward their alternate. *Note:* Attempting to complete all plotting, measuring, and computations involved before diverting to the alternate destination may only aggravate an actual emergency.
- Once established on course, the pilot will note the time and then use the winds aloft nearest to their diversion point to calculate a heading and GS. Once the GS is determined, the pilot can determine their ETA and fuel consumption to the alternate.

340 Aviation Supplies & Academics

Chapter 11 **Cross-Country Flight Planning**

- The pilot should give priority to flying the aircraft while dividing attention between navigation and planning.
- When determining the altitude to use while diverting, the pilot will consider cloud heights, winds, terrain, and radio reception.

[PA.VI.C.K1; FAA-H-8083-25]

2. What are several reasons a pilot might need to divert during a flight?

A few potential reasons a pilot may choose to divert could include unforecasted or unexpected weather conditions, a system malfunction, poor preflight planning, pilot or passenger emergency or health issue, or a closed runway or airport.

[PA.VI.C.K1; FAA-H-8083-25]

3. Explain how a pilot can prepare for a potential diversion before takeoff.

a. Check the charts for airports or suitable landing areas along or near the route of flight.

b. Check for navigational aids that can be used during a diversion.

c. Carry additional reserve fuel for the possibility of a diversion.

d. Ensure updated weather will be available in flight (FSS, FIS-B, etc.).

[PA.VI.C.K1; FAA-H-8083-25]

4. What actions should be taken if you become disoriented or lost on a cross-country flight (with no GPS available)? Condition 1: You have plenty of fuel and weather conditions are good.

- Fly a specific heading in a direction you believe to be correct (or circle, if unsure); don't wander aimlessly.
- If you have been flying a steady compass heading and keeping a relatively accurate navigation log, it's not likely you will have a problem locating your position.
- If several VORs are within reception distance, use them for a cross-bearing to determine position (even a single VOR can be of enormous help in narrowing down your possible position); or fly to the station (there will be no doubt where you are then).

(continued)

Private Pilot Oral Exam Guide 341

Chapter 11 **Cross-Country Flight Planning**

- Use knowledge of your last known position, elapsed time, approximate wind direction, and ground speed to establish how far you may have traveled since your last checkpoint.
- Use this distance as a radius and draw a semicircle ahead of your last known position on the chart. For example, you estimate your ground speed at 120 knots. If you have been flying 20 minutes since your last checkpoint, then the no-wind radius of your semicircle is 40 miles projected along the direction of your estimated track.
- If still unsure of your position, loosen up the eyeballs and start some first-class pilotage. Look for something big. Don't concern yourself with the minute or trivial at this point. Often, there will be linear features such as rivers, mountain ranges, or prominent highways and railroads that are easy to identify. You can use them simply as references for orientation purposes, making them valuable in fixing your approximate position.

Condition 2: Low on fuel; weather deteriorating; inadequate experience; darkness imminent; and/or equipment malfunctioning.

Get it on the ground! Most accidents are the product of mistakes that have multiplied over a period of time, and getting lost is no exception: Don't push your luck. If you do, it could well be the final mistake that adds another figure to the accident statistics. If terrain or other conditions make landing impossible, don't waste time, for it is of the essence: Don't search for the perfect field—anything usable will do. Remember, most people on the ground know where they are, and you know that you do not.

[PA.VI.D; FAA-H-8083-25]

5. If it becomes apparent that you cannot locate your position, what actions are recommended at this point?

The FAA recommends the use of the 4 Cs:

Climb—The higher altitude allows better communication capability as well as better visual range for identification of landmarks.

Communicate—Use the system. Use 121.5 MHz if no other frequency produces results. It is guarded by FSSs, control towers, military towers, approach control facilities, and Air Route Traffic Control Centers.

342 Aviation Supplies & Academics

Chapter 11 **Cross-Country Flight Planning**

Confess—Once communications are established, let them know your problem.

Comply—Follow instructions.

[PA.VI.D.K1; FAA-H-8083-25]

6. What is an ARTCC, and what useful service can it provide to VFR flights?

An Air Route Traffic Control Center (ARTCC) is a facility established to provide air traffic control service primarily to aircraft operating on IFR flight plans within controlled airspace and principally during the enroute phase of flight. Air Route Surveillance Radar allows them the capability to detect and display an aircraft's position while en route between terminal areas. When equipment capabilities and controller workload permit, certain advisory/assistance service may be provided to VFR aircraft (VFR flight following). Frequencies may be obtained from FSS or the *Chart Supplement*. Also, IFR enroute charts have ARTCC sector frequencies depicted. If departing from an airport with a control tower, you can request the appropriate frequency from them.

[PA.VI.D.K2; P/CG]

7. What is the universal VHF emergency frequency?

121.5 MHz; Both 121.5 MHz and 243.0 MHz are guarded by military towers, most civil towers, and radar facilities. If an ARTCC does not respond when called on 121.5 MHz or 243.0 MHz, call the nearest tower.

Note: All aircraft operating in US national airspace are highly encouraged to maintain a listening watch on VHF/UHF guard frequencies (121.5 or 243.0 MHz).

[PA.III.A.K5; AIM 5-6-13, 6-3-1]

8. What should a pilot know about intercept procedures?

Pilots should be familiar with intercept procedures to ensure safety and compliance if intercepted by military or law enforcement aircraft. Intercept procedures are outlined in the *Aeronautical Information Manual* and include specific signals to identify, communicate, and ensure the pilot follows instructions.

a. *Visual signals*—The intercepting aircraft will approach from behind or slightly above and rock its wings to signal the pilot to

Private Pilot Oral Exam Guide 343

Chapter 11 **Cross-Country Flight Planning**

follow. The intercepted aircraft should acknowledge by rocking its wings and then follow the intercepting aircraft.

b. *Radio communications*—Tune to 121.5 MHz (guard frequency) and attempt communication. The intercepting aircraft may provide instructions verbally or using transponder codes.

c. *Follow instructions*—The intercepted pilot must comply with instructions from the intercepting aircraft, which may involve following it to a landing location.

d. *Signals for uncertain situations*—If the pilot cannot comply or does not understand, they should indicate so by rocking their wings or switching lights on and off.

e. *Final signals*—If an intercepting aircraft circles the intercepted plane, lowers its landing gear, and turns toward a runway, it's signaling to land.

Knowing these signals and responding appropriately is critical for safety and preventing escalation. Pilots should also review *AIM* Table 5-6-1 for detailed intercept signals and responses.

[PA.I.D.K6; AIM 5-6-13]

9. When planning a cross-country flight, how can a pilot mitigate the risk of inadvertent flight into IMC?

Flying with advanced avionics can provide significant safety and situational awareness benefits, but it can also lead to potentially dangerous distractions. Pilots can mitigate these risks by adopting best practices to ensure focused and safe operation. Pilots should receive comprehensive training on the specific avionics system in their aircraft. Understanding the features, limitations, and operational procedures helps reduce confusion during flight. Regular practice in using advanced avionics, including simulators, ensures proficiency and minimizes the need for inflight troubleshooting.

Before flight, pilots should configure avionics settings, such as flight plans and frequencies. This minimizes inflight distractions and reduces workload during critical phases of flight.

It is always best to adhere to the principle of "Aviate, Navigate, Communicate." Pilots should prioritize maintaining control of the aircraft and basic flight tasks over interacting with avionics. Utilize automation features like autopilot appropriately to reduce workload

344 Aviation Supplies & Academics

Chapter 11 **Cross-Country Flight Planning**

during high-stress situations. However, remain vigilant to avoid overreliance on automation.

Advanced avionics can tempt pilots to focus excessively on screens. Don't forget to continue to scan outside the flight deck to maintain situational awareness and avoid fixation on instruments.

By combining proper training, preparation, and disciplined flight deck management, pilots can effectively leverage advanced avionics while avoiding distractions that could compromise safety.

[PA.I.H.R3; FAA-H-8083-25]

Night
Operations   **12**

Chapter 12 **Night Operations**

A. Night Vision

1. Name the two distinct types of light-sensitive cells located in the retina of the eye.

Rods and cones are the light-sensitive cells located in the retina.

[PA.XI.A.K1; FAA-H-8083-3]

2. Where are the cones located in the eye and what is their function?

The cones are located in higher concentrations than rods in the central area of the retina known as the macula. The exact center of the macula has a very small depression called the fovea, which contains cones only. The cones are used for day or high-intensity light vision. They are involved with central vision to detect detail, perceive color, and identify far-away objects.

[PA.XI.A.K1; FAA-H-8083-3]

3. What is the function of the rods and where are they located in the eye?

The rods are located mainly in the periphery of the retina—an area that is about 10,000 times more sensitive to light than the fovea. Rods are used for low light intensity or night vision and are involved with peripheral vision to detect position references, including objects (fixed and moving) in shades of gray, but they cannot be used to detect detail or to perceive color. The rods make night vision possible.

[PA.XI.A.K1; FAA-H-8083-3]

4. What is the average time it takes for the rods and cones to become adapted to darkness?

The cones will take approximately 5 to 10 minutes to become adjusted to darkness. Much more time—about 30 minutes—is needed for the rods to become adjusted to darkness.

[PA.XI.A.K1; FAA-H-8083-3]

Chapter 12 **Night Operations**

5. What should the pilot do to accommodate changing light conditions?

The pilot should allow enough time for the eyes to become adapted to the low light levels and then should avoid exposure to bright light, which could cause temporary blindness.

[PA.XI.A.K1; FAA-H-8083-3]

6. What is the night blind spot, and how does it affect a pilot's visual field?

The night blind spot refers to the absence of rods in the fovea, affecting the central 5 to 10 degrees of the visual field under conditions of low ambient illumination. This can cause an object viewed directly at night to go undetected or fade away after initial detection.

[PA.XI.A.K1; FAA-H-8083-3]

7. What is the false horizon illusion, and how can it affect pilots flying at night?

Flying at night under clear skies with ground lights below can result in situations where it is difficult to distinguish the ground lights from the stars. A dark scene spread with ground lights and stars, and certain geometric patterns of ground lights, can provide inaccurate visual information, making it difficult to align the aircraft correctly with the actual horizon.

[PA.XI.A.K8; FAA-H-8083-3]

8. What is autokinesis, and how can it lead to spatial disorientation in pilots?

In the dark, a stationary light will appear to move about when stared at for many seconds. This illusion is known as autokinesis. The disoriented pilot could lose control of the aircraft in attempting to align it with the false movements of this light.

[PA.XI.A.K8; FAA-H-8083-3]

9. What is the featureless terrain illusion, and how can it cause problems for pilots during landing?

A black-hole approach occurs when the landing is made from over water or non-lighted terrain where the runway lights are the only source of light. Without peripheral visual cues to help, orientation

Private Pilot Oral Exam Guide 349

Chapter 12 **Night Operations**

is difficult. The runway can seem out of position (downsloping or upsloping) and in the worst case, this can result in the pilot landing short of the runway.

[PA.XI.A.K8; FAA-H-8083-3]

10. How can bright runway and approach lighting systems create illusions for pilots, and what should pilots do to mitigate these illusions?

Bright runway and approach lighting systems, especially where few lights illuminate the surrounding terrain, may create the illusion of being lower or having less distance to the runway. In this situation, the tendency is to fly a higher approach. Also, flying over terrain with only a few lights makes the runway recede or appear farther away. With this situation, the tendency is to fly a lower-than-normal approach. To mitigate, trust the instruments to determine the correct approach path.

[PA.XI.A.K8; FAA-H-8083-3]

11. What are ground lighting Illusions, and how can they be mistaken for runway and approach lights?

Lights along a straight path, such as on a road or on moving trains, can be mistaken for runway and approach lights. Bright runway and approach lighting systems, especially where few lights illuminate the surrounding terrain, may create the illusion of less distance to the runway. The pilot who does not recognize this illusion will often fly a higher approach.

[PA.XI.A.K8; FAA-H-8083-3]

12. What can a pilot do to prevent the optical illusions that can occur at night and cause landing errors?

a. Anticipate the possibility of visual illusions during approaches to unfamiliar airports, particularly at night or in adverse weather conditions.

b. Use airport diagrams and the *Chart Supplement* for information on runway slope, terrain, and lighting.

c. Make frequent reference to the altimeter, especially during all approaches, day and night.

d. If possible, conduct aerial visual inspection of unfamiliar airports before landing.

350 Aviation Supplies & Academics

Chapter 12 **Night Operations**

    e. Use VASI or PAPI systems for a visual reference or an electronic glideslope, when available.

    f. Utilize the visual descent point (VDP) found on many non-precision instrument approach procedure charts.

    g. Recognize that the chances of an approach accident increase when an emergency or other activity distracts from normal procedures.

    h. Maintain optimum proficiency in night landing procedures.

[PA.XI.A.K8; FAA-H-8083-3]

13. What should the pilot do to maintain good eyesight?

Good eyesight depends upon physical condition. Fatigue, colds, vitamin deficiency, alcohol, stimulants, smoking, or medication can seriously impair vision.

[PA.XI.A.K1; FAA-H-8083-3]

14. What are some self-imposed stresses that can impair vision during flight at night?

Self-imposed stresses such as self-medication, alcohol consumption (including hangover effects), tobacco use (including withdrawal), hypoglycemia, sleep deprivation/fatigue, and extreme emotional upset can seriously impair vision.

[PA.XI.A.K1; FAA-H-8083-3]

15. How does hypoxia impair visual performance during night flight?

Unaided night vision depends on optimum function and sensitivity of the rods of the retina. Lack of oxygen to the rods (hypoxia) significantly reduces their sensitivity. Sharp clear vision (with the best being equal to 20/20 vision) requires significant oxygen, especially at night. Without supplemental oxygen, an individual's night vision declines measurably at pressure altitudes above 4,000 feet.

[PA.XI.A.K1; FAA-H-8083-25]

Chapter 12 **Night Operations**

B. Airport Lighting

1. Describe runway end identifier lights (REIL).

REILs are installed at many airfields to provide rapid and positive identification of the approach end of a particular runway. The system consists of a pair of synchronized flashing lights located laterally on each side of the runway threshold. REILs may be either omnidirectional or unidirectional facing the approach area.

[PA.XI.A.K2; AIM 2-1-3]

2. Describe a runway edge light system.

Runway edge lights are used to outline the edges of runways during periods of darkness or restricted visibility conditions. They are white, except on instrument runways where yellow replaces white on the last 2,000 feet or half the runway length (whichever is less) to form a caution zone for landings. The lights marking the ends of the runway emit red light toward the runway to indicate the end of runway to a departing aircraft and emit green outward from the runway end to indicate the threshold to landing aircraft. These light systems are classified according to the intensity or brightness they are capable of producing. Examples are high intensity runway lights (HIRL), medium intensity runway lights (MIRL), and low intensity runway lights (LIRL).

[PA.XI.A.K2; AIM 2-1-4]

3. Describe a Runway Centerline Lighting System (RCLS).

Runway centerline lights are installed on some precision approach runways to facilitate landing under adverse visibility conditions. They are located along the runway centerline and are spaced at 50-foot intervals. When viewed from the landing threshold, the runway centerline lights are white until the last 3,000 feet of the runway. The white lights begin to alternate with red for the next 2,000 feet, and for the last 1,000 feet of the runway, all centerline lights are red.

[PA.XI.A.K2; AIM 2-1-5]

4. What are touchdown zone lights (TDZLs)?

TDZLs consist of two rows of transverse light bars disposed symmetrically about the runway centerline. The system consists of steady-burning white lights that start at 100 feet beyond the

Chapter 12 **Night Operations**

landing threshold and extend to 3,000 feet beyond the landing threshold or to the midpoint of the runway, whichever is less.

[PA.XI.A.K2; AIM 2-1-5]

5. Describe several different types of taxiway lighting.

a. *Taxiway edge lights* outline the edges of taxiways; consist of blue lights.

b. *Taxiway centerline lights* assist ground traffic in low-visibility conditions; consist of steady-burning green lights.

c. *Clearance bar lights* are installed at holding positions on taxiways; consist of three in-pavement steady-burning yellow lights.

d. *Runway guard lights* are installed at taxiway/runway intersections; consist of either a pair of elevated flashing lights on either side of taxiway or in-pavement yellow lights installed across the taxiway.

e. *Stop bar lights* are used to confirm ATC clearance to enter or cross an active runway in low-visibility conditions; consist of a row of red, unidirectional, steady-burning, in-pavement lights installed across the taxiway and a pair of elevated, steady-burning red lights on each side.

[PA.XI.A.K6; AIM 2-1-10]

6. What are the different types of rotating beacons used to identify airports?

a. White and green—lighted land airport

b. Green alone*—lighted land airport

c. White and yellow—lighted water airport

d. Yellow alone*—lighted water airport

e. Green, yellow, and white—lighted heliport

f. White (dual peaked) and green—Lighted military airport

* "Green alone" or "yellow alone" beacons are used only in connection with a white-and-green or white-and-yellow beacon display, respectively.

[PA.XI.A.K2; AIM 2-1-9]

Private Pilot Oral Exam Guide 353

Chapter 12 **Night Operations**

7. What type of aeronautical lighting is a visual approach slope indicator (VASI)?

VASI is a system of lights arranged to provide visual descent guidance information during the approach to a runway. The basic principle of VASI is that of color differential between red and white: each light projects a beam of light having a white segment in the upper half and a red segment in the lower part of the beam. The lights in a two-bar VASI will be as follows:

- Red over red—Below glidepath
- Red over white—On glidepath
- White over white—Above glidepath

[PA.XI.A.K2; AIM 2-1-2]

8. What is a precision approach path indicator (PAPI)?

PAPI uses light units similar to VASI, but they are installed in a single row of either two- or four-light units. These systems have an effective visual range of about 5 miles during the day and up to 20 miles at night. The row of light units is normally installed on the left side of the runway. The glidepath indications are as follows:

- Four white lights—High (more than 3.5°)
- Three white, one red—Slightly high (3.2°)
- Two white, two red—On glidepath (3°)
- One white, three red—Slightly low (2.8°)
- Four red lights—Low (less than 2.5°)

[PA.XI.A.K2; AIM 2-1-2]

9. Describe several types of obstruction lighting.

a. *Aviation red obstruction lights*—Flashing aviation red beacons and steady-burning aviation red lights during nighttime operations.

b. *Medium and high intensity white obstruction lights*—May be used during daytime and twilight with reduced intensity for nighttime operation. Not normally installed on structures less than 200 feet.

c. *Dual lighting*—A combination of flashing aviation red beacons and steady-burning aviation red lights for nighttime operations, and flashing high intensity white lights for daytime operation.

Chapter 12 **Night Operations**

   d. *Catenary lighting*—Medium- and high-intensity flashing white markers for high-voltage transmission lines and support structures.

[PA.XI.A.K2; AIM 2-2-3]

10. How does a pilot determine the status of a light system at a particular airport?

The pilot needs to check the *Chart Supplement* and any Notices to Airmen (NOTAMs) to find out about available lighting systems, light intensities, and radio-controlled light system frequencies.

Exam Tip: Be prepared to determine and explain the type and status of airport and runway lighting at your departure and destination airports.

[PA.XI.A.K2; FAA-H-8083-3]

11. How does a pilot activate a radio-controlled runway light system while airborne?

The pilot activates radio-controlled lights by keying the microphone on a specified frequency. The following sequence can be used for typical radio-controlled lighting systems:

a. On initial arrival, key the microphone seven times to turn the lights on and achieve maximum brightness.

b. If the runway lights are already on upon arrival, repeat the above sequence to ensure a full 15 minutes of lighting.

c. The intensity of the lights can be adjusted by keying the microphone seven, five, or three times within 5 seconds.

[PA.XI.A.K2; AIM 2-1-8]

Private Pilot Oral Exam Guide **355**

Chapter 12 **Night Operations**

C. Airplane Equipment

1. Explain the arrangement and interpretation of the position lights on an aircraft.

A red light is positioned on the left wingtip, a green light on the right wingtip, and a white light on the tail. If both a red and green light of another aircraft are observed, and the red light is on the left and the green to the right, the airplane is flying in the same direction. Care must be taken not to overtake the other aircraft and to maintain clearance. If red light of another aircraft appears on the right and green to the left, the airplane could be on a collision course.

[PA.XI.A.K7; FAA-H-8083-3]

2. What is the difference between aircraft position lights and anti-collision lights?

Aircraft position lights and anti-collision lights serve distinct purposes and are required under different circumstances to enhance visibility and safety during flight.

Position lights—These are steady, non-flashing lights located on the wingtips and sometimes on the tail of the aircraft. The position lights are color-coded: red on the left wing, green on the right wing, and white on the tail. Their purpose is to help determine the orientation and direction of the aircraft in low-visibility conditions, such as at night or in poor weather. Position lights are required to be illuminated during all operations between sunset and sunrise, regardless of whether the aircraft is on the ground or in flight.

Anti-collision lights—These include strobe lights and rotating beacons designed to make the aircraft more conspicuous. Strobe lights are high-intensity flashing lights typically located on the wingtips, while rotating beacons emit a red flashing light, often mounted on the top or bottom of the fuselage. Anti-collision lights are used to signal the presence of the aircraft to other pilots and are required to be operational during all flight operations, day or night. They are also used when the aircraft is moving on the ground to alert nearby personnel.

[PA.XI.A.K3; FAA-H-8083-3]

Chapter 12 **Night Operations**

3. During what period of time are position lights required to be on?

From sunset to sunrise.

[PA.XI.A.K3; 14 CFR 91.209]

4. When an aircraft is operated in, or in close proximity to, a night operations area, what is required of the aircraft?

The aircraft must:

a. Be clearly illuminated;

b. Have lighted position lights; or

c. Be in an area which is marked by obstruction lights.

[PA.XI.A.K3; 14 CFR 91.209]

5. Explain how a pilot can mitigate the risk present when starting an engine at night on a dark ramp.

a. Before entering the airplane, clear the area around the airplane.

b. Inform ramp personnel and others of the intention to start.

c. Switch on the NAV lights and rotating beacon prior to start.

d. Carefully scan the area around the aircraft.

e. If all is clear, announce "clear prop," pause and listen, clear the area again, then start the engine.

f. While on the ramp, remain alert for activity outside the aircraft.

g. Always be ready for an immediate engine shutdown.

[PA.XI.A.R3; FAA-H-8083-3]

6. Are aircraft anticollision lights required to be on during night flight operations?

Yes; however, the anticollision lights need not be lit when the pilot-in-command determines that, because of operating conditions, it would be in the interest of safety to turn the lights off.

[PA.XI.A.K3; 14 CFR 91.209]

Private Pilot Oral Exam Guide   357

Chapter 12 **Night Operations**

7. What are some common types of flight deck and exterior lighting equipment on a general aviation aircraft?

General aviation aircraft are equipped with a variety of flight deck and exterior lighting systems designed to enhance visibility, safety, and operational effectiveness. These lights serve specific purposes both inside the flight deck and outside the aircraft.

Flight deck lighting:

- *Instrument lights*—Illuminate the flight instruments for easy reading during low-light conditions. These may include backlighting or overhead light sources.
- *Map lights*—Provide focused illumination for charts, maps, or other documents in the flight deck.
- *Panel lights*—Light up various switches and controls to improve accessibility during night operations.
- *Dome lights*—Offer general lighting in the flight deck or cabin area.

Exterior lighting:

- *Position lights*—Steady red, green, and white lights on the wingtips and tail to indicate aircraft orientation.
- *Anti-collision lights*—Flashing strobe lights or rotating beacons to enhance visibility to other aircraft and ground personnel.
- *Landing lights*—High-intensity lights mounted on the wings or fuselage to illuminate the runway or taxiway during landing, takeoff, or taxiing.
- *Taxi lights*—Provide forward illumination during taxiing operations, often mounted on the nose gear or lower fuselage.
- *Recognition lights*—Additional lights, such as wingtip strobes or fuselage-mounted lights, to increase visibility in certain conditions.

[PA.XI.A.K3; FAA-H-8083-3]

8. What are some generally accepted good operating habits concerning the use of aircraft lighting (taxi, landing, strobes) while on the ground at night?

Good operating practice concerning the use of aircraft lighting while on the ground at night is crucial for both safety and compliance with regulations. Proper use of lights helps ensure visibility, avoid collisions, and maintain situational awareness in low-light conditions.

358 Aviation Supplies & Academics

Chapter 12 **Night Operations**

Taxi lights—Use taxi lights when taxiing at night to provide adequate forward visibility of the taxiway, any obstacles, or other aircraft. This is particularly important in poorly lit areas or airports without sufficient ground lighting. However, turn off taxi lights when not needed or when the aircraft is stopped to prevent blinding other pilots or ground personnel.

Landing lights—Landing lights should be turned on during taxiing if they enhance visibility, especially when transitioning to takeoff. However, landing lights should not be used unnecessarily during taxi operations in areas where they might interfere with other aircraft or ground operations. It is generally accepted to not have landing lights on when holding short of a runway awaiting takeoff with other aircraft landing, as it may affect their vision. After landing, pilots should turn off the landing lights once the aircraft is clear of the runway to avoid dazzling other aircraft or personnel if not needed for their own taxi operations.

Anti-collision lights (strobes)—Strobe lights or beacon lights should be used when the aircraft is moving on the ground or in any situation where it could be visible to others. This helps increase visibility to other aircraft, reducing the risk of a collision. For aircraft without a rotating beacon, only strobes, they may be required to be on during all operations. If possible, turn off strobes when taxiing in close proximity to other aircraft or on ramps where other personnel may be working, as strobe lights can be distracting and disorienting.

[PA.XI.A.R2; FAA-H-8083-3]

D. Pilot Equipment

1. What standard equipment should a pilot have for all night flight operations?

At least one reliable flashlight is recommended as standard equipment on all night flights. A reliable incandescent or LED dimmable flashlight able to produce white and red light is preferable. The flashlight should be large enough to be easily located in the event it is needed. It is also recommended to have a spare set of batteries for the flashlight readily available. Some pilots prefer two flashlights, one with a white light for preflight and the other a penlight type with a red light.

[PA.XI.A.K4; FAA-H-8083-3]

Private Pilot Oral Exam Guide   359

Chapter 12 **Night Operations**

2. What color of light is recommended for preflight inspection, general flight deck activities, and chart reading at night?

The white light is used while performing the preflight visual inspection of the airplane, the red light is used when performing flight deck operations, and the dim white light may be used for chart reading.

[PA.XI.A.K4; FAA-H-8083-3]

3. What is the effect of red-light illumination on aeronautical charts?

Red-light illumination distorts colors (magenta and yellow pigments both appear as red, and cyan pigment appears black) on aeronautical charts.

[PA.XI.A.K1; FAA-H-8083-3]

4. What other items should the pilot have on board for night flights?

Aeronautical charts are essential for night cross-country flight, and if the intended course is near the edge of the chart, the adjacent chart should also be available. It is also recommended to have a spare set of batteries for the flashlight readily available. Organize equipment and charts and place them within easy reach prior to taxiing.

[PA.XI.A.K4; FAA-H-8083-3]

5. Explain how use of an EFB for chart reference can increase risk during night operations.

Use of an EFB that hasn't been adjusted for night operations can significantly reduce night vision. When using an EFB on the flight deck at night, ensure that the device brightness has been set so as not to seriously impair night vision.

[PA.XI.A.R2; FAA-H-8083-3]

6. Describe the equipment checks a pilot should prioritize prior to a night flight.

a. Personal equipment such as flashlights, EFBs, and portable transceivers.

b. Spare batteries charged and available.

360 Aviation Supplies & Academics

Chapter 12 **Night Operations**

c. The aircraft's position lights, landing light, and rotating beacon.

[PA.XI.A.K4; FAA-H-8083-3]

E. Night Flight Operational Environment

1. What is the first indication of flying into restricted visibility conditions at night?

The first indication of flying into restricted visibility conditions is the gradual disappearance of lights on the ground. If the lights begin to appear surrounded by a halo or glow, continued flight in the same direction calls for caution. Such a halo or glow around lights on the ground is indicative of ground fog.

[PA.XI.A.K8; FAA-H-8083-3]

2. What are the hazards of crossing large bodies of water at night in single-engine airplanes?

a. In the event of an engine failure, the pilot may be forced to land (ditch) the airplane in the water.

b. Due to limited or no lighting, the horizon blends with the water.

c. During poor visibility conditions over water, the horizon becomes obscure and may result in a loss of orientation.

d. Even on clear nights, the stars may be reflected on the water surface, which could appear as a continuous array of lights, thus making the horizon difficult to identify.

[PA.XI.A.K8; FAA-H-8083-3]

3. What should a pilot pay particular attention to when reviewing weather reports and forecasts for a planned night flight?

Particular attention should be directed toward temperature/ dewpoint spreads to detect the possibility of fog formation.

[PA.XI.A.R6; FAA-H-8083-3]

4. Explain why it is important to determine wind directions and speeds along the proposed route of flight at night.

Perception of drift at night is generally inaccurate, so accurate drift calculations are necessary to prevent drifting off course.

[PA.XI.A.R6; FAA-H-8083-3]

Private Pilot Oral Exam Guide 361

Chapter 12 **Night Operations**

5. Explain how a pilot should prepare aeronautical charts before a flight at night.

a. Study the planned route of flight thoroughly.

b. Mark lighted checkpoints clearly.

c. Obtain charts for the proposed route, as well as any adjacent charts if the intended course is near the edge of the chart.

d. Taxi operations are more challenging at night. Have an airport diagram available.

[PA.XI.A.K4; FAA-H-8083-3]

6. Prior to a night flight, what steps should a pilot take if they are planning on using radio navigational aids or GPS for navigation?

a. Review all radio navigational aids for correct frequencies and availability.

b. If a GPS is being used for navigation, ensure that it is working properly before the flight. All necessary waypoints should be loaded properly before the flight, and the database should be checked for accuracy prior to taking off and then checked again once in flight.

[PA.XI.A.K3; FAA-H-8083-3]

7. You notice an aircraft's green position light at your 10 o'clock, same altitude. In what direction is the aircraft moving?

Green position lights are installed on the right wing (or starboard side of an aircraft); therefore, the airplane is moving from your left to right.

[PA.XI.A.K5; FAA-H-8083-3]

8. Describe several hazards related to the pilot, aircraft, environment, and external pressures when conducting night flight operations.

Remember: PAVE

Pilot—Fatigue, night flying currency and proficiency, deficiencies in night vision, optical illusions.

Aircraft—Airworthiness, inoperative lighting, lack of proper equipment (flashlights, batteries etc.).

Chapter 12 **Night Operations**

EnVironment—Weather, situational awareness, terrain, obstacles, CFIT, airport lighting familiarity.

External pressures—Need to get there, pressure from passengers, someone waiting.

[PA.XI.A.K1; FAA-H-8083-3]

9. When flying VFR at night, what are examples of IFR practices a pilot can use to minimize risk?

When flying visual flight rules (VFR) at night, pilots can adopt certain instrument flight rules (IFR) practices to reduce risks associated with reduced visibility, darkness, and the challenges of navigating in low-light conditions. When flying VFR at night:

a. In addition to the altitude appropriate for the direction of flight, pilots should maintain an altitude which is at or above the minimum enroute altitude as shown on charts. This is especially true in mountainous terrain, where there is usually very little ground reference. Do not depend on your eyes alone to avoid rising unlighted terrain, or even lighted obstructions such as TV towers.

b. Just as in IFR operations, pilots should focus on maintaining a consistent altitude to avoid unintentional altitude deviations. This can be accomplished by regularly checking the altimeter and avoiding reliance on visual references that can be misleading at night.

c. Use instrumentation for navigation: Instead of relying solely on external landmarks, pilots should use navigation instruments such as the GPS, heading indicator, and vertical speed indicator. This helps maintain situational awareness and avoids becoming disoriented, especially when visual references are limited.

d. Monitor heading and course: Pilots should continuously verify their heading using instruments to avoid unintentional deviations caused by wind or other factors. This is similar to the strict heading monitoring required in IFR flights.

e. Preflight planning and alternates: Similar to IFR flight planning, pilots should plan for possible alternate landing sites in case of unexpected weather changes or navigation errors.

f. Avoid scud running: When flying VFR at night, pilots should avoid flying just below clouds or in areas with low visibility to

Private Pilot Oral Exam Guide 363

Chapter 12 **Night Operations**

prevent becoming disoriented, similar to avoiding hazardous conditions under IFR.

[PA.XI.A.R2; FAA-H-8083-3]

10. How can a pilot determine the hours of operation for an ATC tower and whether it is open all night?

A pilot should refer to the *Chart Supplement* to determine the hours of operation for an ATC control tower.

[PA.XI.A.K2; FAA-H-8083-3]

11. How can a pilot determine the proper frequency on which to activate airport lighting at night?

A pilot should refer to the *Chart Supplement* to find the frequency on which pilot-controlled lighting is activated. This will not always be the CTAF frequency.

[PA.XI.A.K2; FAA-H-8083-3]

12. What best practices should a pilot follow when determining waypoints to use at night for cross-country VFR flying?

When planning a cross-country VFR flight at night, pilots should follow best practices to ensure safe navigation and clear situational awareness. Since visibility is reduced at night, careful waypoint selection is crucial.

a. *Choose well-lit waypoints*—At night, visual references are harder to identify. Therefore, pilots should select waypoints that are clearly visible, such as cities, major highways, or large landmarks with lighting. Airports and navigational aids (like VORs) can also serve as reliable waypoints.

b. *Use visual landmarks*—Choose waypoints with distinctive, easily identifiable features such as large bodies of water, mountain ridges, or familiar infrastructure. Pilots should avoid relying on features that may be harder to see or less distinctive at night.

c. *Plan for backup waypoints*—In case a primary waypoint becomes difficult to locate, pilots should have secondary or backup waypoints planned, ideally at a similar distance, to ensure continuous navigation. This helps avoid disorientation if visibility or visual references become poor.

364 Aviation Supplies & Academics

Chapter 12 **Night Operations**

   d. *Maintain situational awareness*—Pilots should constantly monitor their position, using instruments such as GPS, heading indicators, and airspeed indicators to stay on course. Regularly check the flight path to ensure the aircraft remains aligned with the selected waypoints.

   e. *Plan for alternatives*—When flying at night, it's important to plan for potential changes in weather or other unforeseen circumstances. Identifying alternative airports or landing areas along the route is essential for safety.

[PA.XI.A.K5; FAA-H-8083-3]

13. What is the first action to take when an airplane engine fails at night?

The pilot's first action must be to maintain control of the aircraft. This means immediately establishing the correct pitch attitude to maintain airspeed and prevent a stall. Focus on keeping the wings level and ensuring the aircraft remains stable.

Next, the pilot should set the aircraft for the best glide speed to maximize distance and time, allowing more time to troubleshoot and identify a suitable landing area. They should avoid making any unnecessary maneuvers that could further reduce airspeed or control.

Once the aircraft is stable, the pilot can begin troubleshooting the engine failure by attempting to restart the engine, if possible. They should check fuel levels, switches, and other critical systems, but do so systematically and without haste. Simultaneously, the pilot should evaluate potential landing sites using the aircraft's lighting and any available instruments, as finding a safe place to land is crucial, especially at night when visual references are limited.

In an emergency engine-out scenario at night, pilots should look for well-lit areas like airports, airstrips, or open fields with clear approaches. Avoid densely populated areas or obstacles like power lines. Use navigational aids such as GPS, lighting from cities or highways, and any visible landmarks to help identify suitable landing sites. Additionally, consider large, flat fields or roads, ensuring there's enough space to glide and land safely without obstructions. Some advice indicates that dark areas may be indicators of open fields that might be suitable for landing.

(continued)

Private Pilot Oral Exam Guide 365

Chapter 12 **Night Operations**

Engine-out scenarios are much more risky at night and provide
the pilot with fewer options that can be visually identified as
potentially suitable landing locations.

[PA.XI.A.R6; FAA-H-8083-3]

F. Night Regulations and Currency

1. What are the three definitions of *night*?

14 CFR §1.1—The time between the end of evening civil twilight
and the beginning of morning civil twilight, as published in the
Air Almanac, converted to local time. (Use this definition when
logging night flight time.)

14 CFR §61.57—The period beginning one hour after sunset
and ending one hour before sunrise. (Use this definition when
determining currency to act as pilot-in-command of an aircraft
carrying passengers.)

14 CFR §91.209—The period from sunset to sunrise. (Use this
definition to determine when you are required to have position and
anti-collision lights on.)

[PA.XI.A.K3; 14 CFR 1.1, 61.57, 91.209]

2. What additional instruments and equipment are required for an aircraft by regulation for VFR night flight?

For VFR flight at night, all the instruments and equipment for VFR
day flight are required, plus the following:

Fuses—one spare set or three fuses of each kind required
accessible to the pilot in flight.

Landing light—if the aircraft is operated for hire.

Anticollision light system—approved aviation red or white.

Position lights (navigation lights)—approved forward and rear
position.

Source of electrical energy—adequate for all installed electrical
and radio.

Remember: FLAPS

[PA.XI.A.K3; 14 CFR 91.205]

366 Aviation Supplies & Academics

Chapter 12 **Night Operations**

3. When may a pilot log a landing or takeoff as "night"?

A pilot may log a landing or takeoff as "night" when it occurs during the period between one hour after sunset and one hour before sunrise, based on local time. According to the FAA, the "night" time requirement for logging landings or takeoffs is not strictly dependent on the actual darkness but rather on the official time of sunset and sunrise.

For a landing to count as a "night landing," it must occur during the specified time window. The same applies to takeoffs—they must occur within the same period to be logged as night operations. Importantly, the pilot should ensure that they are conducting the flight with sufficient lighting and in compliance with night VFR or other applicable regulations.

[PA.I.A.K1; 14 CFR 61.57]

4. What requirements must a pilot meet to carry passengers in flight at night?

To carry passengers at night, a pilot must meet specific currency requirements set by the FAA. According to 14 CFR §61.57, the pilot must have made at least three takeoffs and three landings to a full stop during the nighttime period (one hour after sunset to one hour before sunrise) within the previous 90 days. These takeoffs and landings must be in the same category, class, and type (if a class or type rating is required) of aircraft that the pilot intends to fly.

[PA.I.A.K1; 14 CFR 61.57]

5. What are the differences in minimum cloud clearance and visibility requirements at night when compared to day clearances?

The minimum cloud clearance and visibility requirements for night flying differ from day operations.

VFR night requirements—Under VFR at night, pilots must still maintain visual separation from clouds and other aircraft, but the minimums are more restrictive than during the day due to reduced visibility. In Class G airspace at all altitudes, the requirements become 3 SM visibility with cloud clearance of 500 feet below, 1,000 feet above, and 2,000 feet horizontally from clouds.

[PA.XI.A.R6; 14 CFR 91.157]

Private Pilot Oral Exam Guide   367

Chapter 12 **Night Operations**

6. May a private pilot fly at night on a special VFR clearance?

Private pilots without an Instrument Rating are limited to day operations under special VFR rules. Instrument-rated pilots may fly special VFR at night, but only if they are instrument current and flying an aircraft that is instrument legal per 14 CFR §91.205(d) and meets the criteria outlined in 91.205(a) and (b).

[PA.XI.A.R6; 14 CFR 91.157, AIM 4-4-6]

Emergency Equipment and Survival Gear 13

Chapter 13 **Emergency Equipment and Survival Gear**

1. What factors should be considered when evaluating the type of survival equipment to carry for a flight over uninhabited terrain?

When flying over uninhabited terrain, pilots should consider several factors when evaluating survival equipment to carry:

a. *Terrain and environment*—Assess the geography, such as mountains, forests, or deserts, and the associated survival challenges. For instance, cold-weather gear is essential for mountainous or winter conditions, while water and shade might be critical for desert areas.

b. *Weather conditions*—Consider the forecasted weather for the route. Extreme temperatures, precipitation, or strong winds may require specialized equipment like thermal blankets, waterproof clothing, or wind-resistant shelters.

c. *Flight route and duration*—Longer flights or those far from populated areas increase the need for extensive survival equipment, including additional food, water, and communication devices.

d. *Emergency signaling*—Always carry signaling equipment like a personal locator beacon (PLB), signal mirror, flares, or a whistle to improve rescue chances.

e. *Communication and navigation*—Ensure backup communication tools, such as a satellite phone or portable VHF radio, are available for contact with search and rescue teams.

f. *Medical supplies*—A well-stocked first aid kit is essential to treat injuries until help arrives.

g. *Legal requirements*—Familiarize yourself with any regulatory requirements for survival gear, especially for flights over remote or international areas.

h. *Aircraft-specific needs*—Consider weight and space constraints in your aircraft and pack appropriately without exceeding limitations.

Proper planning and preparation tailored to the flight environment enhances safety and survivability in the event of an emergency landing.

[PA.IX.D.K3; AIM 6-2-6, CAMI OK-06-033]

370 Aviation Supplies & Academics

Chapter 13 **Emergency Equipment and Survival Gear**

2. What does the FAA recommend a pilot do with regard to survival equipment for flight over land?

For flight over uninhabited land areas, it is wise to take and know how to use survival equipment for the type of climate and terrain. The FAA provides several resources to help pilots prepare for survival situations. *Basic Survival Skills for Aviation*, created by the FAA Civil Aerospace Medical Institute (CAMI), presents the basic knowledge and skills for coping with various survival situations and environments. The FAA Safety Briefing *General Aviation Survival* provides survival tips, training and equipment recommendations, and related resources for GA pilots.

[PA.IX.D.K3; AIM 6-2-6, CAMI OK-06-033, FAA GA Survival]

3. What are some items the FAA recommends having in a survival kit that would be taken on board a general aviation aircraft, especially for flight over non-populated areas?

No matter where you fly, you should always equip your aircraft with a survival kit. There are several that are available commercially, but you can also assemble a personal survival kit that is custom tailored to your mission.

Some common items that you should ensure you have in your aircraft include:

- Clothing appropriate for the environment
- Multi-tool or knife
- Flashlight with extra batteries
- Rope
- Signaling device
- Compass
- First aid kit
- Waterproof matches or method of fire starting
- Bug repellant
- Work gloves

[PA.IX.D.K3; FAA-H-8083-2, FAA-H-8083-3, FAA-H-8083-25; POH/AFM]

Private Pilot Oral Exam Guide 371

Chapter 13 **Emergency Equipment and Survival Gear**

4. What are some things you should have with you for safety or emergency gear, even on a local flight?

While a local flight may not have the same survival gear concerns as a longer flight or one over uninhabited terrain, some considerations may be warranted based on the time of the year and location over which you will be flying. These might include some of the following:

a. *Water*—Dehydration can be a concern for pilots and passengers in many conditions. Be sure to have some water available in flight to counteract this concern. It can also be used for flushing dust from eyes or cleansing a wound if one occurs, such as cutting yourself on a sharp edge during a preflight.

b. *Proper clothing*—Be sure to have clothing appropriate for the conditions. While your aircraft may be heated, a jacket, hat, and gloves may be important for flight in colder climates to protect you if you get stuck on a cold airport ramp or for preflight procedures. In warm and sunny climates, lightweight long-sleeve shirts and/or a hat can help protect against sunburn. When you consider what clothing you wear and additional clothing you take on a flight, think about what would help if you had to evacuate from the aircraft and were stuck outside for a longer period of time.

c. *Sturdy shoes*—A good sturdy pair of shoes or even an extra pair of boots might be important if you are flying where there is snow or rough terrain.

d. *Cell phone*—Having a cellular phone with you and located on your person can be helpful if you get stranded somewhere or are involved in an accident or incident. Having a phone tucked away in a bag in the back of the aircraft will not help you call for help if you are trapped in a crashed aircraft.

e. *First aid kit*—A basic first aid kit that includes supplies like bandaids, tweezers for a sliver, and other minor items can help remedy basic medical concerns.

Exam Tip: Be prepared to discuss your local conditions and concerns with regard to safety and things you might have with you to mitigate some risks if unexpected emergency or concern arises. If you are flying in Arizona in the summer, heat may be a concern. If you are flying in North Dakota in the winter, you might choose to carry different daily flight safety items.

[PA.IX.D.K3; FAA-H-8083-25]

Chapter 13 **Emergency Equipment and Survival Gear**

5. What should a pilot do with respect to briefing passengers about emergency equipment on an aircraft?

Before a flight, a pilot should brief passengers on the location and use of emergency equipment in the aircraft. This includes showing them the location of the fire extinguisher, first aid kit, oxygen masks (if applicable), and emergency exits. The pilot should explain the use of seat belts, life vests, and any other safety equipment, ensuring passengers understand how to operate them.

The briefing should also cover emergency procedures, such as what to do in case of an emergency landing, decompression, or fire. Emphasize the importance of following the pilot's instructions during an emergency.

[PA.IX.D.K3; FAA-H-8083-25]

6. In a privately flown aircraft, must a pilot carry a life raft or life preservers when flying over water?

Technically, a pilot is only required to carry a life preserver or raft for the crew and/or passengers under certain conditions. There are more restrictive requirements for aircraft operated for hire. These will come into effect when the pilot is beyond certain distances from land. Even in overflight of the Great Lakes, these regulations will rarely apply unless a pilot is flying over larger expanses of water such as the oceanic environment.

The regulation in 14 CFR § 91.509 states that:

a. No person may take off an airplane for a flight over water more than 50 nautical miles from the nearest shore unless that airplane is equipped with a life preserver or an approved flotation means for each occupant of the airplane.

b. Except as provided in 14 CFR § 91.509(c), no person may take off an airplane for flight over water more than 30 minutes flying time or 100 nautical miles from the nearest shore, whichever is less, unless it has on board the following survival equipment:

  1. A life preserver, equipped with an approved survivor locator light, for each occupant of the airplane.

  2. Enough life rafts (each equipped with an approved survival locator light) of a rated capacity and buoyancy to accommodate the occupants of the airplane.

  3. At least one pyrotechnic signaling device for each life raft.

(continued)

Private Pilot Oral Exam Guide   373

Chapter 13 **Emergency Equipment and Survival Gear**

4. One self-buoyant, water-resistant, portable emergency radio signaling device that is capable of transmission on the appropriate emergency frequency or frequencies and not dependent upon the airplane power supply.

Note: While not required, best practice would be for a pilot to have flotation gear for each crewmember and passenger if the flight has the potential of not being able to reach land in an emergency. The pilot should be familiar with emergency services in the area for a water rescue and the ditching procedures outlined in *AIM* ¶6-3-3 for such a flight.

[PA.IX.D.K3c; FAA-H-8083-2, FAA-H-8083-3, FAA-H-8083-25; POH/ AFM, AIM 6-3-3, 14 CFR 91.509]

7. Is a fire extinguisher required safety equipment for most general aviation aircraft? What should a pilot know about fire extinguishers and their usage?

For most light general aviation aircraft, a fire extinguisher is not required equipment for aircraft not involved in commercial operations or common carriage. For a few aircraft, the fire extinguisher may be required by the manufacturer, and a pilot should refer to equipment lists, MEL, or KOEL documents if applicable.

A pilot of a light general aviation aircraft should be familiar with the type, location, and operation of the fire extinguisher on board. The extinguisher must be easily accessible to the pilot and passengers in case of emergency. Most general aviation aircraft use a B:C class fire extinguisher, effective against both flammable liquids and electrical fires. Pilots should ensure that the extinguisher is properly charged, check the pressure gauge, confirm that the pin is secure, and know the manufacturer's instructions for the extinguisher's use.

In the event of a fire, the pilot should act quickly, following established procedures for firefighting, which includes shutting off electrical power, controlling airflow, and using the extinguisher as needed. Regular checks of the extinguisher's status and expiry date should be part of routine preflight inspection.

[PA.IX.D.K3; POH/AFM]

374 Aviation Supplies & Academics

Chapter 13 **Emergency Equipment and Survival Gear**

8. What is an emergency locator transmitter (ELT)?

An ELT is a radio transmitter attached to the aircraft structure that operates from its own power source on 121.5, 243.0 MHz, and the newer 406 MHz. It aids in locating downed aircraft by radiating a downward-sweeping audio tone, 2–4 times per second. It is designed to function without human action after an accident. It can be operationally tested during the first 5 minutes after any hour. (*Note:* Digital 406 MHz ELTs should only be tested per the manufacturer's instructions.)

Note: Pilots and their passengers should know how to activate the aircraft's ELT if manual activation is required. They should also be able to verify the aircraft's ELT is functioning and transmitting an alert after a crash or manual activation.

[PA.IX.B.K5; AIM 6-2-4]

9. Is an emergency locator transmitter (ELT) required on all aircraft?

No person may operate a US-registered civil airplane unless the airplane has an attached automatic-type emergency locator transmitter that is in operable condition. Several exceptions exist, including the following:

a. Aircraft engaged in training operations conducted entirely within a 50 NM radius of the airport from which local flight operations began.

b. Aircraft engaged in design and testing.

c. New aircraft engaged in manufacture, preparation, and delivery.

d. Aircraft engaged in agricultural operations.

[PA.IX.B.K5; 14 CFR 91.207]

10. When must the batteries in an emergency locator transmitter be replaced or recharged, if rechargeable?

Batteries used in ELTs must be replaced (or recharged, if the batteries are rechargeable):

a. When the transmitter has been in use for more than 1 cumulative hour; or

b. When 50 percent of their useful life (or, for rechargeable batteries, 50 percent of their useful life of charge), has expired.

(continued)

Private Pilot Oral Exam Guide   375

Chapter 13 **Emergency Equipment and Survival Gear**

Note: The new expiration date for replacing (or recharging) the battery must be legibly marked on the outside of the transmitter and entered in the aircraft maintenance record. This date indicates 50 percent of the battery's useful life.

[PA.IX.B.K5; 14 CFR 91.207]

11. How can a pilot test a traditional ELT transmitter to ensure it would be functional in the event of an off-field landing?

Analog 121.5/243 MHz ELTs should only be tested during the first 5 minutes after any hour. If operational tests must be conducted outside of this period, they should be coordinated with the nearest FAA control tower. Tests should be no longer than three audible sweeps. If the antenna is removable, a dummy load should be substituted during test procedures. At no time are airborne tests authorized.

[PA.IX.D.K1; AIM 6-2-4]

12. Can a pilot test a digital 406 MHz ELT within 5 minutes before or after the hour like a traditional ELT?

No. The newer digital 406 MHz ELTs should only be tested in accordance with the unit's manufacturer's instructions. This is because any triggering of the device initiates an immediate satellite-based notification. At no time are airborne tests authorized.

[PA.IX.D.K1; AIM 6-2-4]

13. If a pilot has encountered an off-field landing or a crash, and an ELT is triggered manually or as a result of the crash, what can they expect with regard to rescue locating efforts?

ELTs of various types were developed as a means of locating downed aircraft. These electronic, battery-operated transmitters operate on one of three frequencies: 121.5 MHz, 243.0 MHz, and the newer 406 MHz. ELTs operating on 121.5 MHz and 243.0 MHz are analog devices. The newer 406 MHz ELT is a digital transmitter that can be encoded with the owner's contact information or aircraft data. The latest 406 MHz ELT models can also be encoded with the aircraft's position data, which can help search and rescue (SAR) forces locate the aircraft much more

Chapter 13 **Emergency Equipment and Survival Gear**

quickly after a crash. The 406 MHz ELTs also transmit a stronger signal when activated than the older 121.5 MHz ELTs.

As of 2009, the Cospas-Sarsat system terminated monitoring and reception of the 121.5 MHz and 243.0 MHz frequencies. What this means for pilots is that those aircraft with only 121.5 MHz or 243.0 MHz ELTs on board will have to depend upon either a nearby air traffic control facility receiving the alert signal or an overflying aircraft monitoring 121.5 MHz or 243.0 MHz detecting the alert and advising ATC.

In the event that a properly registered 406 MHz ELT activates, the Cospas-Sarsat satellite system can decode the owner's information and provide that data to the appropriate SAR center. In the United States, NOAA provides the alert data to the appropriate US Air Force Rescue Coordination Center (RCC) or US Coast Guard Rescue Coordination Center. That RCC can then telephone or contact the owner to verify the status of the aircraft. If the aircraft is safely secured in a hangar, a costly ground or airborne search is avoided. In the case of an inadvertent 406 MHz ELT activation, the owner can deactivate the 406 MHz ELT. If the 406 MHz ELT equipped aircraft is being flown, the RCC can quickly activate a search. 406 MHz ELTs permit the Cospas-Sarsat satellite system to narrow the search area to a more confined area compared to that of a 121.5 MHz or 243.0 MHz ELT. 406 MHz ELTs also include a low-power 121.5 MHz homing transmitter to aid searchers in finding the aircraft in the terminal search phase.

Pilots and their passengers should know how to activate the aircraft's ELT if manual activation is required. They should also be able to verify the aircraft's ELT is functioning and transmitting an alert after a crash or manual activation.

[PA.IX.D.K1; AIM 6-2-4]

Private Pilot Oral Exam Guide 377

Scenario-Based Training 14

by Arlynn McMahon

Chapter 14 **Scenario-Based Training**

Introduction

Pilot examiners are encouraged by the FAA to develop scenarios as part of the "plan of action" used during the practical tests they conduct. Usually, the examiner will ask the applicant to pre-plan a cross-country. The assigned cross-country, then, is the beginning of the scenario and is the basis for this part of the oral exam.

The examiner is not required to follow the order of tasks as they appear in the Airman Certification Standards (ACS). Therefore, the questions in this chapter are presented as they might appear in an actual oral exam, rather than in the order given in the ACS. However, these questions alone do not make a complete oral exam. Usually, examiners will first ask a scenario-based question, and then, building from your response, construct additional questions as they go to further probe into your knowledge of an ACS Task.

Scenario-based questions are intentionally open-ended. Don't get frustrated. They are designed to allow you to go freely in any direction you feel is pertinent in demonstrating your ability to apply aeronautical knowledge and to be a safe pilot.

Answers to scenario-based questions can be lengthy. Feel free to use scrap paper to organize your thoughts before answering. For example, "TOMATO FLAMES" by itself is not a suitable answer to a question, but writing this acronym on a piece of paper will help you organize a better answer as you begin reciting the required equipment. Draw a diagram if that helps you to discuss the fuel system or to more clearly describe a concept to the examiner.

Ideally, your responses to scenario-based questions will demonstrate that you understand the underlying concepts of what's important and why. This is the *Practical Test*. To perform your best, you must show the practical application of *what* to do, *when* to do it, *why* do it, and *how* to do it.

Aeronautical decision making (ADM) is a special emphasis area on the practical test. Feel free to think out loud so the examiner can hear the reasoning in your answers. Discuss the plans you considered but discarded, and why you did so. By all means, include the elements that you feel make a good pilot, rather than one who just meets minimum standards. Show that you are prepared to be a responsible aviation-citizen.

The questions in this scenario-based training chapter are worded similarly to the way that the designated examiner might ask them during your exam, and your answers should reflect the specifics of

380 Aviation Supplies & Academics

Chapter 14 **Scenario-Based Training**

the scenario presented to you. Scenario-based questions don't have one universal correct answer; your correct answers will depend on the presented scenario, the specific aircraft used for the practical exam, and preparations you completed in planning the cross-country. For this reason, the answers provided here indicate the concepts your answer should or could include, but for your exam you should revise them with your specific information, as necessary. Also included with many of the answers are tips, suggestions, or notes (in *italic* type), which draw attention to the specific areas you should address in your responses to the examiner's questions.

Scenario-Based Questions

1. **Your good friend has requested you to fly as safety pilot in his retractable gear Piper Arrow while he practices flight by reference to instruments. What do regulations require for you to be able to do this?**

   Your answer should include knowledge of safety pilot requirements and currency requirements to carry passengers.

   I must meet safety pilot requirements and currency requirements to carry passengers, including:

   • I must hold at least a Private Pilot Certificate in the same category and class of aircraft to be flown.
   • I must hold a valid medical certificate or BasicMed.
   • I must have satisfactorily met the requirements of a flight review, and
   • I must have logged at least three takeoffs and landings in the preceding 90 days to carry passengers.

2. **Your same pilot friend (from the previous question) appreciated your help flying as a safety pilot for him, and he offers to let you borrow his Piper Arrow whenever you want, if you pay for the fuel you use. Can you do that?**

   Here, you must take the answer further, determining that an Arrow is a "complex" aircraft, talk about what that means, and what you would have to do to be able to fly the aircraft.

   You need an endorsement to fly this complex aircraft on your own (or for a high-performance or tailwheel aircraft).

Private Pilot Oral Exam Guide   381

Chapter 14 **Scenario-Based Training**

3. What personal documents will you be required to take with you to ensure that you are legal for this flight, carrying me as your passenger?

- Pilot certificate, photo ID, and a current medical certificate (duration based on age). These must be available in the flight deck.
- While I don't need to take it with me, I would need to be able to produce, upon request, verification in a logbook or training record that the following were completed:
  - › A flight review (or equivalency) within the previous 24 months.
  - › Three takeoffs and three landings within the previous 90 days (to a full stop if at night).

4. Tell me about the FAA Pilot Proficiency Program (WINGS).

A good pilot is always in training, even after passing the practical exam. The FAA Pilot Proficiency Program:

- Is an FAA and industry accident prevention initiative.
- Is based on the premise that pilots who maintain proficiency are safer pilots.
- Encourages ongoing flight training and aviation education.
- Is accomplished in little bits, throughout the year, encouraging pilots to fly in different seasons and in different flight conditions.
- Can be used to satisfy the flight review recency requirement as prescribed in 14 CFR §61.56(e), as long as the requirements for at least a "basic WINGS" level are met within the preceding 24 months.
- Has its official home at faasafety.gov, where free online courses are available.
- Has program specifics outlined in FAA Advisory Circular 61-91, *WINGS—Pilot Proficiency Program.*

382 Aviation Supplies & Academics

Chapter 14 **Scenario-Based Training**

5. **Let's talk about the plane: What three major components of the airworthiness verification process are required to determine an aircraft is airworthy?**

An airplane's airworthiness involves three different levels of verification:

- *Documents*—The pilot needs to verify all required documents for flight are on board the aircraft. This is an application of the "SPARROW" acronym process.

- *Inspections and maintenance*—The pilot will need to show all required inspections and AD compliance in the actual logbooks of the aircraft as completed by an appropriate FAA mechanic. They will need to demonstrate that the aircraft complies with airworthiness requirements at least annually by the "return to service" statement upon completion of the annual inspection and any one-time or reoccurring AD compliance documentation.

- *Preflight inspection*—The pilot certifies airworthiness, and is the final authority, before each flight with a thorough preflight inspection and inspection status review.

6. **Prove to me the airplane is airworthy for our flight today.**

This must include required inspections, documents, and instruments/equipment, as well as your statement that the preflight inspection shows the aircraft to be satisfactory. This will be an actual demonstration of the ability to apply the question above in practice.

Here are my pertinent aircraft documents and papers:

- Supplements
- Placards
- Airworthiness certificate.
- Registration.
- Radio license (if for international flight)
- Operating limitations *[which is probably in the AFM or POH]*—and here are the placards and markings on the instruments *[when appropriate]*.
- Weight and balance data.

(continued)

Private Pilot Oral Exam Guide   383

Chapter 14 **Scenario-Based Training**

Regarding the aircraft maintenance records for this airplane:

- The annual inspection was completed within the past 12 months and a mechanic with an Inspector Authorization stated that the aircraft was "returned to service."
- The 100-hour inspection was completed *[if appropriate]*.
- The transponder inspection was completed within the previous 24 months *[if appropriate]*.
- The ELT battery is current, and the system was inspected within the previous 12 months.
- Airworthiness directives (ADs) are complied with.
- Outstanding maintenance discrepancies have been checked and the status of inoperative equipment verified.

Also, the aircraft has the required instruments and equipment (i.e., day VFR versus night VFR); a thorough preflight inspection has been completed; the aircraft is properly serviced; and it is in airworthy condition—safe for this flight.

7. **The examiner will ask you to plan a cross-country flight. Be prepared to show how you determined your course, both magnetic and true, and what items you considered when choosing this course.**

For extra credit and to demonstrate good ADM, experienced instructors suggest you discuss alternative courses that were considered but discarded, and why.

The chosen course considers:

- Terrain—and I considered circumnavigating extreme high terrain, or areas of dense forest with no possible emergency landing areas.
- Checkpoints that are easy to see and identify.
- Navigation and communication reception—I considered altering course and/or altitude for reliable reception.
- Airspace—I considered altering course and/or altitude to avoid SUA and Class B airspace, etc.
- Weather avoidance—In some cases, a flight may be able to be completed with some deviations around areas of weather. This can be especially true in areas where coastal weather conditions can be localized. *[Be prepared to discuss options with this in mind also.]*

384 Aviation Supplies & Academics

Chapter 14 **Scenario-Based Training**

8. **Immediately after takeoff, you're at 100 feet AGL when your kneeboard falls onto the floor. You reach down to get it and suddenly become aware of a buffeting feeling. What should you be concerned about?**

Demonstrate here that you recognize and understand stalls and spins and know how to recover from them. This is a good example of a focus on "aviate, navigate, communicate," where flying the plane would be the first priority.

My first concern is to immediately get the nose down—reduce the angle of attack.

- The buffeting means the aircraft is on the brink of an unintended stall without having sufficient altitude to recover.

- The distraction may also mean that the aircraft is not in coordinated flight.

My focus should be on flying the plane first and getting to an appropriate altitude where the kneeboard could be safely retrieved; or I could potentially choose to just land, solve the issue on the ground with the aircraft stopped, and then take off again to head en route on my cross-country.

9. **Beginning with takeoff, and along your true course until landing, talk me through the different airspace we will fly through, and what implications each has on our flight.**

Use the sectional chart and begin with the airspace surrounding your departure airport, then proceed along your route, describing each airspace area as you come to it and how it may impact your flight. Continue describing the airspace and special use airspace as you encounter it along your route, and mention how that airspace may impact your decisions and requirements to be there—or not be there!

- Class D airspace extends to the blue dashed line—while in this area I must maintain two-way communications with the control tower.

- Assuming a normal climb, by the time I clear the "D" airspace, I'll be above 700 feet AGL. At this point, I will be at the area depicted on the chart where the base of the Class E airspace is at 700 feet AGL. Therefore, I am required to maintain VFR cloud clearances and 3 SM visibility.

(continued)

Private Pilot Oral Exam Guide   385

Chapter 14 **Scenario-Based Training**

> › If I'm not above 700 feet AGL, then I'll be in Class G airspace where I'm required to remain clear of the clouds and at least 1 SM visibility.

- Further along the course, I'm now in an area where the base of Class E airspace is at 1,200 AGL.

Modify these scenarios to consider other airspaces or potential equipment failures. For example, discuss what would happen if you were flying through or near Class D, C, or B airspace and ATC indicated that they were no longer receiving the altitude output from your transponder, or your ADS-B output. How would this affect your flight in these airspaces? What communications requirements and/or options are available in the airspace you would be travelling? What about if you had to divert?

10. What factors went into choosing your planned cruising altitude?

Consider the following, as appropriate for your planned flight:

- Terrain clearances—High enough to exceed minimum safe altitudes. As a new pilot, I will fly at least 1,500 feet AGL.
- Cloud clearances—It meets the requirements (for example, 500 feet below the clouds).
- Direction of flight—Complies with regulations.
- Airspace—Stays clear of any airspace I'd rather not fly close to or into (such as TFRs, prohibited areas, or restricted areas).
- Favorable winds—A suitable altitude that allows the most favorable ground speed.
- Allows me to see visual checkpoints easily.
- Best for aircraft performance (true airspeed vs. economic fuel burn).
- Personal minimums—This is an altitude that I feel comfortable flying at and that allows safety margins.

11. Looking at your Nav Log, how did you calculate fuel requirements?

Here, demonstrate your ability to use performance charts and graphs located in the POH/AFM. Calculate precisely, but add a safety margin at the end; also, remember to apply any and all pertinent notes included in the performance charts. Show and discuss your precise calculations (do not round-off, do not add "fudge factors").

386 Aviation Supplies & Academics

Chapter 14 **Scenario-Based Training**

Here are my precise calculations for:

- Fuel required for start, runup and taxi.
- Fuel for takeoff and climb.
- The chosen power setting and its associated fuel flow for the duration of cruise.
- Fuel required for descent and landing.
- Potential differences between actual and AFM/POH indicated fuel burn expectations.
- +30 minutes (+45 minutes at night) for required fuel reserve.

In addition to the above, I added fuel as necessary to meet my personal safety minimums. (For example, a new pilot should carry enough fuel to fly to a suitable alternate airport or +30 minutes cruise fuel after that—a total 1 hour reserve.)

12. You are required to prepare a navigation log. Why is having a nav log important?

Demonstrate your own routine use of a nav log.

I use a nav log because:

- All available information is organized on one piece of paper—that's good flight deck management.
- It provides a mental rehearsal and preparation for each aspect of the flight—that's good situational awareness.
- During flight, it is used to monitor the plan by:
  › Verifying ground speeds and fuel consumption.
  › Verifying ETAs to checkpoints and final destination.
  › Helping me to think and plan ahead.
  › Helping to prevent me from getting lost.
  › Reminding me of routine flight deck tasks (change fuel tanks, listen to ATIS, cancel flight plan, etc.).
  › Assisting in diversion to an alternate, if it should become necessary.

Note: If using an EFB for planning, which the ACS allows, be prepared to show where calculated numbers in a digital flight plan are derived from, how you will know they are correct, and what happens if that EFB fails during your flight. A good backup would be to print out the flight plan it generated or have backup power for the device or even a backup device. Of course, backup paper charts can also still be a great option.

Private Pilot Oral Exam Guide 387

Chapter 14 **Scenario-Based Training**

13. When planning a cross-country that will require a fuel stop, what factors do you feel are important in selecting an airport for a stop?

Demonstrate your understanding of aeronautical decision making.

In selecting an airport for a fuel stop, important factors to consider include:

- Airport airspace—airspace similar to my training and/or experience.
- Runways—length and relation to the wind.
- Size of the airport—not too small but not so big that the amount and type of traffic is intimidating.
- Pilot support facilities available (FSS access, weather station, hours of operation, etc.)
- Amenities (restrooms, service, loaner car, restaurant at the airport, etc.)
- Price of fuel or method for payment.

14. Considering your calculated takeoff distance for the planned flight, how would that change if the outside air temperature were 20° warmer or 20° cooler?

Your specific answer to this question will depend on the individual circumstances of your practical exam; but whatever your situation is, the answer should demonstrate your ability to accurately use the performance table and your understanding of the effects of atmospheric conditions on the airplane's performance. You should include the table or chart in your aircraft's POH, specifically:

- *How your calculations were carefully performed. Interpolate as necessary for accuracy and apply any "Notes" that may be applicable.*
- *Recalculate performance using the 20° warmer and 20° cooler scenarios.*

Discuss the differences in performance and effects of density altitude on performance, not only for takeoff but through each of the phases of flight.

Chapter 14 **Scenario-Based Training**

15. Are the runways you plan to use today suitable for us?

Demonstrate your ability to use the performance tables in your aircraft's POH and your understanding of the need to include a safety margin. Show your calculations.

Yes, using the takeoff and landing performance charts, I calculated the required distance to take off and to land. This shows what the aircraft is capable of; however, as a new pilot, I am not always able to achieve takeoffs or landings that precisely. Therefore, I added 50% *[or whatever your safety margin is]* more to my calculations as my personal minimum when determining runway suitability.

Note: Are there charts or calculations available for your aircraft for using a non-paved (potentially grass or turf) runway surface? If not, what performance considerations would you make? Apply reasonable personable minimums and be able to discuss why and how you to got to your numbers.

16. During our flight today, with whom will you communicate?

Demonstrate your knowledge of available resources and your willingness to use them.
- Ground/Tower/Departure (if departing from a controlled airport), or
- UNICOM or MULTICOM (if from an uncontrolled airport).
- Enroute: Flight Following to assist in knowing about pop-up TFRs and to assist with traffic avoidance.
- FSS for updated weather, altimeter settings, and possible revisions to the filed flight plan.
- Destination airport communications *[as appropriate to the destination]*.

17. How did you obtain weather information for our flight?

Your flow might look something like the following:
- Beginning last night, I watched the weather channel on TV. The weather channel is not a specific aviation weather source, but it helps me to hear the meteorologist talk about the weather patterns.
- Then I logged online to Leidos Flight Service and received an outlook briefing or obtained a downloaded briefing on my EFB.

(continued)

Private Pilot Oral Exam Guide 389

Chapter 14 **Scenario-Based Training**

- This morning, I logged on to Leidos Flight Service or onto my EFB for a standard weather briefing to complete my planning and nav log.
- As we got closer to departure time, I wanted to get a more final and thorough briefing, so I called Flight Service and got a full briefing.
- Just before flight, to verify some potentially changing conditions, I called FSS again for an abbreviated weather briefing before I made a final go/no-go decision.

18. Tell me about the weather along our flight.

Demonstrate your understanding of meteorology and what entails a complete weather briefing. Explain all the components of the standard weather briefing you received for the proposed cross-country flight.

- Pressure areas affecting weather.
- Fronts affecting weather and their direction of movement.
- Ceilings, winds, and visibility at departure, at several points en route, and at the destination.
- Wind direction and speed at cruise altitude.
- Significant or adverse weather near the route or during possible flight time, and how it may affect the flight; it includes a plan to escape a possible problem of this kind.
- NOTAMs.

19. Discuss at least two different weather charts that you used in preparing for our flight and describe how you used them.

It's easy to get confused when discussing these charts. To make answering this question easier, bring printouts or have a digital source during the exam of the charts you used and show them as you answer. Following is an example of what your answer to the examiner might include.

- I used the **surface analysis chart** to see the pressure areas, fronts, wind, local weather, and visual obstructions. It is transmitted every 3 hours and covers the country.
- I used the **weather depiction chart** to get an overview of the surface conditions as derived from METAR and other surface

390 Aviation Supplies & Academics

Chapter 14 **Scenario-Based Training**

observations. It gives me an overall picture of the weather across the United States. It is transmitted every 3 hours.

- I used the **significant weather prognostic chart** to see the forecast. The chart has four panels that include 12- and 24-hour forecasts. Charts are issued four times a day. The valid time is printed on each panel. The upper two panels show forecast significant weather, which may include turbulence, freezing levels, and IFR or MVFR weather.

Note: Be prepared to answer a question such as, "What if I decided to postpone the flight for two or three days; what general weather considerations would I be experiencing if that was the case?" This would take you outside the time periods of TAFs and require you to demonstrate knowledge of the information charts that go out a few more days.

20. Discuss the following weather forecasts that you used in preparing for our flight and describe how you used them: GFA, TAF, and winds and temperatures aloft forecast.

Include, as appropriate for your flight planning purposes, details of weather forecasts such as:

- I used the **GFA** to get the big picture about the general weather in the area, what is causing the weather, and how it may change during the upcoming 24 hours.
- I used the **TAF** to get specific weather for certain weather reporting areas along my route, and for information about how conditions at those airports may change. This allows me to evaluate if the clouds and visibility will allow my flight to continue VFR. I could also find areas of VFR in case I run into unforecasted weather that I need to escape.
- I used the **winds and temperatures aloft forecast**. With the wind direction and velocity, I found the most desirable altitude giving the best ground speeds. I also used the temperatures aloft to determine probable altitudes for clouds to form.

Private Pilot Oral Exam Guide 391

Chapter 14 **Scenario-Based Training**

21. Discuss and demonstrate how you will obtain updated weather information while en route.

Demonstrate your understanding of all resources available and how to choose the best resource to use in a given situation. For example:

- Onboard datalink weather options—Either satellite of ADS-B based weather sources that are fed into panel or non-permanent technology can provide a great deal of weather data information. *[Be prepared to show how some of this could be used to update weather information en route, and be prepared to discuss the limitations of the data this provides.]*
- If I only need recorded information (for instance, to update an altimeter setting), I could listen to a nearby AWOS/ASOS/ATIS.
- If I need to ask questions (for example, if I guess that weather is unexpectedly changing), I would contact FSS on 122.2 or one of the remote transmitters associated with a VOR.
- If I'm in a pinch, or if the flight is becoming unsafe, ATC might be of assistance.
- For the best weather update, I would collect information from a variety of resources before making a decision.

22. While en route, we listen to the ATIS of a Class D airport near our course to update the altimeter setting and find that the ATIS is reporting visibility as 2 SM. What does that mean for us?

Demonstrate your understating of VFR weather minimums in Class E and Class G airspace, and the special VFR clearance. Show your aeronautical decision-making ability by evaluating your options and choosing the best option based on the specifics of your flight.

We have two priorities: (1) to remain legal, and (2) as a new pilot, the prudent choice is an immediate diversion to an alternate airport to land.

- Option 1 is to fly in "G" airspace, where regulations allow us to remain clear of clouds with 1 SM visibility while en route to an uncontrolled airport and land.
- Option 2 is to fly in "G" airspace while heading for the Class D airport and request a special VFR from ATC to land there.

392 Aviation Supplies & Academics

Chapter 14 **Scenario-Based Training**

23. You have chosen to divert to an airport that you were not intending to visit. How will you obtain the needed information about your alternate airport?

Demonstrate your understanding of all resources available and how to choose the best resource for a given situation. Be able to demonstrate how you would manage workload while doing this, such as taking advantage of using an autopilot to alleviate flying demands while getting more information.

The most pressing information needed is airport airspace, runway length, airport elevation, and an airport communication frequency. I would:

- Use technology—Most GPS databases include all of this information.
- Use the sectional chart—The needed information is on the airport legend.
- Use the *Chart Supplement*.
- Use EFB data to find updated NOTAM information or any other information about the airport to which I will be flying.
- Use a combination of the above.

24. What deice or anti-ice equipment is your airplane equipped with?

Demonstrate that you know the specific equipment installed on your airplane, as well as when to use it.

- Defrost—Used to keep the windshield clear. I will turn it on in advance of a possible icing situation.
- Pitot heat—Used to keep the pitot/static instruments operational. I will turn it on in advance of a possible icing situation.
- Carburetor heat—Used to keep fuel and air flowing to the engine. It's normally turned on after the first sign of possible carburetor icing.
- The most important piece of equipment is a thinking pilot who, when encountering dangerous icing conditions, can make a timely decision to turn around or land as soon as practical.

Private Pilot Oral Exam Guide   393

Chapter 14 **Scenario-Based Training**

25. **Tell me about the fuel system on your airplane.**

Include the components of your airplane's fuel system, the normal operation of the system, and how you interact with it. Be specific, using the information contained in the POH for your airplane. The following answer, based on an example airplane, illustrates the type of details you might cover.

- Twenty-eight gallons are stored in each wing tank. Three gallons are unusable and a total of 53 gallons are usable. I would order and verify that 100LL is being serviced into the airplane.

- Fuel quantity is measured by float-type quantity indicators, but good pilots always verify the fuel visually. Annunciators show L and R "LOW FUEL" if the fuel quantity is below 5 gallons in a tank.

- The tank has a visual FUEL TAB, allowing verification that 17.5 gallons are on board when takeoffs are performed with less than full fuel.

- The tanks are vented, and I ensure the vents are not blocked during the preflight inspection.

- Also on the preflight inspection, I drain fuel from 13 fuel sumps to verify fuel grade and to remove any possible sediment. Ten of these sumps are on the wings, two are on the belly, and there is a fuel strainer in the cowling that is pulled to collect a fuel sample.

- Fuel flows by gravity from the wing tanks to the fuel selector value. I control fuel to the engine being fed from the L, R or BOTH tanks. I select "BOTH" for takeoffs, climbs, landings, and maneuvers that involve slips or skids of more than 30 seconds.

- From the fuel selector, fuel flows to a reservoir tank, aux fuel pump, fuel shutoff valve, and into the engine.

- I activate the auxiliary fuel pump for start and during engine emergencies.

- The fuel shutoff valve shuts off fuel to the engine. I activate this to decrease the likelihood of fire upon ditching, and during an extended period of aircraft storage.

394 Aviation Supplies & Academics

Chapter 14 **Scenario-Based Training**

26. What method of navigation will you use today, and what are the advantages and limitations of that method?

Demonstrate your understanding of navigation methods and resources available and how to choose the best resource to use in a given situation. For extra credit and to demonstrate ADM, point out that the best way to navigate is by using a combination of methods.

- Dead Reckoning—Advantages are that it is simple. When everything else fails, it will bring us home. The limitations are that it requires accurate winds and performance calculations, and careful timekeeping.
- Pilotage—Advantages are that it builds confidence; you see it on the chart and see it on the ground. Limitations are that it requires prominent checkpoints and enough visibility to see them.
- VOR—Advantages include that it is more reliable than dead reckoning or pilotage; it's an accurate form of navigation over an area where no prominent checkpoints exist. Limitations are that it is line-of-sight navigation, somewhat dependent on altitude, and less accurate when far away from the station.
- GPS—Advantages include that it is not limited to line-of-sight; ground speed and other calculations are provided; and distance is not slant distance. Limitations are that there are occasional outages, and the database must be current for reliable data. Ground speeds are instantaneous but not point-to-point, as is needed for calculating accurate ETAs and fuel remaining.

27. Let's talk about your passenger safety briefing. Assume that I am your good friend who has never been in a small plane. Give me your passenger safety briefing.

The items below (indicated as bold initials of the word "safety") are what you are required to include in a safety briefing. Demonstrate your knowledge of the elements of a complete safety briefing and your understanding that an effective briefing at the start of the flight can add to the safety and enjoyment of the flight for everyone.

(continued)

Private Pilot Oral Exam Guide   395

Chapter 14 **Scenario-Based Training**

S Seat belts—fastened for taxi, takeoff, and landing
Shoulder harness—fastened for takeoff and landing
Seat—adjusted and locked into place
A Air vents—location and operation; you can adjust
All environmental controls—what's available; you shouldn't adjust (ask me)
Action—in case of passenger discomfort
F Fire extinguisher—location and operation
E Exit doors (and windows)—how to secure, how to operate
Emergency evacuation plan
Emergency equipment—location and operation
T Traffic (scanning, spotting, and notifying pilot)
Talking (sterile cockpit expectations)
Y Your questions? There are no dumb questions. It's more fun when you ask.

28. While en route, you notice a discharge on the ammeter. What will you do?

Demonstrate your understanding of the electrical system, using specifics relevant to your airplane.

A discharge on the ammeter indicates the possibility of an electrical problem. If left unchecked, it might exhaust the battery, causing a partial or total loss of electrical equipment. I would:

- Turn off the avionics master switch (if appropriate) and the master switch to reset what may be an overvoltage relay.
- Turn the master switch back on and notice the indication on the ammeter. If it is still not showing a charge, then:
  - › Turn off any unnecessary electrical equipment, and
  - › Re-evaluate how this may affect the safety of continued flight.
  - › Consider landing as soon as practical during the day, or as soon as possible at night, for repairs.

396 Aviation Supplies & Academics

Chapter 14 **Scenario-Based Training**

29. As you approach the airport of intended landing with your battery now dead, are we in danger of the engine quitting? If not, what problems might we encounter while landing with a dead battery?

Demonstrate your understanding of the electrical system, using specifics relevant to your airplane.

- No, the engine will not quit; it derives its electrical ignition power from magnetos—not the electrical system.
- We may have to land without flaps—a slip might be needed to descend.
- We will not have engine gauges—the fuel gauges will show empty which is always uncomfortable to see.
- We will not have lights—if at night, a flashlight will be needed in the flight deck. The landing will be made without a landing light.
- We will not have a turn coordinator, but the pitot/static and gyro instruments will be operational.
- We will not have COM radios—if landing at a controlled airport, we should look for light gun signals. If landing at an uncontrolled airport at night, we might not be able to turn on the pilot-controlled lighting.

30. Are there specific techniques that you normally use for collision avoidance?

Demonstrate the need for good collision avoidance habits during each phase of flight.

- Ensure that the windshield is as clean as possible.
- Organize the flight deck to avoid a lot of "head down" time—pre-fold charts, pre-select frequencies, etc.
- Keep my head up and eyes outside during all ground maneuvering. On the ground, stop while copying ATC clearances.
- Perform clearing turns before performance maneuvers requiring rapid changes in heading or altitude.
- Scan for traffic often when in straight-and-level flight and during maneuvers.
- Don't practice maneuvers over VORs, airports, or other areas where traffic normally converges.

(continued)

Private Pilot Oral Exam Guide   397

Chapter 14 **Scenario-Based Training**

- Enter traffic patterns correctly and at proper traffic pattern altitude.
- Listen on frequencies, especially at uncontrolled airports, to hear possible traffic in the area.
- Visually verify that final approach is clear before taking the runway for takeoff.
- Use anti-collision lights and a landing light at night and during times of low visibility.
- Comply with right of way rules (14 CFR §91.113).
- In the radar environment, if ATC issues traffic, I will look to see it and maneuver to avoid it. If I lose sight of the traffic, I will report that to ATC.
- Use flight following en route as another tool for traffic avoidance.

31. With our head in the flight deck reading the taxi diagram, we accidentally hit a large taxiway light. The prop is chewed up pretty badly, and the lower nose cowling is banged up, but nothing else seems to be damaged. Are you required to report this to the NTSB?

This does not require a report to the NTSB because the damage is limited to the prop and the damage to other people's property probably doesn't exceed $25,000. Therefore, I would:

- Have the airplane towed to the maintenance shop for repairs.
- Contact the airport manager to have possible foreign object debris cleaned from the taxiway.

32. Tell me about the emergency equipment and survival gear that is on board for our flight today.

Show your awareness that the need for emergency equipment and survival gear is not limited to flights over extreme terrain or extreme temperature changes.

If the emergency originates in flight and there is time:

- The autopilot could be considered emergency equipment to help relieve workload.
- The communications radio can be used to send a "mayday."
- The GPS could be used for "NRST" and "DIRECT TO" navigation to an airport.
- The transponder could be used to signal "7700."

Chapter 14 **Scenario-Based Training**

I have the following items on board that could be useful after ditching:

- Fire extinguisher—It is charged, and I know how to use it.
- Cell phone.
- Water and snacks.
- Pocket knife/all-purpose tool.
- First aid kit.
- Emergency locator transmitter (ELT)—I can manually activate it.
- Other items that I routinely carry that would be of use in an emergency are _____ [if relevant].

33. What do you feel are the major differences between the PAVE checklist and the 5P checklist?

Show your awareness of the need to manage the risks of flight and the tools available to help pilots.

- Both checklists are tools recommended for pilots in managing the risks associated with flying.
- Both consider the risk elements; those are: the pilot, the airplane, the environment, and the external factors.
- The PAVE checklist encourages the pilot to react to a risk element that they find unacceptable.
- The 5P checklist encourages the pilot to be proactive—to do surveillance, look ahead for changes in a risk element, and take early action to prevent a problem.

34. For a flight involving first-time fliers as passengers, how would you manage the risks pertaining to their aeromedical factors?

Demonstrate your knowledge of aeromedical factors as well as your understanding of what causes them and how to address them. Also, explain how would you determine when a diversion would be necessary—i.e., discuss where your break points would be in managing a passenger with a challenge.

- If possible, I would sit the passenger most likely to experience motion sickness in the front seat so I can keep their attention focused outside—far, far away on the horizon.
- I keep a Sic-Sac on board in case of motion sickness or hyperventilation.

(continued)

Private Pilot Oral Exam Guide   399

Chapter 14 **Scenario-Based Training**

- If possible, I would sit the passenger most likely to experience ear or sinus problems in the front seat so I can watch for early signs of problems and possibly take corrective action, especially during climbs and descents.

35. **Your friend owns a condo in Colorado ski country. It's a long trip from the East Coast. How would you manage the risks pertaining to the aeromedical factors?**

Demonstrate your knowledge of relevant aeromedical factors as well as your understanding of what causes them and how to address them.

- I would consider each element of the "I'M SAFE" checklist before takeoff.
- Although the regulations require supplemental oxygen when flying over 12,500 feet for more than 30 minutes, if flying at an altitude of more than 10,000 feet MSL, I would carry supplemental oxygen, especially at night to aid my eyesight.
- Unless terrain (as an example) requires otherwise, I would plan to fly below 8,000 feet MSL to prevent possible hypoxia.
- I would carry a small bottle of water to ward off the possibility of dehydration (but not a big bottle because that might create another problem!).
- Rather than planning long legs (more than 4 hours), I'd plan shorter legs with a fuel/rest stop every 2 to 3 hours to prevent stress and fatigue.

Note: Discuss how many legs in a day (or total flight time) you might be willing to do. When does fatigue, even in good weather conditions, become a limiting factor on how far you will fly in a day? How much rest will you require before you start flying again?

36. **You are considering the flight home after a scuba diving vacation during spring break in the Florida Keys. You want to enjoy every minute possible in the water and relaxing on the beach. How would you manage the risks pertaining to aeromedical factors on the flight home?**

Demonstrate your knowledge of the relevant aeromedical factors as well as your understanding of what causes them and how to address them.

- I would consider each element of the "I'M SAFE" checklist before takeoff.

Chapter 14 **Scenario-Based Training**

- Because I am headed back north to where it is colder (winter), the cabin heat will probably be on. I would use a carbon monoxide detector in the aircraft cabin to help with detection of carbon monoxide.
- Winter may involve snow showers. If flying in low-visibility conditions, I scan instruments more often to prevent spatial disorientation. If an autopilot is available, it should be turned on to assist in better aircraft control and keeping the wings level, whenever spatial disorientation is a concern.
- I would wait 12 to 24 hours after scuba diving, depending on if it were a controlled ascent (decompression needed) or not, to ward off possible nitrogen oxide symptoms.
- I would wait at least 8 (or better yet, 12) hours after drinking alcohol before takeoff.

37. Hazardous weather caused you to delay your return flight home by a few days. As a result, the annual inspection and transponder check are now both out of date. Do regulations permit you to fly home with these items out of date?

No, I cannot legally fly home without the transponder inspection, unless it is disabled, placarded, and a maintenance entry is made; and if I did, there would be some limitations: 14 CFR §91.215(c) indicates that "each person operating an aircraft equipped with an operable ATC transponder maintained in accordance with §91.413 shall operate the transponder, including Mode C equipment if installed, and shall reply on the appropriate code or as assigned by ATC..." To operate a transponder, it must have had a current transponder certification.

If this requirement is not met, the pilot would need to have the transponder disabled, placarded, and a maintenance entry made unless a special flight permit was given.

Flight without an annual inspection can be initiated only with the issuance of a special flight permit issued by the FSDO. (Note that a special flight permit will typically require all ADs to have been complied with.) So, I can fly home provided I've been issued a permit and am in compliance with the conditions listed on the permit, which usually also do not allow passenger carriage.

Private Pilot Oral Exam Guide 401

Chapter 14 **Scenario-Based Training**

38. It's Saturday morning and you are ready for the flight home. During your preflight, you find that the landing light is inoperative. Will this affect your ability to fly home?

Demonstrate your awareness that all installed equipment must be operational on the airplane before takeoff, and the two legal ways to fly with inoperative equipment.

Regulations require that:

- All installed equipment be operational before takeoff, unless:
  › The flight is in compliance with an approved minimum equipment list (MEL) or kinds of operations equipment list (KOEL), or
  › The inoperative equipment is not required by type design, regulations, or ADs.
- The pilot can safely operate the airplane without the equipment that has become inoperative.
- The pilot removes or deactivates any inoperative equipment.
- The pilot has placarded any inoperative equipment near the ON/OFF switch and made an appropriate maintenance log entry.

Because the landing light is not required, I feel that I can safely fly the airplane during the day without it. Simply pulling a circuit breaker and placarding it may not be considered "deactivation" of the system, so I will consult with maintenance personnel first before departing on my flight.

Note: Deactivation means to make a piece of equipment or an instrument unusable to the pilot/crew by preventing its operation. Not tie wrapping or collaring a CB would allow for continued operation of that system. A pilot should consult maintenance personnel before deactivating or removing any item of equipment from an airplane.

Chapter 14 **Scenario-Based Training**

39. **You have volunteered to fly a sick child to meet an ambulance at a Class B airport. It's a clear night when at 60 NM out you notice an ammeter discharge. You guess you have about 30 minutes of battery remaining. What will you do?**

There is no right answer; this is simply your opportunity to demonstrate your ADM. You should show a willingness to declare an emergency and divert. Include a discussion of ways to manage the electrical system until landing. Include your thoughts out loud until you make a final decision. You could also mention whether you would you do anything differently if this was a Pilot-N-Paws flight with a sick animal rather than a flight with a sick child.

- Within 30 minutes, I might make Big Controlled Airport, but may not be able to communicate with ATC when I get there.
- I could declare an emergency (to obtain radar assistance and priority handling into Big Controlled Airport).
- It might be safer to divert to the "NRST" airport, but then we would miss the ambulance pre-arranged for the patient. I would reduce the electrical load by turning off all unnecessary electrical system equipment. *[Specify the particular flight deck equipment you would turn off in your training airplane.]*

40. **After an exhausting three-day business meeting, you are loading up the rental airplane for the two-hour flight home when you discover you have lost your reading glasses. You can see in the distance but can't read instruments or a chart very easily. The weather is good, and if you depart in the next 20 minutes you can be home before dark. What will you do?**

There is no right answer; this is simply an opportunity to demonstrate your risk management and ADM. Voice your thought process out loud until you make a final decision.

- I would ask passengers or others (if available) to assist me in searching for my lost glasses.
- If possession of corrective lenses is required on my medical certificate, then takeoff is not permitted.
- How familiar am I with the rental plane? Can I see "well enough" to fly a plane I don't often fly?
- I could spend the night, buy a new pair of glasses, get some rest, and depart fresh in the morning.

Private Pilot Oral Exam Guide 403

Appendix 1

Maneuvers Table

Appendix 1

Private Pilot Airman Certification Standards (condensed)

Task	Objective Minimum acceptable standard of performance			
Takeoff				
Normal/Crosswind	V_Y +10 / -5			
Short/Soft	V_X +10 / -5, then V_Y +10 / -5			
Landing				
Normal/Crosswind	1.3 V_{S0} +10 / -5, touch at or within 400 feet beyond target			
Forward Slip	Min float, touch at or within 400 feet beyond target			
Short	1.3 V_{S0} +10 / -5, touch at or within 200 feet beyond target			
Soft	1.3 V_{S0} +10 / -5, touch at minimum speed and descent rate			
Go Around	Apply Power (Carb Heat Off), pitch for V_X or V_Y +10/-5 kts, then V_Y +10/-5 kts to safe altitude			
Emergency Operations				
Emergency Descent	Bank angle 30°–45°, airspeed +0/-10 kts, level off ±100 feet.			
Emergency Approach and Landing	Best glide airspeed, ±10 kts, recommended descent configuration			
		Heading or bank ±°	**Altitude ± ft**	**Speed ± kts**
Traffic Pattern	Accurate track and safe spacing		100	10
Pilotage/NAV/Diverting	Know position ±3 NM	15	200	ETA ±5min
Instrument Flying				
Straight and level		20	200	10
Constant airspeed climb and descend		20	200	10
Turns and rollouts on heading		10	200	10
Communications, Navigation, Radar Services		20	200	10
Recovery from unusual attitudes	Recover to stabilized flight w/o excesses			
Slow Flight and Stalls (recovery from maneuver no lower than 1,500 AGL)				
Power-off Stalls	S & L or max. 20° bank Full-stall then recover	10		
Power-on Stalls	S & L or max. 20° bank Full-stall then recover	10		
Maneuvering during Slow Flight Straight & level, turns, climbs, descents		10	100	No stall warning +10/-0 kts
Performance Maneuvers				
Steep turns 360° with 45° ±5° bank, coordinated		10	100	10
Ground Reference Maneuvers	Enter downwind 600–1,000 AGL		100	10

Exam Tip: Remember to always perform "clearing turns" prior to beginning any flight maneuver.

Appendix 2
Applicant's Practical
Test Checklist

Appendix 2

Applicant's Practical Test Checklist

Appointment with Examiner

Examiner's Name: _____

Location for test (airport): _____

Date of test: _____

Start time for test: _____

Examiner's fee: _____

Documents to Bring to the Practical Test

___ *Aircraft Maintenance Records*
Logbook record of airworthiness and inspections for engine, aircraft, propeller, and AD compliance:
- Annual inspection
- 100-hour inspection (if applicable)
- VOR test (if applicable)
- Altimeter, pitot static test
- Transponder test
- ELT inspection and battery
- AD compliance documentation
- Current GPS database (if applicable)

___ *Aircraft Required Documents:*
- Supplemental documents
- Placards
- Airworthiness certificate
- Current aircraft registration
- Radio station license
- Owner's manual (AFM/POH)
- Weight and balance documentation

Personal Documents
___ Government-issued photo identification
___ Pilot certificate
___ Aviation Medical Certificate or BasicMed qualification (when applicable)
___ FAA Knowledge Test results
___ Completed FAA Form 8710-1, Airman Certificate and/or Rating Application, with instructor's signature, or completed IACRA form (a best practice is to have both in case of an IACRA system outage)

408 Aviation Supplies & Academics

Appendix 2

Training Documentation
___ Log of ground training meeting FAR requirements*
___ Log of flight training meeting FAR requirements
___ Log of experience requirements meeting FAR requirements
___ Endorsements signed by instructor for practical test eligibility
___ Graduation certificate if test will be conducted based on graduation from a Part 141 approved training provider
___ Log of experience indicating currency for flight (flight review endorsement or current solo endorsement; complex, high-performance, or tailwheel endorsement if applicable)
___ Copy of previous Notice of Disapproval (if the test is a retest)
___ Endorsement for retest (if the test is a retest)

A best practice is to have all of these items tabbed or identified to be able to demonstrate eligibility for the practical test to the examiner. The examiner is required to determine and confirm eligibility prior to beginning the test. If they are unable to determine eligibility or you are missing documentation, they may be unable to begin the test and it may need to be rescheduled.

Equipment and Materials to Bring to the Test
___ View-limiting device
___ Current aeronautical charts (printed or electronic)
___ Flight computer, calculator, and/or plotter
___ Flight plan form and flight logs (printed or electronic)
___ *Chart Supplement*, airport diagrams, or other charting resources
___ Current FAR/AIM

* Note that ground training as logged by an online ground school for the FAA Knowledge Test typically does not meet the requirements for ground training for a certificate or rating. Be sure that you have logged ground training for the practical test and that you have it documented and available for review for the practical test.

Private Pilot Oral Exam Guide 409

Appendix 3

Operations of Aircraft Without/With an MEL

Appendix 3

Operations of Aircraft *Without* a Minimum Equipment List (MEL)

(14 CFR 91.213, AC 91-67, AC 120-71B)

During the preflight inspection, the pilot discovers inoperative instruments or equipment.

DECISION SEQUENCE:

1. Are the inoperative instruments or equipment part of the VFR-day type certification? (14 CFR 91.213(d)(2)(i))

These are the instruments and equipment prescribed in the applicable airworthiness regulations under which the aircraft was type-certificated (Part 23 for newer aircraft and CAR Part 3 for much older aircraft).

Note: Referencing the aircraft certification regulations to determine if instruments and equipment are required can be a complex task. In general, the instruments and equipment required by the aircraft certification regulations can be found in the aircraft's Equipment List and Type Certificate Data Sheet (TCDS).

If YES, the aircraft is not airworthy and maintenance is required before you can fly.

If NO, go to next the step.

2. Are the inoperative instruments or equipment listed as "Required" on the aircraft's equipment list, or "kinds of operations equipment list" (KOEL) for the kind of flight operation being conducted? (14 CFR 91.213 (d)(2)(ii))

Note: Many newer aircraft have a "Kinds of Operations" equipment list which refers to the kinds of operations (VFR Day, VFR Night, IFR Day, IFR Night, Icing) in which the aircraft can operate. The equipment list and KOEL are located in the AFM.

If YES, the aircraft is not airworthy and maintenance is required before you can fly.

If NO, go to next the step.

412 Aviation Supplies & Academics

Appendix 3

3. **Are the inoperative instruments or equipment required by 14 CFR §91.205, §91.207, the type certificate data sheet for the aircraft, the aircraft equipment list, any supplemental type certificates that apply to equipment installed after the original production and delivery of the aircraft, or any other rule of Part 91 for the specific kind of flight operation being conducted?** (14 CFR 91.213(d)(2)(iii))

Note: Other required equipment regulations include: §91.205 VFR Day, VFR Night, IFR; §91.207 – ELTs; §91.209 – Aircraft Lights; §91.215 – ATC Transponders.

If YES, the aircraft is not airworthy and maintenance is required before you can fly.

If NO, go to the next step.

4. **Are the inoperative instruments or equipment required to be operational by an Airworthiness Directive (AD)? Check the aircraft maintenance logs and/or consult with a maintenance technician to determine AD compliance.** (14 CFR 91.213(d)(2)(iv))

If YES, the aircraft is not airworthy and maintenance is required before you can fly.

If NO, go to the next step.

5. **At this point, the inoperative instruments or equipment must be:**

REMOVED from the aircraft (14 CFR §91.213(d)(3)(i)), the cockpit control placarded, and the maintenance record (logbook) updated in accordance with 14 CFR §43.9.

OR

DEACTIVATED and PLACARDED "Inoperative"(14 CFR §91.213(d)(3)(ii). If deactivation of the inoperative instrument or equipment involves maintenance, it must be accomplished and recorded in accordance with Part 43.

Note: Unless the equipment modification is able to be completed under "preventive maintenance" allowances, an FAA-certified mechanic will need to complete and document the change.

Private Pilot Oral Exam Guide 413

Appendix 3

6. **Finally, a determination is made by a certificated and appropriately rated pilot or mechanic that the inoperative instrument or equipment does not constitute a hazard to the aircraft for the anticipated conditions of the flight, e.g., day VFR, night VFR etc.**

Operations of Aircraft *With* a Minimum Equipment List (MEL)
(14 CFR 91.213, AC 91-67, AC 120-71B)

During the preflight inspection, the pilot discovers inoperative instruments or equipment.

DECISION SEQUENCE:

1. **Is the inoperative equipment not included in the MEL, but required by the type certification, AD or other special conditions?**

   If YES, the aircraft is not airworthy and maintenance is required before flight.

   If NO, go to next step.

2. **The pilot performs or has a qualified person perform the appropriate "O" or "M" deactivation or removal procedure.**

   Note: Two categories of maintenance procedures:

   "O" Operations procedures—can be performed by pilot; must be accomplished before or during operation with listed item of equipment inoperative.

   "M" Maintenance procedures—must be done by maintenance personnel and be accomplished before beginning operation with the listed item of equipment inoperative.

3. **The pilot or maintenance personnel placards the inoperative equipment and updates the maintenance record (logbook).**

4. **The pilot confirms that the inoperative equipment does not present hazards to the conditions of flight.**

414   Aviation Supplies & Academics

Stay Informed with ASA's Online Resources

Reader resources and updates for the
Private Pilot Oral Exam Guide:
asa2fly.com/oegp

Visit **asa2fly.com** for ASA's full
selection of aviation books, training
resources, apps, and pilot supplies.

asa2fly.com

Learn to Fly Blog—Where pilots and future
pilots explore flight and flight training:
learntoflyblog.com

Follow, like, share.
- instagram.com/asa2fly
- facebook.com/asa2fly
- youtube.com/asa2fly
- linkedin.com/company/asa2fly